First World War
and Army of Occupation
War Diary
France, Belgium and Germany

58 DIVISION
Headquarters, Branches and Services
General Staff
31 July 1918 - 5 September 1918

WO95/2990

The Naval & Military Press Ltd
www.nmarchive.com
Published in association with The National Archives

Published by

The Naval & Military Press Ltd

Unit 10 Ridgewood Industrial Park,

Uckfield, East Sussex,

TN22 5QE England

Tel: +44 (0) 1825 749494

www.naval-military-press.com

www.nmarchive.com

This diary has been reprinted in facsimile from the original. Any imperfections are inevitably reproduced and the quality may fall short of modern type and cartographic standards.

© Crown Copyright
Images reproduced by permission of The National Archives, London, England, 2015.

Contents

Document type	Place/Title	Date From	Date To
Heading	58th Division General Staff Aug 1918		
Map	Map		
Heading	War Diary General Staff, 32nd Division August, 1918 Volume No.35.		
Heading	General Staff, 58th (London) Division, August, 1918.		
Heading	1st August To 1st September 1918		
Map	Map		
Miscellaneous	Narrative Of Operations		
Miscellaneous	Narrative Of Operations	08/08/1918	08/08/1918
Miscellaneous	History Of The 58th Division,		
Miscellaneous	Battle History Sheet	09/08/1918	09/08/1918
Miscellaneous	Battle History Sheet	08/08/1918	08/08/1918
Miscellaneous	Battle History Sheet	10/08/1918	10/08/1918
Miscellaneous	Battle History Sheet	09/08/1918	09/08/1918
Miscellaneous	Battle History Sheet	08/08/1918	08/08/1918
Miscellaneous	Battle History Sheet	09/08/1918	09/08/1918
Miscellaneous	Battle History Sheet	08/08/1918	08/08/1918
Miscellaneous	Battle History Sheet	09/08/1918	09/08/1918
Miscellaneous	Battle History Sheet	10/08/1918	10/08/1918
Miscellaneous	Battle History Sheet	09/08/1918	09/08/1918
Miscellaneous	Battle History Sheet	08/08/1918	08/08/1918
Miscellaneous	Battle History Sheet	10/08/1918	10/08/1918
Miscellaneous	Battle History Sheet	09/08/1918	09/08/1918
Miscellaneous	Battle History Sheet	10/08/1918	10/08/1918
Miscellaneous		24/08/1918	24/08/1918
Miscellaneous	58 G Ref I.G 1/391	15/08/1918	15/08/1918
Miscellaneous	D.A.G., 3rd Echelon		
Miscellaneous	Addendum No.1 To 58 Th (London) Divisional	06/08/1918	06/08/1918
Miscellaneous	Forthcoming Operations 58th (London) Divisional Instructions No. 6	05/08/1918	05/08/1918
Miscellaneous	Forthcoming Operations 58th (London) Divisional Instructions No. 7	05/08/1918	05/08/1918
Miscellaneous	Forthcoming Operations 58th (London) Divisional Instructions No. 8	06/08/1918	06/08/1918
Miscellaneous	58th (London) Divisional Instruction No 9		
Miscellaneous	58th (London) Divisional Instruction No. 10	07/08/1918	07/08/1918
Miscellaneous	Table "A"		
Map	Map		
Heading	Report On Operations On 8th 9th & 10th August 1918 Of 10th Tank Battalion "B" Coy		
Heading	10th Tank Bn Report On Operations 8th 9th & 10th August 1918		
Miscellaneous	Report On Operations Of 10th Tank Battalion	08/08/1918	08/08/1918
Heading	B Coy 10th Tank Bn. Report On Operations On 8th 9th 10th August 1918		
Miscellaneous	B Coy 10th Tank Battalion	08/08/1918	08/08/1918
Heading	C Coy 10th Tank Bn Report On Operations On 8th 9th 10th August 1918		
Miscellaneous	C Company. 10th Tank Battalion	08/08/1918	08/08/1918

Heading	58th Division Report On Operations Of 173rd Inf Bde For August 1918		
Miscellaneous	58th Division	05/09/1918	05/09/1918
Miscellaneous	173rd Infantry Brigade	05/09/1918	05/09/1918
Miscellaneous	Narrative		
Miscellaneous	General Notes		
Miscellaneous	Appendix "A" Prisoners.	25/08/1918	25/08/1918
Miscellaneous	Appendix "B" Composition of Brigade Group-(Less Affiliated Artillery)	25/08/1918	25/08/1918
Miscellaneous	173rd Infantry Brigade	25/08/1918	25/08/1918
Map	Map "A"		
Map	Map		
Map	Map "C"		
Heading	58th Division Report On Operations Of 174th Inf Bde For August 1918		
Miscellaneous	58th Divisions	21/08/1918	21/08/1918
Miscellaneous	Report On Operations	16/08/1918	16/08/1918
Miscellaneous	174th. Infantry Brigade	08/08/1918	08/08/1918
Miscellaneous	Report On Operations	25/08/1918	25/08/1918
Miscellaneous	Col Courton's Command on the Chipilly Shor Controversy	09/08/1918	09/08/1918
Miscellaneous	Narrative Of Operations	08/08/1918	08/08/1918
Miscellaneous	Narrative Of Operations	22/08/1918	22/08/1918
Map	Map		
Heading	Instructions For Forthcoming Operations		
Miscellaneous	Appendix "A"		
Miscellaneous	Forthcoming Operations 58th (London) Divisional Instructions No. 1	03/08/1918	03/08/1918
Miscellaneous	Distribution		
Miscellaneous	Administrative Instructions No. 1	21/08/1918	21/08/1918
Miscellaneous	Forthcoming Operations 58th (London) Divisional Instructions No. 2	05/08/1918	05/08/1918
Miscellaneous	Forthcoming Operations 58th (London) Divisional Instructions No. 3		
Miscellaneous	Forthcoming Operations 58th (London) Divisional Instructions No.3	05/08/1918	05/08/1918
Map	Map		
Miscellaneous	Tank Routes		
Miscellaneous	Forthcoming Operations 58th (London) Divisional Instructions No. 4	05/08/1918	05/08/1918
Miscellaneous	Forthcoming Operations 58th (London) Divisional Instructions No. 5	05/08/1918	05/08/1918
Diagram etc	Diagram		
Miscellaneous	A Form Messages And Signals.		
Miscellaneous	Gx 334		
Miscellaneous	A Form Messages And Signals.		
Miscellaneous	G.X. 353		
Miscellaneous	GX 358		
Miscellaneous	GX 380		
Miscellaneous	GX 369		
Miscellaneous	G.X. 374		
Miscellaneous	The Following Is A List Of Part Of The War Material Captured By This Division		
Miscellaneous	58th (London) Division	08/08/1918	08/08/1918
Heading	War Diary App "B" Locations		
Miscellaneous	58th (London) Division	04/08/1918	04/08/1918

Miscellaneous	58th (London) Division		
Miscellaneous	58th (London) Division	18/08/1918	18/08/1918
Miscellaneous	58th (London) Division		
Heading	War Diary		
Miscellaneous	GX 211		
Operation(al) Order(s)	58 (London) Division Order No. 145.	15/08/1918	15/08/1918
Miscellaneous	GX 226		
Miscellaneous	GX 227		
Miscellaneous	174th Inf Brigade	20/08/1918	20/08/1918
Miscellaneous	Movement In The Divisional Area	21/08/1918	21/08/1918
Operation(al) Order(s)	58th (London) Division Order No. 146	21/08/1918	21/08/1918
Miscellaneous	58th Divn.	21/08/1918	21/08/1918
Miscellaneous	Messages And Signals		
Miscellaneous	G 500		
Miscellaneous	G. 503		
Miscellaneous	III Corps Orders	22/08/1918	22/08/1918
Miscellaneous	G 562		
Miscellaneous	G.572		
Miscellaneous	G.585		
Miscellaneous	G 596		
Miscellaneous	G 606		
Miscellaneous	A Form Messages And Signals.		
Miscellaneous	C Form Messages And Signals.		
Operation(al) Order(s)	58th (London) Division Order No. 147.	24/08/1918	24/08/1918
Operation(al) Order(s)	58th (London) Division Order No. 148.	24/08/1918	24/08/1918
Miscellaneous	C Form Messages And Signals.		
Miscellaneous	A Form Messages And Signals.		
Miscellaneous	CRE G.605		
Miscellaneous	Administrative Instructions In Accordance With Divisional Order No. 147	24/08/1918	24/08/1918
Miscellaneous	A Form Messages And Signals.		
Map	Map		
Miscellaneous	Message Form.		
Miscellaneous	G 625		
Operation(al) Order(s)	58th Division Operation Order No. 149	25/08/1918	25/08/1918
Miscellaneous	G.233		
Miscellaneous	Messages And Signals		
Miscellaneous	A Form Messages And Signals.		
Miscellaneous	GX 104		
Miscellaneous	GX 115,		
Miscellaneous	A Form Messages And Signals.		
Miscellaneous	G. 645		
Miscellaneous	G 649		
Miscellaneous	G.651 25		
Miscellaneous	G.101		
Operation(al) Order(s)	58th (London) Division Order No. 150.	26/08/1918	26/08/1918
Operation(al) Order(s)	58th (London) Division Order No. 151.	27/08/1918	27/08/1918
Map	Map		
Miscellaneous	Amendment To 58th Division C.O. 151.	27/08/1918	27/08/1918
Operation(al) Order(s)	58th (London) Division Order No. 134.	31/07/1918	31/07/1918
Miscellaneous	Administrative Arrangements Issued With 58th Division Order No. 134	01/08/1918	01/08/1918
Miscellaneous	G.257		
Miscellaneous	G.256		
Miscellaneous	A Form Messages And Signals.		
Miscellaneous		03/08/1918	03/08/1918

Miscellaneous	Relief Table		
Operation(al) Order(s)	58th (London) Division Order No. 152.	28/08/1918	28/08/1918
Miscellaneous	A Form Messages And Signals.		
Miscellaneous	G.S. 152/1.	28/08/1918	28/08/1918
Operation(al) Order(s)	58th (London) Division Order No. 153.	29/08/1918	29/08/1918
Miscellaneous	A Form Messages And Signals.		
Miscellaneous	G.X 273.		
Miscellaneous	G. X.308		
Miscellaneous	Location In New Area		
Miscellaneous	58th (London) Division	31/07/1918	31/07/1918
Miscellaneous	Embussing Programme	02/08/1918	02/08/1918
Miscellaneous	Embussing Programme	04/08/1918	04/08/1918
Miscellaneous	Lorry Programme	02/08/1918	02/08/1918
Miscellaneous	58th Divn. G.S. 134/1	03/08/1918	03/08/1918
Operation(al) Order(s)	58th (London) Division Order No. 135.	03/08/1918	03/08/1918
Miscellaneous	Table To Accompany 58th Division Operation Order No. 135	03/08/1918	03/08/1918
Operation(al) Order(s)	58th (London) Division Order No. 136.	04/08/1918	04/08/1918
Miscellaneous	Table To Accompany 58th Division Order No. 135	03/08/1918	03/08/1918
Miscellaneous	G 350		
Miscellaneous	C Form Messages And Signals.		
Operation(al) Order(s)	58th (London) Division Order No. 137	04/08/1918	04/08/1918
Map	Map		
Miscellaneous	G 360		
Miscellaneous	58th Division	05/08/1918	05/08/1918
Map	Map		
Miscellaneous	Forthcoming Operations 58th (London) Divisional Instructions No. 4	05/08/1918	05/08/1918
Operation(al) Order(s)	58th (London) Division Order No. 138	06/08/1918	06/08/1918
Miscellaneous	Forthcoming Operations. 58th (London) Divisional Instructions No. 10	08/08/1918	08/08/1918
Miscellaneous	A Form Messages And Signals.		
Miscellaneous	58th Battalion Machine Gun Corps.	06/08/1918	06/08/1918
Operation(al) Order(s)	58th (London) Division Order No. 138.	06/08/1918	06/08/1918
Miscellaneous	D.R.L.S		
Miscellaneous	A Form Messages And Signals.		
Operation(al) Order(s)	58th Battalion Machine Gun Corps. Order No. 24.	06/08/1918	06/08/1918
Operation(al) Order(s)	58th (London) Division Order No. 139.	07/08/1918	07/08/1918
Miscellaneous	G.S. 139/2	07/08/1918	07/08/1918
Miscellaneous	Reference 58th (London) Division Order No. 139.	07/08/1918	07/08/1918
Miscellaneous	R.E. Instruction No.1 By C.R.E 58th. Division.	07/08/1918	07/08/1918
Miscellaneous	Addendum No.1 To R.E. Instructions No. 1	07/08/1918	07/08/1918
Miscellaneous	R. E Instructions No. 2	08/08/1918	08/08/1918
Operation(al) Order(s)	58th (London) Division Order No. 140.	08/08/1918	08/08/1918
Miscellaneous	A Form Messages And Signals.		
Operation(al) Order(s)	58th (London) Division Order No. 141.	09/08/1918	09/08/1918
Miscellaneous	A Form Messages And Signals.		
Miscellaneous	GX 71		
Miscellaneous	A Form Messages And Signals.		
Operation(al) Order(s)	58th (London) Division Order No. 142.	09/08/1918	09/08/1918
Miscellaneous	A Form Messages And Signals.		
Miscellaneous	G. X. 76		
Miscellaneous	A Form Messages And Signals.		
Miscellaneous	G. X.81.		
Miscellaneous	A Form Messages And Signals.		
Miscellaneous	G X 90		

Miscellaneous	G X 96		
Miscellaneous	G X 99		
Miscellaneous	G X 103		
Miscellaneous	G X 117		
Miscellaneous	G X 146		
Miscellaneous	G X 161		
Miscellaneous	G X 162		
Miscellaneous	G X 163		
Miscellaneous	A Form Messages And Signals.		
Miscellaneous	G X 173		
Miscellaneous	Form Messages And Signals.		
Miscellaneous	A Form Messages And Signals.		
Operation(al) Order(s)	58th (London) Division Order No. 143.	12/08/1918	12/08/1918
Miscellaneous	G X 200		
Miscellaneous	G X 201		
Miscellaneous	G X 202		
Miscellaneous	G X 203		
Operation(al) Order(s)	58th (London) Division Order No. 144	12/08/1918	12/08/1918
Miscellaneous	G X 206		

58TH DIVISION

GENERAL STAFF
AUG 1918

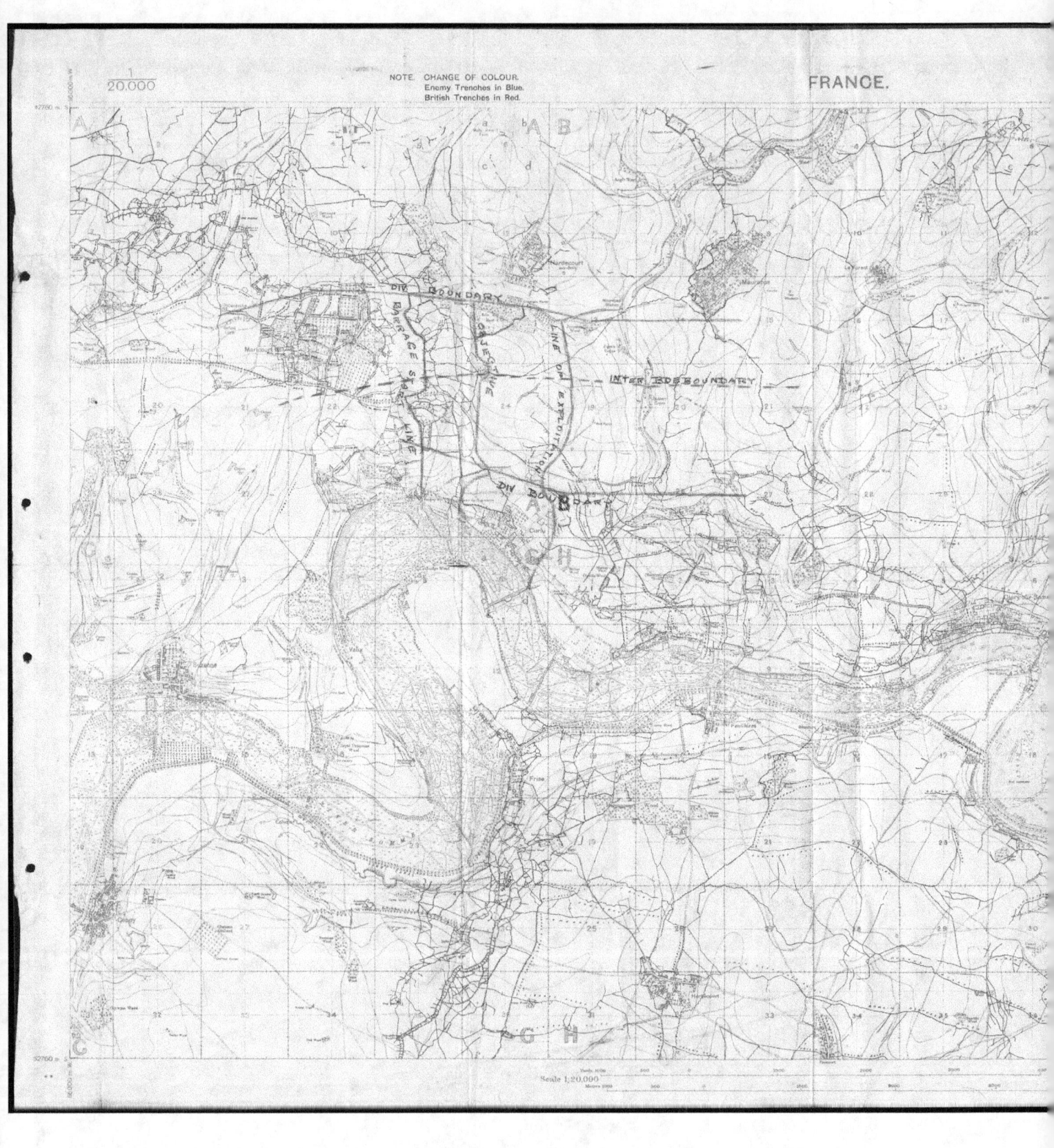

FRANCE. EDITION 4. B TRENCHES CORRECTED TO 6-3-18 SHEET 62c N.W.

CONFIDENTIAL.

WAR DIARY.

GENERAL STAFF, 32nd DIVISION.

AUGUST, 1918.

VOLUME No. 35.

GENERAL STAFF,

58th (LONDON) DIVISION,

AUGUST, 1918.

Appendices only: Narrative of Operations takes place of War Diary as per 58th Div. G.S. letter to D.A.G. 3rd Echelon dated 22.2.1919, filed herein.

1ˢᵗ August
to
1ˢᵗ September
1918

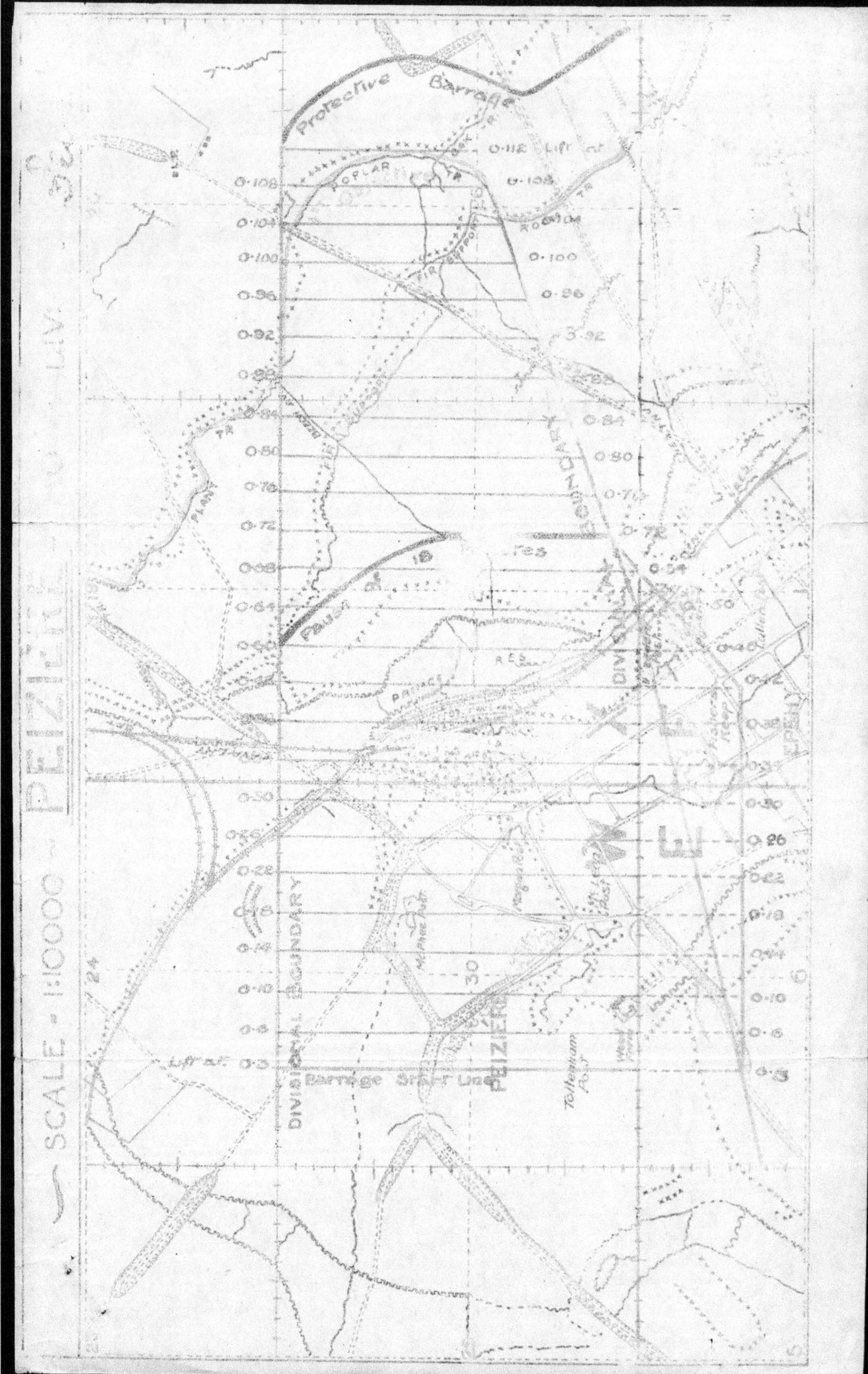

NARRATIVE OF OPERATIONS.

Period 22nd August to 1st September 1918.

INTRODUCTORY.- The Division (less artillery) arrived in the QUERRIEU Area on relief by the 47th Division on August 14th.

Brigade Groups were disposed as follows :-

173rd Inf. Brigade.- QUERRIEU.
174th Inf. Brigade.- ROUND WOOD (W. of FRANVILLERS)
175th Inf. Brigade.- BOIS ESCARDONNEUSE (S. of LA HOUSSOYE)

The Divisional Artillery was still left in the Sector N. of the SOMME and came under the orders of a Composite Force which was introduced to co-ordinate the operations of the III and Australian Corps across the SOMME Valley.

No definite instructions were forthcoming as to how long the Division would be in rest. The time was spent in reorganization, absorption of drafts and training.

On August 17th the Commander-in-Chief visited all Brigades during their training and expressed himself well pleased with the part the Division had taken in the operations just previously carried out.

GENERAL.- On August 18th a conference was held at which proposals were made for an attack by the III Corps with 47th, 12th and 18th Divisions. The objective was approximately a line running from the N. of BRAY to E. of ALBERT. The attack was to be carried out on August 22nd, in co-operation with attacks of the Fourth Army South of the SOMME and the Third Army in the direction of BAPAUME; the object of these attacks being to capture the country re-taken by the enemy on March 21st, so that he might not be able to destroy roads and railways in his intended withdrawal.

NARRATIVE.-
1918.
22nd AUGUST.- The Division (less artillery) was in Corps Reserve.

At Zero hour 175th Inf. Brigade with affiliated M.G. Coy. moved to position of assembly in rear of the old British Front Line W. of MORLANCOURT.

At Zero plus 1 hour 174th Inf. Brigade with affiliated M.G. Coy. moved from ROUND WOOD to a position E. of the HEILLY - FRANVILLERS Road.

23rd " The attack by the III Corps was continued by 47th, 12th and 18th Divisions.

173rd Inf. Brigade moved from QUERRIEU to the Valley S. of MERICOURT at dawn.

174th Inf. Brigade was placed at the disposal of 18th Division and remained in its assembly position E. of the HEILLY - FRANVILLERS Road.

175th Inf. Brigade was placed at the disposal of the 47th Division for an attack at dawn on the 24th August, and moved up to assembly position about the North end of TAILLES WOOD.

At 10-30 pm. 173rd Inf. Brigade moved to assembly position in the Old AMIENS Defence Line.

24th August.— At 1 am. on the 24th August the 175th Inf. Bde. on right and 140th Inf. Brigade (47th Division) on the left continued the attack under the 47th Division in conjunction with the 12th Division on the left and the 3rd Australian Division on the right.

The deep ravine running parallel to the objective line called the HAPPY VALLEY was crossed and "mopped up" in the moonlight and the objective was reached before dawn. Later in the day this valley was heavily shelled with gas and H.E. shells.
109 prisoners were captured representing 12 Coys. of each of the 116th and 117th Inf. Regts.

The 174th Inf. Brigade returned to command of G.O.C. 58th Division and were moved forward to the old British trenches 1500 yards S.W. of MORLANCOURT. The 1/4th Suffolks (Pioneer Battn.) and Field Coys. R.E. of the Division moved from BOIS ESCARDONNEUSE to the Valley S. of MERICOURT.

At 10 am. 58th Division took over the Headquarters of 47th Division and the Divisional Artillery of 47th Division and the command of the Right Divisional Sector of the Corps front passed to G.O.C. 58th Div. at the same time.

To exploit the successful attack carried out in the morning III Corps ordered the Division to make a further attack at 4 pm. on the same day (24th). This was later postponed until 2-30 am. the following morning.

25th " At 2-30 am. 175th Inf. Brigade and 140th Inf. Brigade attacked the objective shown on the attached map "B". The attack was carried out under a barrage moving at the rate of 100 yards in four minutes.

173rd Inf. Brigade moved forward in close support of the attack ready to carry either of the leading Brigades through to their objective if strong opposition was met.

On instructions received from III Corps at 4-37 pm. 173rd Inf. Brigade with 83th Army Bde. R.F.A. attached was ordered to be in readiness to form the advanced guard of the Division should the enemy's defence weaken.

Both Brigades gained their objective with little opposition and consolidated, pushing out patrols to the front. Divisions on the flanks also reported little resistance.

173rd Inf. Brigade was at once ordered to form the advanced guard of the Division and to advance on MARICOURT via BRONFAY FARM and North of BILLON WOOD

A Troop of Northumberland Hussars was at the

disposal /

disposal of 173rd Inf. Brigade.

Divisional Headquarters moved from HEILLY to South of MORLANCOURT at 9-30 am. but was obliged to return to HEILLY owing to a dump of gas shell being exploded near the site of the new Headquarters.

Divisional Headquarters was finally established South of MORLANCOURT about 11-30 am.

3rd Australian Division ordered their advance to proceed in conjunction with 58th Division, keeping touch with the 58th Division's Right.

12th Division on the left encountered little opposition and their action consisted chiefly in following up and keeping touch with the enemy.

140th and 141st Inf. Brigades reverted to the command of 47th Division at 11-44 am.

The C.R.A. 58th Division took over command of the artillery covering the Division from the C.R.A. 47th Division, 115th and 120th Heavy Batteries were placed under the 58th Division.

140th Inf. Brigade was to withdraw when 173rd Inf. Brigade had passed through their position.

The 2/4th Battalion which formed the vanguard encountered opposition when approaching BILLON WOOD and was compelled to deploy.

173rd Inf. Brigade reported the situation at 11am. to be as follows :- 2/4th Battn. attacking BILLON FM. 2/2nd Battn. about BRONFAY FARM, and the 3rd Battalion in Brigade Reserve. M.G. fire was reported from BILLON WOOD and the enemy shelling was becoming severe.

At 12-15 pm. the enemy was still in possession of BILLON WOOD, the 2/4th Battalion was then trying to work round the North side of the Wood.

At 1-30 pm. orders were issued for 173rd Inf. Brigade and 174th Inf. Brigade to push forward to the line COPSE "N" - A.26.o.5.0. - by BILLON AVENUE - SHEFFIELD AVENUE to LAPREE WOOD as soon as the relief of the 175th Inf. Brigade by the 174th Inf. Brigade was completed.

Very heavy fighting was experienced in BILLON WOOD and the vicinity. The enemy's artillery fire was also exceptionally severe. 173rd Inf. Brigade had troops in BILLON AVENUE during the early afternoon but were forced to withdraw owing to M.G. and Artillery fire. The greater part of the Wood was gained before evening but the situation in the South East corner was obscure until dark, and it is probable that the enemy held out there throughout the day.

At 4-30 pm. one Field Artillery Brigade was placed at the disposal of 174th Inf. Brigade.

26th August.- During the night it was thought that the enemy

were /

retiring on the trenches at the West edge of ~~MARICOURT~~.
His main Line of Resistance was probably there but he
still had troops West of COPSE Valley and in the
trenches joining COPSE "E" and LAPREE WOOD.

Patrols of 174th and 173rd Inf. Brigades pushed
out with the object of establishing a line running
N.W. through COPSE "C" by dawn. They were however
prevented in this by many isolated enemy M.Gs.

At 4-30 am. our artillery placed a heavy barrage
on the trenches at the West edge of MARICOURT and on
the trench line running S. from the village to CREST
AVENUE. At the same time 174th and 173rd Inf. Bdes.
advanced over the high ground E. of BILLON Wood and
came under heavy M.G. and artillery fire chiefly from
the village of MARICOURT. Several Field Guns were
firing at close range and it is estimated that about
10 M.Gs. were firing from A.15.central and about 20
to 25 M.Gs. were pouring out fire from CREST AVENUE.

With the help of artillery attached to Brigades
the advance was pressed on and by the afternoon a
line running from "C" COPSE to a point 200 yards S.
of OXFORD COPSE was established.

The 12th Division on the left had not cleared
CARNOY and 173rd Inf. Brigade made a defensive flank
facing North from OXFORD COPSE to LAPREE WOOD. South
of "C" COPSE the line was not continuous but "D"
COPSE and a bank 200 yards N. of it was manned by
174th Inf. Brigade who were in touch with 3rd Aust.
Division on the Right. The Australian Patrols late
in the evening pushed N.E. on the East side of the
MARICOURT Valley towards CREST AVENUE and succeeded
in driving the enemy back to cover in SPUR WOOD.

Arrangements for the following day's attack
were made more difficult as no decision as to the
Divisional Right boundary could be obtained.

After orders for the attack had been sent out
it was decided by Australian Corps that the 3rd
Australian Division would attack the Quarry in
A.28.a. and FARGNY Mill but that III Corps must be
responsible for FARGNY Wood.

It was then impossible, owing to the late hour,
to alter the plan and detail sufficient troops to deal
with FARGNY Wood. The 3rd Australian Division
carried out the barrage as originally arranged.

27th August.- Three German Divisions had been identified as
available to fight in the Sector. III Corps sent
out a warning that stiff opposition was again to be
expected in the MARICOURT Sector.

At 4-55 am in conjunction with the 3rd Australian
Division on the right and the 12th Division on the left
the 58th Division attacked under a creeping barrage.
The barrage dwelt on the Start Line for 20 minutes
and then moved forward at 100 yards in 4 minutes for
500 yards and then at the rate of 100 yards in 6
minutes.

174th Inf. Brigade attacked on the right and
173rd Inf. Brigade on the left.

The /

The Start Line, boundaries, and objectives are shown on the attached map "B", but 74th Inf. Brigade had to detach what troops were available to attack FARGNY Wood from the North.

News of the attack was not received until late owing to enemy shelling.

Both Brigades gained the general line of the objective but could not push forward to the line of exploitation owing to strong enemy resistance in the old German Front Line.

The situation on the right was obscure for some time and the enemy were not driven out of FARGNY Wood.

Front Line Battalions, especially those of 173rd Inf. Brigade, became very disorganised in the advance chiefly owing to mist and the high percentage of officer casualties.

Reorganization of troops on the objective was difficult owing to the accuracy of the enemy's snipers and artillery fire.

The 12th Division gained a general line North and South through the West edge of FAVIERE Wood. Touch with them on the objective was easily obtained.

The 3rd Australian Division gained objectives with the exception of FARGNY Mill. Front Line troops were unable to gain touch with them until late in the day.

A separate operation had to be arranged for the taking of FARGNY Wood, which was reported to be still occupied by the enemy at 9-5 pm.

28th August.— An attack with a creeping barrage was ordered to be carried out, the objective, Start Line etc. for which are shown on the attached Map "B"

Zero hour was 4-55 am, and the 173rd Inf. Brigade was to attack on the left with the 174th Inf. Brigade on the right.

This attack opened very successfully almost all over the Divisional Front. Enemy resistance was on the whole rather weak, though his barrage on the Old British Front Line and on MARICOURT during the attack was distinctly heavy.

By 8 am. the objective was reported as reached all along the Divisional front except at the Northern end, where more determined resistance was offered by the enemy in the BOIS D'EN HAUT. Here the attack entered the Wood but was temporarily held up by considerable enemy M.G. fire, especially from CLAPHAM Fm.

By 8-30 am. an International Post was established by the 8th Battalion Lon. Regt. and the Australians in A.30.b. and by 9-15 am. touch was still reported as definitely established by the two attacking Brigades, on the objective in SUPPORT COPSE.

The enemy M.Gs. in BOIS D'EN HAUT were also reported

by /

by the 12th Division as hanging up their advance at about 10-30 am., but by 12-15 pm, the 173rd Inf. Bde. had fought their way forward through the Wood and had captured CLAPHAM FARM which had been the main point of resistance in this area, and a joint post was established there with the 12th Division.

Other enemy Machine Guns had been causing annoyance and delay to the 174th Inf. Brigade and the Australians on our right from the direction of A.24.b. but by 11-7 am. the 174th Inf. Brigade were able to report that two enemy Machine Guns in this neighbourhood had been dealt with by an encircling movement.

Enemy shelling of the forward area was heavy throughout.

At about 12-15 pm. the enemy was reported to be dribbling back to the valley in B.13 and B.19, and the Artillery was informed accordingly.

At 1-58 pm. the Australians reported the trenches in B.25 and H.1.b. to be strongly held by the enemy with forward M.Gs. near our forward posts.

At 7-30 pm. orders were issued for artillery bombardments to be opened at 10-15 pm. to assist the 173rd and 174th Inf. Brigades in establishing posts at B.13.c.0.0 and B.19.c.0.2. respectively - those posts to be consolidated as soon as established.

29th August -   During the earlier part of the night 28/29th August, forward posts were established as follows -

By 173rd Inf. Brigade at approximately A.24.b.9.9.
By 174th Inf. Brigade in the trench running from
  A.24.d.4.2 to A.24.d.1.2.

After the establishing of the above posts these two Brigades were relieved by the 175th Inf. Brigade with the 4th Suffolks (Pioneers) attached, and the whole Divisional front was then held by this "Composite" Brigade.

After relief the 174th Inf. Brigade became the Support Brigade, and was situated in A.22.a and c. A.28.a and A.21., whilst the 173rd Inf. Brigade passed to Divisional Reserve in L.4., the XXII Corps Cavalry and Cyclists being attached.

Shortly after taking over, the 175th Inf. Bde. established posts at A.18.d.8.8., A.24.b.9.9 and A.24.d.4.2.

No organized attack with a barrage had been ordered for the 29th, and the fighting resolved itself into a series of patrol actions forward to tactical points, followed by the advance of the infantry holding the front line.

At 8-45 am. orders were issued for fighting patrols to be pushed forward to follow up the enemy who was believed to be withdrawing, and by 10-40 am. a line of posts had been established on the general line RED FARM - B.19.a.5.5 - B.13.c.2.0., and touch was established on both flanks. Patrols were then

pushed /

pushed forward to BATTERY COPSE and reported the Copse clear of the enemy.

The enemy appears to have been somewhat demoralised as prisoners stated that during the previous night many ran away and were rounded up in PERONNE, where they were collected and sent back into the front line.

At 1-15 pm. 175th Inf. Brigade was ordered to endeavour to push forward to the trench running S.E. from the South end of MAUREPAS through B.21.central to B.28.a., where touch was to be established with the Australians.

At 1-50 pm. the XXII Corps Cyclists were placed under the orders of B.G.C. 175th Inf. Brigade.

At 3-50 pm. the 2nd Life Guards M.G. Battn. (less 2 Coys.) were moved forward to hold the line of trenches running N and S. through SUPPORT COPSE, and at 6-45 pm. 1 Squadron Northumberland Hussars was also attached to the 175th Inf. Brigade.

At 6-15 pm. 175th Inf. Brigade moved to A.23.b.2.0.

At 6-50 pm. enemy guns were located in MARRIERES WOOD.

At 8-15 pm. 175th Inf. Brigade reported that they had 2 Battalions in the trenches running S.S.W. from MAUREPAS and 2 Battalions in trenches running S.E. from MAUREPAS to B.28.a. where touch was established with the Australians in accordance with orders issued by Divisional Headquarters.

30th August.— Orders were issued on the 29th August for the advance to be continued on the 30th August as rapidly as possible and an advance guard consisting of the following units was ordered to move at dawn from the positions reached on the night of the 29th August.

       175th Inf. Brigade.
       4th Suffolk Regt.
       3 Brigades R.F.A.
       1 Section R.E.
       "C" and "D" Coys. 58th Bn. M.G.C.
       1 Coy. XXII Corps Cyclists.
       1 Sqdrn. Northumberland Hussars.

Divisions on both flanks had similar orders to push forward in co-operation.

During the night 29/30th August a copy of the 3rd Australian Division's Operation Orders showed that they intended to advance in a general N.E. direction, across the front of the 58th Division, cutting the Division out at C.14.central. The III Corps were asked if the boundary had been changed, but at the time they had no knowledge of the contemplated change.

At 8 am. a message was received from III Corps

stating /

stating that if the Australians were successful in crossing the SOMME further South the 3rd Australian Division's advance would be across the 58th Divisional boundaries, taking the system of trenches South of BOUCHAVESNES from the South flank.

The Advance Guard Commander - General COBHAM, 175th Inf. Brigade - was informed, but not sufficiently early to pass it on to the vanguard, which had already pushed ahead. At the same time the advance guard were ordered to continue their advance between the new boundaries as far as C.14.central.

The vanguard (consisting of 1 Squadron of Northumberland Hussars, 1 Coy. XXII Corps Cyclists, 1 Section of R.Es. 1 Section of 291st F.A. Brigade, and 2 Sections of M.G. Coy.) advanced at 5 am. The Cyclists selected the MAUREPAS - LE FOREST Road, the Cavalry Squadron were 1500 yards South of this road and encountered little opposition. One patrol of the cavalry were fired at from B.22.central, and another patrol of the same squadron had linked up with the Australian Cavalry. Both of the latter units reported opposition from B.23. c.5.5 (Hill 110) and considerable shell fire from MARRIERES Wood.

At 10-40 am. two fighting patrols were sent out towards MARRIERES Wood while the Main Guard at this time had reached the line N. and S. of B.22.a., where they were in touch with 47th Division on the left. At 11-10am. the 3rd Australian Division reported that their cavalry had reached Hill 150 (N.W. of MARRIERES Wood) and that squares B.18, 23, and 24 were clear of the enemy.

The advance was not altogether comfortable as the enemy shell fire was heavy in the general area between MAUREPAS and HEM Wood, and in addition long range M.G. fire was directed on our likely routes and avenues of approach.

At 11-50 am. nests of M.Gs. were located and with artillery support the Main Guard advanced towards MARRIERES Wood.

In the afternoon the Mainguard had progressed to the line of trenches from B.18.central to B.24.central, immediately West of MARRIERES Wood, in touch with Flank Divisions. Infantry patrols were forward of this line. The 175th Inf. Brigade were held up on this line by fire from M.Gs. and T.Ms. fired from within the Wood. During the day the line had advanced 3000 yards, the final line being just West of MARRIERES Wood from B.18.central to B.24.central (Map 62C)

In the meantime the Headquarters of the 58th Div. moved from the Quarry at L.1.b.3.0 to old Railway Siding at A.19.b.5.2., opening at the latter place at 3 pm.

At about 7 pm. arrangements were made between III Corps and Flank Divisions to continue the attack on the 31st. with the object of capturing the high ground East of MARRIERES Wood. Orders were issued for 174th Inf. Brigade to pass through 175th Inf. Brigade and to take over the advanced guard of the Division. This order was subsequently cancelled and an attack by the 174th Inf. Brigade accompanied by a creeping barrage was substituted.

At /

At 6-30 pm. the 174th Inf. Brigade moved forward by bus to CURLU, thence by march route to Valley in B.22.

Two Companies of 2nd Life Guards M.G. Battalion were ordered to move to and defend the line B.28.a.5.0. to B.14.b.6.0. from 4 am. on the 31st August.

The Squadron of the Northumberland Hussars attached to the Division were ordered to pass to Corps Reserve but to remain in the forward area.

31st August.- On the morning of the 31st August the attack was launched by 174th Inf. Brigade at 5-10 am. The 3rd Australian Division co-operated on the right and the 47th Division on the left. The Start Line ran North and South about 400 yards West of MARRIERES Wood and the objective was the forward crest of the high ground overlooking BOUCHAVESNES.

The attack continued successfully, though the enemy's rearguards put up a good defence, chiefly with M.Gs. The ground in front of the objective lent itself particularly to defence by M.Gs. which the enemy concealed in the low scrub, ditches and quarries about the BAPAUME - PERONNE Road near BOUCHAVESNES.

The objective on the forward slope was reached under cover of the artillery creeping barrage and touch was maintained with flanking units.

The four Company Commanders of the left Battalion (8th Lon. Regt.) became casualties early in the attack, and most of the heavy casualties were sustained by the left Battalion as they came over the bare crest of the high ground out of the wood. The two weak Battalions - 8th Londons and 6th Londons - which formed the front line of the attack captured nearly 400 prisoners, two 4.2 Howitzers, two 77 mm. guns, a few Light Trench Mortars and many Machine Guns, with a certain amount of ammunition.

The flanking Divisions also captured several prisoners, representing the 447th, 445th and the Augusta Guard Regiments.

Later, the Australians pushed on, capturing Mt. ST. QUENTIN, a conspicuous high landmark which overlooked the back areas of our own and the enemy's front.

Early in the afternoon the enemy's resistance stiffened E. of the BAPAUME - PERONNE Road, and although he shelled our new positions and approaches with light and heavy pieces, no counter-attack developed On the other hand, Divisions of each flank, each repulsed a fairly well organized counter-attack during the afternoon.

Throughout the day, and it had been noticed on several days previously, the enemy aeroplanes made no show at all. Our superiority in the air was most marked by the numbers of our own planes over both lines and the total absence during the day of enemy machines.

At 2 pm. the 173rd Inf. Brigade were ordered to

move /

move forward by busses in readiness to attack on the morning of the 1st September. This was contrary to expectations as the Division had had a warning order that probably the 74th Division would relieve the 58th Division on the night of the 31/1st. During the afternoon orders were issued by the Division ordering the 173rd Inf. Brigade to attack through the 174th Inf. Brigade on the morning of September 1st. in co-operation with 3rd Australian Division on right and 47th Division on the left. The Start Line for the 173rd Inf. Brigade was roughly the BAPAUME - PERONNE Road, along which the barrage would fall at 5-30 am. The objective was the old German Reserve Line running South of MOISLAINS Wood.

The 175th Inf. Brigade moved back to the valley South of MARICOURT with their Headquarters at the QUARRY A.28.a. (Map 62.C)

1st September.— On the morning of the 1st September the attack was continued, the 173rd Inf. Brigade passing through the 174th Inf. Brigade, and attacking in conjunction with 3rd Australian Division on the right and the 47th Div. on the left. The plan was to capture BOUCHAVESNES and the ridge beyond, including the old British Front Line trenches in C.15.b and d. (Sheet 62C N.W.)

The approach march of the 173rd Inf. Brigade was considerably interfered with by the congestion of traffic along all roads and tracks in the forward area; but they reached their assembly positions at 3 am. without interference of the enemy.

At 5-30 am the attack began and troops moved forward under a creeping artillery barrage.

This attack was completely successful and the old British Front Line East of BOUCHAVESNES was captured without much difficulty. Touch with Divisions on each flank however was not made until some hours later. The enemy had opposed the advance by M.G. fire and his barrage put down in response to ours was prompt and heavy.

From the statements of prisoners captured during the day it was evident that it was the enemy's intention to hold the ridge East of BOUCHAVESNES at all costs. The exploitation of the successful attack was hampered by the fact that all movement forward was necessarily on the forward slope of the ridge, and therefore under full view of the enemy, and also that the Divisions on each flank were well in rear of the 58th Division and unable to co-operate. However, the 173rd Inf. Brigade established forward posts along the German trench line 800 yards in front of the final objective.

Considering the low strength of the 173rd Inf. Bde. the number of prisoners captured was large. In all 325 German Officers and men were captured as well as 8 Field guns, numerous M.Gs. and a Motor Ambulance complete with Driver.

The line as given above was handed over on the night of the 1/2nd September to the 74th Division. The Command of the Sector passed from G.O.C. 58th Division to G.O.C. 74th Division at midnight on September 1/2nd.

------o0o------

The following is a list of part of the war material captured by this Division (and the 131st Regt. U.S. Infantry attached) since the commencement of operations on the 8th instant.

Some Trench Mortars and 77 mm. guns in addition are believed to have been taken away by Australian Troops, and there are probably more guns in the area which have not yet been located.

77 mm. Guns.

No.	Location.
8	K.33.b., along Western edge of BOIS CELESTINE.
4	K.29.a.5.5.
3	K.23.c.8.9. to K.23.d.1.8.
5	K.11.b.5.8.
1	K.22.a.2.1.
1	K.21.a.9.9.
3	K.28.d.3.4.
1	K.32.a.3.7.
1	K.26.b.
1	K.32.a.8.6.
2	K.27.a.2.5.
1	K.34.b.8.5.
4	Q.4.d.
2	N.W. end CHIPILLY.
37.	

4.1 inch Guns.

No.	Location.
4	K.33.b.
5	K.27.d.9.1.
3	K.23.c.7.2.
1	K.18.a.5.0.
13.	

4.2 inch Howitzers.

No.	Location.
2	K.33.d.8.8.
2	K.34.c.
2	K.34.a.3.8.
4	K.17.b.2.4.
10.	

5.9 inch Howitzers.

No.	Location.
1	K.28.d.9.3.
2	K.18.c.
2	K.29.a.1.6.
5.	

5.9 inch Guns.

No.	Location.
1	K.18.c.

8 inch Howitzers.

No.	Location.
1	K.29.a.1.0.
1	K.29.a.3.9.
2.	

GRAND TOTAL - 68 Guns and Howitzers.

/It

It has only been possible to obtain the number of Trench Mortars and Machine Guns captured by the 174th Infantry Brigade.
The actual total captured by the Division is very much in excess of these, which are as follows :-

Trench Mortars.

Heavy. .... 9.
Light. .... 27.

Machine Guns.

Heavy. .... 57.
Light. .... 133.

In addition, an enemy aeroplane intact was captured in L.4.b.

Large quantities of S.A.A. and ammunition of all calibres were taken.

Also a large quantity of rifles, equipment and stores were taken, especially in CHIPILLY.

1,825 unwounded prisoners, including 58 officers, were captured by and passed through the cage of the Division (this includes those taken by 131st Regt. U.S.Infantry, but not any captured by other Divisions who passed through Corps Cage).

The number of wounded prisoners cannot yet be ascertained.

Many of the enemy were killed by the fire of the Artillery, Machine Guns and Infantry, and with the bayonet.

(Sd) C.M.DAVIES.   Lt.-Colonel,
General Staff, 58th (London) Division.

12th August, 1918.

```
C.R.A.          6 copies.
C.R.E.          5    "
173rd Inf. Bde. 5    "
174th Inf. Bde. 5    "
175th Inf. Bde. 5    "
Signals.        2    "
58th Bn.M.G.C.  6    "
Div. Train.     4    "
A.D.M.S.        4    "
1/4th Suffolks. 2    "
"A" and "Q"     1 copy.
D.A.D.O.S.      1    "
D.A.D.V.S.      1    "
A.P.M.          1    "
```

NARRATIVE OF OPERATIONS.

Period 8th to 13th August 1918.

THE CONCENTRATION OF THE 58th DIVISION FOR THE ATTACK ON AUGUST 8th.

During the period August 1st - 6th, the concentration of the Division for the attack was carried out, the greatest secrecy being observed throughout. All movements of troops took place by night, and men, transport and guns remained carefully concealed in woods and villages during the day.

On the night of August 4/5th, the 173rd and 174th Brigades together with the 4th Suffolks, the 504 Field Coy and 511 Field Coy. and affiliated M.G. Companies were moved by bus and road to the FRANVILLERS area whence the 174th Brigade marched straight to bivouacs in deep Valley running up from the SOMME just west of SAILLY-LE-SEC.

On the following night, 5/6th, this Brigade relieved that portion of the front held by the 18th Division between CHIMP LANE (see map "C" attached) and the SOMME, and on the night of the 6th the 173rd Brigade moved into the Valley vacated by the 174th Brigade. The 175th Brigade were meanwhile being bussed up from VIGNACOURT to the BOIS ESCADOEUSE and completed their move on August 7th.

During this period all the Divisional Artillery together with three attached Brigades of Field Artillery who were to cover the attack, were moving up ammunition and preparing positions into which the guns were to be moved during the night before the attack.

On the evening of August 7th the concentration of the Division and its neighbours was complete.

The dispositions of the Division in detail at dawn on the 8th being as shown on the attached map.

GENERAL PLAN OF THE ATTACK.

The whole operation composed an attack to be made from MORLAI COURT to MORBUIL the primary objective being the old AMIENS Defence Line constructed in 1914; the recapture of which would release the important Railway and road junctions of AMIENS from gun fire. The front of the attack included the whole of the Fourth British Army under Sir H. RAWLINSON and of a French Army on their right.

The special role of the III Corps composed of the 18th and 58th Divisions was - operating North of the SOMME - to form a protective flank to the more extended advance of the Australian and Canadian Corps South of the river.

This was to be effected by capturing and holding a strong defensive position facing N.E. on the general line BOIS GRESSAIRE - BRIQUETERIE, and by forming a defensive flank along the heights overlooking MORLANCOURT from the South. The 58th Division was entrusted with the carrying out of the first part of the operation whilst the 18th Division on their left were ordered to form a defensive flank overlooking MORLANCOURT. The importance of the III Corps' operation, to a successful advance by the Australians South of the River, was obvious from a study of the ground.

The reaches of the SOMME between CORBIE and BRAY have very steep banks rising to cliffs in places and a resolute enemy

/entrenched

entrenches anywhere along the heights on the North bank, between SAILLY LAURETTE and CHIPILLY would be able to enfilade with deadly effect troops advancing on the Southern Bank of the River.

THE SPECIAL PLAN OF THE 58th DIVISION.

The boundaries and objectives of the 58th Division and the 18th Division on its left are shewn on Map "C" attached.

The plan provided for the first objective the GREEN line being captured by the 174th Brigade and the 2/10th London Regt. attached, the latter under command of Lieut.-Colonel E.P. CAWSTON, were given the special mission of capturing SAILLY LAURETTE, whilst the assault on the GREEN line itself was entrusted to the 6th and 7th London Regts. with the 8th London Regt. moving in close support to the leading Battalions. That portion of the GREEN line allotted to the 18th Division was to be attacked by two Brigades, the 53rd and the 55th, each attacking with two Battalions leading.

After the capture of the GREEN line there was to be a pause of one hour after which the 173rd Brigade with the 53rd Brigade on their left were to pass through the Battalions of the 174th Brigade and capture the RED line, which comprised the whole of the CHIPILLY SPUR - a bare upland commanding a wide expanse of country South of the river.

The attack by the 173rd Brigade was entrusted to the 3rd London Regt. under command of Lieut.-Colonel SANDARS, MC. on the left and the 2/4th London Regt. under command of Lieut.-Colonel Grover, DSO. on the right with the 2/2nd London Regt. moving in close support. Simultaneously with the advance of the 173rd Brigade the 53rd Brigade of the 18th Division on their left were to complete the day's work by the capture of GRESSAIRE WOOD and the brickyard.

The attack was to be covered by a Field Artillery creeping barrage giving an average intensity of one gun to every 25 yds. (90 - 18-pdrs. and 30 - 4.5"Hows. were allotted to the 58th Division for the attack) whilst the deep valleys and gulleys running into the SOMME were to be dealt with by a Howitzer barrage jumping from valley to valley. The heavy artillery bombarding all known gun positions, machine gun nests and villages known to be strongly held.

The attack was further supported by 12 Tanks two were specially detailed to co-operate with the 2/10th London Regt. in their attack on SAILLY LAURETTE, subsequently assisting in the clearing of the Southern end of MALARD WOOD, whilst the remaining ten were detailed to co-operate with the 174th Brigade and subsequently to assist the attack of the 173rd Brigade on the CHIPILLY SPUR.

The 4th Suffolks, (Pioneer Bn.) of the 58th Division under the command of Lieut.-Colonel COPEMAN, CMG. were specially detailed to dig a series of strong posts along the BROWN line, (see map "C" attached) so as to provide a strong line of resistance in case of strong counter attacks forcing back the leading troops.

The Machine Gun Battalion were given such tasks as providing covering fire for the advancing Infantry and to assist in holding the ground when captured. In addition each of the assaulting Battalions was accompanied by one section of Machine Guns.

/Other

Other features of the attack were the use of Supply Tanks and of low flying aeroplanes both to drown the noise of the assembling tanks and for dropping ammunitions for the use of the leading troops and machine guns.

The 175th Infantry Brigade were in Corps Reserve for the attack and were concentrated in the BOIS ESCARDONEUSE at Zero on August 8th.

THE GERMAN ATTACK ON THE 18th DIVISION.

Before going on to describe the events of August 8th it is important to give some account of the German attack delivered on August 6th against the 54th Brigade.

At 4.15 a.m. the enemy put down a heavy barrage of shrapnel and trench mortars on our trenches from about 300 yards South of CRUMP LANE to about the line of the MORLANCOURT-CORBIE ROAD and followed it up with an attack with about 3 battalions.

At the time the 8th London Regt. were in process of relieving the 2nd Bedford Regt. from CRUMP LANE Southwards and the attack extended South of CRUMP LANE sufficiently far to involve the frontage occupied by the two left Companies. On this two Company frontage the enemy was repulsed, but North of CRUMP LANE about three lines of trenches were penetrated and number of prisoners taken by the enemy, and this penetration made it necessary to withdraw the outpost line on the Divisional front although the front line remained intact.

The immediate counter attack by troops of the 18th Division partially restored the situation but at 11.30 a.m. on August 6th the enemy still held AIMMONS and CLONCURRY Trenches.

A further organised counter attack by troops of the 18th Division delivered at 4.40 a.m. on August 7th retook all the ground lost except a pocket towards the North end of CLONCURRY Trench.

The enemy's penetration of the 18th Divisional front admitted him into some of the forward dumps and gun positions awaiting occupation for the attack, and two men of the 50th Divisional Artillery in charge of these dumps were captured.

It seemed inevitable that the enemy would now become aware of the great attack that was impending either from his examination of prisoners or any way from the discovery of dumps and gun positions so far forward. As it turned out, however, the significance of these dumps appears to have completely escaped him and the statements of all prisoners agree that the attack on August 8th came as a complete surprise.

The only serious consequence of this attack was that the heavy losses incurred by the 54th Brigade both in the original attack and in their subsequent counter attacks to regain the lost trenches made it necessary to replace them by the 36th Infantry Brigade of the 12th Division for the attack on August 8th.

The withdrawal of the outpost line and the belief that the enemy might have recognized our gun positions made it necessary to recast the Artillery programme with new gun positions and a start line about 300 yards further West.

This was, however, successfully completed in spite of the shortness of time available.

HISTORY OF THE 58th DIVISION.

THE BATTLE ON AUGUST 8th.
(The capture of MALARD WOOD).

The hour for the attack (Zero) was fixed for 4.20 a.m. A dense mist prevailed at this hour and increased in density until about 8.30 a.m. after which it rapidly lifted so that by 10 a.m. it had entirely cleared. This mist undoubtedly saved us many casualties from machine gun fire, as all movements in the earlier stages of the attack were completely screened; on the other hand it just as certainly contributed to the loss of direction, and confusion, which took place after the first objective had been taken.

The Tanks were affected to an even greater extent than the Infantry, as their field of vision is limited at the best of times.

The 174th Brigade carried out their assembly undetected by the enemy and casualties during the forming up were slight.

The attack started punctually, with all troops moving forward close up to the barrage and although the enemy put up a stout fight his resistance in the front trenches was quickly overcome, and groups of prisoners were soon hurrying down the tracks leading from the front line, many running in their anxiety to get out of range of their own Artillery fire.

Identifications showed that we were opposed by the 27th WURTEMBURG Division - first class troops, who had only just come into the line after 8 weeks rest.

The chief resistance was encountered on the right where the 6th Battalion, assisted by one Tank had to fight hard all the way to MALARD WOOD, arriving there about 7.30 a.m. Very little opposition was actually encountered in the Wood and eventually the line was established along its Eastern edge.

The advance of the 174th Brigade was closely followed by the front Battalions of the 173rd Brigade so much so that in the dense fog some of their leading troops over-ran and became mixed up with the Battalions of the 174th Brigade.

The original intention had been for the leading Battalions of the 173rd Brigade (the 3rd and 2/4th Londons) to work round the Northern edge of MALARD WOOD to their assembly positions on the GREEN Line but owing to their being so mixed up with the 174th Brigade, this plan had to be abandoned and they passed through MALARD WOOD with the leading Brigade.

Immediately on debouching from the Wood both Battalions came under very heavy machine gun fire and were unable to reach their forming up line, in addition the 2/4th Londons in trying to overcome the opposition on their forming up line lost direction and became mixed up with units of the 18th Division.

In consequence of this difficulty in reaching the GREEN line only a few troops reinforced by the 2/2nd London Regt. were able to continue the advance when the barrage lifted, and only a few of these appear to have reached the steep cliff overlooking the SOMME.

The 2/2nd London Regt. moving forward to reinforce this line came under heavy machine gun fire from the CHIPILLY SPUR and after suffering severe loss had to retire to the cover of MALARD WOOD. Meanwhile on the right the enemy was still in

/possession

possession of the CHIPILLY SPUR from which he was interfering considerably with the advance of the Australians South of the river. Many machine guns were installed on this ridge and in some cases batteries of guns with their triggers bound together were worked by single men from the security of deep dug-outs. Any attempt to advance towards CHIPILLY was met with a storm of machine gun fire.

No change in the general situation occurred during the day and the line remained just outside MALARD WOOD. The 2/10th London Regt. were therefore ordered to attack and capture CHIPILLY at 7.30 p.m. so as to clear the way for the Australians South of the river. Under cover of a heavy bombardment the leading troops forced their way into the outskirts of the Village but were unable to advance further in the face of heavy machine gun and rifle fire and eventually they had to withdraw to a position just outside it. The attack by the 2/10th Londons on CHIPILLY brought to an end the first day's fighting and the approximate line held is shewn by the start line (in VIOLET) on attached Map "C".

Although the full objectives of the day had not been attained very considerable results had been attained and a severe blow dealt to the enemy who was now considerably disorganised. A large number of prisoners had been counted and number of guns, Field and Heavy, not to mention hundreds of machine guns, trench mortars and masses of equipment abandoned by the enemy in his flight had been captured. Large numbers of his dead and wounded were also scattered over the newly captured ground.

In concluding this account of the first day's fighting it will be of interest to record certain details of the fighting not included above.

Although the contact aeroplanes constantly reported the arrival of our men on the final objective it does not appear in the light of subsequent knowledge that these reports were correct, at the most only a handful of men could have reached the bluff overlooking the SOMME and ETINEHEM and these must speedily have either become casualties or been forced to withdraw in the face of the heavy machine gun fire from both CHIPILLY and GRESSAIRE WOOD.

The Tanks rendered very valuable assistance, and their sudden appearance out of the mist in the middle of the enemy infantry caused a panic in several cases. One Tank under Lieut. Mc.GUIRE after losing its way in the mist came in contact with enemy machine-gun nests S.E. of MORLANCOURT and destroyed these taking 300 prisoners. Several Tanks were knocked out by direct hits and at the end of the day only six were fit for further action.

Captured enemy machine guns were used on several occasions with good effect against retreating parties of Germans.

The capture of SAILLY LAURETTE by the 2/10th Londons under Lieut.-Colonel E.P.CAWSTON, was a very well executed manoeuvre and by 6.30 a.m. not only had the whole village been cleared but this Battalion had captured the QUARRY and sunken road N.E. of the Village with a large number of local reinforcements. In all it is estimated that this Battalion accounted for 150 killed and about 500 prisoners of which 150 came from the QUARRY.

/The

The attack of the 18th Division was successful in attaining its first objective but as in the case of the 58th Division the confusion and loss of direction on the first objective prevented the attack being pressed home.

The attack by the Australians and Canadians on the right met with great success and all objectives were attained except on the left where resistance of the Germans on the CHIPILLY SPUR made an advance on the South bank of the SOMME past this Village very difficult.

The need for an immediate resumption of the offensive whilst the enemy was still in his present state of disorganization was paramount. Orders were, therefore issued for the attack to be resumed at dawn by the 175th Infantry Brigade and the 131st American Regt. on their right.

The 175th Infantry Brigade, although it had not been engaged in actual fighting on August 8th had, nevertheless done a considerable amount of marching. In the first instance the 9th and 12th Battalions were placed at the disposal of the 18th Division, and ordered by them to move up to the BALLARAT - ROMA Line. Later on, the 9th London Regt. were sent to the assistance of the 173rd Brigade and eventually dug themselves in on the Eastern edge of MALARD WOOD. The 12th London Regt. were sent at the same time to fill a gap on the front of the 36th Brigade (18th Div) but by the time they arrived it was dark and the gap had already been filled so they dug in behind the advanced troops of the 36th Brigade.

The attack ordered for dawn on the 9th had eventually to be postponed as in the darkness it was found impossible to collect the troops concerned or to move forward the American Regt. in time to co-operate.

THE CAPTURE OF GRESSAIRE WOOD AND THE CHIPILLY SPUR.

The attack that it had been intended should take place at dawn on the 9th was finally ordered for 5.30 p.m. on that afternoon. Orders to that effect could not be got out to the Brigades concerned until 12 noon, so very little time was available for making preparations. The assaulting troops consisted of the 131st American Regt. on the right and the 175th Brigade on the left whilst the 36th Brigade of the 18th Division attacked on the left of the 175th Brigade.

The boundaries and objectives of the day's attack are set forth on map "C" attached.

The 175th Brigade for the purpose of this action was composed of the 9th Londons and 12th Londons, 8th Londons and 5th Royal Berkshires, the latter two Battalions being lent by the 174th and 37th Brigades respectively.

The actual assaulting troops reading from left to right were the 8th Londons, 12th Londons, 3 Bn. 131st American Regt., 1st Bn. 131st American Regt.

In conjunction with this attack the 173rd Brigade were first to sideslip and take up a line between the QUARRY just East of MALARD WOOD and the SOMME to be in position by 3.30 pm. and then to advance and capture the RED line and CHIPILLY SPUR, at the same time as the attack further North, therefore forming a defensive flank for the Americans and clearing the way for the Australians South of the river.

The whole attack being covered by a creeping barrage which, after dwelling for 25 minutes on the Start Line was to creep forward at the rate of 10 yards in 4 minutes.

During the morning Brig.-General MAXWELL-SCOTT had to relinquish the command of the 175th Brigade owing to ill-health and was succeeded by Lt.-Colonel POWELL, Commanding the 9th London Regt.

Owing to the shortness of the notice received, verbal instructions had to be conveyed to all the Commanders concerned, neither was there any time to reconnoitre a forming up line, and to add to the difficulties the enemy continued to shell MALARD WOOD and its vicinity heavily throughout the day. The American Battalions taking part had to double the last mile in order to reach the forming up line in time. Notwithstanding all these difficulties, the assaulting troops were formed up only eight minutes after Zero, and went forward with great dash immediately the barrage lifted.

The Germans were completely surprised and many of their infantry seized with panic abandoned their arms and equipment and surrendered or ran away as soon as our men appeared. An hour after the attack started, the track running from the North end of MALARD WOOD to the line was thick with returning German prisoners many of these unaccompanied by any escort were running in panic to escape the heavy Artillery fire which the German Artillery was now directing on to this track, whilst the huddled heaps by the side of the track bore witness to the accuracy of this fire. By 8 p.m. it became clear that all objectives had been captured but both the 8th and 12th Battalions had suffered fairly severe casualties from machine gun fire and the 8th Londons had not obtained touch with the 12th Division.

In view of this situation the 5th Royal Berkshire were ordered to proceed to the assistance of the 8th Londons either by consolidating in depth behind them or by prolonging their

/left

left flank to join up with the 12th Division, and the 8th Londons were ordered forward in close support to the 12th Londons. Meanwhile the Battalions of the 173rd Brigade had reached the sunken road running North from CHIPILLY but had been unable to get further in face of enfilade machine gun fire from the terraces North of CHIPILLY. However the 2/10th Londons who were acting under their orders in close support working their way through CHIPILLY and all its Northern edge took the enemy machine guns on the terraces in flank and reverse. Fierce fighting took place for these guns but eventually they were all silenced, and the crews killed or captured, about 100 prisoners being taken in all.

The capture of CHIPILLY and the terraces soon brought about the fall of the whole SPUR and by 11 p.m. that night all objectives set for the day had been taken.

The artillery barrage for this action was very good and the enemy only retaliated with desultory shelling. Machine gun fire however was very intense and caused many casualties especially among the Americans. Most of the machine guns were installed in the sunken road near the brickyard and on the CHIPILLY terraces. The chief difficulty experienced was the keeping of direction in such featureless country. The Officer Commanding the 8th Londons to assist in preserving direction specially detailed officers to march in front of his attacking troops. These officers, however, were all killed or wounded and the whole attack edged off to the right causing a gap to appear on the left of our line.

The attack, however, was a complete success and the dash with which all ranks went forward in spite of the heavy marching and fighting of the previous day is deserving of the highest praise.

In one part the retreat of the Germans was so precipitate that the German Battalion Commander left his orders, maps, and telephone installation behind in his dugout.

THE CAPTURE OF TAILLES WOOD AND THE OCCUPATION OF THE OLD AMIENS DEFENCE LINE.

Early on the 10th information was received from the III Corps that the attack had been successful on the whole front and that the enemy was everywhere in retreat. The attack was to be continued without respite and the Division in conjunction with the 12th Division would rush on at once and occupy the old Amiens Defence Line. The 9th Londons and the 131st American Regt. had already pushed out strong fighting patrols early in the morning and at noon these patrols sent back word that TAILLES WOOD was clear of the enemy, and the American patrols further reported the Old Amiens Defence Line trenches on their front empty. Owing to a strong gas concentration in the TAILLES WOOD however it was not possible to reach them on the 175th Brigade front. Arrangements were therefore made for these trenches to be attacked at 6 p.m. in conjunction with the 12th Division on our left, however news was received from the 9th Londons at 3 p.m. that they had already been occupied without opposition although the enemy was still holding them strongly opposite the 12th Division. The attack of the 12th Division therefore took place by itself and was successful except on a small portion of the front immediately on our left and this subsequently cleared by fighting patrols of the 8th Londons, so that by 11 p.m. the Old AMIENS Defences

/had

had been occupied on the whole front of the 58th and 12th Divisions.

On August 11th the line became stabilised, and certain reorganizations of the line were carried out, a part of the 12th Division's front was taken over and reorganized that night on a three battalion front held by the 12th, 9th and 2/10th London Regts from right to left. At the same time the Australians took over the 131st American Regt's front and this Regiment passed under their orders.

The 5th Yorkshires and 8th Londons returned to the command of their respective Brigades and the 173rd and 174th Brigades were withdrawn to the old trench system to reorganize.

The capture of the Old Amiens trench system brought to an end the First Phase of the 3rd Battle of the SOMME and on the night of August 12th the 175th Infantry Brigade was relieved by the 142nd Infantry Brigade and marched on the following day to the BOIS ESCARDONEUSE, the 173rd and 174th Brigades having moved on the previous day to QUERRIEU and ROUND WOOD respectively.

On August 10th Brig.-General COBHAM, DSO. arrived to take command of the 175th Brigade.

The Division had now been in action for 4 days during which they had made a total advance of 6,000 yards all in the face of strong opposition. 1,925 prisoners including 58 Officers had actually been counted through the cages and many more undoubtedly found their way back through other Divisional areas.

Some attempt has been made overleaf to record a list of the guns, machine guns and other booty captured during these four days but the Division was withdrawn from the area of the fighting before anything like a complete count could be made, neither was it possible to count the enemy dead, although all who subsequently examined the battle field are agreed that the numbers were unusually large.

In every way, therefore, the actions of August 8th - 12th deserve to rank as amongst the greatest and most successful fought by the 58th Division up to date, and on August 17th the Commander-in-Chief himself visited all Brigades of the Division and congratulated them on their performance, and to these congratulations must be added those of the Corps Commander, Sir A. BUTLER and Sir H. RAWLINSON, Commanding the Fourth Army.

----- o**o -----

BATTLE HISTORY SHEET.

Crew No. 3   Tank No. J 46   Date. 9.8.18
Commanded by 2/Lieut. N. Kerr A Coy 10th Bn.
Unit to which attached   5th   Divn.   15 Bde.
Zero hour.   3.30 pm.
Hour Tank started for action.   3.10 pm
Proceeded in front of Infantry.
Reached objective at   4.10 pm
Condition of the ground.   Good, steep banks in places
Condition of the enemy's trenches.   Very narrow. not ditched. M.G. pits

Weather conditions.   Fine hot day - very clear
Condition of crew after action.   Exhausted.
Condition of Tank after action.   Burnt out at K.34.a.70.20.
Casualties.   one man

Number of messages sent by pigeon.   nil
Anti-Tank measures adopted by the enemy?   Bombs
6-pdr ammunition expended.   60 rds.
S.A.A. expended.   9000 do
No of hours Tank was in action.   5½ hrs
Approximate mileage covered.   8 miles
Position of Tank after action.   K.34.a.70.20
Orders received at 2.45 pm. on 9.8.18. were as follows :-
To follow J5 along road to K.34.c.20.10. then branch NORTH through CELESTINS WOOD and clear banks of enemy Machine guns

REPORT OF ACTION:- Followed Lt Gender in taking road, then patrolled round CELESTINS WOOD for 4 hrs. also patrolled banks at K.34.a. and cleared enemy machine guns. Tank was set on fire by enemy bombs thrown at close range. Crew evacuated tank and formed a strong point & held the enemy off till our Infantry arrived two hours later. He then reorganized Infantry & went on with them till he was wounded.

F.A. Robinson
Major

Suggested that in future :-

Signature L.J. Lambert Capt.
Time   2.45 pm.
Date   15.8.18.
Place   POULAINVILLE

BATTLE HISTORY SHEET.

Crew No. 12   Tank No. 9160   Date. 8-8-18
Commanded by   F Sharp 2nd Lt   10th Bn.
Unit to which attached   -   Divn. -   Bde.
Zero hour.   4.20 a.m.
Hour Tank started for action.   -
Preceeded   -   Infantry.
Reached objective at   -
Condition of the ground.   -
Condition of the enemy's trenches.   -

Weather conditions.   Thick ground mist
Condition of crew after action.   -
Condition of Tank after action.   -
Casualties.

Number of messages sent by pigeon.   -
Anti-Tank measures adopted by the enemy?   -
6-pdr ammunition expended.   Nil
S.A.A. expended.   Nil
No of hours Tank was in action.   -
Approximate mileage covered.   -
Position of Tank after action.   -
Orders received at   pm. on 6-8-18 were as follows :-

To reach the Green Line for the 1st objective and the Red Line for the 2nd objective

REPORT OF ACTION. Owing to my tank breaking down at J.19.c.80.20, I did not part in any action.

I suggest that in future :-

            Signature F Sharp 2nd Lt
            Time   10 A.M.
            Date   12-8-18
            Place   K.24.b.80.20.

BATTLE HISTORY SHEET.

Crew No. 3   Tank No. J __ (9444)   Date 6.8.17
Commanded by 2/Lieut W Tait   10th Bn.
Unit to which attached 7th Batt. Royal Sussex   Division 12th Div.   Bde. 35th
Zero hour 4.20 am
Hour Tank started for action 4.20 am
Proceeded behind Infantry
Reached objective at
Condition of the Ground Good
Condition of the enemy's trenches Good

Weather conditions Bad   Thick ground mist
Condition of crew after action Very bad (gassed with fumes)
Condition of tank after action Good
Casualties nil.

Number of messages sent by Pigeon nil
Anti-Tank measures adopted by enemy? nil
6 Pdr ammunition expended nil
S.A.A. expended nil
No. of hours tank was in action nil
Approximate mileage covered ½ mile
Position of Tank after action K21 C20 ⅘
Orders received at 6.0 p.m. 6.8.17 were as follows:-
First to attack and take the green line (2d) K21 D50 50 +
as a second objective to take the red line at 62 D K 24. a 0 0 20.
  REPORT ON ACTION:- This tank was ditched
                    and never actually got
                          into action

Suggest that in future -

                        Signature W.P. Davy Capt 4 o/c
                        Rank Tank Comm. 2/Lt W Tait
                        Time 10.0 am
                        Date 12.8.1917
                        Place J24 A 20 20

BATTLE HISTORY SHEET.

Crew No.   Tank No. J 30   Date 8.8.18.
Commanded by   2/Lt Wright   10th Tank Bn.
Unit to which attached 9th Dessex 18th   Division   53rd Bde.
Zero hour
Hour Tank started for action 3.50 a
Proceeded In front of Infantry
Reached objective at
Condition of the Ground   Good
Condition of the enemy's trenches
                        Shallow & unpainted
Weather conditions   Very misty.
Condition of crew after action Exhausted.
                the Tank do Burnt out, direct hit
Casualties 2 Lt Wright killed, 4 O.R. wounded
                    + 1 O.R. missing.
Number of messages sent by Pigeon Nil
Anti-Tank measures adopted by enemy? Anti Tank Rifle, A.P.
                        Ammun. & Shell fire.
6 Pdr ammunition expended 6 Case 27 H.E
S.A.A. expended   1000 Rounds.
No. of hours Tank was in action 8
Approximate mileage covered   11-12 miles
Position of Tank after action   K 15 d.
Orders received at 5.0 p.m.   - were as follows:-

The tank went in at Zero, but owing to mist was an hour & half before getting into touch with enemy. The tank then proceeded North of the BRAY-CORBIE Rd. firing on Machine guns & riflemen. The first objective was reached about 10.30 a.m. The tank then went on & met a machine gun but could not be located. Twenty minutes were spent here & then the tank went on to the following objective. The petrol then began to run short, the tank was swung the rear. The tank then received a direct hit that set her alight.

Lieut Wright ordered the tank to be abandoned. The fire was so rapid that no guns were saved. The crew then occupied a dugout, taking their wounded with them.

They captured about 30 Germans who were made to carry their wounded with them back.

It is not known when Lieut Wright was killed. Pte Sil Kent is the only member of the crew with the Battn at present & the above is the only statement available.

(Signed) J Jordan Lloyd Capt.

15.8.18

Battlefield

BATTLE HISTORY SHEET.

Crew No.　　　　Tank No. J25　　Date 8.8.18.

Commanded by 2/Lt Todd　　　　　　　　　Bn.

Unit to which attached　12th　Division　36th　Bde.

Zero hour　4.20 a.m.

Hour Tank started for action　3.55 a.m.

Proceeded　in front of　Infantry

Reached objective at

Condition of the Ground　Good

Condition of the enemy's trenches　Shallow & unfinished.

Weather conditions　Very misty

Condition of crew after action　Exhausted.

Casualties　2/Lt Todd wounded.

Number of messages sent by Pigeon

Anti-Tank measures adopted by enemy?　A.P. ammunition & shell fire

6 Pdr ammunition expended

S.A.A. expended

No. of hours Tank was in action

Approximate mileage covered

Position of Tank after action

Orders received at 5.0 p.m.　　　were as follows:-

(Signed) J. Jordan Lloyd
Capt.

BATTLE HISTORY SHEET.

Crew No.   Tank No. J25   Date 8.8.18

Commanded by 2/Lt Klee   10th Tank Bn.

Unit to which attached — 18th Division 53rd Bde.

Zero hour 4.20 a.m

Hour Tank started for action 3.50 a.m

Proceeded Infront of Infantry

Reached objective at

Condition of the Ground Good.

Condition of the enemy's trenches Fair. Very few finished.

Weather conditions Very misty

Condition of crew after action Exhausted by heat.
do Tank do Knocked out.

Casualties 2/Lt Klee killed + 2 OR wounded.

Number of messages sent by Pigeon Nil

Anti-Tank measures adopted by enemy? A.P Ammunition & Anti Tank Rifles & bombs.

6 Pdr ammunition expended Unknown believed 20 rounds

S.A.A. expended Unknown 7500 Rds

No. of hours Tank was in action

Approximate mileage covered

Position of Tank after action K2.a.9.2. (62d NE 1/20,000)

Orders received at 5.0 p.m.   were as follows:-

Tank went into action at Zero.

Owing to mist targets were hard to find. About 6.0am hostile machine guns were located & fired on the BRAY CORBIE Rd.

At about 9.30am the tank had gear trouble. The gears were put into neutral & could not be got into mesh again. Lt. Klee organised an Infantry party to clear a machine gun nest to his direct front.

He led this attack & then kept up fire with a Hotchkiss gun from the top of his tank.

The crew in the meantime got the tank into running condition.

Shortly after this the first driver was wounded. More machine guns were met & Lieut Klee took over his seat where he was killed by a shot through the telescope slot. The gears then jibbed again & could not be got into action again. The tank was then evacuated under heavy fire & fired.

———

I suggest that in future :-

There should be better ventilation & a more reliable gun.

(Signed) J Jordan Lloyd Capt
C o By.
15.8.18.
In the field.

BATTLE HISTORY SHEET.

Crew No.   Tank No. J~~ 9417   Date 8.8.18.

Commanded by 2/Lt Duffy.   11th Tank Bn.

Unit to which attached 10th Essex 18th Division 55th Bde.

Zero hour 4.20 a.m.

Hour Tank started for action 3.30 a.m.

Proceeded behind Infantry

Reached objective at 7.10 a.m.

Condition of the Ground Good.

Condition of the enemy's trenches Shallow + unfinished

Weather conditions Very misty

Condition of crew after action Fatigued
     do Tank do Good.

Casualties Nil

Number of messages sent by Pigeon Nil
Anti-Tank measures adopted by enemy? A.P. Ammunition, Anti Tank Rifles & bombs
6 Pdr ammunition expended 8 Case 25 H.E.
S.A.A. expended 800 Rounds
No. of hours Tank was in action 3½
Approximate mileage covered 10.000 Yds
Position of Tank after action J.18.d.3.3
Orders received at 5.0 p.m.   were as follows:-

Report on Action —

Tank went into action about 3.30 a.m. & proceeded along the BRAY-CORBIE road & then swung along the north side.

Crossing the first line German machine guns were engaged & put out of action.

Owing to the mist targets were hard to find. The tank reached the Brickyard K.16.c & then mopped up the trenches about that neighbourhood. The tank was then swung back to the brickyard & cleared a M.G. nest on the north.

A party retreating were caught & wiped out.

The tank was then swung round & reported back to the Coy.

Report obtained from crew owing to absence of 2nd Lieut. Duffey in hospital.

(Signed) J. Jordan Lloyd
Cpl.

BATTLE HISTORY SHEET.

Crew No.　　　　　Tank No. J19　　　Date 8.8.18
Commanded by 2Lt. S. A. Price
　　　　　　　　　　　　　　　　　　　　　　Bn.
Unit to which attached 4th R.W.K. Division 53rd Bde.
Zero hour 6·30 am
Hour Tank started for action 6·20 am
Proceeded *in front of* Infantry
Reached objective at 7·12 am
Condition of the Ground Shelled but dry
Condition of the enemy's trenches No definite line

Weather conditions Thick fog
Condition of crew after action Exhausted
　　　　　　　　　　Tank　　Two direct hits on left side
　　　　　　　　　　　otherwise fit
Casualties Three men wounded.

Number of messages sent by Pigeon Nil
Anti-Tank measures adopted by enemy? A.P. bullets, Anti Tank
　　　　　　　　　　　　　　　　　　　　　guns & rifles
6 Pdr ammunition expended 51 Common shell 9 Case shot
S.A.A. expended 1050
No. of hours Tank was in action 4 hours
Approximate mileage covered 12000 yds
Position of Tank after action 62d NE. J 24 d 61
Orders received at 5.0 p.m. 7·8·18 were as follows:-
To proceed in front of Infantry from K. 20 b. 80·80
along the BRAY-CORBIE Rd. to Brickyard at K 16. c & patrol
until Infantry had consolidated & then return to
Rallying Point.

Report on action:-
　　Zero hour was 6.30 a.m.
　　Owing to mechanical trouble, I left my
starting point @ Zero + 10 & proceeded along the
BRAY-CORBIE Rd in fourth speed. I overtook the
Infantry at the cross roads at K 21. & 60.90.
　　The Infantry followed my Tank until
held up by Machine Gun fire.
　　On ascertaining the position of the M.G. I
engaged same with 6 pdr. causing the gun
team to retire. At the same time they Machine
Gunners opened fire.

After reaching my objective I patrolled the ground in front until the infantry were consolid[ated]

During this time I engaged four machine guns which were harassing our troops & succeeded in silencing them.

The Infantry reported that they were being worried by M.Gs on the left & asked me to go & clear them.

I proceeded to a ridge on the left front & found the enemy forming a line of resistance. On opening fire they retired.

I gave chase & broke the enemy formation & inflicted many casualties.

Owing to magneto trouble my engine stopped delaying me for 30 minutes. When the trouble was remedied I turned about & made for the Rallying Point under heavy shell fire receiving two direct hits.

During this action three of my crew were wounded, two by machine gun fire & one by shell fire.

At 4 P.m. I received orders to proceed to the valley on the S.E. side of MORLANCOURT & engage the enemy who were reported to be massing for a counter attack.

I patrolled the valley & opened fire with my Lewis at suspected Machine Gun posts, but no enemy were sighted.

Shell fire was the only resistance offered.

I suggest that in future:-

Better ventilation be provided for the Mark V Tank

(Signed) Talbot H. Price

3. 50 p.m
15-8-18
In the field.

Battle History Sheet.

Crew No............   Tank No....9396/J22. Date...8/8/18.....
Commanded by........Lieut..J.A.McGuire."B".Coy..10th.Tank Battalion.
Unit to which attached .....18th and 12th......... Division.... 53&55 Bde.
Zero Hour....4.20 a.m. and 12.55 p.m.
Hour Tank started for action.....4.24 a.m. and 12. 0 p.m.
Proceeded....with...... Infantry ....
Reached objective at....about 6.0a.m. and 2 Objective 12.35 p.m.
Condition of the Ground....Good with occasional shell holes.
Condition of the Enemy's trenches....fair...........

Weather conditions....Heavy Mist to about 8.0 a.m.
Condition of Crew after action.....Fair..........
Condition of Tank after Action.......Fair.........
Casualties.........3 Members of Crew slightly scratched with bullet splashes.

Number of messages sent by Pigeon......None.......
Anti-Tank measures adopted by Enemy ?...Only Shell and M.G. Fire
6Pdr Ammunition expended ....20 Rounds............
S. A. A. expended........200 Rounds.....
No. of hours Tank was in action....5. to. 4............
Approximate mileage covered......18000 yds....
Position of Tank after action....J.12. A55. S of TREUX

Orders received at..4. & 11 a.m. on Aug. 8th... 1918 were as follows:-
At 4.0 a.m. Move forward to K14 D49 and deal with enemy found there. At 11.0 a.m. move forward to K14 A56 at 12.35 p.m. and clear up pocket of enemy.

Report on Action.

Tank J22 moved forward at 4.24 a.m. toward first objective, but owing to dense mist was lost in the vicinity of first objective and until fog lifted about 8.0 a.m. did not know locality and then reported to G. O. C. 35th Inf. Bde, 12th Division. Received instruction then to clean up pocket of enemy South East of MORLANCOURT and at 12.35 p.m. when barrage lifted went forward with Infantry and cleared up this Section. Between 300 and 400 Prisoners resulted from this Action.

Signature... Lt. James McGuire.
Time.......2.0 p.m.
Date......14.8.18...

Querrieu Wood near   Place....Allonville.

BATTLE HISTORY SHEET.

Crew No. A.　　　Tank No. ???　　Date ???

Commanded by Lieut F. Gatin　　　　　　　　　Bn.

Unit to which attached　???　Division　???　Bde.

Zero hour . 2.20 am.

Hour Tank started for action　3.55 am

Proceeded　ahead　Infantry

Reached objective at　—

Condition of the Ground　Good

Condition of the enemy's trenches　narrow

Weather conditions　Thick mist

Condition of crew after action　In exhaustion petrol fumes + gas

Condition of Tank after action　Bad — petrol fumes coming inside

Casualties　Nil.

Number of messages sent by Pigeon　Pigeons not used.

Anti-Tank measures adopted by enemy?

6 Pdr ammunition expended　—

S.A.A. expended　—

No. of hours tank was in action　2

Approximate mileage covered　5

Position of Tank after action　Tny at 3 (Bf 2a)

Orders received at S.O. p.m. ??? were as follows:—

To leave my starting point at 3.55 am. and reach the barrage at 4.20 am. + continuing behind the barrage to the first objective.

REPORT ON ACTION. At 3.55 am I left my starting point with the object of reaching the barrage when it opened at 4.20 am. At daybreak a very thick mist arose so that it was impossible to see more than a few yds from the Tank. Owing to this mist + ??? deviations ??? I was unable to reach the barrage at zero hour. During this time my exhaust pipe had been damaged with the result that the petrol fumes came into the Tank affecting the crew. I was outside the Tank trying to ??? my route in the mist + was not affected in this manner. The crew ??? ??? my crew were all so exhausted on account of the petrol fumes that I had to drive the tank myself. After trying to find ??? ??? in the mist for about two hours, my Section Commander ordered me to go back to the Tnx, as it was useless going to continue with my crew in such a condition. I therefore direct the Tank back to Battalion Headquarters, where I handed her over to a Officer there, who was to take charge of same, & my crew received medical attention.

I suggest that in future — some means be devised for better ventilation of the tank, as the heat of the present tank is overpowering.

That the exhaust pipes be so arranged as not to be in the drivers face or the interior part, in the case of the back cruiser faint, etc.

Signature A.H. [illegible]
Time 1-20 pm
Date 15.8.18
Place In the Field

BATTLE HISTORY SHEET.

Crew No.　　　　　Tank No. 9390/J24.　Date 8·8·1918.

Commanded by 2/Lt. C. E. Cyphus, B Coy 10th Tank Bn.

Unit to which attached　18th　Division　53rd Bde.

Zero hour　4·20 a.m.

Hour Tank started for action　4·24 a.m.

Proceeded　W.H.　Infantry

Reached objective at　7·15 a.m.

Condition of the Ground　Shelled but dry.

Condition of the enemy's trenches　No definite line held.

Weather conditions　Misty. Fine after mist cleared.

Condition of crew after action　Exhausted.

Condition of Tank after action　Good.

Casualties　2 Wounded 1 Gassed.

Number of messages sent by Pigeon　Nil.

Anti-Tank measures adopted by enemy?　Armour piercing bullets.

6 Pdr ammunition expended　26 Common Shell. 12 Case Shot.

S.A.A. expended　750 rounds.

No. of hours Tank was in action　4.

Approximate mileage covered　12000 yards.

Position of Tank after action　Withdrew to rallying point.

Orders received at 4·30 p.m. Aug 7/8 were as follows:-

Proceed along the left of the Bray Corbie Rd. keeping as far as possible to the route marked as near the barrage as possible and aid the Infantry.

Report on Action.

From the starting point we moved in a zig-zag fashion through the enemy lines keeping as near the barrage as possible. At first it was difficult to discover our position or find any landmarks owing to the intense mist but after a short time we were able to find the Bray Corbie Rd. and keep to our route about 500 yds to the left of it. We were at a slight disadvantage from the start by the loss of a 4/C/1 (2nd Driver) who was wounded at the starting point. During this action we were able to put out of action about 8 Machine Guns & 2 Trench Mortars and so clear the way for the Infantry.

P.T.O.

Report continued.

We reached a point about 200 yards past our first
objective and then had to return for petrol.
The crew behaved well but were exhausted from
the heat and exhaust fumes at the finish.

Signed.
C E Cyphus Lt
3 o F.H.
14 . 5 . 1918.

BATTLE HISTORY SHEET.

Crew No.　　　　Tank No. 9020.　　　Date 8 8 1918

Commanded by Lt. A. J. Hawkins B Coy 10th Bn.

Unit to which attached　18th Division　53rd Bde.
　　　　　　　　　　　7th R. W. Kent.

Zero hour　4.20 a.m.

Hour Tank started for action　3.30 a.m.

Proceeded in front of　Infantry

Reached objective at K.10c Ref 62D. 7.10 a.m.

Condition of the Ground　Good.

Condition of the enemy's trenches　Little damaged by shell fire
very short in length most being small M.G. strong point

Weather conditions　Very misty until 10 a.m.

Condition of crew after action　Very tired

Condition of Tank after action　Mechanically fit and holes through
R. H. Track also requiring spring on sprocket, Gun broken, 18
holes from A.P. bullets through observers plate.

Casualties　One Killed Three Wounded.

Number of messages sent by Pigeon　Nil.

Anti-Tank measures adopted by enemy?　Cannons firing M.G. bullets

6 Pdr ammunition expended　70 rounds

S.A.A. expended　500 rounds.

No. of hours Tank was in action　3½ hours.

Approximate mileage covered　6 miles

Position of Tank after action　J.18.d.2.4.(62D)

Orders received at 5.0 p.m. 7/8/18　were as follows:-

To advance with 7th Royal West Kent towards
K.20.b.8.7 then take the position round the
Brickyard by advancing eastwards near the
Bray Corbie Rd leaving K.20.b.8.7 at 6.30 a.m.

Report on Action

Moving along the Bray Corbie Rd we saw
the enemy barrage at J.18.d.5.7.
At about K.19.c our Infantry, who were scouting
for us, reported a pocket of enemy machine
guns which were holding up the advance on the
right of the road.
As there were no Tanks there I swung right
and after encountering heavy M.G. fire located
their position in the wheat. Several bursts of
case shot roused them. Then I swung left
and joined Tanks J.18 and J.29 and advanced
towards the Brickyard in K.16.
Reaching J.14.d we came under heavy M.G. fire
from half left and I turned the Tank in
that direction.
Owing to the mist and the well concealed
positions it was difficult to see these M.G. posts.
Time after time we came within 50 y of a
post before they fired, then they fired thro'
various openings.
Against us the M.G. fire was so heavy that
bullets came through the armour and pierced the
water tanks and damaged the ammunition.
My driver was killed by what seemed to be an explosive
bullet through the head. The 6 Pounder Gunners found
their targets well and kept up a good fire until the
enemy retired along a communication trench.
We waited for our Infantry and meanwhile ran over
several enemy M.G. already located. Then we followed
the communication trench towards K.10.c, cleared up a M.G.
nest here and moved toward the Bray-Morlancourt Rd.
Here we did some mopping up of trenches and worked
for half an hour until the Infantry had consolidated
behind us.
When the situation seemed secure we moved back
to J.18.c.

I suggest in future:-
Better ventilation in the tank for gunners; the crew trained in
first aid work - a more reliable machine gun to give a
steadier volume of fire. Sgd. Arthur J. Hinks Lt.

BATTLE HISTORY SHEET.

Crew No.   Tank No. Jeu 9059   Date 8-8-18.

Commanded by Capt. Wardrop.   10th Tank Bn.

Unit to which attached 7th Queens 18th Division 55th. Bde.

Zero hour   4-20 am.

Hour Tank started for action   3.55 am.

Proceeded *in front of*   Infantry

Reached objective at

Condition of the Ground   Good.

Condition of the enemy's trenches   Shallow and unfinished with frequent machine gun nests.

Weather conditions   Very misty.

Condition of crew after action   Very exhausted.

Condition of tank after action.   Very good.

Casualties   Captain Wardrop. (Crushed finger)

Number of messages sent by Pigeon

Anti-Tank measures adopted by enemy?   Anti-tank rifles & A.P. ammunition.

6 Pdr ammunition expended

S.A.A. expended

No. of hours Tank was in action

Approximate mileage covered

Position of Tank after action

Orders received at 5.0 p.m.   were as follows:-

Suggestions in future:-

Signature.
Time.
Date.
Place.

BATTLE HISTORY SHEET.

Crew No. 1. Tank No. 9404 (J.18) Date. 10-8-18
Commanded by 2/Lt. Aaron Evans. 10th Bn.
Unit to which attached 9th Essex Divn. Bde.
Zero hour. 6 p.m.
Hour Tank started for action. 2.30 p.m.
Proceeded in front of Infantry.
Reached objective at. 6.50 p.m.
Condition of the ground. Good.
Condition of the enemy's trenches. There were few trenches - his defences consisting mostly of scattered posts in shell holes etc.
Weather conditions. Very good.
Condition of crew after action. Good.
Condition of Tank after action. The lugs on lip of track plate were strained, in one case broken.
Casualties. One man wounded twice.
Number of messages sent by pigeon. Nil.
Anti-Tank measures adopted by the enemy? A.P. bullets.
6-pdr ammunition expended. 60 rounds
S.A.A. expended. 1000 rounds.
No of hours Tank was in action. 4½ hrs
Approximate mileage covered. 7.
Position of Tank after action. J.24 b 5.5.
Orders received at 5 pm. on 10/8/18 were as follows :-

To proceed in front of Infantry to line running from E 28 a 0.8. to K.5 c 9.5 and then patrol high ground (105 contour) in front

REPORT ON ACTION :- I was detailed as the right hand tank of the 4 operating with 9th Essex. I took the road running E of MORLANCOURT, as far as the Aeroplane sheds at K 10 a 8.6 and then proceeded towards objective. It was necessary to wait some little time for our standing barrage to lift, when we were about 200 yards south of the railway line.

We crossed the railway line and engaged M.G's which were firing from the cornfields to our front. I patrolled the high ground in front and assisted a company of the 6th Queens which was moving forward on the left of the

P.T.O.

9th Essex to the commanding ground in front of the railway.

My second driver was wounded both in going into and coming out of action.

When returning the enemy put up a rather heavy barrage on the South side of the railway line. His artillery fired for the most part from the MÉAULTE direction.

A. Evans. 2/Lt.

I suggest that in future :-

① Another sort of strip be used for the Hotchkiss guns. Several instances of jamming occurred.

② The percentage of case shot be raised.

Signature. A. Evans. 2/Lt.
Time. 3.30pm
Date. 11-8-18
Place. K.24.b.5.5.

BATTLE HISTORY SHEET.

Crew No. 1.   Tank No. J 13.   Date. 10-8-18

Commanded by   2nd Lt. A. Evans   10th Bn.

Unit to which attached   9th Essex   Divn.   Bde.

Zero hour.   6 pm

Hour Tank started for action.   2.30 pm

Proceeded in front of Infantry.

Reached objective at   6.50 pm

Condition of the ground.   Good

Condition of the enemy's trenches.   Narrow trenches and scattered posts in cornfield

Weather conditions.   Good

Condition of crew after action.   Fit

Condition of Tank after action.   Lug on one track plate broken, tracks appear generally strained

Casualties.   One man (2nd Driver) wounded twice

Number of messages sent by pigeon.   Nil

Anti-Tank measures adopted by the enemy?   A.P. bullets

6-pdr ammunition expended.   20

S.A.A. expended.   1000

No of hours Tank was in action.   3 hours

Approximate mileage covered.   5000 yards

Position of Tank after action.   J 24 b 55

Orders received at 6 pm. on 10-8-18 were as follows :-

To proceed with Infantry to line running from K 4 b 8.5 to K 5 d 0.6 and then patrol high ground in front of this line

__REPORT ON ACTION__: I was detailed as the right hand tank to take infantry forward to their objective and then patrol the high ground in front. I took the MORLANCOURT - MÉAULTE road as far as the aeroplane sheds at K 10 a 9.6 and then swung towards the objective. The infantry had by this time advanced from the sunken road running south from MORLANCOURT.

We crossed the railway line and then I patrolled the few trenches and the ground to the right, from which direction M G fire was directed against us.

One of the two tanks which were to patrol the left

P.T.O.

sector having been knocked out, I then went forward in the direction it should have gone, when I met a company of the 6th Queen's who were waiting to go forward to occupy the high ground. I then went forward and saw everything clear for them to advance.

One man of my crew was twice slightly wounded, as we were crossing the railway line, but was fit to carry on until we returned to the starting point.

The artillery fire directed against us came mostly from the direction of MÉAULTE. The enemy put up a barrage when we were returning.

A. Evans. 2nd L.

I suggest that in future -

Short strips be substituted for the belts now in use on the Hotchkiss guns.

Signature: A. Evans. 2nd L.
Time   2.30 pm
Date   12-8-18
Place   J.24.b.55.

BATTLE HISTORY SHEET.

Crew No. 1   Tank No. J13   Date 9.8.18.

Commanded by   Capt. N. R. Murphy   10th Tank   Bn.

Unit to which attached   Division   Bde.

Zero hour   5.30 p.m.

Hour Tank started for action   3.30 p.m.

Proceeded   In front of Infantry

Reached objective at   E.27b.69.   Sheet 62d.N.E.

Condition of the ground   Good going over hills: some steep banks.

Condition of the enemy's trenches   Narrow trenches and scattered posts: few Tank obstacles.

Weather conditions   dry and clear

Condition of crew after action   Morale, high. Crew Commander gassed by Petrol Fumes. Others affected, many splash wounds.

Condition of Tank after Action:- Good running order, some holes from A.P. and Anti-Tank Bullets, external fittings damaged.

Casualties   5 men lightly wounded by bullet splash.

Number of messages sent by Pigeon   -

Anti-Tank measures adopted by enemy?   Numerous: Anti-Tank rifle A.P. Bullets, T.M.S. and some small Gun like a Pom-Pom.

6 Pdr ammunition expended   30/40 rounds

S.A.A. expended   1000/1500 rounds.

No. of hours tank was in action   2½ hours

Approximate mileage covered   1000 yards

Position of Tank after action   J.24.b.55.

Orders received at 5.0 p.m. 9.8.18. were as follows:-

This Tank to pass by left side of MORLANCOURT and precede Infantry to a line of trenches running through E.27b. and 28c. after clearing enemy out of this Sector to return to R.P. at J.24b.

Report on Action:- J13 started off at 5.0 p.m. but was stopped at Jumping off Line and told that Zero hour was altered to 5.30p.m. After this false start S.O.S. signals were observed going up from the hill behind MORLANCOURT and T.M. and Gun Fire was directed on the Tank, which spent the next half hour swinging from side to side of a valley in 4th Speed in order to make a more difficult target.

The jumping off line was crossed again at 5.30 p.m. the Tank passed the left of MORLANCOURT and preceded Infantry towards first objective. Shortly after passing the village it was seen that a Tank to the left was overturned in a trench and that very much more opposition than had been anticipated was coming from the ANCRE valley in the direction of DERNANCOURT. The Tank was accordingly turned in this direction to fill up the Gap, and ran for a considerable distance along the railway at the top of the ANCRE valley. Nests of M.G. were found along and between the two lines of railway and were demolished. 6 Pdr fire from the left Sponson (Composite tank) was directed at more distant targets in the valley, where much movement was observed. Targets were difficult in this Sector owing to the good cover

Crew No.1. Tank No. J13. (Capt. N.R.Murphy.

Report on action, 9.8.18. contd. No.2.

provided by Trees and Banks.   The Infantry came on steadily behind
the Tank without many casualties: They were held up at one point
by M. G. and T. M. fire from a Post which I passed without noticing
until afterwards, when I swung about and dealt with it.
At the BLUE line of the original scheme the Tank was taken accidentally
through our own barrage over some works about E.27.b.49, at that time
un-occupied. No further targets of an obvious nature, were seen,
and I realised that I had got beyond the barrage line, so I ordered the
Driver to turn about and go back along the valley.
Troubles from inside the Tank came from two sources.

    1. Petrol fumes in the Tank.
    2. All the Hotchkiss Guns jammed repeatedly although very
       great care had been taken in filling and cleaning
       belts.

I suggest that in future:-

1. Some improved device should be provided for clearing the Tank
   of Petrol Fumes.
2. That at any rate a considerable proportion of short strips
   should be provided for Hotchkiss Gun in lieu of metallic
   belts.
3. That the proportion of Case Shot in 6Pdr Ammunition should be
   increased to about 50% of the total number of rounds.

Signature.   N. R. Murphy,

Time.   1.30 p.m.

Date.   12.8.18.

Place.   J.24.b.55.

BATTLE HISTORY SHEET.

Crew No. 13   Tank No. J7   Date. 9.8.18.
Commanded by 2/Lieut G.P.Walker   10th Bn.
Unit to which attached   5th   Divn. Composite Bde.
Zero hour.   5.20 pm
Hour Tank started for action.
Proceeded in front of Infantry.
Reached objective at
Condition of the ground.   Good
Condition of the enemy's trenches.   Very narrow

Weather conditions.   Very clear.
Condition of crew after action.   Exhausted
Condition of Tank after action.   Hit
Casualties.   2/Lieut Walker killed Pte Ralphs wounded.

Number of messages sent by pigeon.   nil.
Anti-Tank measures adopted by the enemy?   Bombs
6-pdr ammunition expended.   100 rds
S.A.A. expended.   11,000 rds.
No of hours Tank was in action.   6 hours
Approximate mileage covered.   6 miles
Position of Tank after action.   Rallying point at T.14.c.

Orders received at 4.0 pm. on 9.8.18 were as follows :-
To proceed to P.P.K.27 Central & then along route due E until the road at K.29.c.5.10. is reached. Follow this road running S of Gressaire Wood up to objective. Special attention to be paid to GRESSAIRE Wood.

REPORT ON ACTION :- Followed route detailed, and engaged enemy machine guns. Patrolled GRESSAIRE Wood for four hours till Tank was set on fire by enemy A.P. bullets. 2/Lieut Walker got out of tank & was killed. Pte Dickenson managed to put fire out & repaired Auto-Vac & then carried on, capturing 200 prisoners & bringing them back to our lines.

H.A Robinson
Major.

Suggestion for future :-

Signature   F.P.Lambert Capt
Time.   2.15 pm
Date   15.8.18.
Place   POULAINVILLE

BATTLE HISTORY SHEET.

Crew No. 9   Tank No. J4   Date. 9.4.18

Commanded by 2nd Lieut B Clinton   10th Bn.

Unit to which attached   58th   Divn. 175 pith Bde.

Zero hour. 5 30 pm

Hour Tank started for action. 5 15 pm

Preceded   Infantry.

Reached objective at:

Condition of the ground. Good

Condition of the enemy's trenches. Very narrow — few of them

Weather conditions: Very good.

Condition of crew after action. Exhausted.

Condition of Tank after action. Running. Direct hit through left
Casualties. 2/Lt Blinton sponson. 6 pdr gun out of action.
wounded 302755 Pte Pinkney W. 302739
Pte Powell R.E. 110147 Pte Harding L.J. wounded.

Number of messages sent by pigeon. Nil.

Anti-Tank measures adopted by the enemy?

6-pdr ammunition expended.   55 rds

S.A.A. expended.   1500 rds.

No of hours Tank was in action.

Approximate mileage covered.

Position of Tank after action.   R.P. J24 c

Orders received at 4 0 pm. 9.9.18. were as follows :—
To follow Bray-Corbie Rd 100' on S side cross road at K16D
24. thence N.W. through big Railway system to objective. See
Infantry well consolidated & return to R.P.

REPORT ON ACTION. Started according to orders and had
good targets at retreating enemy. Tank was then hit in
left sponson, which wounded 4 of the crew, including the officer. As
tank was temporarily unfit Mr Blinton went on ahead leaving
his 1st Driver in charge of the tank. On his return he went to the
dressing station with the men of his crew who were wounded. This
left the tank with only three men, and as the shell had damaged
the Engine in several places, the 1st Driver took the tank to the R.P.

F.F. Lambert Capt.
O.C. No 2 Coy.

Suggest that in future —

Signature F.F. Lambert Capt.
Time 2 15 pm
Date 15.4.18
Place Bussu-ville

BATTLE HISTORY SHEET.

Crew No. 11   Tank No. J.5   Date. 9-8-18
Commanded by   Capt J. Henderson   10th Tank Bn.
Unit to which attached   58th Divn. 175th Bde.
Zero hour.   3.30 pm
Hour Tank started for action.   3.10 pm
Proceeded in front of Infantry.
Reached objective at   3.50 pm
Condition of the ground.   Hard road.
Condition of the enemy's trenches.   Nil

Weather conditions.   Fine, hot day, very clear.
Condition of crew after action.   All wounded.
Condition of Tank after action.   Burnt out, owing to enemy bombs.
Casualties.   All the crew.

Number of messages sent by pigeon.   Nil
Anti-Tank measures adopted by the enemy?   Stick bombs tied in threes.
6-pdr ammunition expended.   98 rounds
S.A.A. expended.   11,000 "
No of hours Tank was in action.   Five
Approximate mileage covered.   7 miles
Position of Tank after action.   K 34 b. 40. 40. Sheet 62d N.E.
Orders received at 2.45 pm. on 9-8-18 were as follows :-

To proceed along road EAST from MALARD WOOD to K.35 c. 30. 90.

REPORT ON ACTION :- Left starting point at K 32. b. 80. 50 and proceeded along road running EAST to CHIPILLY and thence to K 35 c. 30. 90.

Patrolled up and down road, engaging enemy machine guns for five hours, then as enemy machine gun fire was coming from the direction of K. 34. b 40. 40. I proceeded there and blew up enemy machine guns.

Whilst I was at K 34 b 40. 40 an enemy bomb blew a hole through top of tank, killing my 1st Driver and setting tank on fire. The crew evacuated tank and were taken prisoners.

We remained prisoners for two hours and then managed to take our guard prisoners and kept them till our infantry arrived at 8.30 pm

P.T.O.

I then made my way back to Company H.Q's and reported. Capt Henderson and over were all wounded by enemy bombs and have since been evacuated.

        F. A. Robinson. Major.

I suggest that in future :-

    Signature :- F. J. Lambert. Capt
    Time   2. 15 p.m
    Date   15 - 8 - 18.
    Place   POULAINVILLE.

BATTLE HISTORY SHEET.

Crew No. 16   Tank No. J9   Date. 9. 8. 18
Commanded by 2/Lieut Garrad D.C.W.   10 Bn.
Unit to which attached   5th Divn.   145 Bde.
Zero hour,
Hour Tank started for action.   3.10. pm
Proceeded in front of Infantry.
Reached objective at
Condition of the ground.   Good
Condition of the enemy's trenches.   Good

Weather conditions.   Good
Condition of crew after action.   Slightly gassed owing to the petrol
Condition of Tank after action.   fumes from the engine
Casualties.

Number of messages sent by pigeon.   Nil
Anti-Tank measures adopted by the enemy?   Anti-tank guns & Armour piercing bullets
6-pdr ammunition expended.   145 rnds
S.A.A. expended.   1,000 do
No of hours Tank was in action.   4
Approximate mileage covered.   3
Position of Tank after action.   K24. B.10. 20.

Orders received at   pm. on 9. 8. 18   were as follows :—
To clear the machine guns from the left side of the village of CHIPILLY & to clear the gully running from the above village to GRESSAIRE WOOD

REPORT OF ACTION :—   Starting from K52.B 30.30 at 3.30 pm proceeded along side the SOMME RIVER through a small wood along a road to the village of CHIPILLY, where I branched off along the gully running up to GRESSAIRE WOOD. On my way up the gully I was fired on from both sides of the gully by machine guns. I swept the bushes on both sides of the gully with case shot & hotchkiss guns finally knocking out the machine guns & causing heavy casualties in the enemy. After my first journey along the gully, I returned back along the gully & swept the little wood on the left of the gully with machine gun fire. I then returned along the gully again sweeping both sides of the gully. On returning back along the gully, I knocked out three machine guns in the village of CHIPILLY.

Suggest that in the future :— Strips should be used in the place of letters in the Hotchkiss guns.

Signature.   E.S. Garrad 2/Lt
Time.
Date.
D.C.W.   15. 8. 18

BATTLE HISTORY SHEET.

Crew No. 14   Tank No. 9253.   Date. 8-8-18
Commanded by   Lieut. McKinstrey   10th Bn.
Unit to which attached 7th Batt Royal Sussex. 12th Divn. 36th Bde.
Zero hour.   4.30 am
Hour Tank started for action.   4.20 am.
Proceeded   behind   Infantry.
Reached objective at   —
Condition of the ground.   Good.
Condition of the enemy's trenches.   Good.

Weather conditions.   Thick ground mist.
Condition of crew after action.   Slightly gassed owing to the petrol fumes from the engine.
Condition of Tank after action.   Forward turret knocked in, trying to unditch the tank.
Casualties.   Nil
Number of messages sent by pigeon.   Nil
Anti-Tank measures adopted by the enemy?   —
6-pdr ammunition expended.   Nil
S.A.A. expended.   Nil
No of hours Tank was in action.
Approximate mileage covered.
Position of Tank after action.   K.26. c 20.40.
Orders received at   pm. on 6-8-18.   were as follows :-

To reach Green Line - first objective
   "   "   Red Line - second objective.

REPORT ON ACTION :-   Started from rallying point at 4.20 am on the morning of the 8th with the intention of reaching the first objective, but was ditched in our front line.

I suggest that in future :-
"That strips should be used in the place of belts in the Hotchkiss gun"

Signature.   E.S. Garrod. 2" Lt. D.C.M.
Time   10 am.
Date   12-8-18
Place.   62.D.K.24.B. 80.20.

BATTLE HISTORY SHEET.

Crew No. 13.   Tank No. 9334   Date. 8-8-18.

Commanded by 2nd Lt. Walker. G. L.   10th Bn.

Unit to which attached 7th Royal Sussex 12th Divn. 36th Bde.

Zero hour.   4. 30 a.m.

Hour Tank started for action.   4. 20 a.m.

Proceeded in front of Infantry.

Reached objective at

Condition of the ground.   Good.

Condition of the enemy's trenches.   Good.

Weather conditions.   Thick ground mist.

Condition of crew after action.   Slightly gassed owing to petrol fumes from the engines.

Condition of Tank after action.   Broken pushrod.

Casualties.   Nil

Number of messages sent by pigeon.   Nil

Anti-Tank measures adopted by the enemy? —

6-pdr ammunition expended.   15

S.A.A. expended.   180.

No of hours Tank was in action.   3.

Approximate mileage covered.   3½

Position of Tank after action.   K. 26 c 20. 40.

Orders received at   pm. on 6. 8-18   were as follows :-

First objective :- The Green Line.

Second objective - the Red Line.

REPORT ON ACTION :- Starting from K 24 b 80.20 on the morning of the 8th with the intention of reaching the Green Line, but owing to the thick mist lost direction.

I suggest that in future :-
    That strips should be used in the place of belts in the Hotchkiss gun.

                        Signature: E. S. Garrod. 2 L. D.C.M
                        Time .   10 A.M.
                        Date.   12-8-18
                        Place.   K 24 b 80. 20.

BATTLE HISTORY SHEET.

Crew No. 18.   Tank No. J11 (9254)   Date. 8.8.18

Commanded by 2ⁿᵈ Lt W J Sampson   10ᵗʰ Tank Bn.

Unit to which attached 7ᵗʰ Bn Royal Sussex 12ᵗʰ Divn. 36ᵗʰ Bde.

Zero hour.   4.20 a.m

Hour Tank started for action.   4.20 a.m

Proceeded   behind   Infantry.

Reached first objective at   5.10 a.m

Condition of the ground.   Good.

Condition of the enemy's trenches.   Good

Weather conditions.   Bad. thick fog prevailing

Condition of crew after action.   Good.

Condition of Tank after action.   Broken down, Engine having been on fire three times

Casualties.   Two (slightly). remaining at duty

Number of messages sent by pigeon.   Nil

Anti-Tank measures adopted by the enemy?   A P bullets — Anti Tank gun

6-pdr ammunition expended.   Nil

S.A.A. expended.   250 rounds

No of hours Tank was in action.   4 hours

Approximate mileage covered.   3 miles

Position of Tank after action.   62D K 25 a. 20.20

Orders received at 6 pm. on 6-8-18 were as follows :—

First to attack and take the Green Line 62D K 21 d 38.50 and as a second objective to take the Red Line at 62D K 25 a 00.20

REPORT ON ACTION

I left the copse at 4.20 a.m and was immediately enveloped in a dense fog and lost touch with my section. Being unable to hear the engines of other Tanks, I proceeded to steer due East by the compass and was badly ditched in the junction of Commando Support and Crump Line at K 19 c 40 10. This occurred about 5 a.m and I eventually dug out at 7.10 a.m. During this time I found 11 Bosche in a dug-out and sent them to the rear in charge of an infantry Lce/Cpl. After this I lead my tank towards some firing (the fog still prevailing) and got into touch with our line when

P.T.O.

I again became ditched but got out under 15 minutes, with the help of J 4 (2nd Lt Walker). Soon after getting under way for the third time my engine commenced to give trouble and took fire in the Crank-case. The fire having been put out I again moved on, and after having the Crank case on fire again, I received a chit from some infantry that a M.G was still giving trouble in copse at J 26. c 4 5. so I pushed across and found the gun which I put out of action. As my engine continued to give trouble I decided to make for our lines and reached K 25 a 20 20 when a serious fire occurred and burned all rubber joints and washers. It was then impossible to move my tank under her own power, so I waited for another tank (returning from action) to tow me back. After being stationary some 15 minutes my tank was shelled so I temporarily abandoned it and attached my crew with their guns to a M G C Coy in a trench near by. Eventually Lt Laster's tank arrived and pulled me back to K 24 a 50 50.

I suggest that in future —

Something be done to prevent crews being overcome by fumes from the Engine.

Signature W J Sampson. 2 Lt
Time   10. 0 a.m
Date   11 - 8 - 18
Place   J 24. b 50 20

BATTLE HISTORY SHEET.

Crew No. 16.   Tank No. 9342 J.9   Date. 8-8-18
Commanded by   E. S. Garrod 2 Lt. D.C.M   10th Bn.
Unit to which attached 7th Batt. Royal Sussex. 12th Divn. 36th Bde.
Zero hour.   4.30 a.m
Hour Tank started for action.   4.20 a.m
Proceeded in front of Infantry.
Reached objective at   6.30 a.m
Condition of the ground.   Good.
Condition of the enemy's trenches.   Good.

Weather conditions.   Thick ground mist
Condition of crew after action.   Slightly gassed owing to petrol fumes from the engine.
Condition of Tank after action.   Good.
Casualties.   Nil.

Number of messages sent by pigeon.   Nil.
Anti-Tank measures adopted by the enemy? A.P. bullets
6-pdr ammunition expended.   10.
S.A.A. expended.   400.
No of hours Tank was in action.   4
Approximate mileage covered.   3½
Position of Tank after action.   62 D:K 26c 20.40.
Orders received at   pm. on 6-8-18   were as follows :-

First to attack the Green Line 62.D.K. 21. d. 50.50.
Second objective to take the Red Line at 62.D.K. 24 a.0.20.

<u>REPORT ON ACTION</u>:- Starting from rallying point at 4.20 a.m. the mist was very thick and I could hardly see a yard in front of my tank. I swung my tank East and reached enemy defences. The tank on my left was ditched, so I drew my tank up in front of it, and hauled it out, then carrying straight on over the enemy defences. operating with the infantry. I received information from an infantry major, saying that they were held up on the left of the Bray-Corbie Road - Map reference approx. 62 D K 14 c 20.50 to 14 c. 90.40. I then drove in that direction, crossing the Bray-Corbie Road and

P.T.O.

-got in touch with the infantry that were held up and operated with them, taking the trench. I then patrolled in front of the trench.

My engine had then been running for 14 hours and had to return for water. On my journey back to the rallying point I towed back one of our tanks which had broken down.

I suggest that in future:-
That Hotchkiss strips should be used in the place of belts.

Signature. C. S. Garrod. 2nd D. D.C.M.
Time.   10.a.m
Date.   12-8-18
Place.   62.D.J 24 A 80.20.

BATTLE HISTORY SHEET.

Crew No. 8   Tank No. J.5.   Date. 9.8.18.

Commanded by 306591 Corp. T. Wood   10th. Bn.

Unit to which attached   58th   Divn. Corps 10 Bde.

Zero hour.   5.30 pm

Hour Tank started for action.   5.20 pm

Proceeded in front of Infantry.

Reached objective at

Condition of the ground.   Very Dry.

Condition of the enemy's trenches.   Very narrow. No obstacle to Tanks.
    Bad.

Weather conditions.   Very Good.

Condition of crew after action.   Exhausted and suffering from gas fumes.

Condition of Tank after action.   Unfit. Gear & lever broken.

Casualties.   306591 Corporal Wood T. killed.

Number of messages sent by pigeon.   Nil.

Anti-Tank measures adopted by the enemy?   Elephant Guns.

6-pdr ammunition expended.   30 rds.

S.A.A. expended.   20 Strips.

No of hours Tank was in action.   3

Approximate mileage covered.   1

Position of Tank after action.

Orders received at 8.P. pm. on 9.8.18 were as follows :—
To follow route as shown on map. To pay special attention to GRESSAIRE Wood.
Route as follows. Follow Bray-Corbie Rd for 1000x + 600x to So of R. Meridian F. 15
Gressaire Wood, Thence along N.edge of wood to objective.
REPORT ON ACTION:— Started off at 5.15 pm for barrage line. Carried on towards
GRESSAIRE WOOD and at 6.15 pm found myself ahead of the barrage. All guns had good
targets as retreating enemy & M.G.s, several of which were knocked out. We were dead
ahead of our own Infantry & barrage when the Primary gear lever broke & we could not
move the Tank. We evacuated the Tank & formed a strong point round it. The
retreating enemy attacked with considerable force but they were held off with M.G.
fire. They eventually retreated round our flank leaving a M.G. in our
hands. Our Infantry then passed us & one of the crew went back for a part to replace that broken. Before he returned, we forced the gears in mesh by hand &
returned to R.P.
    I suggest that in future —

        Signature.   F. J. Lambert & Capt.
        Time.   1-10. p.m.
        Date.   15.8.18
        Place.   Poulainville.

BATTLE HISTORY SHEET.

Crew No. B Tank No. 9435 Date 8.8.18

Commanded by Sgt Raffel M.M. Bn.

Unit to which attached 7th R.W.K. 18th Division 53rd Bde.

Zero hour 4.20 a.m.

Hour Tank started for action 3.30 a.m.

Proceeded without Infantry

Reached objective at Map location uncertain. S.E. of MORLANCOURT

Condition of the Ground Perfect

Condition of the enemy's trenches Comparatively undamaged narrow seldom more than 6' deep occasionally protected by wire

Weather conditions 5.30 to 10.00 am owing to thick mist extreme visibility 50 to 100ˣ

Condition of crew after action do. Tank don't tired but fit more especially to. Requiring minor adjustments poles due to anti aircraft gears. Two small holes due to anti tank rifle fire.

Casualties 3 Wounded in morning. 1 in afternoon

Number of messages sent by Pigeon one

Anti-Tank measures adopted by enemy? Anti tank rifle M.G. firing A.P. Johnson

6 Pdr ammunition expended Case & rounds Shell 25 rounds

S.A.A. expended 1000 Rounds

No. of hours Tank was in action 3½ hours

Approximate mileage covered 10,000 Yd

Position of Tank after action 18d.70.30 62 NE

Orders received at 3.0 p.m. 8.8.18 were as follows:- To prepare tank for immediate further action.

Report on Action

J18 along with J17, 19 & 29 forming No.5 Section B. Coy 10th Bn. had orders to leave the Tank Park at HEM1 at Z-70 min (3.30am) & to rally at K20.b.80.80. 62 NE before Z+130 min. A line running N. & S. through J16d.70.00 was not to be crossed before Z+70. In J14a. difficulty was caused by the obliteration of Track by other Transport (Previous reconnaissance having been rendered impossible by the local tactical situation. J16d.70.00 was however reached to time. Here Tanks halted for 30 mins and petrol etc filled in. At about this time 5. to 5.30 am the mist which had previously been fairly thin, thickened and visibility was reduced to 10ˣ — As difficulty was experienced in keeping direction the Tank was taken to the BRAY-CORBIE Road along which it proceeded to about K13.d.70.20.

2.

Crew to Tank 9435.
Report on Action :- (cont'd)

~~The Tank left the road~~

where considerable hostile M.G. Fire from foot S of the Road was encountered. The Tank proceeded E and on reaching the Trees at K 20 a 70.95. the Tank left the road and patrolled the area K 20 a 70.95, K 9d, K 16a, K 15d. In this Area some of our Infantry were met, these were unable to get any definite information as to locations or Enemy dispositions owing probably to the thick Mist. Many Enemy M.Gs. opened Fire on the Tank and hits were twice received from Enemy rifle. One bullet penetrating the right sponson setting fire to a 6 Pdr Charge breaking the hun Ration. Many of these M.G's were engaged case shot proving very effective. At least about 6 were destroyed by running the Tank over them. Hotchkiss Guns were very unsatisfactory and stoppages on many occasions allowed parties of the Enemy to escape into the mist. Lead splash in the Tank when under M.G. Fire wounded both Gunners on the Female Side early in the action. At about 9.30 a.m. the Mist began to clear. No further M.G. Pockets or Enemy Infantry could be found but Shell Fire was concentrated on the Area in which the Tanks were operating. Tanks therefore rallied after first instructing Infantry as to where they could be found in event of a Counter Attack.
—————"—————"—————"—————"

At about 5.30 p.m. information was received that the Enemy were concentrating for a Counter Attack in K 10. The Tank moved in this direction. On crossing the Ridge at about K 13 b. the Tank came under heavy Shell Fire. No Enemy Infantry were encountered though two

BATTLE HISTORY SHEET.

Crew No.   Tank No.   J58   Date   8. 8. 18.
Commanded by   2/Lt. G.T.L.Bayliff   10th Tank   Bn.
Unit to which attached   55th Division   174th Bde.

Zero hour   4.20 a.m.

Hour Tank started for action   3.55 a.m.

Proceeded   In front of Infantry

Reached objective at

Condition of the Ground   Standing crops, few trenches.

Condition of the enemy's trenches   Shallow and small.

Weather conditions   From 4.0 a.m. - 7.30 a.m. very thick fog
Condition of crew after action   Exhausted from Heat and Petrol Fumes
          Badly shaken by Hit from Shell.
Condition of Tank after Action:-   Burnt Out.

Casualties   NIL.

Number of messages sent by Pigeon

Anti-Tank measures adopted by enemy?   -

6 Pdr ammunition expended   -

S.A.A. expended   -

No. of hours Tank was in action   35 minutes

Approximate mileage covered   800 yards.

Position of Tank after action   -

Orders received at 5.0 p.m.   were as follows:-
         XXX   7.8.18.

To proceed with Infantry to GREEN LINE position East of MALARD WOOD to valley at LES CELESTINS, thence to attack the RED LINE final objective.
    Report on Action. Left Jumping Off Point J2437.5. at 3.55 a.m. with crew of four, two men having fainted from Fumes and Heat. Heavy Mist made it impossible to keep direction, or see the attacking Infantry.
         Drove on in search of Front line and attacking Infantry, till at 4.30 a.m. the Tank received a direct Hit under the Engine setting it on Fire.

         The Crew escaped being slightly scratched and shaken; but it was impossible to save any Guns or Equipment.
              I then joined J.42. 2/Lt. Cronshaw M.C. with three of my Crew.

                                    Signature;- G.T.L.Bayliff 2/Lt.
                                    Time....... 11.0 a.m.
                                    Date.   14.8.18.

                                    Place.   In the Field.

BATTLE HISTORY SHEET.

Crew No. 6   Tank No. F36   Date 8.8.18

Commanded by Cpl. F.P. Tyers   10th Bn.

Unit to which attached 15th Division 174 Bde.

Zero hour 4.20 a.m.

Hour Tank started for action 4 a.m.

Proceeded with Infantry

Reached objective at

Condition of the Ground Shell holes and craters

Condition of the enemy's trenches Nil

Weather conditions Very misty

Condition of crew after action Completely exhausted, driver delirious

Condition of Tank after action Auto-vac trouble

Casualties Nil

Number of messages sent by Pigeon Nil

Anti-Tank measures adopted by enemy? A.P. & T.Ms.

6 Pdr ammunition expended 14 rds.

S.A.A. expended 300 rds.

No. of hours Tank was in action 9 hrs.

Approximate mileage covered 8 miles.

Position of Tank after action Chipilly.

Orders received at 5.0 p.m. 7.8.18 were as follows:—
To take the village of Chilly-Lavette, and after barrage lifts, to proceed to Chipilly.

REPORT ON ACTION:— Tank left starting point at Zero hour. Owing to the heavy fog, the journey to Chilly-Lavette was obscured. The Infantry had already taken the village when the tank arrived. The tank proceeded down the Chilly-Lavette–Chipilly road, dealing with isolated M.G. posts. When approximately half way between these two villages, contact with our Infantry was lost, so the road was patrolled by the tank. The Infantry appearing, and auto-vac trouble developing, the tank was taken back to Chipilly. The crew were overcome with breathing the fumes, on the halfway position between the two villages, the officer & 4 men fainting simultaneously. This prevented the tank from reaching the final objective.

Suggestions for future:—

Signature F.P. Tyers (Cpl.)
Time
Date 14-8-18
Place In the Field

BATTLE HISTORY SHEET.

Crew No. 9.   Tank No. J 44.   Date. 9-8-18

Commanded by 2/Lt. A.E.M. Creswell.   10th Bn.

Unit to which attached   12th Divn.   Bde.

Zero hour,   5.30.p.m.

Hour Tank started for action.   5.30.p.m.

Proceeded   with   Infantry.

Reached objective at

Condition of the ground.   undulating.

Condition of the enemy's trenches.   Deep and narrow.

Weather conditions   Good.

Condition of crew after action.   Fair.

Condition of Tank after action.   In good order, apart from Armament.

Casualties.   1. O.R. wounded

Number of messages sent by pigeon.   NIL.

Anti-Tank measures adopted by the enemy?   A.P. T.M's.

6-pdr ammunition expended.   80 rounds.

S.A.A. expended.   1800 rounds.

No of hours Tank was in action.   2½ hours

Approximate mileage covered   5 miles

Position of Tank after action.   J 23 b 9.0.

Orders received at 3.30.pm. on 9-8-18   were as follows :-

To proceed in front of Infantry and take BLUE LINE.

REPORT ON ACTION :- Tank moved off fit from Starting point at Zero hour.

Contact with the enemy was made 10 minutes after and casualties inflicted. The objective was gained in a very short time.

After encountering very heavy M.G. fire we engaged a strong enemy post consisting of 10 M.G's + 4 T.M's and cleared it. At this time the 6 Pdr + 2 Hotchkiss guns were put out of action and the Tank took up a position under a bank to endeavour to get the guns repaired.

The Tank took no further part in the action and subsequently was ordered to return to the rallying point.

I suggest that in future :-

Signature. A.R. Chivers. Cpl

Time

Date. 14.8.18

Place. Field.

BATTLE HISTORY SHEET.

Crew No. 13.   Tank No. 9265. J.41.   Date. 9-8-18.

Commanded by 2/Lt. C.S. Oday   10th Bn.

Unit to which attached   12th   Divn.   Bde.

Zero hour.   5.20. p.m.

Hour Tank started for action. 5.20. p.m.

Proceeded in front of Infantry.

Reached objective at; 6.35 p.m.

Condition of the ground.   good, but very difficult

Condition of the enemy's trenches.   good.

Weather conditions   good.

Condition of crew after action.   exhausted.

Condition of Tank after action.   good, but plates pitted and one gun out of action

Casualties.   Nil.

Number of messages sent by pigeon.   Nil (no pigeons)

Anti-Tank measures adopted by the enemy?   Anti-tank guns – Field guns and A.T. bullets.

6-pdr ammunition expended.   40 rounds

S.A.A. expended.   1600 rounds

No of hours Tank was in action.   3 hours.

Approximate mileage covered   6.

Position of Tank after action.   J.23.b.9.0.

Orders received at 4.30. pm. on Aug 9th/18   were as follows :—

Proceed to Blue line to South of Morlancourt, and await orders.

REPORT ON ACTION :—   At 5.25 p.m. I started at approx. K.14.c.2.3 and got to the enemy front line and got Infantry past, but noticed that Infantry on my left in front of Morlancourt had not made much progress. On communicating with them, found they were being held up by M.Gs from (in) Morlancourt. This was due to the fact that the tank on my left had been knocked out and so couldn't dispose of this flank of village. I immediately made for village from South and working enemy side of village North. It was very strongly held by M.Gs and Infantry, but we cleared it with 6.pdr and case shot by 6.10 p.m. causing about 200 (approx) prisoners to go into our lines.

During this fighting we knocked out 3 M.Gs and captured a battery of French mortars and killed personnel of same, also inflicted very heavy casualties on the enemy in village.

I then went back and got Inf: through village. After this I worked with Infantry, mopping up posts etc. etc, until dusk when I had orders to go back to Rallying Point. During one of these smaller excursions we again got numerous prisoners.

P.T.O.

I suggest that in future :-

Signature. C. G. Oddy Lt.
Time.   11.30 a.m
Date.   14/8/18
Place   In the field.

BATTLE HISTORY SHEET.

Crew No. 8   Tank No. J.46   Date. 9-8-18
Commanded by Capt. M.C. Keynes   10th Tanks Bn.
Unit to which attached   12¾   Divn.   Bde.
Zero hour.   5.30 p.m
Hour Tank started for action.   5. 0 p.m
Proceeded   Infantry.
Reached objective at   —
Condition of the ground.
Condition of the enemy's trenches.

Weather conditions.   Good.
Condition of crew after action.   very shaken
Condition of Tank after action.   Six direct hits and burned out.
Casualties.   1 O.R. badly burned.

Number of messages sent by pigeon.   Nil.
Anti-Tank measures adopted by the enemy?   probably Field Guns
6-pdr ammunition expended.   +
S.A.A. expended.   —
No of hours Tank was in action.   10 minutes
Approximate mileage covered.   300 yards
Position of Tank after action.   K 8 c 2.2.
Orders received at 4.30 PM. on 9-8-18 were as follows :-

Proceed to Blue line to South of MORLANCOURT and await orders.

REPORT ON ACTION :- Owing to not being notified of revised Zero hour, I started at 5 p.m. I had been going for 10 minutes when I received simultaneously 2 direct hits. The Tank caught fire. I evacuated the Tank and put the fire out. Within ten minutes the Tank received 4 more direct hits and was subsequently burned out.

I suggest that in future —

Signature.- M.C. Keynes. Capt
Time
Date   9-8-18.
Place   Field.

BATTLE HISTORY SHEET.

Crew No.   Tank No. 9059   Date 9-8-18

Commanded by 2nd Lt. P.D. Cameron   16th Bn.

Unit to which attached 9th Bn 13th Division   15th Bde.

Zero hour   5.0 p.m.

Hour Tank started for action   5.30 p.m.

Proceeded in front of Infantry

Reached objective at   6.30 p.m.

Condition of the Ground   Perfect but dry

Condition of the enemy's trenches   Indefinite line. There were a few shallow trenches & several isolated pockets.

Weather conditions   Very good.

Condition of crew after action   Very fatigued.

Condition of Tank after action   So badly damaged by shell fire as to make it unfit for further action until overhauled.

Casualties   Four wounded — two severely, two slightly.

Number of messages sent by Pigeon   Nil.

Anti-Tank measures adopted by enemy?   Armour piercing bullets & shell fire.

6 Pdr ammunition expended   110 rds.

S.A.A. expended   6000 rds.

No. of hours Tank was in action   1½ hours.

Approximate mileage covered   6000 yds.

Position of Tank after action   Trench C.2.a.30. Ref map 1.25

Orders received at 5.0 p.m. 9-8-18 were as follows:—
You will proceed with your Tank to Rt. K.10.b.4 & form left flank of action & advance along the S. side of Ville-sur-Ancre, Meaulte Rd.

REPORT ON ACTION:— On arriving a Tolle Hill I observed too many machine gun nests, therefore I proceeded coming down about R.21 Central. By proceeding to their rear I found it strongly occupied by machine guns. I destroyed this nest & inflicted heavy casualties to them at bare of one of their strong points. The casualties to the crew were caused by direct fire on the corner of the R. flank from a field gun. The services flap of the Sponson door.

Suggestions for the future:—   Signature P.D. Cameron
More ventilation is necessary.   Rank 2nd Lt.
                                     Date 15-8-18
                                     Place Lutz

BATTLE HISTORY SHEET.

Crew No. _____ Tank No. 9137 Date 10/7/17

Commanded by F. Sare 2/Lt 10th Bn.

Unit to which attached 9th Essex 13th Division 35th Bde.

Zero hour 6 am

Hour Tank started for action 12 am.

Proceeded in front of Infantry

Reached objective at 7.30 am.

Condition of the Ground Shelled - but dry

Condition of the enemy's trenches He held no definite line

Weather conditions Fine.

Condition of crew after action Fatigued.

Condition of tank after action Good.

Casualties 3 men wounded.

Number of messages sent by Pigeon Nil.

Anti-Tank measures adopted by enemy? Use of Anti Tank rifle. Plating his road twice.

6 Pdr ammunition expended 65 rds.

S.A.A. expended 3400.

No. of hours Tank was in action 2 hrs.

Approximate mileage covered 6000 yds.

Position of Tank after action at 18.D.2.1.

Orders received at 5.0 p.m. 10.7.17 were as follows:—
To attack enemy strong points & return to base.

REPORT ON ACTION:— Ref. Map. 62d. N.E. The attack was to be on the following points of the enemy. 1. Trenches K.5.c. 2. Pill box contained in E.28.d. and E.29.b. At zero I proceeded on in front of the infantry to the 1st objective (Railway cutting in K.5.c.) Here we were held up for half an hour by our own barrage. It was estimated it would take both Tanks & infantry until Zero + 60 to reach objective. Actually they were there at Zero + 30. When the barrage lifted we engaged the trenches at K.5.c. I then proceeded to the crest where we patrolled until the infantry had consolidated their final objective. We then withdrew & returned to our base.

Suggestions for future:—
1. A better machine gun be mounted in Tank
2. n.s. officers.
3. Better ventilation be provided.
4. One man in crew to trained in First Aid.

Signature
Time
Date
Place.

BATTLE HISTORY SHEET.

Crew No. Tank No. F21 Date 9-8-18

Commanded by 2/Lieut Copperson Bay 10th Bn.

Unit to which attached 5th Division ?? Bde.

Zero hour 6.30 p.m.

Hour Tank started for action

Proceeded in front of Infantry

Reached objective at —

Condition of the Ground Good

Condition of the enemy's trenches they seemed to attack to ??

Weather conditions Very good

Condition of crew after action Exhausted

Condition of Tank after action Ditched at R.29.C

Casualties Nil

Number of messages sent by Pigeon Nil

Anti-Tank measures adopted by enemy? A.P. bullets

6 Pdr ammunition expended Nil

S.A.A. expended 100 rounds

No. of hours Tank was in action 1 hour

Approximate mileage covered 2 miles

Position of Tank after action R.29.C

Orders received at 5.0 p.m. 9-8-18 were as follows:—
To follow route shown on map and deal with any M.Gs in GRESSAIRE Wood. S.P. N.27 Central, thence to X roads R.27.A.3.6. From there along road running N.W. through GRESSAIRE Wood.

REPORT ON ACTION:—
Proceeded along route detailed to GRESSAIRE Wood. Going down steep bank, clutch broken and tank ran away & ditched in large shell hole. Infantry passed me & tank was salved next day.

H.B. Robinson
Major

Suggestions in future:—

Signature F.C. Lambert Capt
Time 2.15 p.m.
Date 15-8-18

3.

two M.G's & 3 M.G. emplacements were destroyed.
No attack materialized and after patrolling S.W of
MORLANCOURT. for an hour during which time the
Tank received two direct hits one on the front
towing shackle which blew out many rivets in the
Cab and the other a glancing blow on the left
side by the fan louvres. The Tank returned to its
S.P.

___

I suggest that in future:-
Tanks be armed with Vickers M.G's or Captured Maxims
these being the only Guns on which definite stoppages
can be taught with hard and fast remedies.
One Vickers Gun on the Female Side would be
sufficient. That splinter Masks be fitted with
easily changed triplex eye-pieces, spares being
carried. Conning Tower to be at least 9in. higher
Circular in shape with slit for all round vision
with internal movable ring with one hole. If
possible an electric fan in the top of Conning Tower.
Speaking Tubes to Drivers & Gunners being fitted.

Sig. K.H Bailey. Capt.
Time. 6.30 p.m.
Date. 15. 8. 18.
Place. In the field

BATTLE HISTORY SHEET.

Crew No.　　　　　Tank No. 9020.　　　Date 9.8.18

Commanded by　Lieut A.S. Dunkin.　10th Tank Bn.

Unit to which attached　9th Essex 12th Division　35th Bde.

Zero hour　　　　　　　　　　　　5 p.m.

Hour Tank started for action　　　3.30.p.m.

Proceeded　in front of　Infantry

Reached objective at　　　　　　K.2. b.3.8

Condition of the Ground　　　　　Good

Condition of the enemy's trenches　Not much damaged by shell fire. They were chiefly M.G. posts posted by the railway.

Weather conditions　　　　　　　　Fine weather.

Condition of crew after action　　Fairly fresh

　　"　　"　TANK　"　　　　　　　Fit, but on her side.

Casualties　　　　　　　　　　　　None

Number of messages sent by Pigeon

Anti-Tank measures adopted by enemy?　Heavy fire from light field guns

6 Pdr ammunition expended　　　　10 rounds.

S.A.A. expended　　　　　　　　　40 rounds.

No. of hours Tank was in action　1½ hrs

Approximate mileage covered　　　2 miles

Position of Tank after action　　K.2. b. 3.8

Orders received at 5.0 p.m. 2.30 9/8/18　were as follows:-

To advance from K.1.c in a direct N.E. by E and take the strong position on the hill by the railway in K.2, then to move on to K.28.c, so that the infantry could consolidate that line.

　　REPORT ON ACTION:- There was heavy shelling as soon as the tank moved up the valley at K.7.d which followed us to K.1.b.6.0 where we crossed our front line. Moving to K.2.b.6.6 we ascended the slope to the Quarry, crossing it to the left. Here we felt enemy M.G fire from K.26.c.8.8 and we fired several rounds of 6 pdr shells at a strong point. My gunners then saw the enemy retiring from this position so they opened on them with the Hotchkiss .303. This permitted the

　　　　　　　　　　　　　　　　　　　　　　　　P.T.O.

infantry to advance up the slope on my right. Swinging right I ascended the slope with the Infantry following. We located a nest of enemy M.G's on the slope at K.2. & 5.5 and my gunners started firing on them. To make sure of what was happening I turned to the R.H. gunner to see exactly where they were firing. On resuming my seat by the driver in front, the tank suddenly turned over sideways over a false escarpment in a wheatfield and settled on her side at an angle of about 80°. With great difficulty we all got out, as the engine stopped. We tried to restart the engine but owing to the Induction side being down it was impossible to get petrol from the Carburetter into the Inducing chamber. I got the three good Hotchkiss guns from the tank and took up a position in a small trench by the tank and waited in the event of a counter attack. I went to see two other tanks to get towed out, but owing to their own difficulties they could not help me. I sent a message back to my company commander telling him of my position and intentions. My crew and I stayed in the trench all night and eventually with the aid of another tank moved her on her side. Then she came back under her own power to the company rendezvous.

I suggest that in future :-

Signature. Arthur T. Hunker, Lt
Time 4 p.m
Date 15/8/18.
Place In the field.

BATTLE HISTORY SHEET.

Crew No.　　　　　　Tank No. J21 9390　Date 9-8-18

Commanded by 2/Lt C.E. Gyles　　　　　　　　Bn.

Unit to which attached　　　　Division　　　　Bde.

Zero hour　　　　　　　　　　5.30 p.m

Hour Tank started for action　5.25 p.m

Proceeded　　　　Infantry

Reached objective at　　　　Objective not reached.

Condition of the Ground　　　Dry but very much shelled

Condition of the enemy's trenches　No definite line - ground very much shelled

Weather conditions　　　　　　Fine

Condition of crew after action　Exhausted

　"　　TANK　"　　"　　Ditched and clutch slipping

Casualties　　　　　　　　　　Nil

Number of messages sent by Pigeon　Nil

Anti-Tank measures adopted by enemy?　Nil

6 Pdr ammunition expended　　40 common shell. 15 case shot

S.A.A. expended　　　　　　　2040 rounds

No. of hours Tank was in action　One

Approximate mileage covered　　One

Position of Tank after action　I 22 d 8.1

Orders received at 5.0 p.m. Aug 9th/18 were as follows:-

Proceed in front of Infantry through Gressaire Wood and hold off the enemy until ground was consolidated.

REPORT ON ACTION:- About 5 minutes before zero we commenced to climb the steep hill to the left of Mallard Wood, and in 20 minutes time we had trouble with a slipping clutch, which could not be satisfactorily adjusted at the time. A few minutes afterwards the tank was ditched in a huge shell hole in the valley at the near corner of Gressaire Wood I.22.d.8.1. During this time we found ourselves surrounded by the enemy. We were able to do good work with the 6pdr on the right and the front Hotchkiss gun. Our two other guns (Hotchkiss) on the left and behind became jambed and we kept the enemy away on this side with revolvers.

P.T.O.

After the infantry had advanced in front of us, we withdrew to the rallying point and the tank was brought out of action on the following night.

The crew worked well, especially the front gunner Pte White, who stuck to his guns and inflicted considerable loss on the enemy's infantry.

I suggest that in future :-

    Signature   C.B. Cryphas 2/Lt
    Time   3 p.m.
    Date   14/8/18.
    Place

BATTLE HISTORY SHEET.

Crew No.   Tank No. J.42.9411   Date 8. 8. 18.

Commanded by 2/Lt. D.H.Crenshaw M.C.   10th Tank Bn.

Unit to which attached   58th   Division 174th Bde.

Zero hour   4. 20 a.m.

Hour Tank started for action   4. 0 a.m.

Proceeded   behind   Infantry

Reached objective at

Condition of the Ground   Good Ground. Cultivated ground growing crops

Condition of the enemy's trenches   Slightly broken in, otherwise in good condition.

Weather conditions   Very misty.

Condition of crew after action   Very weak owing to intense heat in the Tank and heavy Petrol Fumes

Condition of Tank after Action:-   Right epicyclic spring broken
Casualties Plates covering right epicyclic gearing broken. Hole in side.
          NIL

Number of messages sent by Pigeon   NIL

Anti-Tank measures adopted by enemy?   Field Guns Firing from Commanding Positions.

6 Pdr ammunition expended   5 rounds.

S.A.A. expended   NIL

No. of hours Tank was in action   9 hours

Approximate mileage covered   12 miles.

Position of Tank after action   J23.b.9.0.

Orders received at 5.0 p.m.   were as follows;-
          7.8.18.

To proceed to the GREEN LINE position on the EAST edge of
MALARD WOOD and then rally at CHAUSSIONS and then attack the
RED LINE, NORTH of CHIPILLY.
REPORT ON ACTION:-

I started off at 4.0 a.m. along with Tanks, J38, 41, 43. These
Tanks were soon lost to sight in the Mist. After going for
about 25 minutes J38 which was about 20 yds in front of me
was observed to be on fire. At 4.30 a.m. 2/Lt. Bayliff
along with four of his Crew joined my Tank I manouvred about
in the mist endeavouring to find the line. About 4.50 a.m.
I was told the right direction by a party of Infantry. I
proceeded in the given direction and offered my services to the
8th Royal Fusileers. After hunting about for snipers for some
time I met Capt. Keynes with his Tank. I then attached myself
to him. Together we went further forward to about K21.0.9.1.
At this position I handed over my spare S. A. A. to the Infantry.
While I was stationary, getting the ammunition off the Tank
I received a hit which broke the spring of the right
epicyclic gear. It was however possible to bring the Tank
back under its own power. It was not at any time at close
range with the enemy in large numbers.

BATTLE HISTORY SHEET.

Crew No.   Tank No. J55   Date   8.8.18.

Commanded by Lt. G. Garnham   10th Tank Bn.

Unit to which attached   58th Division   174th Bde.

Zero hour   4.20 a.m.

Hour Tank started for action   5.0 a.m.

Proceeded   Infantry   —

Reached objective at

Condition of the Ground   Cultivated

Condition of the enemy's trenches

Weather conditions   Very foggy

Condition of crew after action   Slightly gassed.

Condition of Tank after Action.:-   Mechanically unfit.

Casualties   1 Wounded 1 Shock 2 gassed.

Number of messages sent by Pigeon   Nil.

Anti-Tank measures adopted by enemy?   —

6 Pdr ammunition expended   —

S.A.A. expended   —

No. of hours Tank was in action   —

Approximate mileage covered   —

Position of Tank after action   1 Mile.

Orders received at 5.0 p.m.   52d.S.E. J24.c.7.5.
                                were as follows:-

Report on Action.:-   On arrival at breaking off point my Tank developed mechanical trouble with brake and gears. The defects were remedied and proceeded at 5.0 a.m. On reaching the top of ridge, could not ascertain how far Tanks had reached, this was owing to thick fog. This being first opportunity I decided to put spare petrol into Tank. The Mist looked like lifting and what information I could get was very vague so waited for a few minutes. Unfortunately during this time one man was hit by bullet and remainder of crew were not feeling at all fit. On being examined by an M.O. one man was sent to Hospital with shock - one sent back suffering from effects of Gas, also another man for the same reason. This did not leave sufficient men to take Tank into action and after trying to get information, for some time, as to position of other tanks - decided to return to rallying point.

Later I reported to O. C. Coy and was instructed to bring Tank back for repairs same being mechanically unfit.

Signature. G. Garnham.   Time. 12.0 p.m.(mid-day)
                           Place. In-the-Field.

BATTLE HISTORY SHEET.

Crew No.　　　　　Tank No. J.45.　　Date 8-8-18.

Commanded by Sec. Lieut. Biss.　　　　10th Bn.

Unit to which attached　58th　Division　17/4 Bde.

Zero hour　4.20 A.M.

Hour Tank started for action　4.0 A.M.

Proceeded *in front of* Infantry

Reached objective at

Condition of the Ground　　Fairly level - high crops.

Condition of the enemy's trenches　Good.

Weather conditions　Thick fog.

Condition of crew after action　Exhausted - owing to heat and long hours.

Condition of Tank after action. Bullet holes in flaps in front of tank.

Casualties　— Nil.

Number of messages sent by Pigeon　Nil.

Anti-Tank measures adopted by enemy?　Anti-tank guns & rifles.

6 Pdr ammunition expended　30 rds.

S.A.A. expended　300 rds.

No. of hours Tank was in action　8 hrs.

Approximate mileage covered　10 miles.

Position of Tank after action　J.25.B.9.0.

Orders received at 4:30 p.m. 7.8.18. were as follows:-
To go to green line and N.E. of Malard Wood, and later, to attack RED LINE just South of Quesnine Wood.

REPORT ON ACTION.-

Left starting point (J.24 c.9.1.) at 4.0 A.M. and proceeded [illegible] riding to top [illegible] about [illegible] before [illegible] made for Malard Wood. On the way [illegible] a message [illegible] say the Batt. had done all to the [illegible] that he was held up [illegible] enemy [illegible] point [illegible]. I proceeded to this point, guided by a runner, [illegible] the enemy in strong numbers with M.G.s and T.M.s. We drove them from the crest, down the embankment and were just about to go down this very steep slope, when the enemy surrendered. The Infantry closed up, resulting in the capture of about 100 prisoners. After this, proceeded to Malard Wood, where I got instructions to return.

I suggest that in the future :-

Signature　C.W. Biss 2/L.
Time　9.30.
Date　11.8.18.
Place　In the field.

BATTLE HISTORY SHEET.

Crew No. 4　　　　Tank No. J.47　　　Date 8.8.18.
Commanded by 2/Lt. C. B. Loxton　　　10th Tank Bn.
Unit to which attached　　　　　Division　　　　Bde.
　　　　　　　　　　58th　　　　　　　　　174th

Zero hour　　　　4. 20 a.m.
Hour Tank started for action　　3. 55 a.m.
Proceeded　with　Infantry
Reached objective at　　8. 0 a.m.
Condition of the Ground　　steep banks, very bad ground.
Condition of the enemy's trenches　　very few, very narrow.

Weather conditions　　Very heavy mist until 8. 0 a.m.
Condition of crew after action　　Very exhausted
Condition of Tank after Action :-　overheated with bullet through Autovac.
Casualties　　1 Officer and 5 O. R.'s wounded.
Number of messages sent by Pigeon
Anti-Tank measures adopted by enemy?　NIL
6 Pdr ammunition expended　　50 rounds
S.A.A. expended　　80 rounds.
No. of hours Tank was in action　　5½ hours
Approximate mileage covered　　5000 yards
Position of Tank after action

Orders received at 5.0 p.m.　were as follows;-
　　　　7.8.18.

To advance behind barrage with Infantry to MALARD WOOD and from there to the RED LINE on the SOMME RIVER.

REPORT ON ACTION :-　Left starting point and met practically no opposition until about 350 yds from MALARD WOOD. Cleared a nest of Machine Guns and knocked out a T. M. Battery at this Point. Shortly afterwards received a bullet through the Autovac - and hand-fed the Tank back to our lines.

　　　　　　　　　　　　Signature;- Fawcett J. L/Cpl.
　　　　　　　　　　　　Time. -
　　　　　　　　　　　　Date 14.8.18.
　　　　　　　　　　　　Place In the Field.

BATTLE HISTORY SHEET.

Crew No. 2 Tank No. J40 Date 8.8.18.

Commanded by Lieut. D.G.B.Day 10th Tank Bn.

Unit to which attached 58th Division 174th Bde.

Zero hour 4.20 a.m.

Hour Tank started for action 4.0 a.m.

Proceeded In front of Infantry

Reached objective at

Condition of the Ground Good cultivated ground with high Crops in places.

Condition of the enemy's trenches slightly smashed in.

Weather conditions From 4.0 a.m. - 7.30 a.m. a very dense mist prevailed.

Condition of crew after action Very exhausted from intense heat and petrol fumes.

Condition of Tank after Action:- A few bullet holes in front- Engine slightly hot but in good running order.

Casualties Two.

Number of messages sent by Pigeon -

Anti-Tank measures adopted by enemy? Anti-Tank Guns and Field Guns.

6 Pdr ammunition expended

S.A.A. expended

No. of hours Tank was in action 9 hours.

Approximate mileage covered 9 miles

Position of Tank after action J23' B9.0.

Orders received at 5.0 p.m. 7.8.18. were as follows:-

To proceed to GREEN LINE at N.E. of Malard Wood and later to attack RED LINE just South of GRESSAIRE WOOD.

Report on Action:- Left Jumping Off Point at J2409.1 at 3.55 a.m. Three Tanks of my Section left together with orders to keep together. Owing to the very heavy mist that prevailed this was impossible and after advancing about 100 yards I found myself alone. I got out of my Tank and had a look round but could see nothing so lead the Tank on by Compass. Went over a big bank and here I met a party of M.G.C. and Infantry. I called the two Officers and found that they were both trying to get to my objective MALARD WOOD but were completely lost. We set our Maps and found direction. I told Infantry to follow my Tank. I had trouble in getting over Bank again and came under M.G. Fire. Later I met my Section Leader - Lt. Larter - his crew were exhausted and he was waiting until they were fit to go on again. I said I would push on.

Owing to heavy Mist direction was difficult to find and the going was very slow and direction difficult to find. I led Infantry on until I reached K26.C.1.4. My Crew were now exhausted and overcome with the fumes. I left Tank in valley and advanced with Infantry to

eramble/

Report on Action (continued)

enable personal Reconnaissance. The Mist was now clearing. When
I returned came under very heavy barrage so brought Tank
into Bank. I had one man hit and one man gassed. At 8.30 a.m.
Lt. Larter and 2/Lt. Cresswell arrived and we all came back together
as the Infantry in front of us were consolidating.

Signature.	D.W.B.Day. Lt.
Time.	11.0 a.m.
Date	14.8.18.
Place.	In the Field.

BATTLE HISTORY SHEET.

Crew No.   Tank No.   Date
        Composite   9306J46   8.8.18.   Bn.
Commanded by
        Lieut. C. B. Larter   10th Tank
Unit to which attached   Division   Bde.
                58th   174th

Zero hour
        4.20 a.m.
Hour Tank started for action
                                5.55 a.m.
Proceeded   Infantry
                with
Reached objective at
                                —
Condition of the Ground
                        long grass, very steep banks
Condition of the enemy's trenches
                        very few, very narrow

Weather conditions
                Heavy Mist till 8.0 a.m.
Condition of crew after action
                        absolutely exhausted and suffering
                from Exhaust Fumes and Gas.
Condition of Tank after action.:-   in good running order.
Casualties
                NIL.

Number of messages sent by Pigeon

Anti-Tank measures adopted by enemy?   Nil.

6 Pdr ammunition expended   M. G. Fire

S.A.A. expended   5 Rounds

No. of hours Tank was in action   500 rounds

Approximate mileage covered   4

Position of Tank after action   4000 yards.

Orders received at 5.0 p.m.   rallying point follows:- 1/20,000
                                                         J24d.3.1.
                XXX   7.8.18.

To advance behind barrage with Infantry to MALLARD WOOD and
from there to the RED LINE on the SOMME RIVER.
REPORT on ACTION. The long approach March had greatly heated the
Tank and on arrival at jumping off point a very heavy mist came down
so that we could neither see nor smell any Gas. Visibility extended
for only five yards, so I drove on a Compass Bearing, crossed the
front line at Zero and went in with the Infantry who were in scattered
parties. Owing to having to swing several times to negotiate
obstacles I lost direction in the mist and at 5.45 a.m. I and the
Crew M were overcome by Exhaust Fumes and Gas. With difficulty
I stopped the Tank, got the Crew outside and revived them. I got
into touch with the Infantry who were also lost, found our position
which was K.86.c.1.4 and arranged to go on. At 8.15 a.m. I started
again, driving myself, but ten minutes later succumbed to fumes
again. On reviving I got into touch with other two Tanks and
finding that the Infantry were digging in, we returned to the
Rallying Point.

I suggest that in future:- More attention be paid to the ventilation
                of the Tank.

                                Signature. C.B.Larter. Lt.
                                14.8.18. In the Field.

BATTLE HISTORY SHEET.

Crew No. 8   Tank No. 46   Date 8.8.18.

Commanded by Capt. M. C. Keynes   Bn. 10th Tank

Unit to which attached   Division 58th   Bde. 174th

Zero hour   4.20 a.m.

Hour Tank started for action   5.55 a.m.

Proceeded with   Infantry

Reached objective at

Condition of the Ground   long grass, very steep banks

Condition of the enemy's trenches   very few, very narrow.

Weather conditions   Heavy Mist till 8.0 a.m.

Condition of crew after action   absolutely exhausted and suffering from exhaust fumes and gas.

Condition of Tank after Action.   In good running order.

Casualties   NIL

Number of messages sent by Pigeon

Anti-Tank measures adopted by enemy?   NIL

6 Pdr ammunition expended   M. G. Fire

S.A.A. expended   5 rounds

No. of hours Tank was in action   300 rounds

Approximate mileage covered   6

Position of Tank after action   4000 yards

Orders received at 5.0 p.m.   rallying point 1/20,000. 324.d.6.1.
were as follows:-
xxx 7.8.18.
To advance behind barrage with Infantry to CHIPILLY and from there to the RED LINE on the SOMME RIVER.

Report on Action.   Owing to the thickness of the Mist I was unable to follow my Course. About 6.15 a.m. when the mist lifted I fell in with small parties of Infantry and rendered them all possible assistance.

Signature.   M. C. Keynes Capt.
Time   ......
Date   14.8.18.
Place.   In the Field.

BATTLE HISTORY SHEET.

Crew No. 9   Tank No. J44   Date 8.8.18.

Commanded by   2/Lt. A. E. M. Cresswell   10th Tk. Bn.

Unit to which attached   58th   Division   175th Bde.

Zero hour   4.20 a.m.

Hour Tank started for action   3.55 a.m.

Proceeded   with   Infantry

Reached objective at

Condition of the Ground   long grass, steep banks.

Condition of the enemy's trenches   very few and very narrow

Weather conditions   Heavy Mists until 8.0 a.m.

Condition of crew after action   Exhausted

Condition of Tank after Action.   Good running order.

Casualties   NIL

Number of messages sent by Pigeon   NIL

Anti-Tank measures adopted by enemy?   A. P. Bullets.

6 Pdr ammunition expended   NIL

S.A.A. expended   NIL

No. of hours Tank was in action   10 hours

Approximate mileage covered   4000 yards

Position of Tank after action   62D.N.E. 1/20,000 J.24d.6.1.

Orders received at 5.0 p.m. 7.8.18.   were as follows:-

To advance behind barrage with Infantry to MALARD WOOD and from there to the RED LINE on the SOMME RIVER.

Report on Action. Tank moved from starting point at ZERO hour, fit, owing to the heavy fog however, travelling was slow and consequently our Infantry got ahead of the Tank. All the Crew suffered very much from Petrol fumes and three fainted in the Tank.
When about 300 yards from our first objective the Officer decided not to proceed further and we returned to rallying point.

          Signature.   A. R. Chivers Crpl.
          Time   ...
          Date   12. 8. 18.
          Place.   In the Field.

BATTLE HISTORY SHEET.

Crew No. 15 Tank No. 9305 Date 8.8.18.

Commanded by 2/Lt. C. G. Oddy. Bn.

Unit to which attached 58th Division 174th Bde.

Zero hour 4.20 a.m.

Hour Tank started for action 6.0 a.m.

Proceeded Infantry

Reached objective at MALARD WOOD

Condition of the Ground Good

Condition of the enemy's trenches Good

Weather conditions Very heavy fog

Condition of crew after action Exhausted – due to Petrol Fumes.

Condition of Tank after Action Good.

Casualties Nil.

Number of messages sent by Pigeon — (No Pigeons)

Anti-Tank measures adopted by enemy? Light Field Guns, Anti-Tank Guns and A.P. Bullets.

6 Pdr ammunition expended 10 rounds.

S.A.A. expended 500 rounds.

No. of hours Tank was in action 8 hours

Approximate mileage covered 12.

Position of Tank after action J.23.p.9.0.

Orders received at 5.0 p.m. 7.8.18. were as follows:-

To proceed to Green Line at Eastern edge of MALARD WOOD, rally and afterwards attack the RED LINE North of CHIPILLY.

Report on Action. At starting point J.24.c.7.5.x. I had mechanical trouble and got into Enemy Barrage, but after remedying trouble, there was a very dense fog which was too thick to get direction, so waited until it cleared and about 6.0 a.m. started and went to assist Infantry but owing to fog got out of my Sector and got up in direction of GRESSAIRE WOOD. After cruising around I eventually reached MALARD WOOD. During the time we rendered assistance to Infantry in mopping up and captured two M.G's. At MALARD WOOD it was decided to return to rallying point to re-organise and re-fill.

Signature. C.G.Oddy 2/Lt.
Time 11.20 a.m.
Date 14.8.18.
Place. In the Field.

BATTLE HISTORY SHEET.

Crew No. 11   Tank No. J.43   Date. 8.8.18.
Commanded by 2/Lt. F. Harper   10th Bn.
Unit to which attached   58th   Divn.   174 Bde.
Zero hour. 4-20 a.m.
Hour Tank started for action. 3.55 a.m.
Proceeded   with   Infantry.
Reached objective at
Condition of the ground.
Condition of the enemy's trenches.

Weather conditions.   Thick fog.
Condition of crew after action.   Exhausted.
Condition of Tank after action.   Broken track.
Casualties.   1 officer & 1 O.R. wounded.

Number of messages sent by pigeon.   nil.
Anti-Tank measures adopted by the enemy?
6-pdr ammunition expended.
S.A.A. expended.
No of hours Tank was in action.   Ten minutes.
Approximate mileage covered.   500 yds.
Position of Tank after action.

Orders received at   pm. on 7.8.18.   were as follows :-
To go to green line N.E. of Malard Wood & later to attack the red line S. of Gressaire Wood.

REPORT IN ACTION :- Tank moved off from starting point at zero hour in a heavy fog. After about 10 mins travelling a shell burst under the left sponson door, breaking the track & wounding one of the crew. The officer & crew got out to look to the wounded man, & while doing so the officer was wounded and shortly afterwards the tank was again hit by a shell on top of the male sponson. The crew saw the wounded to the first aid post & and returned to the tank & salvaged the Hotchkiss guns. They then attached themselves to the crew of Tank No 9265 as ordered.

Suggest that in future :—

Signature D. Colvin Cpl.
Time.
Date.   14-8-18.
Place.   Field.

BATTLE HISTORY SHEET.

Crew No.   Tank No. J. 19. 9346   Date. 10-8-18

Commanded by   2nd Lt. C. A. Price.   10th Bn.

Unit to which attached   Australian   Divn.   Bde.

Zero hour.   9.45 p.m.

Hour Tank started for action.   9.40 p.m.

Proceeded   with   Infantry.

Reached objective at   10.10 p.m.

Condition of the ground.   Road.

Condition of the enemy's trenches.   No definite line

Weather conditions.   Moonlight.

Condition of crew after action.   Fit.

Condition of Tank after action.   Fit.

Casualties.   Nil

Number of messages sent by pigeon.   Nil

Anti-Tank measures adopted by the enemy?   Bombs. A.P. bullets.

6-pdr ammunition expended.   Nil

S.A.A. expended.   650

No of hours Tank was in action.   1

Approximate mileage covered.   2½

Position of Tank after action.   62ᴰ N.E. J.24 d 6.1

Orders received at 9.30 pm. on 10-8-18 were as follows :-

To proceed from cross roads L.13 central, along BRAY-CORBIE road to crucifix L.15.20.40.

REPORT ON ACTION :-

Zero hour was 9.45.

I left my starting point at zero, and proceeded with the Infantry along the road towards BRAY sweeping the road in front with machine gun fire. My gunners on the left kept up a steady fire at enemy flashes until we reached the crucifix. The enemy offered a feeble resistance. When I saw that our troops were consolidating, I turned about and reported to the Officer Commanding the operations, who told me to wait further orders.

At 12 midnight I received orders to proceed back

P.T.O.

to my Company.

I suggest that in future:—

Better ventilation be provided for the Mark V tank

Signature. Gilbert A Grice
Time.   3.40 pm
Date   15-8-18
Place   In the field.

BATTLE HISTORY SHEET.

Crew No. Composite   Tank No. 9366. J.48   Date. 9-8-18.
Commanded by   Lieut: C.B. Carter.   10th Bn.
Unit to which attached   12th   Divn.   Bde.
Zero hour.   5.30.p.m.
Hour Tank started for action.   5.30.p.m.
Proceeded   with   Infantry.
Reached objective at   —
Condition of the ground.   crops and long grass, undulating.
Condition of the enemy's trenches.   few and narrow.

Weather conditions,   bright and clear
Condition of crew after action.   with the exception of the casualties, fit
Condition of Tank after action.   Auto-vac pierced and 6 pdr out of action.
Casualties.   2 wounded
    1 wounded but at duty.
Number of messages sent by pigeon.   Nil.
Anti-Tank measures adopted by the enemy?   M.G. fire with A.P. bullets.
6-pdr ammunition expended.   3 rounds
S.A.A. expended.   400 rounds
No of hours Tank was in action.   3.
Approximate mileage covered.   3000 yards
Position of Tank after action. rallying point 62 DNE 1/20,000. U 23 b. 9.0.
Orders received at   pm. on   9-8-18.   were as follows :-

To advance behind barrage with Infantry between MORLANCOURT and the CORBIE-BRAY road to first objective just E of BRICKYARD in K.16.c.

REPORT ON ACTION :- Left jumping off point at K.20.a.1.1 at Zero, crossed main road at K.20.b.3.9 and turned E. picking up Infantry, and following our barrage. Engaged enemy machine gun nests on the left front with case shot, which was very effective in the crops. After two rounds, the firing mechanism broke. Repaired the damage. fired another round, and it broke again. While repairing it again. gunner and loader were wounded by splinters. Carried on, engaging enemy with Hotchkiss and revolver fire. About K.15 d.6.8 I found that the Auto-vac had been pierced in two places and was leaking badly. I plugged the holes as best I could, turned about and brought the tank out of action.

C.B. Carter. Lieut

P.T.O.

I suggest that in future:—

More case shot should be carried for open fighting.

6 pdr sponsons should be fitted with telescope shields and splash felting.

Signature: C.B. Carter. Lieut.

Unit:

Date: 14-8-18.

Place:

BATTLE HISTORY SHEET.

Crew No. 7.   Tank No. J.45   Date. 9-8-18
Commanded by Sec Lieut: G. Biss.   10th Bn.
Unit to which attached   12th   Divn.   Bde.
Zero hour.   5.30 p.m
Hour Tank started for action.   5.30 p.m
Proceeded in front of Infantry.
Reached objective at   8.0 p.m
Condition of the ground.   Level (wheat crops)
Condition of the enemy's trenches.   Fair

Weather conditions.   Good.
Condition of crew after action.   Exhausted, owing to heat.
Condition of Tank after action.   In running order
Casualties.   Nil.

Number of messages sent by pigeon.   Nil.
Anti-Tank measures adopted by the enemy?   Light guns.
6-pdr ammunition expended.   50 rounds
S.A.A. expended.   400 rounds
No of hours Tank was in action.   3½ hours
Approximate mileage covered.   7 miles
Position of Tank after action.   J.23.b.9.0.
Orders received at 3.30 pm. on 9-8-18 were as follows:—
   To proceed in front of Infantry and take Blue Line.

REPORT ON ACTION:— Left starting point (K.30.a.1.1) at 5.30 p.m and caught up infantry, working with them until reaching objective. The infantry were in position but were being worried by M.G fire. I then received a message from O.C. "A" Coy 6th Buffs asking me to deal with M.Gs on his right which I promptly did.

I suggest that in future:—

Signature.   G.W. Biss. 2nd Lt
Time.   9.30 a.m.
Date.   14-8-18
Place.   In the Field

BATTLE HISTORY SHEET.

Crew No. 2.   Tank No. J.40.   Date. 9-8-18.
Commanded by Lieut. D.Q.B. Day.   10th Bn.
Unit to which attached   12th Divn.   Bde.
Zero hour.   5.30. p.m.
Hour Tank started for action.   5.40 p.m.
Proceeded in front of   Infantry.
Reached objective at   8.0. p.m
Condition of the ground.   Level good ground with high crops.
Condition of the enemy's trenches.   Fair.

Weather conditions.   Clear and bright
Condition of crew after action.   Exhausted, owing to intense heat and petrol fumes.
Condition of Tank after action.   Bullet holes in male sponson and in right side and a number in exhaust pipe.
Casualties.   One.

Number of messages sent by pigeon.   Nil.
Anti-Tank measures adopted by the enemy?   Light guns
6-pdr ammunition expended.   90 Ball. 30 Case Shot.
S.A.A. expended.   1500 rounds
No of hours Tank was in action.   3½ hours.
Approximate mileage covered.   4 miles
Position of Tank after action.   J.23.B.9.0
Orders received at 3.30. pm. on 9-8-18 were as follows :-

To proceed in front of Infantry and take Blue Line.

REPORT ON ACTION :- Leading up to Starting Point I was held up by engine trouble. Put this right and passed Starting Point at K.20. A.1.1. at 5.40 (10 minutes after other Tanks) Crossed main Road at K.21. A.3.4 and came under heavy machine-gun fire. Silenced this gun and made straight for objective. I saw the Infantry on right of main Road were held up, so went up and found that they were being held up by strong point. I took Tank forward and put 12 rounds of 6 Pdr ammunition into S.P. and blew it up. The Infantry then advanced. I met Lt Biss (J.45) at K.15.D. and we pushed on together dealing with a number of machine guns in the high crops. Reached Objective at 8.0 p.m and received message from O.C. 'A' Coy 6th Buffs to deal with machine Gun in front.

P.T.O.

I acted on this and cruised in front of the Infantry for 300 yards. Turned back and arrived at J.23.B.9.0 about 9.30 p.m.

                 D.Q.B. Day. Lt.

I suggest that in future :—

           Signature :- D.Q.B. Day. Lt.
           Time.   11.30 a.m.
           Date.   11-8-18
           Place.   In the Field.

1918 AUG

BATTLE HISTORY SHEET.

Crew No. Composite. Tank No. J 35. Date. 10/8/18.
Commanded by Lt. G. Garnham. 10th Bn.
Unit to which attached 12th Divn. Bde.
Zero hour. 6 p.m.
Hour Tank started for action. 6 p.m.
Proceeded in front of Infantry. 9th Battn. Essex Regt.
Reached objective at —
Condition of the ground. Cultivated
Condition of the enemy's trenches. —

Weather conditions. Clear and dry
Condition of crew after action. —
Condition of Tank after action. Knocked out.
Casualties. 3 killed, 1 wounded, 2 missing

Number of messages sent by pigeon. —
Anti-Tank measures adopted by the enemy? —
6-pdr ammunition expended. —
S.A.A. expended. —
No of hours Tank was in action. ½
Approximate mileage covered. 1000 yds.
Position of Tank after action. 62 DNE. — K 4d central.
Orders received at pm. on were as follows :—

REPORT ON ACTION :— Received orders to go into action at 6 p.m on 10th inst. and started fit. After proceeding approximately 1000 yds my tank was hit by a large shell — the right sponson being very much damaged.

This unfortunately killed 3 men and wounded 1. Two others more or less suffering from shock were reported missing — one has since turned up.

The Tank was left behind our front line at 62 DNE. K 4d central. I returned with one man to Coy Hdqrs. arriving at 11.20 p.m.

I suggest that in future :—

Signature G. Garnham
Time 12 - mid-day
Date 14th Aug. 1918
Place In the field

SATURDAY 24th AUGUST 1916.   Sheet No. 1.

Time	W/re No.	Phone Message To	From	Subject	Action
am.				Headquarters opened at HEILLY 10 am.	
10-40	G.611		Office.	Move of 174th Bde. completed. Units located in K.13 and K.14.a. and b. Bde. H.Q. established K.14.b.2.2.	III Corps. Q.
11-5	G.612		"	Map dropped from aeroplane timed 10-10 am. shows British seen on line K.14.c.5.5 to F.2.a.0.0. Discs shown F.8.c.3.5 to F.13.d.5.0. Discs seen on line F.20.a.3.3.- also in trenches F.13.b. Aeroplane fired on from F.22.c. and F.20.d.0.4 - F.21.d.3.3. Aeroplane fired on from F.22.c. and F.23.a and b, also from line L.14.central. L.16.central.	140, 175th Bdes III, G.R.A. III, V Corps, 18th Div.
10-30	GX100		"	"G" Coy. 2 L.G. M.G. Bn. placed under 175th Bde. for consolidation purposes for to-day's attack. "B" Coy. placed under 140 Bde.	
11-30	G.599		174th Bde.		
11-30	G.220		174th Bde.	Bde. Group in new position 8-30 am. Bn. H.Q.- 6th Bn. K.13.a. 6.3. 7th K.13.d.1.3. 8th K.13.b.4.3. Bde. H.Q. K.14.b.2.2.	
11-30	SM.12		175th Bde.	Our troops definitely hold final objective.	
12noon	G612		Office	Zero hour given in para: 1 of O.O.147 cancelled. Zero hour will now be 2-30 am.25th.	Recipients O.O.147.
11-30			Aeroplane.	Line runs E.side BECOURT WOOD - F.8.a and c. - F.14. a and d. - F.20.b and d. - F.27.central - L.3.b and d. - L.9.b and d.	
2 pm.	G.614		Office.	Zero hour 2-30 am 25th. Para: 6 Order 147 cancelled further orders for Sqdrn will be issued early. Assembly position K.18.a.	"D" Sqdrn 22 Corps Cav.

SUNDAY 25th AUGUST 1918.   Sheet No. 14

Time	Wire No.	'Phone Message To.	From.	Subject.	Action.
am 5-35	-	G.II		175th Bde. reported they were on final objective. R. and Centre Bns. no opposition. L. Bn. very little opposition. Pushing patrols out and digging in on final objective.	
5-40		G.II	140 Bde.	Reported that they believed there had been little opposition but had not yet got definite report as to whether they were on objective or not.	
7-40				173rd Bde. informed of the situation.	
"				Gen. RAMSAY told C.R.E. that the Pioneers would not be employed for the present and would remain in K.10.	
				Arranged with Corps that C.R.A. 58th Div. should take over from C.R.A. 47th Div. at new H.Q. and that the latter should go there in the first instance.	
				Col. WYLIE was told to move "D" Coy. M.G. Bn. forward so that it would be available to relieve or reinforce.	
8-50		G.II	47th Div.	re 141st Bde. None of the Bdes. of 47th Div. are to go back to refit. To refit where they are. We informed 47th Div. that we did not want to use 141st Bde. and that it was at 47th Divs disposal for refitting. Corps have not made it definite yet under whose orders 141 Bde. are.	
pm. 4-30				Coy. Commander 174th Bde. reports 12-55pm. that our troops are through BILLON Wood and meeting with considerable resistance East of it..	

SUNDAY 25th — AUGUST 1916.   Sheet No. 2

Time	Wire No.	Phone Message To.	From.	Subject.	Action.
pm. 1-30			173rd Bde.	Message from B.M. to say that there is no artillery shelling of MARICOURT. Asks for as much as possible to be turned on.	C.R.A. told to comply.
1-50			140. Bde.	Report 4 enemy balloons up.	C.R.A. is asking Army Wing to deal with them.
"			173rd Bde.	Just had message from Company Commander 174 Bde that they had got BILLON WOOD. No other news of situation on any other part of the front. They are pushing on now. Major Webster informed that bombardment of MARICOURT would take place as soon as guns could be put on it - as soon as they had decided what artillery fire they wanted they were to inform D.H.Q. what they wanted shelling, where our troops were what time the bombardment was to start and what time it was to lift.	
2.10		G. I.	173rd Bde.	Says that 4th Battn. are in A.19.b. and d. and in A.25.b. with their right at COPSE "H". 2 Coys. 2nd Bn. have gone up through A.19.d. N. of BILLON WOOD with other 1½ Bns. in neighbourhood of BRONFAY FARM.	
2.20		G. II.		Adjt. 2/2nd Bn. who was up when they were attacking on E. edge of BILLON WOOD said that they met considerable fire from W. of MARICOURT - BILLON AVENUE and S.W. corner of BILLON WOOD.	
			Maj. Kitchen rang up for orders.	Major Kitchen was informed that he was BILLOW WOOD was recaptured definitely report situation as soon as	

SUNDAY 25th. AUGUST 1916. Sheet No. 3.

Time	Wire Message No.	Phone Message No.	From	Subject	Action
p.m. 2.40		III x Corps		III Corps informed of general situation.	
3.30		G. I.	Major Kitchen.	Asks for instructions. Told to remain with 173 Bde. and bring back accurate result of attack being made at 4.30 p.m.	
			175 Bde. asks that 175 Bde. be informed of their attack as they were not in touch. Said all arrangements for attack 4.30 p.m. had been made and that they would push through as far as possible.		
4.0		G. I.	175 Bde.	The position of 173 Bde. explained to General Cobham. Informed that the G.O.C. wished 175 and 174 Bde. to co-operate if possible. General Cobham explained that his men were dead beat. He sent for Gen. Maxwell who was 50 yds. away. General Maxwell promised to push on as fast as he could with his Brigade Eastwards. Said that our No. G.X. 104 had not been received although O.O. 149 had. Gist of missing wire explained also dividing lines.	
4.30			Aeroplane No. 5	Report up to 1.55 p.m. - See typed report.	
4.25		G. I.	174 Bde.	Sent forward B.M. and part of B.H.Q. to end of cable - F.29.c. B.G.C. will move immediately Communication is established. Has not yet got Group Commander with him - Told him that Bde. of artillery was placed at his disposal and that Group Commander had call on a second Brigade.	
6.45			Capt. Spencer 47th Divn.	Map from aeroplane observation dropped HEILLY at 6.15 p.m. gave line as follows :- G.7.d. & b.- G.1.d. & b.- E. of BILLON WOOD and along Grid line between A.19. & F.24. and between CAFTET WOOD and CARNOY.	

Sheet No. 4.

SUNDAY -- 25th -- AUGUST 1918.

Time	Wire No.	Phone Message To.	From.	Subject.	Action.
p.m. 7.20		X	173 Bde.	Troops .2/2nd Bn. are at trench A.21.a.cent. - Copse "B" Flank defence LA PRIE WOOD. No one on left. Heavy shelling from OXFORD AND CAMBRIDGE COPSES. Parties of enemy seen 10-20 (?) retiring S.E. through approx A.23.cent. and further to the N. Wanted to know whether 3rd Bn. would support. Bn. gone forward or right Bn. at BILLON WOOD. Told them that 174 Bde. would be ordered to take over BILLON WOOD from them as soon as possible up to the Bde. boundary as laid down, also that they could use the last Bn. to support the 2nd Bn. .22 Corps Cavalry Sqdn. attached 58th Divn. have their H.Q. at HAPPY VALLEY.	
7.20					
7.25			B.M. 173 Bde.	2 Coys. 2/2nd Bn. are on their final objective - probably A.21.a.central and a Coy. N. of them.	

=*==*==*==*==*==*==*==*==*==*==*==*==*==*==*==*==*==*==*==

26th AUGUST 1916.   Sheet No. 5.

Time	Wire No.	Phone Message To.	From.	Subject.	Action.
a.m. 9.15		G.I.	175 Bde.	Can give no information re situation.	
9.30				Corps Conference postponed until 10.30 a.m.	
9.45			L.O.	Our troops hold BILLON AVENUE and trench running down S. to Copse "N", in strength, we also hold trench E. of A.26.cent. down to Copse "J".	
10.10				Australian line now runs E. of SUZANNE through G.2.cent. to Copse "N". They are pushing forward Eastwards with River as objective of their patrols, left on A.28.central. They are in touch with our Right Bde.-some of our troops reported in A.26.central	
1.27		G.I.	III Corps.	Asks for situation. We are informed V Corps are doing very well, they have got LONGUEVAL, and pushing down E. of TRONES WOOD towards ARROWHEAD COPSE (at least orders have gone out for them to do that). Cut off the pocket which is holding up our left (18th Divn)	
p.m. .20		G.I.	174 Bde.	Verify positions reported. They were told to reorganise.	
.45			III Corps.	Said that 18th Divn. had advanced half-way through MONTAUBAN and that 38th Divn. on their left were in DELVILLE WOOD	
.30			B.G.G.S. Corps.	Rang up to know what our intentions were for tomorrow. Gave him the original proposed objective but said the plan was at present under discussion. The aeroplane map gives the line A.15.cent.-E. of Copse "B" to A.28.a.3.0. to A.28.c.0.0.	

Sheet No. 6

26th AUGUST.   AUGUST 1918.
XXXXXXX

Time	Wire No.	'Phone Message To.	From.	Subject.	Action.
P.M. 7.5		G.I.	B.G.G.S. Corps	Genl. Fuller was informed of proposed attack tomorrow.	
7.15		G.I.	3rd Aus. Divn.	Gave start line — asked if it would suit them — gave suggested boundary as practically continuation of our old boundary A.28.a. (QUARRY incl) to AUSTRALIANS — A.24.c.2.6. also gave details of our attack tomorrow. Objective A.29.a.8.0. — Northwards along trench to ROUND STREET A.29.a.7.8. — due N. along trench following trench line round A.23.c. — along trench line in that trench system (old British front line) — A.23.a. — Road A.17.c. following front line all the way round up to A.16.b.

Making general line A.18.a.0.2., general line of exploitation BOIS D'en HAUT — Western edge of SUPPORT COPSE — due S. line to Chat. de GENDARME.

12th Divn. have gist of order explained for attack of 58th Div on morning 27th — 12th Divn. also informed us of their intention to advance in two bounds this evening — 1st bound from present positions to the line BRIQUETERIE — MARICOURT Road thenceforward if no opposition encountered. In the event of opposition in strength being made 12th Divn. propose to advance in co-operation with 58th Divn. with a barrage on morning 27th. | |
| 8.20 | | | | | |
| 9.5 | | | 3rd Aus. Divn. | State that the Div. Genl. has gone down to arrange details of attack, with Brigadiers and that he could not give strengths with which they would attack, but we may reckon that 3rd Australians will do it with at least two Coys. and one in support. G.O.C. 3rd Aus. Divn. will not take on FARGNY WOOD. | |

Sheet No. 7

26th AUGUST 1918.

Time	Wire No.	'Phone Message To.	From.	Subject.	Action.
pm. 10-30		G.I to	3rd Aust. Div.	Informed 3rd Aust. Div. that we received order from III Corps saying that the new boundary suggested by us was to come into force for the attack tomorrow.	
10-45		G.I	B.M., R.A.	Arranged with C.R.A. 3rd Aust. Div. to cover front with protector barrage because Aust. Arty. cannot reach.	
11-45			173rd Bde.	Wanted to know if H.A. could be placed under them so that in the event of enemy withdrawal guns could be ordered to move forward at once. Informed them that Arty. Group should be informed if enemy withdraws and he will take necessary action. 173rd Bde. were given time for synchronization of watches by telephone as officer detailed to take watch round had not arrived. (The both wires at midnight)	

----------oOo----------

TUESDAY 27th AUGUST 1918.   Sheet No. 8

Time	Wire No.	Phone Message To	From	Subject	Action
am 12-25			12th Div.	Compared watches with 12th Div. who were a shade fast. They had synchronized with Corps.	
6-10			B.M. 173rd Bde.	Reports that one of 173rd Bn. Commanders rang up at 6-5 am. to say that the attack was going well. A batch of 20 - 30 prisoners were being sent on from his H.Q.	
6-15				Above message passed on to III Corps.	
6-50			B.M. 173rd	States through Village. Light casualties. Prisoners 117 Regt. 25th Div.	
6-52				Above message passed to Corps and 12th Div.. Corps report that 18th Div. are pushing on speedily. Captured 150 prisoners two of which were of fresh and unexpected Divs. Int. however was sceptical of 18th Div. report.	
			173rd Bde.	117 I.R. 3 Offr. 40 O.R. of 1st and 4th Bns. 1-4, ard 10th Coys. Div. distributed from N to S. 115 I.R. 116th I.R. 117th I.R. S. of Regt. 201st I.R. 203rd I.R. Prisoners state enemy's intention to retire to ridge N. of PERONNE .Coys. strength 49. All Regts. of 25th Div. identified.	Information passed to III Corps. They have no further information.
7-30 7-45			174th Bde.	From wounded officer. Attack going well up to line A.22.a.9.5 and A.22.d.1.6. Well up to barrage. In touch with 173rd. 6th Bn. casualties from M.Gs.	
7-45			3rd A.I.F.	11th Bde. occupy QUARRY. Enemy transport seen going East at gallop. Heavies assisting. 11th Bde. propose to use Light Horse to assist exploitation on N. bank of River.	
8-30			173rd Bde.	4th Bn. rept 7-15 am. taken objective. 200 yards front astride railway.	

Sheet No. 9

TUESDAY — 27th — AUGUST 1918.

Time	Wire No.	'Phone Message No.	From.	Subject.	Action.
am. 9.0		G.I.	12th Divn.	Report their troops at MALTZ HORN FARM – Hill A.6. where their post is rather isolated – not in touch on either flank.	
9.30			173 Bde.	Report they are in touch with 37th Bde. H.Q. and state that 37th Bde. line runs A.6.a. & c. – A.12.a. and c. 18th Division report general counter-attack is developing in neighbourhood of BERNAFAY WOOD.	
			184th Bde.	Report left Bn. 2 Coys. on objective. 2 Coys moving forward to line of exploitation. Position of right Bn. obscure. C.O. gone forward to elucidate. Heavy enemy barrage between Copse C and A – A.28.a. interfering with messages. 8th Bn. in support in A.28.a.	
		III Corps.	Major Kitchen.	Reported to Corps that we are in touch on our left but not cert ain of our right. That there is no reason to suppose that there is anything wrong. Enemy barrage from Copse C. to A.28.a. prevents messages getting through. Patrols gone forward to line of exploitation, general Line NAMELESS WOOD to SUPPORT COPSE.	
9.45		174 Bde.	G. I.	Told them that boundaries are likely to be aslaid down originally; i.e. due E. and W. line, and that we shall have to extend further to the right so that they should not go further N. than MAUREPAS Station. Right Divl. Boundary Grid line through A.30.central – B.25.central. – B.26.central. Left Boundary Grid line through B.13. and 14. central.	

Sheet No: 10

TUESDAY 27th AUGUST 1918.

Time	Wire No.	'Phone Message To.	From.	Subject.	Action.
am. 10-5		G.I.	3rd Aust. Div.	Report many enemy are still in A.23.c and d., and A.29, and have been asked by their Brigade for artillery support.	
10-20		Major KITCHIN	12th Div.	Say their main line of resistance will be BRIQUETERIE - MARICOURT Rd. Asked what ours was. Informed Front Line trench E. of MARICOURT in A.17.a and c, through &23.a and c. They will join with us at the SQUARE. 35th Bde. being moved up for that purpose.	
10-20				Army Commander to visit G.O.C. 4 or 5 pm. today.	
10-40		Major KITCHIN	Corps.	Ask if we can make our main line of resistance our objective line and join with 12th Div. about the SQUARE. Informed them that as far as the Right Bde. concerned position still obscure but main line of resistance will be made as far forward as possible up to the objective line when re-organization takes place.	
11		G.I.	174th Bde.	For the time being and until situation cleared line of resistance would be along trench line - RAVINE Avenue - BLACK St. thence old British Front line.	
11-7			G.O.C. R.A. Corps.	Promised that he would turn on what artillery he could on to likely hostile assembly positions and lines of approach.	
11-15		3rd Aust. Div.	L.O.	Informed 3rd Aust.Div. of situation.	
11-22		173rd Bde.	G.I.	173rd Bde. fixed their line of resistance Old British Line. Established defensive line Old British Line. Not quite certain as to whether they are in touch with 174th on their right but endeavouring to establish communication. Not in touch with 12th Div. on their left. 175th Bde. to move up to A.19 - 25 in readiness to take up position as support.	

TUESDAY 27th .... AUGUST 1916.   Sheet No. 11

Time	Wire No.	'phone Message To.	From.	Subject.	Action.
am 11-30		12th Div.	G.I.	Informed that we have definitely established line of defence along old British Front Line. From a personal reconnaissance of Bty. Commander 12th Div. have a line definitely established from A.11.c.4.0 - A.11.c.0.5. A.11.a.6.6 - A.5.d.2.0 - A.5.a.central - A.5.a.8.7. Main Line of Resistance will be along BRIQUETERIE - MARICOURT Rd. with Right thrown forward to connect with us at the SQUARE.	
11-57			173rd Bde.	Report touch with 12th Div. SQUARE Tr. to line A.17.a.5** 2.5 where there are 25 men of 3rd Bn. Thence A.17.c.5.7. 3 Offrs. 6 M.Gs. 120 O.R. 4th Bn. In touch on Right with weak Coy. 3rd Bn. They state that 174th Bde. are in Scots St. and S Works, but are not in touch with 174th. 2/2nd are helping and organizing N. side Line, from U works - A.21.a. 3rd Bn. H.Q. are in COPSE B. Old German Front Line is strongly held	
12-30 pm.		Corps	G.I.	Reported situation.	
1-10		Major KITCHIN	175th Bde.	Intend to move their H.Q. at 3 pm. to F.28.d.0.8. Their Bns. are moving to positions of assembly w. of BILLON WOOD ready to occupy defensive line through A.20 and A.26 if necessary; when they would be disposed as follows :- SHEFFIELD AVE. 1 Bn. plus some M.Gs. BILLON AVE. *** and S. to A.26.c.4.9 1 Bn. A.26.c.central 4 M.Gs. to deal with any enemy enveloping moves from the South West of BILLON WOOD. 1 Bn. and 1 M.Gs. ready to reinforce either N. or S. of BILLON WOOD or to stop any possible break through through BILLON WOOD.	
1-25		G.I.	173rd Bde.	Estimate prisoners to be total 120 including 1 Bn. Commander.	

TUESDAY 27th AUGUST 1916.   Sheet No. 12

Time	'Phone Message To.	From.	Subject.	Wire No.	Action.
pm. 2-55	Major KITCHIN	174th Bde.	6th and 7th Bn. both on objective. 6th in touch with Fusiliers on Left and with one another. Elements 8th Bn. on right of 7th (not in touch with Australians. Whole Bde. objective gained. B.G.C. wishes to move B.H.Q. to F.30.c.3.0. There is already line to it.		
3-35	174th Bde.	G.I.	Gen. MAXWELL informed of tomorrow"s operations.		
4-10	174th Bde.	G.I.	Informed that Australians take over from 174th up to KING ST. in A.23.c. and then straight line to trench junction A.29.b.95.95 then on to the QUARRY.		
4-30	Capt. SPENCER	173rd Bde.	Report touch with units on both flanks. Links with 12th Div at the SQUARE.		
5-15	Major KITCHIN	12th Div.	As their men will be advancing further ahead than ours tomorrow they will require a gap between our left and their right or our barrage which will be behind theirs may drop on their own men. Their barrage is moving 100 yards in 4 mins. They therefore propose to make their Southern boundary the line from S. edge of FAVIERE Wood. to the South edge of HARDECOURT. As to eir objective should take up that runs through East edge of HARDECOURT they want to know how we propose to effect junction in view of our objective being West edge of BOIS D'EN HAUT.	Reptd. to G.I. 12th Div. 5-35 pm. in addition suggested that we should take 6 for the whole of BOIS D'EN HAUT. 6-30 p.m. informed
5-40	Major KITCHIN	173rd Bde.	Said that they told B.G.G.S. Corps this morning that they estimated their strength at 800. Now think they can only find about 550. They ask us to please inform Corps lest Gen FULLER be mislead.		
6-40		12th Div.	Report 4-5 Hows. firing short in A.16.b.central.		B.M., D.A. informed.

Sheet No. 13.

TUESDAY 27th AUGUST 1916.

Time	Wire No.	'Phone Message To.	From.	Subject.	Action.
pm 8-5		Major KITCHIN	12th Div.	Report location of their Right Bde. H.Q. A.10.b.5.3.	
9-5		"	174th Bde.	State that their right is in front line trench about ROUND St. where they are in touch with Australians and as far as they know that is still the situation.	
9-20		G.I.	Aust. Div.	Say the enemy is reported to be in FARGNY Wood which will entail their undertaking a preliminary operation before zero hour. They suggest that Bdes. should arrange direct between themselves how this is to be carried out. (First reported 9-5 pm)	
9-20		G.I.	173rd Bde.	Asked whether the Coy. sent out forward had got to be in exact place named in order. It was pointed out that the position was only approximate and that the whole Coy. should not be concentrated together.	
9-30		G.I. to Gen. MAXWELL		Informed that FARGNY Wood occupied by enemy and that arrangements for prelininary operation would be arranged direct between Australians and 173rd Bde.	
10-35		G.I.	12th Div.	(Mmss-&) A.18.b.1.3. A.30.b.1.6. B.7.b.6.4. Captured map with pencil marks where M.Gs. were firing to-day and this map shows similar pin holes at above co-ordinates.	
10-45		3rd Aust. Div.	G.I.	Informed them that 12th Div. had captured map as above and that point which affected them was the one at A.30.b.1.6.	

---------oOo---------

WEDNESDAY 28th AUGUST 1918.

Time	Wire No.	'phone Message To.	From.	Subject.	Action.
am 8-15		G.II	173rd Bde.	Right Platoon at 6-45 am. reported entering SUPPORT Copse. Left Centre Platoon A.18.c.1.3. Believed Left Platoon in BOIS D'EN HAUT.	
12-18			3rd Aust. Div.	Report FARGNY Wood taken and Australians now in touch with us on proper objective.	
9-45		B.G.C.175 Bde.	G.I.	Situation explained.	
9-50			174th Bde.	6th Bn. now on objective. In touch with Fusiliers in SUPPORT Copse and with 8th Bn. on Right. Are pushing out posts. Good deal M.G. fire from Crest about B.19.a.	
9-55			12th Div.	Report CLAPHAM FM. holding them up. G.O.C. informed them that CLAPHAM FM. was in their area and that our men near it: exact position not known, therefore artillery fire cannot fire on it. Situation must be cleared up by Os.C. of the 2 Bns. on the spot.	
9-5		Major KITCHIN	174th Bde.	8th Bn. (R. Bn.) on objective, in touch with Australians. Joint Post established in A.30.b. 6th Bn. (L. Bn.) have established Post with Vickers guns at A.23.b.9.4. Position of remainder of 8th Bn. uncertain. C.O. is now there and going forward to objective.	
10-15			173rd Bde.	Report CLAPHAM FM. held by us and in touch with 12 Div. Post at A.18.b.4.2. Enemy trying to push forward towards CLAPHAM FM. Arty. turned on to E. of CLAPHAM FM.	
10-30		Corps.	G.O.C.	G.O.C. asked Corps for Coy. L.G. M.G. Bn. Corps are sending us 2 Coys. Are being ordered to take up the defence of the line BILLON AVE. A.20.a.2.6.	

Sheet No. 15.

WEDNESDAY 28th AUGUST 1918.

Time	Wire No.	'Phone Message To.	From.	Subject.	Action.
am 11		Corps	Major KITCHIN	We are now holding the front line trenches running N. and S. through SUPPORT Copse. In touch with Australians on Right with an International Post established forward in QUARRY A.30.h. Patrols have pushed through BOIS D'EN HAUT and CLAPHAM FM. is now reported in our hands, after having hung us up for some time.	Also w red to Corps GX217.
11-5		Major KITCHIN	174th Bde.	6th Bn. have now put to flight two enmy M.Gs. in A.24.b. which were holding up advance and have established Lewis Gun Post at approx. B.19.a.4.2.	
11-25		G.I.	173rd Bde.	Are not quite certain of position of CLAPHAM FM. When Bde. Major was there it was held by us. He thinks the enemy have only a few M.Gs. and Snipers in front of it.	
pm 4-30				3rd Aust. Div. rang up to say that they had heard our post had been withdrawn in A.24. 174th Bde. stated this to be true. Line to run on the objective with post at the QUARRY. 3rd Aust. Div. informed.	

---o0o---

THURSDAY 29th AUGUST 1918.

Time Wire No.	'Phone Message To.	From.	Subject.	Action.
am. 9-15	G.I.	Gen. COBHAM.	Stated that the Brigade on his left was not advancing at all. He was pushing out patrols himself and would conform with any form of forward movement by the Australians.	
9-20	Major KITCHIN	Corps	Contact Patrol Machines report 6-50 am. our troops seen in trench system N.10.b. and d. N.4.b. and d. Advancing in H.22.d. H.16. QUARRY H.13.central held by us. Advancing in H.2.c., H.1.b. B.25. Apparently no opposition.	
9-30	G.II	Corps.	State aeroplane shows our troops in B.25.d and H.2.	
9-50	3rd Aust. Corps G.I.		Told 3rd Aust. Div. that 12th Div. on our left were not advancing at present. We were pushing forward on right to connect up with them (Australians) and should have to throw back our left to the East of BOIS D'EN HAUT.	
11	Major KITCHIN	3rd Aust. Div.	Aeroplane reports our troops strongly hold trenches in A.8.b and d. and A.12.b. No enemy shelling, little of ours. Enemy M.G. post in B.14.d.9.5.	
11-5	do.	175th Bde.	Informed of above. 175th Bde. said post established at A.13.a.3.0 pushing out patrols MAUREPAS STN. Endeavouring to establish posts B.19.a.central. RED FM. HINDLEG WOOD.	
11-10	Capt. SPENCER	175th Bde.	Confirmed above. Established Post RED FM. B.13.c.2.0. In touch on both flanks. Patrolled to BATTERY Copse. No sign of enemy there.	
11-15	do.	12th Div.	Informed of above. 12th Div. say that an Advance Guard of 1 Bde. Group have been ordered to move forward and pass through their present line and engage the enemy wherever met. Latest information is that the enemy hold line COMBLES - OAKHANGER WOOD MAUREPAS STN. Cavalry with M.Gs. sent to FALFEMONT FARM (B.28)	

Contd. page 17.

Sheet No. 17

THURSDAY 29th AUGUST 1918.

Time	Wire No.	'Phone Message To.	From.	Subject.	Action.
am 11-15	Contd.			to enfilade this line. 12 Division will move to Adv. H.Q. at HIDDEN WOOD at 1 pm. today.	
11-20		12th Div.	Capt. SPENCER.	Informed them that 1/4th Suffolks would most likely be at MAUREPAS STATION very shortly.	
11-55		Major KITCHIN	18th Div.	18th Div. patrols in touch with 12th Div. at FALFEMONT FARM. Patrols 18th Div. advancing from LEUZE WOOD. V Corps pushing on Eastwards also. 4th Cavalry 18th Div. long way ahead in touch with enemy. Enemy transport seen retiring from COMBLES, being shelled by Heavies. One of prisoners captured LEUZE WOOD said he was ordered to hold out to the last. He did not feel like it and handed himself up.	
12 noon		Corps.	Major KITCHIN	Reported general situation to Corps, including Australians on our right.	
12 "		Capt. SPENCER	B.G.C. 175th Bde.	Rang up to speak to G.O.C. in accordance with instructions from the latter. B.G.C. 175th reports that they now hold posts RED FM. (A.19.a.central) - A.13.c.3.0. He considers he can advance to Trench line running South from MAUREPAS to A.20.central. As G.O.C. was not in, B.G.C. 175th Bde. took on the responsibility of advancing to that line.	175th Bde. informed.
noon pm-		Capt. SPENCER	12th Div.	Report that Advance Guard just entering MAUREPAS with no opposition.	do.
12-50		Aust. L.O.	Aust. Div.	Aust. line advancing in H.17, 23, 29, 35 (central) One Bde. crossing Canal at H.17.b.3.5 and another at BRIE.	12-10 12th Div. informed.

THURSDAY 29th. AUGUST 1918.   Sheet No.   18.

Time	Wire No.	'Phone Message To.	From.	Subject.	Action.
pm. 12-10			3rd Corps.	Report Aust. line runs H.17.a. H.23.a and c. H.29.a and c. H.30, 36, 35 b and d. N5 a and c, N.11.a and c. N.30.d, 35 d. T.6.c, T.12.a and c, T.11.d, T.17.d. T.18.c, T.23.b, T.24.c.	
1-50		G.I.	do.	Asked whether a Bde. Group of busses would be any use to us. Replied that it would be of great use in bringing up reserve Bde. when going forward.	
3-3				G.I. had conversation with G.O.C. (at 175th Bde. H.Q.) was told to ask for Sqdrn. N/Hussars to go up at once to 175th Bde. H.Q. as Inf. Being too tired could not keep up with the enemy.	
3-40		Corps	G.I.	Explained situation. Asked Corps to send up Sqdrn N/Hussars as quickly as possible.	
4-45			12th Div.	Report that they have reached line B.9.d. - B.15.b. and are pushing on towards LE FOREST. Officer's patrol reports the enemy on high ground East of LE FOREST.	Repeated to III Corps, C.R.A.
5-10		Corps	Major KITCHIN	3rd Corps when asked about Sqdrn. N/Hussars said they are all up in HAPPY VALLEY burying horses. They have sent up to them and told them to report to 175th Bde.	
5-20		G.II Corps.	G.I.	Informed that we should urgently require busses tomorrow. Corps said that they had already promised them to 18th Div. but they would try to let us have busses for 1,000. men tomorrow.	
6-30		Capt. SPENCER	G.I. 12th Div.	Stated that at 5-40 pm. troops of 12th Div. were about to attack trench line immediately West of LE FOREST from line N. to S. through OLD WINDMILL.	

Sheet No. 19

THURSDAY 29th AUGUST 1918.

Time	'Phone Message To.	From.	Subject.	Action.
pm. 6-50	Major KITCHIN	175th Bde.	H.Q. established A.23.b.2.0. Rear H.Q. closing. Enemy showing more activity. Certain amount of shelling forward. Enemy on high ground in B.18 and 24. Reported that enemy has fair number of guns in neighbourhood MARRIERES WOOD.	
8-10	Capt. SPENCER	12th Div.	State line of resistance from Right agrees along East side of MAUREPAS and trench line runningS.E. from South end of MAUREPAS. 175th Bde. to join up with 12th Div. at trench junction B.14.b.6.0 and Liaison Post for foremost troops to be established at B.16.b.8.1.	
8-15		175th Inf. Bde.	Informed of above and replied that they will try but they do not think our troops are as far forward as that.	
10 9-20	G.I.	12th Div.	12th Div. say previous report is incorrect. Their line runs from B.16.b.7.0 by trench W. of LE FOREST through B.10.a.8.0.	
9-20	Major KITCHIN	12th Div.	Report their line runs approx. B.5, 11, 17. (all central)	
11-5	B.G.G.S. Corps	G.I.	Agrees to proposal for using XXII Corps Sqdrn. as in our Operatn on Order.	
9-20	G.II. Corps.	G.I.	Told G.II. Corps that we were going to send out order to alter zero hour from 5-30 to 5 am. and cut down dwell on Start Line from 15 to 10 minutes.	

---------------o0o---------------

FRIDAY 30th AUGUST 1918.

Sheet No. 20

Time	Wire No.	Phone Message To.	From.	Subject.	Action.
9-15		Major KITCHIN	175th Bde.	Right. patrol in touch with 3rd Australians. Cavalry appears to be in B.23.c.5.5. Our Cavalry being heavily shelled from direction of MARRIERES WOOD. 13 Enemy preparing to counter-attack from LEG OF MUTTON WOOD C.7.a.a. We have pushed forward strong patrols to keep in touch and support our cavalry. Our guns got on to MARRIERES WOOD.	
9-15		do.	12th Div.	Enemy preparing to counter-attack from LEG OF MUTTON WOOD C.13.a.	reptd. to 47th Div.
10-20		Major KITCHIN	Capt. SPENCER	Reported had been in touch with 1/4th Suffolks - H.Q. at B.14.d.9.6. Reptd. to 2 Fighting Patrols sent out towards MARRIERES WOOD. Main body Corps. GX304. probably on N and S. line through B.22.a. Report they are in touch with Right Bn. 47th Div. at B.15.a.8.3. where 47th Div. Right Bn. H.Q. are. 2 of our 18-pdrs. firing from B.16.c.8.0. Enemy M.Gs. believed to be on high ground B.18, B.24.	
11		G.I.	Corps	Move forward of Australians only temporary. They will move South again and we are to carry on our our old boundaries. We may use XXII Corps Cavalry. tomorrow as arranged. N/Hussars going into Corps Reserve to be kept well forward.	
11-15		G.II	47th Div.	Report 1 Bn. on HILL 150. 1 Coy. on Track in C.7.a. 1 Coy. in B.12.a. 1 Bn. from B.11.h.5.5 to T.30.c.5.0.	
11-40		B.G.1	B.G.G.S.Corps	Says Australians have orders not to go forward N. of line BOUCHAVESNES - MOISLAINS. Wants special precautions taken that our Heavy Arty does not fire on any ground occupied by the Australians.	
12-5		Corps Commdr.	G.I.	Explained fully the situation.	

FRIDAY 30th
~~TUESDAY 27th~~ AUGUST 1918.   Sheet No. 21

Time	Wire No.	Phone Message To.	From.	Subject.	Action.
am 12-50		G.I.	175th Bde.	Bde. is now moving forward with Suffolks on Left, 10th Bn. on Right, 9th Bn. in Support, to capture Ridge B.19 - 24 central, then to push on through and to the East of MARRIERES WOOD.	Information repeated to 47th Div.
1		175th Bde.	G.I.	47th Div. say they are on HILL 150 and will push on with 175th. Corps anxious to get BOUCHAVESNES to-day if possible. 175th are to push on to BOUCHAVESNES.	
4				New Liaison Offr. from Aust. Div. explained scheme of Australians was to move tomorrow with their left on ~~our~~ the boundary given this morning running ~~approx.~~ N.E. from C1.a.9.central. They were to move N.W. roughly on to a line running from C.20, 21, 22. central.	
4-30		174th Bde.	G.I.	Explained situation and told them that we would let them know more definitely later. Also about position of Headquarters.	
5		G.I.	Gen. COBHAM.	Our line is on the original line from B.18. central B.24. central just W. MARRIERES WOOD. In touch with 47th Div. on Left, Aust. Div. on Right, neither of whom are in advance of us. All being held up by M.G. and T.M. fire. Preparations are being made for another attack. Probably it will not take place before dark.	
7-45		Major KITCHIN	47th Div.	Objective tomorrow from C.14.a.3.0 - Trench System - C.7.d.9.0 Trench junction C.7.d.2.7 -- cross to B.13.b.2.3. Propose to have 5-30 Zero and barrage 100 yards in 4 minutes, starting on S.O.S. Line.	
10-15		Corps.	G.I.	Told G.II. Corps our plans for tomorrow and they are going to see that it is co-ordinated with 47th Div.	

FRIDAY 30th AUGUST 1918.

Sheet No. 22

Time	Wire No.	Phone Message To.	From.	Subject.	Action.
10-25		G.I.	C.R.A.	Confirmed rate of barrage 100 yards in 6 mins. and not 8 mins.	
11-25		47th Div.	G.I.	Told 47th Div. that we had not got their Operation Order 266; they say that there is nothing in it which will affect us, and that it fits in quite well with our order which they had got.	

---o0o---

Sheet No. 23.

SATURDAY 31st AUGUST 1918.

Time	Wire No.	'Phone Message To.	From.	Subject.	Action.
am. 12-25		174th Bde.	Major KITCHIN	Told them Australians will make an attack tomorrow in co-operation with them, advancing in N.E. direction to the line OLD QUARRY C.20.central QUARRY FM. C.31.c. and that a barrage S. of line from B.24.d.0.2 through C.13.central to Road junction C.20.a.9.8 would be fired by Australian Arty. but at the same rates, lifts etc. as per our barrage programme already issued.	
6-35		Major KITCHIN	B.M., D.A.	Asked if they were responsible for covering the whole front between the old boundaries. Question referred to Corps & 3rd Aust. Div. who say that as a temporary measure they will be responsible for artillery protection of all ground S. of the line B.26.d.0.2, C.19.central, C.20.a.8.8. and thence due East. 58th D.A. to be responsible for all artillery North of that line. B.M., D.A. informed and agreeable.	
8-30		G.II	174th Bde.	Wounded Offr. says our Left Battn. on objective but considerable opposition was encountered, chiefly from M.G. fire from the Right. He states our casualties heavy, especially amongst officers. No information as to Right Battn. Number of prisoners taken.	
10-40		G.I.	3rd Corps.	Says that 2 Bdes. 74th Div. will probably come up by bus by daylight. First one will relieve Support Bde. and subsequently going into the line.	
11-50		G.II.	174th Bde.	State Patrols only up to the RANCOURT - BOUCHAVESNES Rd. but unable to get further forward owing to heavy M.G. fire from C.9 and C.15.b. Told them that we were going to arrange for H.A. preparations on above squares and patrols were to get forward under this and to keep touch with Australians.	174th Flank Divs C.R.A. informed by wire.
11-55		47th Div.	G.I.	47th Div. have no objection to our H.A. going on to squares C.9., C.15.b. and C.16.a.	

Sheet No. 24

SATURDAY 31st AUGUST 1918.

Time	'Phone Message To.	From.	Subject.	Action.
pm. 12-40	174th Bde.	G.II	Informed 174th that the following is the situation. The chief thing is to keep touch with Australians Left. As far as is known there will be an attack this afternoon. Any ground gained between C.15, so much the better. Dont want to do an organized attack.	
1-5	B.G.G.S. Corps	G.I.	The Reserve Bde. 74th Div. is to be embussed up to MARICOURT as soon as it can be. Then if possible after that Leading Bde. 74th Div. is to be bussed up to CLERY. After that as soon as possible Support Bde. is to be bussed up to CLERY line also.	
1-10	174th Bde.	Major KITCHIN	174th Bde. informed of proposed attack this afternoon at 6 o/c. Also 175th Bde.	
1-30	G.I.	D.A.	Our troops in C.27.a. and moving forward from QUARRY C.21.c. Still held up on Left flank. Do not know exactly where, but they are pushing forward.	
5	G.I.	Gen. COBHAM.	Our line is on the original front B.18.central B.24.	
10-5	Corps.	G.I.	Aust. Corps on Right fixed Zero 5 am. Ours was fixed for 5-30 Trying to fix up the matter.	
10-12	Aust. Div.	G.I.	Told Australian Div. that our message GX.369 was suspended. Also told them that Div. on our left was starting at 5-30 and that our Corps would not lets us alter our Zero. to 5 am. as we wanted to. Also that we were trying to fix up the matter.	

---------o0o---------

Sheet No. 25

SUNDAY 1st SEPTEMBER 1918.

Time	Wire No.	'Phone Message To.	From.	Subject.	Action.
am 8-20		Major KITCHIN	3rd Corps	47th Div. attacks going well. PRIEZ FM. taken. Prisoners estimated over 100.	
8-40		do.	173rd.	Our men well beyond BOUCHAVESNES - going strong. Prisoners estimated 200 with proportion of Offrs.	
9-20		G.I.	F.O.O.	Reports through 173rd - Our troops pushing on beyond objective.	
10		Major KITCHIN	B.G.G.S. Corps.	74th Div. Will take over from 58th Div. and Australians N. of Corps Southern boundary as soon as can be arranged. Boundaries as given to Gen. GIRDWOOD.	
10-10		do	Div. Observers	Div. Observers rang up to ask if they were to hand over to 74th Div. Told to hand over to 224th Bde. as 74th Div. have no Observers.	
10-15		G.I.	47th Div.	Say they are being fired at by M.Gs. from C.15 and 16.	
10-15 "		G.I.	47th Div.	Report they are in old British front line on Right and are on objective on Left. M.G. fire reported from about between squares C.15. and C.16.	
10-45		G.I.	do.	On final objective on Right (confirmed). Bde. is very weak.	
10-55		Major KITCHIN	3 Corps.	Corps asked for situation. Reported that er were on final objective with patrols pushed out East. In touch with 47th Div. on final objective on Left.	
11-20		Corps.	G.I.	Corps were asked what was to become of L.G. M.G. Bn., Sqdrn. XXII Corps Cavalry and XXII Corps Cyclists, on relief of 58th Div. Corps directed that they were all to be handed over to 74th Div.	

Aug 15th 1918

To 58 G.

Ref. I.G. 1/391 dated 14th inst

Enclosed herewith report on the action of the Divl Observers during the operations from 8th - 12th inst

A.W. Ethridge Lieut

o/c Div. Observers

AUGUST 1918

7th — Div. Observers moved to BEHENCOURT. Attached 173 BRIGADE for ration etc. Moved with Brigade to H.Q's at J 28 A.8.9.

8th — 4.00 AM - Heavy mist - standing by Z+2 hrs. Sent 3 parties out for information

1 party N.E. of SAILLY LAURETTE
1 " E.S.E HAMEL

Informed that an Australian report centre was being established at RECORD WOOD in P12A.

The above parties to work forward.

Took third party to MALARD WOOD.

7.50 AM — Reported (from statements of wounded officer of the 2/10th London Regt.) we had captured SAILLY LAURETTE with 30 odd

prisoners & several M/Gs
also at 7am our troops were
on the N outskirts of
MALARD WOOD

10-45AM Single white light sent
up from well to the N
of MALARD WOOD

11-5am 4 TANKS - appeared to be
on fire S.E. of CERISY-GAILLY

11-5am was heavily fired upon
at K33 c 4.9 from an
ENEMY M/G from MALARD
WOOD.
   An officer & 12-15 men
6th L.N. advancing in an
E direction at K33 c & d
This M/G also fired on
movement on high ground
K32 b.
   Saw few individual
GERMANS on the road
& marshy ground in
K33 c. Stalked these
& found all were wounded
- removed rifles &
ammunition from them

3.

& informed first party of
stretcher bearers we met

11-10am Met an officer i/c of a
cavalry patrol on the
road in K32d. Gave
him all available
information

11-15am Mixed party of troops under
an officer of 2/3rd L.R. was
advancing E on high
ground in K32A. Party
were heavily fired upon
by ENEMY M/G from
MALARD WOOD. Warned him
about this gun & lead
him round to dead
ground in K33c. He was
then trying to locate
& silence this gun.

11-55am Met Col. ———
G.S.O.2. & gave him
all information we had
also some GERMAN
correspondence picked
up

11.45 am We were heavily shelling ETINEHEM.

12.35 pm We heavily shelled CHIPILLY.

1 pm AUSTRALIAN officer reported their advance gone very well. Could not give location of his troops except that they were among the ENEMY - heavy guns.

During the morning and afternoon informed stretcher bearers location of our wounded.

Withdrew all men at dusk.

9TH Established an O.P. in K 31 d 2.4 - near Brigade H.Q.s also Heavy Art O.P. who were on the phone.

Little individual movement at K 34 d.8.6.

5.

5.5pm — Luminous white lights appeared to be dropped from a plane over ENEMY'S lines at K34d 8.8. approx.

4.30pm to / AMERICAN troops marching
5.30pm / towards MALARD WOOD on the CHIPILLY – SAILLY LAURETTE ROAD.

5.30pm — Our Artillery opened fire – heavy barrage to the N. of MALARD WOOD – very weak barrage by CHIPILLY

Our troops seen advancing S. of MALARD WOOD

5.50pm — Informed an American Brigadier location of American troops

Little information gathered – sent to 173 Brigade HQ.

6.

8.50 pm. At the request of the G.O.C. 173 Brigade went on a reconnaissance patrol with 1 officer & 2 runners 173 Brigade.

Verify an ENEMY M/G reported active on the bluffs in K 34 central

Find out dispositions & strength of our troops

Advanced to a point on the road at K 34 d 5.5. Heard an ENEMY M/G firing to our right rear. Also another to our left. As we faced E. M/G on our left was firing on the E slope of BOIS les CELESTINS — reconnoitred the bluffs & vicinity. No enemy seen. Found out approx strength of our troops & dispositions

Informed C.O. 10th K.R. on our way back to Hire we had been etc. the same

7

also gave us information.
returned to Brigade H.Q.
I reported to G.O.C. 173 Brigade
who told us we had done
good work.

10TH   5am went round front line
with the Brigade Major &
Staff Captain - etc.
Established an O.P. at
K 35 c. 5.5.

Little enem. movet. seen at
CATEAUX WOOD

3.00pm 30 men seen E of BRAY.

Enem. movet. seen at road R8b
R1c. 3.7.

4.30pm Convoy of vehicles on
road L17A going S.W.

ENEMY shelled GRESSAIRE WOOD
from direction of CATEAUX
WOOD & further N.

11TH   OP withdrawn on relief of 173 Brigade by AUSTRALIANS

12TH   Reported back to adv. Div. H.Qs. & moved to QUERRIEU.

All reports from to 173 Brigade.

CASUALTIES

8TH   L/Cpl. Bishop to G
2/4" London Regt.
att/ Div. Observers wounded.

A.B. Ethridge Lieut
o/i Div. Observers

[Stamp: 58th (LONDON) DIVISION GENERAL STAFF — 22 FEB. 1919]

D.A.G.,
   3rd Echelon. G.H.Q.
=================

      Herewith "Narrative of Operations" of this Division for period August 8th to November 11th 1918. This will take the place of the Monthly War Diary for the above mentioned period.

                                                    P de Fonblanque Major GS
                                        Major-General,
                          Commanding 58th (London) Division.

22nd February, 1919.

[Stamp: ADJUTANT GENERAL'S BRANCH, G.H.Q. 3rd ECHELON, CENTRAL REGISTRY — 27 FEB 1919]

ADDENDUM NO. 1 To 58th (LONDON) DIVISIONAL
INSTRUCTIONS No. 5. - "ARTILLERY"

Copy No. 26

1. The Arty. support for the attack will consist of :-

    A Creeping Barrage.
    Protective Barrages.
    A Howitzer Barrage.
    Special Smoke Screens.
    Counter-Battery work and gas bombardments.
    Engagement of distant objectives by long range guns.
    Special bombardments for 60-pdrs. and howitzers.

2. SMOKE IN THE BARRAGE.-

Smoke will be used in the artillery barrage if the weather is wet. Troops must be warned that this smoke is not a signal but is only used to replace dust.

3. HOWITZER BARRAGE.-

In order to ensure that the valleys running North from the valley of the River SOMME are engaged by artillery fire, Field and Medium Howitzers will bombard these valleys. These Howitzers will jump from valley to valley in advance of the 18-pdr. barrage as per Table "A" issued with Divisional Instructions No. 5, and Addendum to Table "A" attached which shows action of 6" Hows.

4. COUNTER-BATTERY WORK AND GAS BOMBARDMENTS :-

Heavy Counter-Battery work will be carried out against groups of hostile guns. For this purpose two-thirds of the heavy artillery available will be employed during the operation.

(a) A neutralising programme will be arranged to subdue the hostile artillery fire during the attack and consolidation of the final objective.

For this purpose the following number of guns will be employed :-

Hostile Group of Guns.	No. of Medium and Heavy Hows. to be employed.
MALARD WOOD.	22
BOIS DE TAILLES.	40
BRICKYARD.	6
BECORDEL VALLEY.	28

In addition to these numbers, 2 super-heavy, 8 heavy, 6 Medium Hows., and 24 60-pdrs., will be available to reinforce this programme and engage more distant H.V. targets.

Gas or Gas and H.E. will be employed on all hostile batteries with the exception of those West of the Final Objective and South of the Grid Line running East and West through K.16.central.

For batteries in the BOIS DE GRESSAIRE a small proportion of the gas shell, C.G.. and J.B.R. only will be employed at the commencement of the programme to induce the enemy to put on their gas masks.

(b)

- 2 -

(b) The maximum amount of counter-battery work possible will be continued until zero plus 48 hours.

(c) Before Zero hour.-

If the enemy commences a heavy bombardment on the front of the attack a short time before Zero, all the guns and Hows. detailed for counter-battery work after Zero will carry out a neutralizing programme.

Before this time only the normal number of guns will be employed.

5. SPECIAL BOMBARDMENTS.-

Bombardments will be carried out by 60-pdrs. and 6" and 8" Hows. as per Table "B" attached.

6 60-pdrs. and 4 6" Hows. will be detailed to search and sweep the valleys and approaches between 500 and 1000 yards beyond the 18-pdr. barrage.

This fire will be carried out by bursts of 5 mins. duration every 20 mins. at a rapid rate.

6. S.O.S. CALLS.-

(a) Before Zero.-

These will only be answered by the normal number of guns, i.e. 2 Bdes. R.F.A. on each Divisional Front, and by the normal number of Heavy Arty. guns.

(b) After Zero during the Barrage Programme.-

In the case of an S.O.S. Call being received from the air or from the ground during the barrage programme, all the Arty. Bdes. in the Divisional Area affected will at once switch one battery per brigade on to the threatened area for 5 mins. at the rate of 4 rounds per 18-pdr. per minute. Then for 5 mins. at the rate of 3 rounds per 18-pdr. per minute. After 10 mins. the fire will be slowed down and return to the barrage programme as the situation permits.

If the call is near a Divisional boundary the flank brigade will co-operate as above.

7. AMENDMENT TO 58th (LONDON) DIVISIONAL INSTRUCTIONS No. 5.- "ARTILLERY" -

Para: 6., Sub-para: (c).-

For "Remaining 5 minutes of this barrage" read -

"Remaining 12 minutes of this barrage."

8. ACKNOWLEDGE.

AWDavis
Lieut-Colonel,
General Staff 58th (London) Division.

6th August 1918.

DISTRIBUTION.

See Slip attached.

S E C R E T.

Copy No. _____

FORTHCOMING OPERATIONS.

58th (LONDON) DIVISIONAL INSTRUCTION No.8.

FIREWORK SIGNALS.

1. The following firework signals will be employed :-

  (i) **No.32 Grenade.**

      GREEN over GREEN over GREEN ... S.O.S.

  (ii) **No.32 Grenade.**

      WHITE over WHITE over WHITE ... SUCCESS Signal, i.e. OBJECTIVE GAINED.

30 of these grenades will be issued to each 173rd and 174th Infantry Brigades.

2. With regard to para.1 (ii) above, the following points will be clearly impressed on all ranks :-

The only objectives for which the signal is to be fired are those laid down in G.X.21 dated 2/8/18, namely :-

    (i) SAILLY LAURETTE.
   (ii) The GREEN Line K.33.c. - K.27.d. - K.27.b.
  (iii) The RED Line K.35.c. - K.29.c. - K.29.b.

3. ACKNOWLEDGE.

[signature]

Lieut. Colonel,
General Staff, 58th (London) Division.

5th August, 1918.

    NOTE. The Left Flank Division will fire single White Very lights to denote that the barrage is about to lift.

DISTRIBUTION.

Copy No.			
1.	C.R.A.	10.	O.C. Div. Sig. Coy.
2.	173rd Inf. Brigade.	11 & 12.	III Corps.
3.	174th Inf. Brigade.	13.	III Corps H.A.
4.	175th Inf. Brigade.	14.	18th Division.
5.	C.R.E.	15.	3rd Australian Div.
6.	58th Bn. M.G. Corps.	16.	4th Australian Div.
7.	A.A. & Q.M.G.	17.	10th Tank Bn.
8.	1/4th Suffolk Rgt.	18.	"C" Coy. 10th Tank Bn.
9.	A.D.M.S.	19.	35th Squad. R.A.F.

S.E.C.R.E.T.   Copy No. _____

FORTHCOMING OPERATIONS.

58th (LONDON) DIVISIONAL INSTRUCTIONS No.7.

ACTION OF AUSTRALIAN CORPS.

1. The attached map (forwarded to C.R.A., 173rd and 174th Inf. Brigades) shows the objectives and barrage lines of the Australian Corps.

   The tracing attached (forwarded to 175th Inf. Bde. C.R.E., and M.G. Battn.) shows the objectives only of the Australian Corps.

2. The 3rd Australian Division on the Left of the Australian Corps assisted by Tanks will take the GREEN Line under a Creeping Artillery and M.G. Barrage, and will reach the GREEN Line at about Zero plus 2 hours.
   The 11th A.I. Bde. will be on the Left of the 3rd Australian Division.

3. The 4th Australian Division assisted by Tanks will pass through the 3rd Australian Division, starting from the GREEN Line at Zero plus 4 hours, and expects to reach the final objective at Zero plus 6½ hours.
   The 4th A.I. Bde. will be on the Left of the 4th Australian Division.

4. The 3rd and 4th Australian Divisions are both to send strong patrols along the North Bank of the Canal in order to assist in keeping touch with the 58th Division.

5. On advancing at Zero plus 4 hours, the 4th Australian Division is to detach one Battn. for the attack and mopping up of CERISY.

6. Every endeavour will be made to establish communication by visual signalling with the Australian Division on the Right. Signal Stations in the neighbourhood of MALARD Wood and the CHIPILLY Spur will be given special instructions to look out for Australian Signal Stations.

7. At Zero.-   The Battle H.Q. of 11th A.I. Bde. will be at
   P.4.a.5.5.
               The Battle H.Q. of 4th A.I. Bde. will be at
   P.7.a.05.15.

   After Zero.- The Battle H.Q. of 11th A.I. Bde. will be in vicinity P.17.central.
               The Battle H.Q. of 4th A.I. Bde. will move to
   P.17.central during the attack on the GREEN Line, and after will move to location to be selected later.

                                           CM Davis
                                           Lieut-Colonel,
                                General Staff 58th (London) Division.

5th August 1918.

Distribution.

As per Divisional Instructions No. 5.

SECRET.   Copy No.......

FORTHCOMING OPERATIONS.

58th (LONDON) DIVISIONAL INSTRUCTIONS No.8.

AIRCRAFT.

1. In addition to the 35th (III Corps) Squadron R.A.F., a proportion of other units R.A.F. will be operating on the Corps front as follows :-

    (a) Scout Squadrons will be exclusively employed in bombing and machine-gunning ground targets.

    (b) Bombing Squadrons will operate by night and by day.

    (c) Reconnaissance machines will constantly patrol the whole front of the attack.

2. The following are the only Signals to be used by infantry to communicate with aeroplanes :-

    (a) RED Flares of which 500 have been issued to 173rd and 174th Infantry Brigades.

    (b) TIN DISCS which will be issued to 173rd & 174 Bdes.

    These discs must be turned about to catch the reflection of the sun. They are ineffective in dull weather.

    (c) Groups of 3 rifles placed on the ground with not less than 10 yards interval between groups.

    All the above Signals denote -

    "I AM HERE."

3. The following method of giving warning of a counter-attack will be employed by aeroplanes :-

    The aeroplane will fly in the direction of the enemy, dropping a WHITE parachute flare as near the counter-attacking troops as possible.

4. A contact aeroplane will fly along the front calling for signals (a) (b) and (c) above -

    from Zero plus 90 minutes to Zero plus 100 mins.

    from Zero plus 240 minutes to Zero plus 250 mins.

    All ranks must be impressed with the importance of displaying these Signals.

5. A maximum of 10,000 S.A.A. for the Divisional Machine Guns will be dropped by parachute from aeroplanes not before Zero plus 4 hours.

    The Signal calling for the S.A.A. will be a white cloth V displayed at point where the ammunition is required.

    Two of these Signals will be carried by each Section of Machine Guns.

    No ammunition for Infantry will be dropped.

6. ACKNOWLEDGE.

Signature
Lieut.-Colonel,
General Staff, 58th (London) Division.

3/8/18.

DISTRIBUTION - see attached.

58th (LONDON) DIVISIONAL INSTRUCTION No. 8

DISTRIBUTION.

Copy No. 1.	Br.-Genl. J.McC. MAXWELL, C.B., D.S.O.	Comdg.	C.R.A.
2.	" G.E.CORKRAN, C.M.G.	"	173rd Bde.
3.	" A. MAXWELL, D.S.O.	"	174th Bde.
4.	" W. MAXWELL-SCOTT, D.S.O.	"	175th Bde.
5.	Colonel E.A.WRAITH, D.S.O.		A.D.M.S.
6.	Lt.-Col. A.J.SAVAGE, D.S.O.		C.R.E.
7.	" C.J.WILEY, D.S.O.		M.G.Bn.
8.	" A.G.P. McNalty, C.M.G.		A.A.& Q.M.G.
9.	" H.C.COPEMAN, C.M.G. D.S.O.		1/4th Suffolks.
10.	Major G.M.HENDERSON, M.C.		O.C., Div. Signals.
11 & 12.	III Corps.		
13.	Br.-Genl. A.E.J.PERKINS, C.M.G.	Comdg.	III Corps H.A.
14.	Maj-Genl. R.P. LEE, C.B.	G.O.C.,	18th Division.
15.	"	G.O.C.,	3rd Aust.Div.
16.	"	G.O.C.,	4th "
17.	Lt.-Col. J. MICKLEM, D.S.O., M.C.	Comdg.	10th Tank Bn.
18.	"	"	"C" Coy. 10th Tank Bn.
19.	Major K.F. BAMAINE.	"	35th Sdrn. R.A.F.
20.			
21.			

SECRET.

Copy No. 21

58th (London) Divisional Instructions No. 9.

FORTHCOMING OPERATIONS — EXAMINATION OF PRISONERS OF WAR.

1. Prisoners of War will be sent back from the line in accordance with para. 3, Administrative Instructions No. 9. It is essential that there should be no delay if their examination is to be of value.

2. The identifications of the first batch of Prisoners of War and if possible, the place of capture, will be forwarded by URGENT OPERATIONS PRIORITY to Divisional Hd. qrs. whether the identifications are normal or not.
   Further identification need not be forwarded by the above means unless they ARE OF A DIFFERENT UNIT.

3. The Divisional Intelligence Officer will be at the Cage where prisoners will be examined.
   Except to obtain the information mentioned in para. 2 above no examination will be made by Battalion or Brigade Intelligence Officers.

4. The following points must be clearly impressed on all ranks:—

   (a). Unwounded prisoners are to be spoken to by and searched in the presence of the following officers only:—

   Officers of the Intelligence Corps.
   Brigade and Battalion Intelligence Officers.
   Staff Officers.

   (b). If reliable information is to be obtained without delay it is essential that prisoners should not be put at their ease by being conversed with.

Lt. Colonel,
General Staff 58th (London) Division

8th August, 1918.

Distribution :—(see overleaf)

56th (LONDON) DIVISIONAL INSTRUCTIONS No. ___

DISTRIBUTION

Copy No. 1.	Brig-Genl. J.McC. HAMWELL, C.B., D.S.O.		C.R.A.
2.	" G.T. COPEMAN, C.M.G.	Cmdg.	173rd Bde.
3.	" A. MAXWELL, D.S.O.	"	174th "
4.	" V. MAXWELL-SCOTT, D.S.O.	"	175th "
5.	Colonel E.A. WRAITH, D.S.O.		A.D.M.S.
6.	Lt-Colonel A.J. SAVAGE, D.S.O.		C.R.E.
7.	" G.E. WILEY, D.S.O.	"	M.G.Battn.
8.	" A.G.P. McNALTY, C.M.G.		A.A.& Q.M.G.
9.	" H.C. COPEMAN, C.M.G., D.S.O. Cmdg. 1/4th Suffolks.
10	Major C.L. PATTERSON, M.C.		O.C. Div. Signals.
11-12		III Corps.
13	Brig-Genl. A.E.J. PERKINS, C.M.G.	Cmdg. III Corps H.A.
14	Major-Genl. R.P. LEE, C.B.	G.O.C. 19th Division.
15	"	G.O.C. 3rd Aust. Div.
16	"	G.O.C. 4th "
17	Lt-Colonel J. BIGELOW, D.S.O., M.C.	Cmdg. 10th Tank Bn.
18		" "C" Coy. 10th Tank Bn.
19	Major M.F. BALMAINE.	Cmdg. 55th Sqdrn. R.A.F.
20		
21		

S E C R E T.   Copy No. 2

FORTHCOMING OPERATIONS.

58th (LONDON) DIVISIONAL INSTRUCTIONS No. 10.

- GENERAL INSTRUCTIONS CONTINUED -

1. / With reference to 58th Divisional Instructions No. 10 dated 6th August.

   Aircraft will make noise to drown the sound of the Tanks at the following hours :-

   (a) Noise from Zero - 3½ hours to Zero - 30 minutes.

   (b) Continuous noise from Zero - 30 minutes to Zero.

2. 2 No Tanks will move during Y/Z night except between Zero - 3½ hours and Zero.

3. 3 ACKNOWLEDGE.

                                                    Lieut.-Colonel,
                              General Staff, 58th (London) Division.

7th August, 1918.

   Distribution as per Divisional Instruction No. 10.

TABLE "A".

4.5" HOWITZER BARRAGE.

ISSUED WITH 50th DIVISIONAL INSTRUCTION No. 5.

Formation.	Hows.	Times.	Tasks.	Rates of Fire.
50th Division.	2 Batteries (4.5" Hows.)	Zero to Zero plus 4 mins.	Bombard SAILLY-LAURETTE and valley in area K.31.c.2.7 – K.31.a.0.3 – K.31.b.5.7 – K.31.c.6.5.	INTENSE.
	do.	Zero plus 4 mins. to Zero plus 10 mins.	SAILLY-LAURETTE S. and E. of line J.36.d.5.0 – J.36.d.5.2 – K.31.c.6.5.	RAPID.
	do.	Zero plus 10 mins. to Zero plus 20 mins.	Bombard valley in area K.32.b.6.8 – K.32.b.3.8 – K.27.c.4.0 – K.27.d.0.7 – K.33.a.5.7 – K.33.a.0.0.	First 5 mins. NORMAL. Last 5 mins. RAPID.
	do.	Zero plus 20 mins. to Zero plus 128 mins.	Bombard valley in area K.34.c.2.0 – K.34.a.5.5 – K.28.d.0.1 – K.34.c.7.0.	First 40 mins. SLOW. Next 10 mins. RAPID. Last 58 mins. SLOW.
	do.	Zero plus 128 mins. to Zero plus 135 mins.	Bombard valley in area K.34.c.2.0 – K.54.c.3.4 – K.34.c.9.5 – K.34.c.7.0.	First 2 mins. SLOW. Last 5 mins. RAPID.

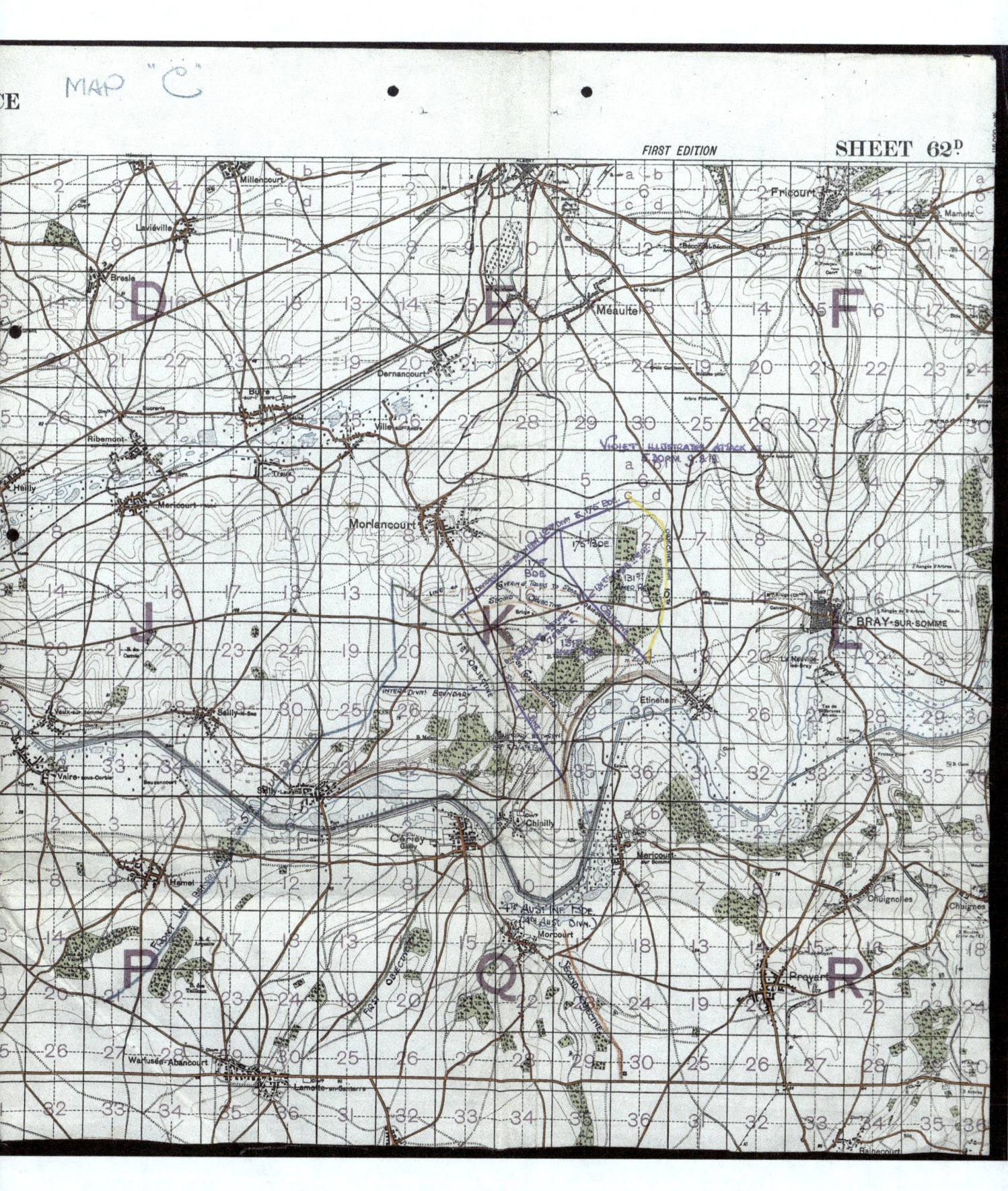

Bassin de radoub	Dry dock.
Bateau phare	Light-ship.
Blanchisserie	Laundry.
B.M. (borne militaire)	Mile stone.
B⁹ (borne kilométrique)	
Boulonnerie	
Fab⁹ de boulons }	Bolt Factory.
Bouée	Buoy.
Brasserie, Brass⁹	Brewery.
Briqueterie, Briq¹⁹	Brickfield.
Brise-lames	Breakwater.
Bureau de poste	Post office.
Butte	Custom house. Butt, Mound.
Cabane	Hut.
Cabaret, Cab¹	Inn.
Câble sous-marin	Submarine cable.
Calvaire, Cal⁹	Calvary.
Canal de dessèchement	Drainage canal.
Canal d'irrigation	Irrigation canal
Fab⁹ de caoutchouc	Rubber factory.
Carrière, Carr⁹	Quarry.
" de gravier	Gravel-pit
Caserne	Barracks.
Champ de courses	Race-course
" " manœuvres	Drill-ground.
" " tir	Rifle range.
Chantier	Building yard. Ship yard. Dock yard.
Chantier de construction	
Chapelle, Ch¹⁹	Chapel.
Charbonnage	Colliery.
Château d'eau	Water tower.
Chaussée	{ Slip-way. Causeway. Highway.
Chemin de fer	Railway.
Cheminée, Ch⁹⁹	Chimney.
Chêne	Oak tree.
Cimetière, Cim⁹⁹	Cemetery.
Clocher	Belfry.
Clouterie	Nail factory.
Colombier	Dove-cot.

Coron	{ Workmen's dwellings.
Cour des marchandises	Goods yard.
Couvent	Convent.
Croisier	Slag heap.
Croix	Cross.
Dans	Inner dock.
Démoli·e, Dét·⁸	Destroyed.
Détruit·e, Dét··⁸	
Déversoir	Weir.
Digue	Dyke, causeway.
Distillerie, Dist¹⁹	Distillery.
Douane	Custom-house.
Bureau de douane	
Entrepôt de douane	Custom warehouse.
Dynamitière, Dynam⁹	Dynamite magazine.
Dynamiterie	Dynamite factory.
Ecluse	Sluice, Lock.
Ecluseste, Ecl¹⁹	Sluice.
Ecole	School.
Ecurie	Stable.
Eglise	Church.
Emaillerie	Enamel works.
Embarcadère, Emb⁹	Landing-place.
Estaminet, Estam¹	Inn.
Etang	Pond.
Fabrique, Fab⁹	Factory.
Fab⁹ de produits chimiques	Chemical works.
Fab⁹ de faïence	Pottery.
Faïencerie	
Ferme, F⁹⁹	Farm.
Filature, Fil⁹⁹	Spinning mill
Fonderie, Fond¹⁹	Foundry.
Fontaine, Font⁹	Spring, fountain.
Forêt	Forest
Forme de radoub	Dry dock.
Forge	Smithy.
Fosse	Mine, Pit.
Fossé	Moat, Ditch.
Four	Kiln.
" à chaux	Lime-kiln.

Four à coke	Cake oven.
Ganterie	Glove Factory.
Gare	Station.
Garenne	Warren.
Garnison	Garrison.
Gazomètre	Gasometer.
Glacerie	
Fab⁹ de glaces }	Mirror Factory.
Glacière	Ice factory.
Grue	Crane.
Gué	Ford.
Guérite	Sentry-box, Turret.
" à signaux	Signal-box (Ry.)
Halte	Halt.
Hangar	Shed, Hangar.
Hôpital	Hospital
Hôtel-de-Ville	Town hall
Houillère	Colliery.
Huilerie	Oil factory.
Imprimerie, Impr⁹⁹	Printing works.
Jetée	Pier.
Laminerie	Rolling mills.
Ligne de haute marée	High water mark.
Laisse de basse marée	Low " "
Maison Forestière Mⁿ Fⁿ⁹	Forester's house.
Malterie	Malt-house.
Marbrerie	Marble works.
Marais	Marsh
Marais salant	Saltern, Salt marsh.
Marché	Market.
Mare	Pool.
Meule	Rick.
Minière	Mine.
Monastère	Monastery.
Moulin, Mⁿ	Mill
" à vapeur	Steam mill
Mur	Wall.
" crénelé	Loop-holed wall.

P/a in 58th Div: G.S. box.
Agst 1918.

Report on Operations

on

8th 9th & 10th August 1918,

of

10th Tank Battalion.

"B" Coy: 10th Tank Bn,
"C" Coy: -"- -"- -"-.

10th Tank Bn:

Report on Operations.
8th 9th & 10th August 1918.

REPORT ON OPERATIONS OF 10TH TANK BATTALION.
8th, 9th, & 10th August 1918.

August 8th, 1918.

1. Battalion was allotted to III Corps.

   The general plan of III Corps was to form a defensive flank to IV Army to protect the flank of the advance south of the SOMME.
   III Corps allotted one Company to 58th. Divn. and 2 Coys. to 18th Divn.
   58th Divn. detailed all tanks for 1st objective and all tanks still in action for 2nd objective.
   18th Divn detailed all tanks less one section for first objective and all tanks still in action plus one fresh section for second objective.
   Tanks were ordered to move close to barrage and to patrol in front of objectives with the exception that on the left they were not to go over the ridge where they would come under direct artillery fire from MEAULTE Ridge.

2. I and Bn. Reconnaissance Officer arrived at III Corps H.Q. three days before the Bn. moved. I was present at all Corps and Division conferences and was in close touch with Divisional and Brigade Commanders up to and during operations.

3. I and Bn. Reconnaissance Officer reconnoitred the ground previous to the arrival of Bn. Coy. Reconnaissance Officers and Coy. Commanders were taken over ground as soon as they arrived in area. In addition each Section Commander and one Tank Commander per Section were able to visit the ground. Remainder of Tank Commanders could not go up owing to shortness of time and necessity of limiting number of Officers visiting forward area.

4. (a) Battalion detrained at POULAINVILLE on morning 3rd August, trains arrived very late but owing to bad visibility tanks were able to move to QUERRIEU WOOD in daylight. Last train arrived 8-30 am. Tanks were all in wood by 12 noon. Approximate distance 4 miles.

   (b) Two tanks remained at QUERRIEU with engine trouble. Remainder (40) moved to HEILLY on night 4/5th. Tanks left QUERRIEU 9-15 p.m. and last tank was in HEILLY at 5-0 a.m. Distance approximately 9 miles of which 3500 yds was on roads through villages.

   (c) 36 Tanks left HEILLY at 10-0 p.m. and moved slowly to assembly points by 3-45 a.m. Distance approximately 5 miles.
   36 Tanks started from position of deployment.
   30 Tanks went on from starting points, 6 failed to start owing to mechanical trouble.

   (d) Reasons of failure.   1. Big end seized.
                             2. Carburettor & exhaust.
                             3. Ditched.
                             4. Autovac.
                             5. Mechanical trouble.
                             6. Brake trouble.

-2-

5. COMMUNICATIONS.

Pigeons were carried on the scale of two pigeons per Section. Pigeons brought in some messages but on the whole did not fly well, probably due to fumes in tank.

Runners were employed between section and Company Commanders and from Company Commanders to Bn. Report Centre. Runners worked well and proved to be by far the most reliable means of communication. Wireless was carried up in a fighting tank and dumped with personnel as tank passed proposed rallying point. Owing to failure to take 2nd.objective this point was eventually in our front line and tanks had to rally further back.

The wireless sent one useful message for tanks and a few for infantry.

Company Commanders had their H.Q. with Brigadiers with whom they were operating from start of operation till first objective was captured. They then moved to rallying points and remained in that neighbourhood as second objective was never taken.

Bn. H.Q. was with Adv.H.Q. 18th. Divn. with a direct speaking line to 38th. Divn. Adv.H.Q. and III Corps.

6. RALLYING POINTS.

After capture of GREEN LINE in valley immediately WEST of GREEN LINE.

After capture of RED LINE, 2 Companies about Northern end of MALLARD WOOD, 1 Company near copses in M.26.c.

7. SUPPLIES.

150% fills of petrol, oil and grease for 40 tanks was dumped at HEILLY also 50% fills of ammunition.

This proved sufficient to fill after first day's fighting and balance was then moved forward to J.24.a. and one further fill was drawn from railhead and dumped at HEILLY.

Tank Supply tanks provided were Mk.IV with sledges which proved most unsatisfactory as they were very difficult to drive and the sledges broke away. One did good work by taking fills to "A" Company about MALLARD WOOD on Z/Z+1 night. Mk.IV tanks with soft sponsons did very good work carrying for the infantry.

8. Going was generally good and over sound country. The area was cut up by numerous steep banks and sunken roads particularly on the right.

Ground was not affected at all by bombardment.

Up till Y day weather was extremely wet. From Y day on weather was very good, no rain at all.

At Z - 15 minutes a very thick ground mist came down and lasted till 8-0 a.m. This seriously affected the operation, as both Tanks and Infantry lost direction at the start.

9. 30 Tanks came into action.
    15 " reached their objective.
    23 Tanks fired 500 rds 6-pdr, 14,880 S.A.A.

The assistance rendered to the Infantry was considerable as a very strong M.G. defence was put up by the enemy. Large numbers of machine gun nests were disposed of and many of the enemy surrendered on the approach of the Tanks.

10. 17 Tanks rallied and were ordered to fill and repair to be be fit for action next day.

11. 1. Casualties to personnel in Tank. 36
    "   "   outside Tank. 12

    2. Casualties to Tanks. Direct hits. 4. (3 moving, 1 stationary)
                             Ditched. 5.
                             Mechanical   (Autovac & Epicyclic)
                              trouble. 5
                             Left on Field. 5.

9th August 1918.

1. On the 9th August under orders of III Corps the attack was continued with the object of reaching the RED LINE on the right and of capturing the ridge E. of MORLANCOURT on the left.
   All available tanks were ordered to co-operate.
   12 Tanks were allotted to 58th Divn. on the right.
   8 Tanks   "   "   " 12th Divn on the left.
   All Tanks were ordered to advance to objectives as close to barrage as possible.

2. Company Commanders were in touch with Brigade and Bn. Commanders and details of the action were arranged by Divisional and Brigade Commanders through me.
   This attack was ordered at very short notice and Zero was changed three times. The last change of Zero did not reach the left Coy. as they had to start at Z - 60 to reach the barrage at Zero.

3. Section and Company Commanders were able to see the ground in the morning.

4. The approach march to starting points was simply a move across the front. The left Coy. had to go roughly 2000 yds.
   20 Tanks moved off and 20 started into action.

5. Runner only.
   Battalion H.Q. on speaking line to 12th and 58th Divn. and III Corps.
   Company Commanders with Bn. Commanders of attacking infantry.

6. J.24.a.

7. No change.
   No Supply Tanks used for tank supplies. Supply Tanks did good work carrying for infantry.

8. As on 8th August.

9. 20 Tanks came into action.
   10 reached objective.
   12 fired 1251 rds. 6-pdr and 45,780 S.A.A.

10. 14 Tanks rallied and were ordered to fill and repair to be fit for action next day.

11. 1. Casualties to personnel.
          In Tank   37
          Outside Tank. 18

-4-

11. (2) Casualties to Tanks.
    (a) Direct hit. (3 moving, 2 stationary).
    (b) Ditched. 2.
    (c) Mechanical trouble. 4 (Autovac & oiling).
    (d) Left on field. 5

10th. August 1918.

1. By orders of G.O.C. 111 Corps 4 Tanks were sent to operate with 12th. Divn the objective being the AMIENS defence line East of MORLANCOURT.
   The plan was that the Tanks were to lead the Infantry and to pay particular attention to two known pockets of the enemy between the starting point and the final objective.
   Under orders of 5th. Tank Bde. 4 Tanks were sent to operate with 13th. Australian Bde. with the object of clearing the spur between ETINEHEM and the CORBIE-BRAY road.
   This was a night operation the plan being for Tanks to advance along the road as far as BRAY firing to their front and left with the object of clearing the way for the Infantry.

2. In both these operations Section Commanders made arrangements on the ground with the Infantry Bn. Commanders concerned after the general plan had been arranged by Division and Bn. Headquarters.

3. The operation in the afternoon was over known ground and the night operation was a purely road operation.

4. Approach marches in each case were about 600 yds and were done in roughly 100 minutes. 4 Tanks started in each case and 4 Tanks went into action.

5. Runner only.

6. After both operations Tanks rallied at Coy tankodromes at about J.34.

7. Dumps were at Company tankodromes.
   No Supply Tanks were required.

8. Good going and good weather.

9. 8 Tanks went into action.
   6 Tanks reached objective.
   6 Tanks fired 185 rds 6-pdr and 3350 rds S.A.A.

   The assistance rendered to the Infantry was great as both operations were successful and the Infantry suffered very slight casualties.

10. 6 Tanks rallied, filled and got ready for action again.

11. (1) Casualties to personnel.
        In Tank. 11
        Outside Tank. 1
    (2) Casualties to tanks. 2 Direct hits. (Moving).
        2 Tanks remained on field.

LESSONS.

(a) TACTICAL.

1. Support Tank in each Section should be at least 1000 yds. in rear of leading Tanks, otherwise it becomes involved at the start and is not available for clearing pockets left by leading Tanks and Infantry.
2. Infantry N.C.O's in Tanks proved valueless as without training they were very quickly overcome by heat and fumes.
3. Owing to speed of Mk.V.Tank long range shooting with 6-pdr is practically impossible. Common shell proved useful solely for village fighting and dealing with M.G's behind walls. For fighting in the open case shot proved very effective at the ranges at which it was found possible to shoot. I consider Tanks should carry 50% shell and 50% case shot.

(b) TECHNICAL.

1. A fan for drawing fumes from inside of tank should be fitted if possible.
2. Hotchkiss short strips should be substituted for metal belts as these seem to have been a great source of trouble.
3. Unditching beam should be given up. It is quicker to dig.

(c) TRAINING.

1. Crews should do more driving with tank shut down to accustom them to fumes and heat.
2. Hotchkiss difficulties were largely due to inexperience. Results will probably be better with more training.
3. Tank crews as a whole showed remarkable powers of endurance and recovered very quickly after being apparently quite prostrated by heat and fumes. Too much attention cannot be paid to physical fitness as with present personnel crews may frequently be called on to fight on three or more consecutive days.

J. Mickle
Lieut. Col.
Commanding 10th. Tank Battalion.

17-8-18.

"B" Coy: 10th Tank Bn:

Report on operations on
8th 9th 10th August 1918.

"1" Coy. 10TH TANK BATTALION.

REPORT ON OPERATIONS on the 8th, 9th & 10th August 1918.

Tanks left the Coy. Tank park at HEILLY at 9-45 p.m. on 7-8-18 following "A" Coy. tracks. The ground was very favourable and all 8 Tanks arrived at the starting point with only one casualty, one man being wounded in the arm by indirect machine gun fire.

All 8 Tanks left the starting point in J.18.d. at 3-35 a.m. on 8-8-18. About half an hour before this a heavy mist had fallen that made all observation impossible over about 10 yards distance.

The Tanks all proceed as far as possible in the directions laid down for them by the Coy. Reconnaissance Officer. The Tank on the extreme left commanded by Lieut. McGuire lost direction in the mist owing to a defective compass and joined the 35th. Bde. farther to the north. Lieut. McGuire realising the impossibility of rejoining in time for action reported to the O.O.C. 35th. Bde. who sent him into action at 12-35 pm. Lieut. McGuire then cleared up a machine gun nest in the south-east of MORLANCOURT taking about 300 prisoners.

Apart from the above and with the exception of J.26 and J.27 all Tanks arrived at their first objective without much trouble. J.26 had a damaged silencer that allowed a certain amount of petrol fumes to collect inside putting all the drivers out of action. The crew were all slightly gassed at the same time and the Tank was withdrawn under orders of the Section Commander, Captain Mackenzie. J.27 developed engine trouble and only got a short distance before receiving a direct hit. The remainder of the Tanks engaged any hostile machine guns that could be located and helped on any Infantry that could locate the places that were holding them up.

The reserve Section were due to leave their starting at 6-30 am. and arrived up to time under Captain Bailey. The situation was still very uncertain owing to the dense mist and the O.C. Coy. decided to move forward with his Section towards the Rally Point. On arrival there fighting was still in progress and the reserve Section was sent in to help clear up the situation. The Tanks of this Section went on and all reached the final objective although through the mist the Infantry were unable to advance at the same pace.

On starting for the second objective the original 2 Sections had 3 and 4 Tanks respectively. After proceeding a short way the Tank commanded by 2/Lt. Klee had serious gear trouble and came under very machine gun fire. 2/Lt. Klee was killed and most of his crew were wounded. The Tank was abandoned under fire and burned out. About half way to the second objective 2/Lt Weights took his Tank on cleaning up machine gun pockets but ran out of petrol and on swinging round to go back to refill he received a direct hit that set his Tank on fire. 2/Lt. Weights gave orders to abandon the Tank but owing to the spread of flames no guns could be salved. 2/Lt Weights was killed on his way back to report.

The remaining Tanks rallied at the starting point J.18.d. There were 4 of No. 3 Section and 1 of No. 2 Section, of those only 3 were fit for further action. The crews were very fatigued but at once set about repairing the engines, and guns.

At about 4-30 pm. Major Williams of the Royal West Kents reported a large party massing for a counter-attack on his front. Two fit Tanks J.18 and J.19 at once went forward to deal with this. They arrived at their objective at 5-3 pm. and returned again to the Coy. at 6-0 pm. having broken up any signs of counter-attack that appeared.

At 4-15 pm. on the 9th 3 Tanks started under command of Captain Mackenzie to attack the high ground between MERICOURT and MORLANCOURT. The original Zero given to the Tanks was 5-0 pm. and at 4-50 pm. orders were received postponing Zero to 5-30 pm. These orders did not reach the Tanks owing to the distance that had to be covered between the time the orders were received and the time the Tanks got into action. Of the 3 Tanks Captain Mackenzie's became badly ditched on the objective after doing all the work laid down for it. That commanded by Lieut. Runkin got ditched after passing the German Front Line. 2/Lt. Cameron's Tank received two direct hits from our own barrage but carried out the programme and returned to the Coy. Tank Park. This Tank was then totally unfit for further action.

No action took place until 6-0 pm. on the 10th

Report by "B" Coy. (continued).

J.20 and J.29 were attached to Captain Murphy who attacked the railway infront of MORLANCOURT. All objectives were reached without serious casualties the action lasting about an hour and a half.

The same night J.19 under 2/Lt. Price was attached to the Australians for a night attack on the outskirts of BRAY. He proceeded down the BRAY-CORBIE ROAD and held his position until the Infantry were satisfied with their position. He then returned to the Company. Zero was at 9-30 pm. and the attack as far as Tanks were concerned ended about 10-30 pm.

This concluded the operations undertaken by this Coy.

(Sgd). H.C.F.DRADER. Major.
Commanding "B" Company. 10th. Tank Battalion.

"C" Coy: 10th Tank Bn.

Report on Operations on
8th 9th 10th August 1918.

"C" Company. 10TH TANK BATTALION.

REPORT ON OPERATIONS. 8th, 9th & 10th August 1918.

8th. August 1918.

Sir,
I have the honour to report on operations carried out by Tanks of this Company in co-operation with troops of the 174th and 173rd Bdes. on 8-8-18.

Order of Battle.

Coy. Commander.   Captain. W.S.Ponsford.

	Left Section.		Right Section.
Tank.		Tank.	
J.43.	2/Lt.T.Harper. MC.	J.44.	2/Lt.A.E.M.Cresswell.
J.38.	2/Lt.G.T.L.Bayliff.	J.45.	2/Lt.G.W.Biss.
J.42.	2/Lt.L.H.Cronshaw. MC.	J.46.	Capt.M.C.Keynes.
J.41.	2/Lt.C.G.Oddy.	J.36.	2/Lt.F.S.Lyne.

Centre Section.

Tank.	
J.40.	Lieut.D.G.B.Day.
J.48.	Lieut.C.B.Larter.
J.47.	2/Lt.C.B.Loxton.
J.35.	Lieut.G.Garnham.

Zero was at 4-20 am. and Sections left jumping-off points at the following times.

Left.	Zero	- 23 minutes.
Centre.	"	" "
Right.	"	- 21 "

During forming up at jumping-off point the Company came under fairly heavy shell fire. J.41 (2/Lt.C.G.Oddy) and J.35 (Lt.G.Garnham) failed to leave the jumping-off point owing to mechanical trouble. On account of dense mist no Tank was able to follow the actual course laid down for it. The mist however cleared about 8-40 am. and the Tanks rendered all possible assistance wherever required by the Infantry.

Within 200 yards of the starting point J.43 sustained 2 direct hits one breaking the track and the Officer (2/Lt.T.Harper.MC.) and 1 Other Ranks were wounded and sent to dressing station. One man was left to guard the Tank and the remainder of the crew were transferred to Tank J.41. which had in the meantime been made fit and was ready to go forward.

J.35 whilst repairing mechanical trouble had 1 Other Rank wounded, 1 Other Rank suffered from shock and 2 Other Ranks slightly gassed. Not having sufficient crew to go forward the Tank returned to rallying point.

Within 300 yards of the jumping-off point J.38 received a direct hit which set the Tank on fire. 3 members of the crew of this Tank had been left behind suffering from petrol fumes and the Officer and the remainder of the crew joined Tank J.42. Later in the day close to MALLARD WOOD J.42 sustained a hit injuring the epicyclic gear on the right side and returned to rallying point.

J.47 owing to hole through the autovac had to be evacuated and was brought in the following day by the Coy. Tank Engineer.

J.36 took the route to CHIPILLY and after being in action 9 hours returned to HEILLY.

The remaining Tanks returned to rallying point about 2-0 pm. The Tanks fit at the end of the day's operations were J.41, J.40, J.48, J.44, J.45 and J.46.

Report by "C" Coy. (Contd).

9th August 1918.

Sir,

I have the honour to report on operations carried out by Tanks of this Company in co-operation with some troops of the 12th. Divn. on 9-8-18.

Order of Battle.

Coy. Commander. Capt.W.S.Ponsford.

Left Section.   Right Section.

J.46. Capt.M.C.Keynes.   J.48. Lieut.C.B.Larter.
J.44. 2/Lt.A.E.F.Cresswell.   J.45. 2/Lt.C.T.Biss.
J.41. 2/Lt.C.H.Oddy.   J.40. Lieut.D.C.R.Day.

Zero was at 5-50 pm. and Tanks moved forward with the Infantry at the various times before Zero as ordered. J.40, owing to mechanical trouble was late in starting but was able to get up to the barrage line in time. J.46 had only proceeded 300 yards when it sustained 2 direct hits which set the Tank on fire. The Officer was slightly burned and the Sergeant severely burned during the operation. It was found impossible to put out the fire in this Tank.

J.44 after having engaged enemy M.G's and T.M's returned with the 6-pdr and 2 Hotchkiss guns out of action, took up a position under a bank but was unable to take any further part in the action. J.41 owing to the left and centre Tanks being casualties entered the village of MORLANCOURT and assisted the Infantry.

J.48 after having engaged the enemy received 3 holes through the autovac and retired from the action. J.45 and J.40 carried on as arranged. Tanks returned to rallying point by 10-30 pm. and the following Tanks were fit for further operations:-J.41,J.45,J.40.

J.37 & J.39 (which were both fit) joined the Company at this rallying point.

Tanks were instrumental in dealing with machine gun nests and T.M. positions and rendered assistance to the Infantry when required. Large numbers of prisoners were secured by the Infantry owing to the action of the Tanks.

Great credit is due to the Coy. Reconnaissance Officer (Lieut.E.Whiteside) and the Coy. Tank Engineer for the efficient manner in which they carried out their duties. They rendered very valuable services.

10th August 1918.

From Officer Commanding Composite Section.

Sir,

I have the honour on operations carried out by Tanks in this Section in co-operation with troops of the 12th. Divn.on 10-8-18.

Order of Battle.   Section Commander. Lieut. G.Garnham.

Left.   Right.
Tank No.J.29. 2/Lt.T.Duffy.   Tank No.J30.2/Lt.F.Frere.
Tank No.J.35. Lt.G.Garnham.   Tank No.J12.2/Lt.A.Evans.

Zero was fixed at 8-0 pm. Tanks moved off with the Infantry at that time and were all able to reach first objective.

J.35 received a direct hit on right sponson - 3 other hands being killed and 1 wounded necessitating this Tank being abandoned.

The remaining 3 Tanks cruised about in front of the objective dealing with heavy machine gun fire from the right and finally patrolling the ground on the left flank and returned safely to their respective Coys. They had in these Tanks slight casualties but only 1 O.R. had to be evacuated.

(Sgd). G. GARNHAM. Lieut.

58th Division.

Report on Operations of 173rd Inf: Bde: for August 1918.

58th Division

[Stamp: 58th (LONDON) DIVISION G.S.330/5 - 6 SEP 1918 GENERAL STAFF]

B.M. 66.

    Herewith one copy of Report on Operations carried out by this Brigade between August 24th and September 1st.

    Certain of the General Notes, especially those on Infantry, are included primarily for the benefit of units of this Brigade, to each of whom a copy of the full report is being issued.

Charles Cokran
Brigadier-General,
Commanding 173rd Infantry Brigade.

5/9/18

SEEN BY:-
G.O.C.........
G.S.O.I.......
G.S.O.II......
G.S.O.III.....
....

173rd INFANTRY BRIGADE.

REPORT ON OPERATIONS, 25th, 26th, 27th, 28th AUG.
AND 1st. SEPT. 1918.

CONTENTS.

Part I.   NARRATIVE.
Part II. GENERAL NOTES.
Appendix "A" - Prisoners.
   "   "B" - Composition of Brigade Group.
   "   "C" - Casualties.

Charles Corkran

Brigadier-General,
Commanding 173rd Infantry Brigade.

5th Sept. 1918.

Distribution:-
    O.C. 2/2nd London Regt.
    O.C. 3rd London Regt.
    O.C. 2/4th London Regt.
    O.C. 173rd L.T.M. Battery.
    58th Division "G".
    War Diary.
    File.

PART I

NARRATIVE

Prior to the operations the Brigade was training in QUERRIEU area, moving thence on August 23rd to positions of assembly immediately South of HERICOURT L'ABEE, and arriving at this latter place about 7 a.m. the same day.

About 8 a.m., 23rd, orders were received for the Brigade to move forward at once to positions of readiness on the plateau immediately East of MORLANCOURT with a view to taking part in an attack at 4 p.m., 24th.

This move was not completed until dawn 24th, owing to the guides furnished being unfamiliar with the ground.

Brigade Headquarters closed at HEILLY HALTE at 10 p.m., 23rd, and reopened at the QUARRY half a mile South of MORLANCOURT (Sheet 62D: K.14.b.) at midnight 23rd/24th.

At 7 a.m., 24th, a conference of Commanding Officers was held at Brigade H.Q. at which the plans for the forth-coming operations were explained.

The role allotted to the Brigade was that of supporting an attack by 175th Inf. Bde. (on the Right), and 140th Bde. (on Left) on enemy's positions North of BRAY (see Map A). All units of the Brigade were to move forward at ZERO (4 pm.)

Orders issued to units of the Brigade were in effect as follows :-

    2/2nd Bn. was to move in rear of 175th Inf. Bde.
    3rd Bn. in rear of 140th Inf. Bde.
    2/4th Bn. was kept in Brigade Reserve, and was to move in rear of the other two Battalions, but not to advance beyond HAPPY VALLEY without orders from Brigade H.Q.

One section "A" Coy., 58th Bn. M.G.C., was attached to each Battalion, the remaining section, 173rd L.T.M.Bty., Detachment of New Zealand Cyclists, and One troop Northumberland Hussars, were retained under direct orders of Bde. H.Q.

At 10 a.m., 24th, information was received from Division that ZERO hour had been altered to 2.30 a.m., 25th.

No great alteration in Brigade Orders was necessitated by this change. Bde. H.Q. moved during the night to K.17.a.5.5.

At ZERO, 25th, the Brigade moved forward according to plan, Bde. H.Q. opening at QUARRY L.1.b.3.0. at 3.30 a.m.

At 5.45 a.m. a message was received from Division to the effect that should 140th and 175th Inf. Bdes. reach their final objective (see Map A) without gaining touch with the enemy, 173rd Inf. Bde. would pass through these two Brigades and form an Advanced Guard of the Division in an advance via North of BILLON WOOD on MARICOURT.

At about 6.30 a.m. capture of objectives by 140th and 175th Inf. Bdes. was confirmed, and at 7 a.m. orders for their advance were despatched by runner to all units

In accordance with this order Bde. H.Q. moved at once to the Starting Point.

During all this time a thick fog existed, and considerably hampered communications by runner, while visual signalling was, of course, out of the question, and it was on account of this difficulty that the rearmost battalion, i.e.:- 2/4th Bn., were ordered to form the Brigade Advanced Guard since their unit was the closest to Bde. H.Q., and could, moreover, be approached by a known track.

On Brigade H.Q. reaching the Starting Point the fog had cleared considerably, and the 2/4th Bn. could be seen immediately ahead with elements apparently engaged in fighting round BRONFAY FARM. Considerable hostile M.G. fire was also coming from the ridge immediately West of BILLON WOOD.

Orders for the Brigade Advanced Guard were accordingly modified, and O.C., 2/4th Bn. was ordered verbally to attack BILLON WOOD. 2/2nd Bn. were ordered to support 2/4th Bn., while 3rd Bn. were ordered to take up position of assembly in valley and remain in Brigade Reserve.

By 1 p.m. the 2/4th Bn. had captured the greater part of BILLON WOOD, but were held up by enemy M.G. on the Eastern and Northern edges.

At 2.40 p.m. orders were accordingly issued to 2/2nd Bn. to attack via the high ground to the North of BILLON WOOD, and to 2/4th Bn. to continue attack in conjunction with 2/2nd Bn. and to clear up the WOOD. Both Battalions were given BILLON AVENUE as their ultimate objective.

This attack was timed for 4.30 p.m., and met with considerable success. BILLON WOOD was finally captured, together with BILLON AVENUE from approximately A.26.a.3.4 to A.15.c.3.2. Further advance was not practicable owing to absence of any touch on our Left flank with 12th Division - the enemy still holding CARNOY - and to the fact that the enemy also held the Western outskirts of MARICOURT in considerable strength.

Our line as it now stood (see Map A) was over extended, and the following readjustments were carried out at dusk :-

174th Inf. Bde. relieved 2/4th Bn., and 3rd Bn. reinforced 2/2nd Bn. with two Companies.

The remaining two Companies of the 3rd Bn. were ordered to take up defensive positions on the high ground North of BILLON WOOD.

4.

During the night orders were issued for the advance to be continued at 4 a.m., 26th, it being understood that 12th Division would co-operate on our Left flank, while 174th Inf. Bde. were to attack on our Right at the same time.

3rd Bn. were ordered to lead the advance, and to endeavour to capture MARICOURT. 2/2nd Bn. were to support the 3rd Bn. 2/4th Bn. were to remain as Brigade Reserve about the GREAT BEAR. This attack was accompanied by an artillery barrage. The 3rd Bn. actually succeeded in penetrating into MARICOURT, but were unable to remain there, being entirely unsupported on their Left flank, while 174th Inf. Bde. on the Right had met with considerable opposition from CREST AVENUE, and were held up West of their line.

At 2.30 p.m., 26th the situation was as shewn on Map "B". Earlier in the day a German counter-attack was reported to be imminent against our Left flank in the neighbourhood of LAPREE WOOD, and to meet this danger 2/4th Bn. was moved forward from GREAT BEAR to vicinity of CONTOUR WOOD, and were ordered to deny the high ground North of BILLON WOOD to the enemy.

The counter-attack, however, did not materialise, and the remainder of the day was spent in consolidation and preparation for continuing the advance the next day.

The orders for the attack on the 27th were issued in the afternoon of 26th, and were briefly as follows :-

3rd Bn. to carry out the attack closely supported by the 2/4th Bn. - 2/2nd Bn. to remain in Brigade Reserve and to hold the trench system running North and South through U WORKS. The objective for this attack was the OLD BRITISH FRONT LINE immediately East of MARICOURT - exploitation was to include the OLD GERMAN FORWARD SYSTEM further East.

The attack started at 4.55 a.m. and met with immediate success. MARICOURT was reported captured early, and at 8 a.m. a summary of reports received shewed our troops to be on the objective line throughout the Brigade Front (see Map "C"). Messages from 12th Division and 174th Inf. Bde. were similar in effect, and according to instructions received, orders were issued for 2/4th Bn. to push patrols through 3rd Bn., and to continue the advance in the direction of MAUREPAS Station. The order was, however, cancelled on information being received that (i) the enemy was holding the OLD GERMAN FRONT SYSTEM in strength and that all endeavour on the part of the 3rd Bn. to exploit success, had met with vigorous opposition; (ii) three fresh enemy Divisions had been located on the Divisional Front.

Instead, the 3rd Bn. were ordered to continue their efforts to reach the line of exploitation, while 2/4th Bn. were ordered to complete consolidation of the OLD BRITISH FRONT LINE.

All efforts on the part of the 3rd Bn. to advance further were unsuccessful, and the situation was unchanged at nightfall.

During the afternoon 27th, reports were received that isolated bodies of the enemy were still at large in MARICOURT. This village was accordingly "raked" from front to rear by a Company 2/2nd Bn., but only some six or seven enemy were discovered. These were duly captured. Total prisoners captured for the day amounted to approximately 120, with one battalion commander.

In the evening of the 27th, orders were issued for a further short advance to be carried out at 4.55 a.m., 28th. 2/2nd Bn. were to attack supported by 3rd Bn., 2/4th Bn. were to remain in occupation of the OLD BRITISH FRONT LINE, and were kept in Brigade Reserve.

Actual written orders did not reach Commanding Officers until after 1 a.m., 28th, owing to runners having great difficulty in finding the various Battalion H.Q. in the dark.

The essential part of the orders were, however, communicated verbally to Commanding Officers by a Staff Officer from Brigade H.Q. and the attack was accordingly launched at ZERO 28th, preceded by a creeping barrage. The attack was entirely successful, and all objectives were gained (see Map "D").

In addition, by way of exploitation, posts were established in advance of the objective (shewn on Map "D").

Little enemy opposition was met with on this day, but numerous casualties were caused by enemy shelling, which was extremely heavy, and by M.G. fire from direction of Sunken Road in A.24.b.

During the afternoon, 28th, orders were received that the Brigade was to be relieved by 175th Inf. Bde. with 1/4th Suffolks attached. This relief was duly carried out and completed by 6 a.m., 29th, at which hour command of the Brigade Sector passed to G.O.C., 175th Inf. Bde.

After relief the Brigade Group concentrated in the valley L.4.a. with Bde. H.Q. at F.21.d.3.0.

Here the Brigade remained until the afternoon of the 31st, when, ~~contrary to expectations~~, orders were received for the Brigade to move by buses to the neighbourhood of HEM WOOD, and thence by march route to BOUCHAVESNES, in order to attack the enemy positions in this neighbourhood the following morning.

The attack was to be carried out in conjunction with 47th Division on Left, and 3rd Australian Division on Right.

The first intimation as to the impending operation was received at Bde. H.Q. about 4 p.m. A Commanding Officers'

Conference was assembled at 5 p.m., when the general plan was explained.

3rd Bn. was to carry out the attack supported by 2/4th Bn., with 2/2nd Bn. in Brigade Reserve.

This was subsequently altered at the suggestion of G.O.C., 58th Division. Final written orders were handed to C.Os. at the ombussing point at 7 p.m., and were briefly as follows :-

3rd and 2/4th Bns. were to attack, 2/4th Bn. on the Right, 2/4th Bn. on the Left.

2/4th Bn. was allotted one section "A" Coy., 58th Bn. M.G.C.

3rd Bn. was allotted two sections "A" Coy. 58th Bn. M.G.C. 2/2nd Bn. were to move in support to the assaulting battalions, passing valley B.23.d., B.24.c., at ZERO, accompanied by one section "A" Coy. 58th Bn. M.G.C. 173rd L.T.M.Bty. were also placed under orders of O.C., 2/2nd Bn.

The approach march of all units was considerably interfered with by the congestion of traffic along all roads and tracks in the forward area throughout the night, but notwithstanding this 3rd and 2/4th Battalions reached the neighbourhood of the assembly positions (see Map E) at 3 a.m., 1st September, in excellent order.

The assembly was carried out without hitch, and the attack duly launched under a creeping barrage at ZERO, i.e.:- 5.30 a.m., 1st September.

This attack was again entirely successful, and final objectives were reached up to schedule time along the whole Brigade Front. A certain amount of difficulty was experienced by Divisions on either flank, and for this reason complete touch with both flanks was not established until 10 a.m. At this hour situation was as shewn on Map E.

8.

Considerable enemy opposition was overcome in the course of this attack, and the enemy barrage was prompt and heavy.

Nearly 400 prisoners were captured on the Brigade Front, and there is no doubt that it was the enemy's intention to hold the ridge East of BOUCHAVESNES at all costs.

Exploitation of this success was immediately attempted, but could not progress far owing to the fact that all movement had to be carried out on a forward slope exposed to full view of enemy, and also to the fact that the brigade was well in advance of units on both flanks, who were in each case held up and unable to co-operate.

The line therefore remained stationary for the remainder of the day, and was handed over to the 47th and 74th Divisions at midnight as shewn on Map "E".

****

PART II

GENERAL NOTES

1. **INFANTRY.**

All ranks shewed the greatest courage and determination throughout the operations, but there is no doubt that had more attention been paid to the recognised principles of open warfare, casualties would have been fewer, and the results greater.

The greatest fault lies in the lack of application of the principles of protection, whether at the halt or on the move.

Too much attention cannot be paid to the principle that the Commander of any unit, however small, is responsible for protection against surprise.

In the attack on BILLON WOOD on the morning of August 25th, whole platoons were observed to advance into the open in 'lumps' against close range M.G. and rifle fire (within 300 yards) and to suffer accordingly. It must be impressed on all Company, Platoon and Section Commanders, that in open and semi-open warfare as now obtaining, every body of troops, whether it be a Company, Platoon or Section, must be preceded by its ground scouts.

The role of such scouts is simple, and is in brief to reconnoitre the ground ahead, and to the flanks of their unit, and to prevent their unit being surprised in any way whatever.

The operation on 25th August also brought to light the tendency on the part of junior infantry commanders to commit the whole of their command to a frontal attack on small enemy posts, the moment these were located. This was probably due to the lack of protection mentioned above, in that Companies were caught in artillery formation by close rifle and M.G. fire, and had no opportunity to manoeuvre left to them. The result of these tactical errors was that :-

1. An unnecessary amount of casualties was incurred in merely locating the enemy, and before any plan of action could be determined upon.

2. Such plan of action was perforce confined to a costly frontal attack, since all movements to a flank under close range M.G. or rifle fire are useless and must never be attempted.

As a general rule, every unit should endeavour to keep a small reserve in hand, and this reserve should never be employed until the local situation has been finally cleared up and the attack launched on a definite plan.

2. MACHINE GUNS.

Throughout the operations the system of attaching one or more sections of Machine Guns to each battalion was adhered to. At the same time it was made clear to Commanding Officers that the tactical handling of these guns was to rest with the M.G. Officer in charge. In other words, it was for the infantry commander to intimate to the M.G. Commander the nature of assistance required, and for the latter to decide how much assistance could be given, and in what manner it should be carried out.

In the attack at BOUCHAVESNES on September 1st the Brigade was allotted an additional Company of M.Gs. - "D" Coy., 58th Bn. M.G.C. This Company was kept intact under orders of Bde. H.Q., and was allotted a definite role at the suggestion of O.C., 58th Bn. M.G.C. The role was that of advancing after ZERO to a position just East of BOUCHAVESNES, and of bringing indirect fire to bear from this position on the MOISLAINS VALLEY, which lay approximately 1,000 yards East of our final objective. This task was duly carried out by the Company, and it is considered that it was to a great extent owing to this use of M.Gs. that the enemy was unable to remove a considerable number of Field Guns, which were in position just N.W. of MOISLAINS. These guns were still in position unmanned when the

Sector was handed over to 47th Division, and it is believed that they have now been definitely captured.

3. ARTILLERY.

Artillery co-operated in all attacks, with the exception of the initial assault by 2/4th London Regt. on BILLON WOOD, and from August 25th (inclusive) onwards, all attacks were proceded by a creeping F.A. barrage at a pace varying from 100 yards in four minutes to 100 yards in six minutes. The co-operation of the Field Artillery was in every way satisfactory. In the attack on BOUCHAVESNES on September 1st, one Field Gun under an officer, was attached to each of the attacking battalions. Only the action of the gun allotted to 2/2nd Bn. can, however, be traced. This gun was ordered to take up a position at the S.W. corner of MARIERES WOOD, from which point it could effectively engage over open sights any enemy counter-attack developing from ST. PIERRE VAAST or MOISLAINS WOOD on to the heights N.W. of BOUCHAVESNES.

As regards the H.A. it is felt that liaison of this branch with the foremost infantry still leaves much to be desired. In the attack on MARICOURT on 27th August a liaison officer from 71st Bde. R.G.A. was attached to Bde. H.Q., and was of great assistance throughout the day. In the attack on BOUCHAVESNES, however, no heavy artillery liaison officer reported although a section of 60-pdrs. was placed under the orders of the F.A. Group Commander. This section of guns was undoubtedly of the greatest value, but was quite unable of itself to cope with the demands made for counter-battery work. Throughout the operation from August 25th to September 1st, our infantry suffered severely from the enemy heavy artillery fire, and urgent calls for counter-battery work were constantly being received at Bde. H.Q. These calls were frequently extremely vague in their information as to the calibre and position of the active hostile batteries. This is nearly always the case. Infantry officers find great difficulty in distinguishing between the many kinds of shell now in use by the enemy, and with so many other matters to attend to, are seldom reliable judges as to direction. It is suggested that at least one H.A. officer could be spared to

assist the forward infantry in this respect. It is recognised
that the supply of Heavy Artillery officers is not unlimited,
and it is also recognised that such an officer will be of
little use unless he can maintain a line either directly or
indirectly to his guns. At the same time, in the present type
of fighting, the main bulk of enemy shell fire is directed for
reasons of range (the enemy guns being placed well in rear of
his front line) on to our forward troops, while our communications
rearward from about 1,000 yards from the front line are
seldom interfered with. This fact should often enable an
artillery line to be maintained as far as Battalion H.Q., while
it could invariably be maintained up to the Brigade Advanced
Command Post which, whenever possible, is selected at a point
where the greater portion of the Brigade Front can be observed.
In any case it is suggested that the principle of keeping the
bulk of the heavy artillery under the orders of Corps H.Q.
during an advance is hardly conducive to a perfect liaison
between the infantry and that branch, and that command of
weapons so essential to the fighting infantry should be de-
centralised as far as possible. It is also suggested that
if possible a certain amount of gas shell should be available
for counter=battery work during an advance, to be used subsequently to the capture of the final objective, when an exact
location of enemy active batteries is a matter of great
difficulty.

4. CAVALRY.

On the 25th August one Squadron, Northumberland Hussars
(IIIrd Corps Cavalry) were attached to the Brigade. These were
replaced on the 26th by one Squadron XXII Corps Cavalry -
Australian Light Horse. Both Squadrons did excellent work
so far as the difficult nature of the ground permitted. From
the first it was obvious that such a small body of cavalry
could not hope to break through the type of L.G. defences
employed by the enemy, which defence was materially assisted

by the mass of shell-holes existing in the battle area, and by the enormous amount of old wire entanglements. It was therefore decided to use the cavalry entirely for patrol work on the flanks of the Brigade, and in this work the Australian Light Horse were of the greatest value. The actual patrolling was carried out on foot, the horses being used merely as a rapid means of transmitting information to and from flank Brigades, and to Brigade H.Q.

5. CYCLISTS

A detachment of New Zealand Cyclist Corps (XXII Corps) was attached to the Brigade throughout the operations. These men were, however, even more hampered than the cavalry, by the difficult nature of the country. Numerous reports were, however, received from them, and served to confirm the information received from the Cavalry and other sources. On the 25th and 26th August, the three Lewis Guns carried by the detachment were used to assist in the consolidation of the ground won from the enemy.

6. LIGHT TRENCH MORTARS.

Four guns only of 173rd L.T.M.Bty. were taken into action, this being the greatest number that, together with sufficient ammunition, can be carried in the limbers now provided for this unit. These guns were, as a general rule, ordered to advance in rear of assaulting infantry, and to take successive positions on tactical features of special importance captured during each day's advance. The battery was invariably placed under the command of the Support Battalion Commander, in order that should one or more Mortars be required forward for offensive purposes, they could always be obtained without time being lost by applying to Bde. H.Q.

7. COMMUNICATIONS

These, on the whole, were not a success. The supply of cable was always a difficulty, and even when lines were established they speedily became practically useless owing

to their being laid on the ground across tracks in use
by advancing artillery, etc. It would appear essential
that in future, wherever a line crosses a used track, rough
uprights should be erected at once and the line carried
overhead at this point. A certain amount of time would
certainly be lost, but this would be more than compensated for
by the final results.

In the earlier battles on the HARICOURT PLATEAU there
was little scope for visual work, but during the BOUCHAVESNES
operation some chain of communication by this method should
undoubtedly have been established. The Brigade Signal
Section spent many hours on September 1st endeavouring to
establish a chain of visual stations, but without success.
This failure was probably due to lack of practice, and
orders have been issued to O.C., Brigade Signal Section to
take the present opportunity of exercising both his own
and battalion sections in visual schemes.

Runners, as usual, formed the most reliable method
of communication. These men, however, frequently experienced
difficulty in locating the various H.Q. of units which,
owing to rapid advance in progress, were constantly taking
up fresh positions in unreconnoitred country. To meet this
difficulty each battalion and company in the Brigade now
carries a H.Q. flag of small dimensions, and it is hoped
that these flags will in future be of considerable assistance
to Staff Officers, Runners, etc. They will not, of course,
be placed in positions open to enemy ground observation.

8. INTELLIGENCE

Battalion Intelligence Officers did their work well.
Identifications secured were passed at once to Brigade H.Q.
and on to Division on almost every occasion. A certain
tendency was noticed on the few occasions that prisoners
were captured late in a day's operations, to delay reports
as to their identity; this was probably due to the fact that

the prisoners in question were of the same unit as those captured earlier in the day. It must be clearly understood in future that all identifications are of value, even if repeated time after time on the same day, and identification messages will in all cases be sent by the quickest possible method to Brigade H.Q. There were also many cases of prisoners being employ on stretcher work. It is recognised that this work is of the greatest importance, but by employing prisoners for this purpose, many a valuable piece of information may reach the higher authorities too late to be of use, and many a life that might otherwise be saved, may be lost in a subsequent surprise attack by the enemy, an attack, the probability of which might possibly have been intimated to us by the very prisoners whose examination is being delayed by our own action. In future all prisoners as soon as captured must be sent at once under a small escort to Brigade H.Q. There they will be collected under Brigade arrangements, and despatched in batches to the Divisional Cage.

****

APPENDIX "A"

PRISONERS.

Date of Capture.	No.	Identifications.
25-8-18.	1.	116 R.I.R. (25th Divn)
26-8-18.	3.	116 R.I.R. (25th Divn)
	6.	77 M.G.Marksmen Detachment.
27-8-18.	Approx: 120.	115, 116, 117 R.I.R. (25th Divn)
28-8-18.	1 Off. 3 O.R.	117 R.I.R.
	6 O.R.	201 R.I.R. (23rd Res. Divn)
	2 O.R.	157 R.I.R. (117 Divn).
1-9-18.	325 Unwounded Prisoners -	445 R.I.R.)
		446 R.I.R.) 232 Divn.
		447 R.I.R.)

A few 2nd Guard Grenadier Regt.

1 2nd Guard Grenadier Field Artillery Regt.

1 2nd Guard Pioneer Coy.

Also many wounded prisoners.

※※※※※※※※※※※※※※※※

APPENDIX "B".

COMPOSITION OF BRIGADE GROUP - (LESS AFFILIATED ARTILLERY).

Aug. 25th.
    2/2nd London Regt.
    3rd London Regt.
    2/4th London Regt.
    173rd L.T.M.Battery.
    "A"Company, 58th Bn. M.G.C.
    No.2 Troop, "C" Squadron, Northumberland Hussars.
    Detachment New Zealand Cyclist Corps.

Aug. 26th.
    27th.
    28th.
    2/2nd London Regt.
    3rd London Regt.
    2/4th London Regt.
    173rd L.T.M.Battery.
    "A"Company, 58th Bn. M.G.C.
    Squadron, Australian Light Horse.
    Detachment New Zealand Cyclist Corps.

Sept. 1st.
    2/2nd London Regt.
    3rd London Regt.
    2/4th London Regt.
    173rd L.T.M.Battery.
    "A"Company, 58th Bn. M.G.C.
    "D"Company, 58th Bn. M.G.C.
    One Squadron, Australian Light Horse.
    Detachment New Zealand Cyclist Corps.

✱✱✱✱✱✱✱✱✱✱✱✱✱

APPENDIX "C"

173rd Infantry Brigade.
CASUALTIES.

Period - Aug.25th to 28th 1918.

	OFFICERS.			OTHER RANKS.			TOTAL.	
	Killed.	Wounded.	Missing.	Killed.	Wounded.	Missing.	Off.	O.R.
2/2nd London Regt.	2	9	-	53	252	59	11	364
3rd London Regt.	2	8	-	23	236	74	10	333
2/4th London Regt.	-	10	-	26	257	54	10	337
173rd L.T.M.B.	-	1	-	1	4	3	1	8
Totals -	4	28	-	103	749	190	32	1042

Period - Sept.1st to 2nd.1918.

	OFFICERS.			OTHER RANKS.			TOTAL.	
	Killed.	Wounded.	Missing.	Killed.	Wounded.	Missing.	Off.	O.R.
2/2nd London Regt.	-	1	-	5	24	2	1	31
3rd London Regt.	2	4	-	10	75	34	6	119
2/4th London Regt.	4	5	-	11	49	36	9	96
173rd L.T.M.B.	-	-	-	-	1	-	-	1
Totals -	6	10	-	26	149	72	16	247

TOTALS.

	Officers.	Other Ranks.
First Period	32	1042
Second Period	16	247
	48	1289

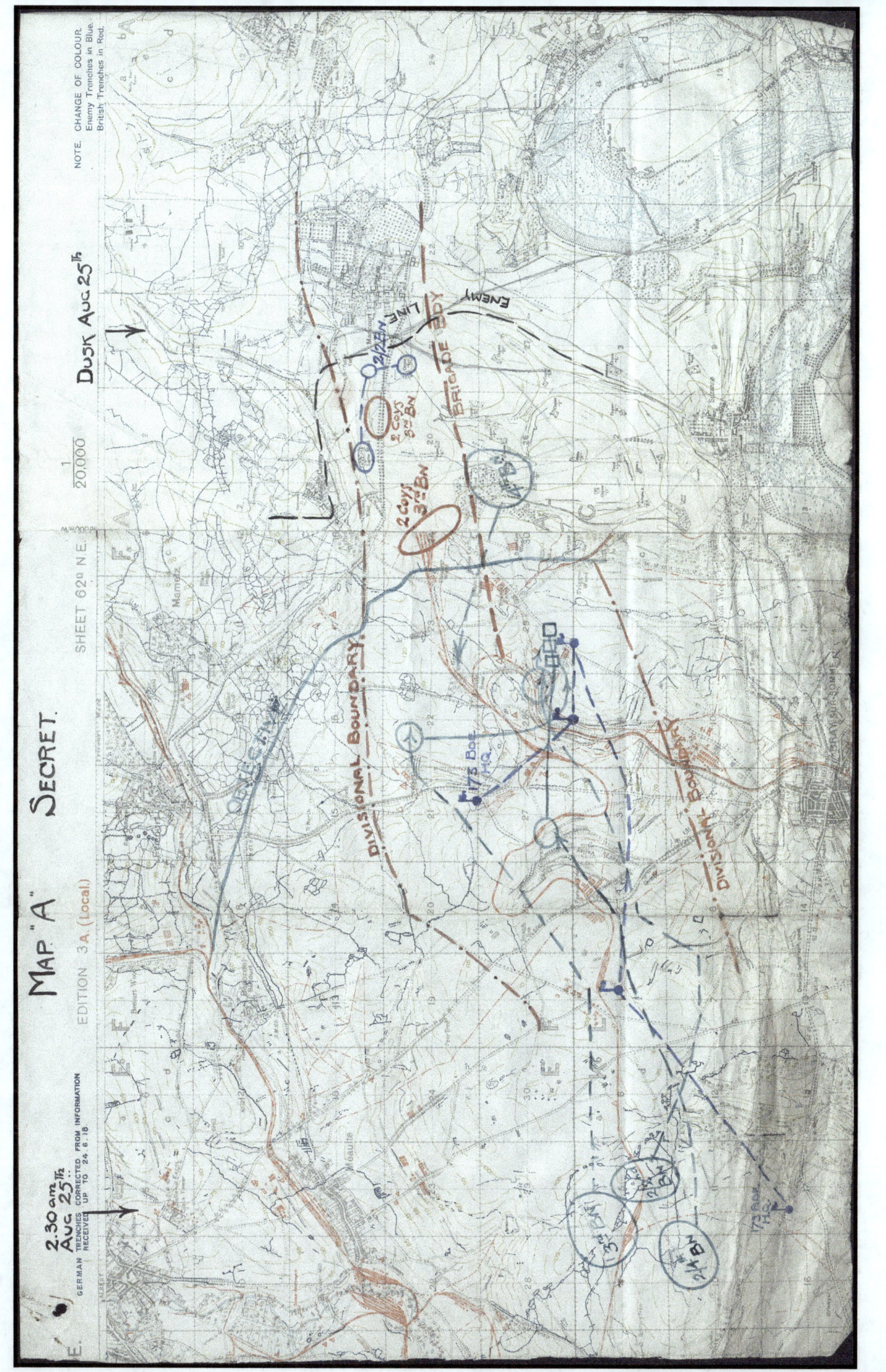

MAP "E".

SHEET 62c N.W.

TRENCHES CORRECTED TO 6·3·18

EDITION 4. B

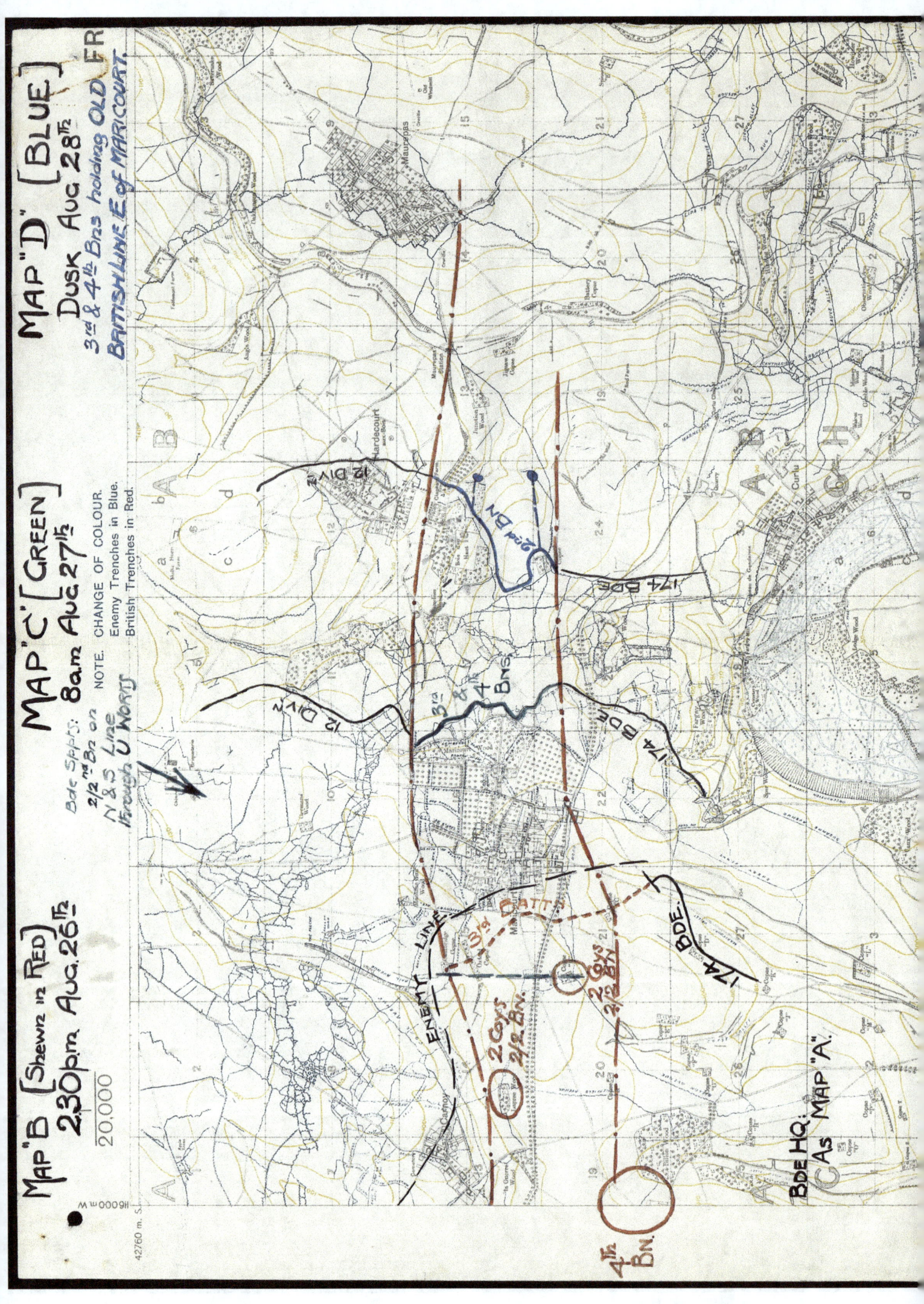

58th Division.

Report on Operations

of

174th Inf: Bde:

for

August 1918.

SECRET.

58th Division.

Herewith report on recent operations.

                                                    [signature] Brigadier General,
                                            Commanding 174th. Infantry Brigade.

21st Aug., 1918.

REPORT on OPERATIONS.

August 6th to 10th

1918.

1. Preliminary.

   On the night 4/5th. August the Brigade proceeded by busses to the LA HOUSSOYE Area arriving at the Debussing Point at 2 a.m. The Brigade was under orders to take over the Line from the River SOMME to K.25.a.9.6. preliminary to taking part in a large offensive by the Fourth British and First French Armies on the morning of August 8th. Only Commanding Officers were aware of the contemplated attack.

2. Relief of 54th. Infantry Brigade.

   On the night of the 5/6th. August the Brigade took over the Line, the 8th. Londons relieving the 2nd Bedfords in the Front Line with the 6th. Londons in Support and the 7th. Londons in Reserve. All four Companies of the 8th. Londons were to garrison the Front Line. The relief was successfully accomplished by the two Right Companies but while the relief was still in progress the two Left Companies were attacked simultaneously with the Troops on their Left. In accordance with orders previously given the Outpost Line was withdrawn and the Front Line was held intact and nine prisoners taken. These two Companies suffered considerable casualties chiefly from T.M. fire, they were afterwards continually shelled until the morning of the 8th. and owing to the muddy state of the trenches and absence of any shelter they were severely tested. The relief was finally completed on the night of the 6/7th. when the remaining elements of the 2nd. Bedfords side-stepped to their Left. The Right Company of the 8th. Londons was relieved by a Company of the 2/10th. Londons on the night 6/7th. in order to facilitate the forming up of the Brigade Group.

3. General Plan of Attack.

   The 174th. Infantry Brigade was ordered to lead the attack on the 58th. Divisional Front, their objectives being a line East of MALARD WOOD from K.27.b. to the SOMME a distance of about 2,500 yards from the British Front Line. The 173rd. Infantry Brigade was then to pass through, capture GRESSAIRE WOOD and the high ground North of CHIPILLY. The 54th. Infantry Brigade were to attack on the Left, the left flank of the General Advance being just South of MORLANCOURT while the attack was to extend as far as MOREUIL to the South. There was no preliminary Artillery preparation, and every precaution was taken to make the attack a complete surprise for the enemy. The 10th. Londons, one Section "C" Company, and "B" Company 58th. M.G. Battalion and one Company 10th. Tank Battalion were attached to the Brigade for the operation.

4. Details of Plan of Attack of 174th. Infantry Brigade.

   (a) Infantry.

   The 10th. Londons were given the task of capturing the village of SAILLY LAURETTE and were to assemble for the attack in the Front Line Trench. The 6th., and 7th. Londons were given the task of capturing MALARD WOOD and taking the first objective. They were to assemble on a tape line 100 yards behind our Front Line in the following order from

/right

-2-

right to left. Two Coys of the 6th. Londons supported by one Coy of the 8th. Londons : One Coy. of the 7th Londons: two Coys of the 6th Londons on a one Company frontage: Two Coys of the 7th Londons with one Coy of the 7th Londons behind them. The remaining three Coys of the 8th Londons were to be behind the Left Companies. The assembly Positions and objectives of each Company are shown on the Map attached.

(b) Machine Guns.

One Section of "B" Coy. 58th M.G. Bn. was attached to each of the assaulting Battalions and followed the assaulting Troops. They took up positions carefully considered beforehand and as soon as the mist cleared performed very useful work in covering the re-organization and consolidation and protecting the Flanks. The remaining two Sections were also pushed forward at an early hour to cover in conjunction with the Forward Sections the advance of the 173rd. Brigade. Both in the initial stages and later in the day the M.Gs. were disposed in depth. The Section of "C" Coy. 58th M.G. Battalion supported the 2/10th. Londons in the attack on SAILLY LAURETTE by covering fire.

(c) Tanks.

Two Sections of Tanks were to proceed to the West edge of MALARD WOOD and after handing over to the Infantry were to go round the Northern edge of the WOOD, clear up any enemy on the Eastern outskirts of the WOOD and assist in consolidating the positions. Of the remaining Section one Tank was to assist in the capture of SAILLY LAURETTE and one to mop up the Copse North West of the Village. These two Tanks were then to proceed along the Valley Road to CHIPILLY. The other two Tanks after dealing with intervening Copses were to proceed to the Southern edge of MALARD WOOD. One was to remain there until the situation was clear and the other to proceed to the East side of the WOOD. On completion of their tasks the Tanks were to rendezvous in the Valley West of MALARD WOOD.

(d) Artillery.

The Artillery Barrage was to come down at Zero. The Divisional Artillery was considerably strengthened and the guns worked out to about one Gun to 25 yards. The barrage lines was not exactly parallel to the line of advance. A large number of heavy Guns were also brought up for the attack and kept silent till they engaged the enemy Batteries on the day of the attack.
[The Artillery Barrage is shown on the attached Tracing.]

5. The Assembly.

At 10.20 p.m. the 6th. and 7th. Londons started off to their Assembly Positions. Although the enemy put down no concentrated Artillery Shoot the troops had to pass through a considerable amount of Gas and H.E. Shelling, especially in the Valley in K.25. This, and the muddy state of the Trenches delayed the march up. The 6th. Battalion was also interfered with by the troops of the 173rd. Infantry Brigade, but their last Companies were lined up on the tape before Zero. In consequence two Companies of the 8th Londons holding the Line were not able to withdraw and in accordance with orders previously given followed the attacking wave picking up their correct positions after the 6th. and 7th. Londons had passed through.

Our casualties on the tape were light and we were subjected only to normal Machine Gun and Artillery Harassing Fire.

6. <u>The Scene of the Attack.</u>

The Country over which the attack took place was typical of the SOMME Area. The ground consisted of gentle slopes cut by fairly steep Ravines running obliquely to the line of advance. Numerous copses were scattered over the Country which were known to be full of M.Gs. - MALARD WOOD itself was situate on the slope of a Hill directly facing the line of advance. The ground was dry and there was little enemy Barbed Wire and his trenches were shallow and not constructed on any organized system.

7. <u>The First Assault.</u>

Zero was fixed for 4.20 a.m. August 8th. and at 4 a.m. a thick mist came down and from then until 8.30 a.m. visibility was extremely bad. Our Troops went over punctually and kept closely behind the barrage which they followed thus being diverted slightly to the South. The enemy put up a stout resistance in his Front Line but this was rapidly overcome and prisoners immediately began to come in.

After the capture of the enemy Front Line the chief resistance came from the Right flank of the attack - the 6th. Londons, assisted by a Tank, having to fight the whole way forward to MALARD WOOD in K.33.b. Owing to the mist the three attacking Battalions soon got mixed up. The parties of the 8th. Londons detailed to mop up the copses captured many prisoners and Captain R.R. POULTON's Company of the 8th. Londons had heavy fighting in the Ravine in K.27.a. and b. where many prisoners were taken. Captain POULTON who led his Company ably and gallantly in this critical part of the fighting was shot in the back and killed here.

By 8 a.m. MALARD WOOD was held by Units of the Brigade. The Tanks were late in arriving but subsequently came up to the Infantry and rendered valuable assistance. The mist undoubtedly favoured the attack though direction was often lost, but the enemy M.Gs. were comparatively useless against our attacking Troops.

The 10th. Londons completed the capture of SAILLY LAURETTE about 7 a.m. and secured a large number of prisoners, Machine Guns and Trench Mortars. After securing the Village the Battalion advanced 1,000 yards and at 9.30 a.m. they held a commanding position on the Spur towards MALARD WOOD with half a Section of M.Gs. on either Flank and captured M.Gs. were trained along the Road down the Valley from the QUARRY at K.31.c.9.1.

8. <u>Consolidation of First Objective.</u>

As far as can be ascertained our attacking Troops reached MALARD WOOD between 7 and 8 a.m. and parties of the 6th and 8th. Londons pushed through as far as the QUARRY East of MALARD WOOD. At 6.20 a.m. Col. JOHNSTON of the 7th. Londons went forward and finding his Battalion in the Ravine in K.27.a. and b. he ordered them to push forward to the high ground in K.27.b. and get in touch with their flanks. MALARD WOOD was not at this time occupied by our Troops but no enemy were there and two Companies of the 2/2nd. Londons deployed and went through the WOOD without opposition. At 10 a.m. a Company of the 6th. Londons were sent to secure the high ground South of MALARD WOOD and connect up with to the North with the 7th. Londons. This was carried out. No enemy were encountered in MALARD WOOD but Troops moving East of MALARD WOOD came under Rifle and Machine Gun fire. Subsequently the line was reorganized

/by

by Commanding Officers of the 6th. and 7th Londons. The 7th. Londons being on the Left and the 6th Londons on the Right with elements of the 8th. Londons in Reserve, The Line that was held was the Eastern edge of MALARD WOOD. Later in the day touch was obtained on the Left with the 5th. Royal Berks.

At 7.30 p.m. an abortive attempt to carry on the attack was made by the 2/2nd. Londons but they were held up by M.G. fire and withdrew to MALARD WOOD leaving a gap which was filled by the arrival of the 9th. Londons just as the 6th. Londons were moving to the positions.

9. Attack on CHIPILLY.

As the occupation by the enemy of CHIPILLY and the high ground to the North of the Village was a considerable menace to the advance South of the SOMME the 2/10th. Londons were ordered with the aid of a preliminary bombardment to attack at 7.30 p.m. and take CHIPILLY from the West. The leading troops reached the outskirts of CHIPILLY but came under heavy fire from well sited M.Gs. in the Village and on the RIDGE and were driven back after sufferring considerable casualties. It was evident that not only was CHIPILLY held but that there was an appreciable force of the enemy with many M.Gs. holding the high ground which it would be necessary to attack at the same time as the village. Patrols were sent out during the night and reported the enemy on the alert and in the early morning by direction of the Brigadier the Commanding Officer of the 2/10th. Londons saw the Australian Commander on the South of the River and made a personal reconnaissance of the position.

10. Capture of CHIPILLY and CHIPILLY RIDGE on August 8th.

At 11.55 a.m. orders were issued by the 58th. Division for the resumption of the attack at 5.30 p.m. with the object of taking the Second Objective. For this purpose the 8th. Londons were attached to the 175th. Infantry Brigade and the 10th. Londons to the 173rd. Infantry Brigade. The attack was to be carried out by the 175th. Infantry Brigade and the 12th. Division on their Left.

In consequence of reports received that an Australian Patrol had eneterd CHIPILLY during the night of 8/9th. and found it unoccupied and that the Australians in fact then held the Village or part of it, it was decided to capture CHIPILLY RIDGE. At 2 p.m. Brigadier General MAXWELL gave verbal orders to the O.C. of the 6th. Londons to concentrate his Battalion in the S.E. corner of MALARD WOOD and to occupy CHIPILLY and capture the RIDGE to the North with the assistance of three Tanks. One Tank was to go on the North of the Attack the other two along the Road through the Valley, one to CHIPILLY the other to the slopes in K.34.b. The attack was to be supported by a strong patrol of the 7th. Londons on its Left Flank and was to be carried out without Artillery Support. Our Troops were known to be holding posts in CELESTINS WOOD. At 4.15 p.m. the attack was launched and on debouching from CELESTINS WOOD heavy fire was encountered from the CHIPILLY RIDGE and the South West corner of CELESTINS WOOD resulting in heavy casualties. Meanwhile O.C., 10th. Londons moved up his troops under the covering fire of the 6th. Londons towards CHIPILLY Village. After seizing CHIPILLY Village and capturing M.Gs and prisoners his troops pushed their way up from the South and Lieut. IDRIS who was in command of the 6th. London Troops moved North East through CELESTINS WOOD and worked round the

/CHIPILLY

CHIPILLY RIDGE from the North. Both forces reached their objectives simultaneously and at 6 p.m. the success signal was fired. Meantime American Troops had arrived and Lieut. IDRIS handed over to them and withdrew his very tired men to K.31.d.8.2. where they arrived about 5 a.m. on the 10th. Of the three Tanks which took part in the attack one had its exhaust pierced in CHIPILLY after accounting for 4 M.Gs., one was burnt out at K.34.c.5.5. while endeavouring to come to the help of the Infantry while the fate of the third is not known. The task set the 6th. Londons was recognized to be a severe one even if CHIPILLY had been unoccupied. The flat country in the Valley East of CELESTINS WOOD was exposed to heavy fire from the banks on the CHIPILLY RIDGE which overlooked it and after heavy casualties in the initial attack the enveloping movement was carried out with great determination and ability.

11. The Attack of the 7th. Londons on August 9th.

The 7th. Londons were ordered to attack with the main attack at 5.30 p.m. under an Artillery Barrage their objectives being the heights overlooking the SOMME at K.29.central in conjunction with an attack by American Troops on their Right and 175th. Infantry Brigade on GRESSAIRE WOOD on their Left. The 7th. Londons advanced punctually behind the barrage and ahead of the American Troops and encountered severe M.G. fire. They advanced steadily gallantly led by Captain HALLEY-JONES until he fell mortally wounded. On reaching the edge of the WOOD in K.28.central the opposition was less severe and finally the Troops reached K.29.a.10. without officers. Captain JACKSON followed by the C.O. and Adjutant with five Lewis Guns and 35 Other Ranks went forward to command and advanced to the top of the RIDGE at K.29.c.5.7. With the exception of two M.Gs. on the left flank no further opposition was encountered. A party of Americans under Captain PEPPIATT of the 7th. Londons disposed of these and during the night the Line was consolidated with the assistance of American Troops on either flank. Heavy fighting took place further North in GRESSAIRE WOOD and touch was not finally established with the 175th. Infantry Brigade until 5 a.m. on the morning of the 10th.

12. Attack by the 8th. Londons on GRESSAIRE WOOD.

On the afternoon of the 9th. the 8th. Londons were ordered to concentrate and to come under the command of the 175th. Infantry Brigade for the attack on GRESSAIRE WOOD. Very little time was given for any preparation to be made and consequently the advance was not made with the Barrage. The Battalion was placed on the left of the 175th. Infantry Brigade and the whole Brigade went slightly to the Right of their proper Line of advance. This was at once reported by O.C. 8th. Londons and steps were taken to fill the gap which had been created between the 8th Londons and the 12th. Division. The 8th. Londons finally reached a line about 100 yards short of their objective with their Right Flank resting on the BRAY - CORBIE Road. On the way to and on reaching their final positions the Battalion came under considerable Artillery fire. This Battalion was witgdrawn into Support on the night of the 9/10th. having been engaged since taking over the Line on the night 5/6th. August. They had been constantly shelled whilst holding the Line in exposed and extremely muddy trenches.

- 6 -

13. **Enemy Resistance.**

The Barrage put down by the enemy on our Front Line in reply to our Barrage at Zero on August 8th. was not heavy and he did not put down a Machine Gun Barrage. Until the evening of the 8th. August our new positions were not shelled but afterwards our positions in, and in front of MALARD WOOD and the Valleys immediately behind were shelled at intervals, SAILLY LAURETTE was not shelled at all. Both on the 8th and 9th of August the enemy Infantry and Machine Guns fought well, hand to hand fighting took place, and in many instances the enemy's resistance was only broken down at the point of the Bayonet.

14. **Relief of the Brigade.**

On the morning of the 10th. the Line was re-organized on the CHIPILLY RIDGE and patrols were sent out to the East of the SOMME. At dusk American Troops commenced to relieve the Brigade and, as relieved the Units bivouaced in the neighbourhood.

15. **Captures.**

It is impossible to state precisely the captures made by the Brigade. It is estimated that at least 1,000 unwounded prisoners were taken, Large quantities of S.A.A. and Field Artillery Ammunition were also captured and stores of all kinds. In addition 23 Guns, 36 Trench Mortars and 182 Machine Guns were counted. A considerable number of these were however removed by Battalions of the Australian A.I.F.

16. **Casualties.**

The casualties in the Brigade were as follows :-

	Officers.	Other Ranks.
6th. London Regiment.	12	308
7th. London Regiment.	14	314
8th. Londons Regiment.	11	292
174th. L.T.M. Battery.	1	6
TOTAL -	38	920
10th. London Regiment (attached.)	11	185

17. **Conclusion.**

The Brigade met with success in the attack on 8th. August and captured their objectives. Owing to the mist and difficulties of communication and observation it cannot be precisely stated at what time their objectives were reached but advanced troops were in their final Line at an early hour. On the 9th. August the Brigade was called upon to take a difficult position with tired troops and depleted Battalions. The task set them was accomplished though with heavy casualties - the C.O'S. of the 6th. and 7th. Londons showing great determination and skill in the difficult operation. The 10th. Londons who had suffered least on the first day, though no longer under the orders of the Brigade on August 9th. by co-operating with the attack of the 6th. Londons on the CHIPILLY RIDGE very greatly contributed to the success of this operation.

/The

The Tanks though late in arriving on August 8th. rendered valuable assistance in destroying M.G. nests. Owing to the mist no exact account of their performances can be given and during the whole of the operation close liaison was not established between them and the Infantry. Valuable assistance was given by "B" Coy. 58th. M.G. Bn. both in the attack and in consolidating our positions. The Brigade suffered a considerable loss on the afternoon of the 9th. when Major PALLISER (Commanding "B" Coy.) was killed whilst xxxxxxxx organizing the advance on CHIPILLY RIDGE. The 174th. L.T.M.Battery unfortunately lost their Guns by Shell fire and subsequently filled the role of moppers up and captured many prisoners.

Throughout the operation the leadership of Officers and N.C.O's was good, and junior as well as Senior Officers showed initiative in dealing with unexpected situations. The spirit of the men was excellent, they closed with the enemy unhesitatingly and showed great determination in overcoming the resistance of the enemy.

A Report on Communications is attached.

Emmanuel
Brigadier General
Commanding 174th Inf Brigade

21 August 1918

174th. Infantry Brigade.

Report on Signal Communications during operations 8th. to 12th. August 1918.

(1) The proposed scheme was as follows:-
A main trunk route, including lines, visual, wireless and runners, was to be established from Brigade Headquarters, J22 d2.3 to "Crump Exchange" K19 c4.1 (before Zero) and thence to "Malard Exchange" near K27 a2.5 (after Zero), this trunk route was to be run under Divisional arrangements, and units could use any point on the route as most convenient.

(2) Crump Exchange was not established in working order till about 8.0 a.m. on the 8th. This was due in part to faulty organisation and in part to unexpected difficulty in maintaining the armoured cable running up COOTAMUNDRA TRENCH.
Once established Crump Exchange worked fairly well till closed (lines being put through) on 10th. inst.

(3) Malard Exchange was established at K26 b8.2 about 10.0 a.m. on the 8th. Units had trouble in finding it.
This exchange had a very great press of messages but worked well on the whole.
Visual could not be established to Crump Exchange but was eventually obtained to the Gully Visual Station.

(4) When Brigade Headquarters moved to the Quarry K21 c8.3 on the evening of the 8th., communication forward depended on a single line to Malard Exchange, and was very slow.

(5) Visual was useful on many occasions, especially during the attack on the afternoon of the 9th. when flags were used.

(6) Wireless was most useful, especially to Division when the Divisional lines were overcrowded with calls.

(7) Runners worked well, except for two or three runs where the runners lost their way.

(8) Pigeons worked excellently, every message sent arriving. More pigeons needed in future.

(9) **Faults and Difficulties.**
  (a) Better organisation of the pre Zero communications, and of the Forward party was needed, the instructions for the latter were changed at the last moment.
  (b) Tanks break and carry away most lines that they cross. This is going to be a serious problem in all Tank attacks.
  (c) All parties and Exchanges should be established by an officer, who should be in charge of the whole party, and not merely of one branch of its work.
  (d) Runners, even when trained in map reading, often fail to find their way off a map. This is understandable at night, but should not occur by daylight. This difficulty was specially found with mounted orderlies.

(10) Great assistance was given to the Signal Officer of 174th. Infantry Brigade by O.C.Signals 58th. Divisional Arty., and by the Officer in Charge of wireless 58th. Division.

Lieut.
Brigade Signal Officer.
174th. Infantry Brigade.

Ref. Sheet 62c N.W.

174th Bde

REPORT ON OPERATIONS.
(August 25th - 31st).

1. **Preliminary.**

    The Brigade who had moved up in stages from ROUND WOOD were concentrated in bivouacs in L.2. and L.3. on the morning of August 25th. The 175th Brigade, after a successful attack at dawn were holding a line running from the West of TRIGGER WOOD to BRONFAY FARM. The 173rd Brigade, who had received orders to provide an advance guard, were held up. Their advanced troops being in portion of BILLON WOOD where severe fighting took place during the day. At 2.25 p.m. the Brigade received orders to relieve the 175th Brigade in the Line. At 6 p.m. this order was cancelled and the Brigade was ordered to advance to the support of the 173rd Brigade, and push out patrols as far as possible.

2. **The approach march, 25/26th August.**

    Units left their assembly positions in L.2. and L.3. at 7 p.m. and moved forward. The 7th Londons on the right, the 8th on the left with the 6th in support. The approach march was accomplished with difficulty, the night was very dark, a violent thunder storm drenched our troops from 9 p.m. to 10.30 p.m. and they came under strong hostile artillery fire on the march up, especially in BILLON WOOD and its vicinity. Major PRIESTLEY Commanding 8th Londons, was severely wounded and the 8th and 6th Londons for a time lost touch. Touch, however, was eventually obtained and also with the Australians on the right.

3. **The attack 26th August.**

    At 1.30 a.m. orders were issued for the enemy positions to be attacked at 4.10 a.m. A barrage was to be put down at that hour on the enemy trench line CREST AVENUE A.27.d.8.7. - A.28.a.4.9. On our left the 173rd Brigade was to co-operate and on the right the 9th Australian Brigade was to make a similar attack. The Northern Brigade Boundary was the north edge of BILLON WOOD. The Southern Boundary from F.26.c.1.0 to F.27. Central and thence due East. The 7th Battalion were ordered to carry out this attack with the 8th in close support and the 6th in Reserve.

    The attack was accordingly launched, the 7th Battalion in spite of the short notice moving forward at the appointed time closely supported by three companies of the 8th Battalion, the remaining company of the 8th having already pushed through BILLON WOOD. As the attack developed elements of the 8th Battalion got mixed up with the 7th Battalion but the 8th Battalion as a whole moved up on the left of the 7th Battalion, establishing themselves between the 7th and the 173rd Brigade. The enemy replied to our attack by heavy shelling of BILLON WOOD and desultory shelling of the surrounding country. The infantry resistance was overcome but the attack was held up in places by well-placed M.G's in the banks and copses with which the country abounded.

/At 9 a.m.

- 2 -

Para. 2 (Contd.)

At 9 a.m. we held a general line in touch with the Australians at Copse "N" to Copse "D" with posts out in front and the 8th Battalion in close support in Copse "B" and protecting our left flank, the position of the troops on our left flank being at the time uncertain.

The enemy M.G's were in considerable strength on the road and old huts in A.27.b. and d. Touch was subsequently obtained with the 173rd Brigade in Copse "C" and the Australians working round to the road in A.27.d. our line was finally established on the general line of the SUZANNE - MARICOURT Road.

3. The attack of the 27th August.

At 8.50 p.m. orders were issued to carry on the advance. The assaulting Battalions were the 7th Londons on the right and the 6th Londons on the left. The 9th Australian Brigade on the right and the 173rd Brigade on the left also attacking. The scheme of the attack was explained verbally to C.O's and the starting point and general scheme of the barrage. The actual barrage map was not received at Bde.H.Q. until 3.15 a.m.

The objective of the Brigade was originally fixed as the old British trenches from the N.E. corner of FARGNY WOOD to F.23.a.5.9. Subsequently an alteration was made, the 9th Australian Brigade taking no part in the operation on FARGNY WOOD, but supporting the attack by proceeding along the North bank of the SOMME to FARGNY MILL.

The attack was launched under a creeping artillery barrage at 4.55 a.m., each assaulting Battalion having two companies in front and two in support. The 6th Londons were reported at an early hour to have reached their objective, one company under Captain BURT-SMITH on the left of the attack taking 100 prisoners. The 7th Battalion had a more difficult task; they came under considerable M.G. and Artillery fire on the High ground in F.28.a. and from the Northern edge of FARGNY WOOD, and at 11.30 a.m. were apparently not East of BLACK STREET and were not in touch with the troops on their flanks. Subsequently one company of the 7th worked down BRIDGE STREET and established themselves on the N.E. corner of FARGNY WOOD and, obtaining touch with the 6th Battalion on the left, reached the line of their objective.

None of our troops were in the ground east of FARGNY WOOD and a report that the Australians were in FARGNY MILL subsequently turned out to be false, but posts were established by the Australians at the S.E. corner of the wood, and by our troops North of the wood. The situation in the Wood remained obscure but at the close of the day the wood was cleared without resistance, a few prisoners being captured.

4. The attack on August 28th.

At 9.45 pm. orders were issued to carry on the attack at 4.55 a.m. next morning. The objectives being the trench line A.24.e.3.0. to SUPPORT COPSE. Any success was to be exploited if possible and posts were to be established at the QUARRY A.30.b.5.3. in Liaison with the Australians and at A.24.d.9.1. The 9th Australian Brigade

/attacked

Para. 4. (contd.) attacked on the right and the 173rd Brigade on the left. The attack was carried out by the 8th Londons on the right and the 6th Londons on the left. The two Battalions had to advance across a deep valley and up the slopes beyond where they met with considerable resistance. The attack was, however, carried out with complete success and reports were received at 9.15 a.m. at Bde. H.Q. that all objectives had been taken, and many prisoners. The 8th Londons pushed out a strong patrol and established posts in touch with the Australians in QUARRY in A.30.b. and subsequently put out posts from there along the PERONNE Road to the objective in A.24.c.

The 6th Londons on reaching their objective were subjected to heavy M.G. fire from the East and N.E. Major VENNING, O.C. 6th Londons proceeded with six men and a Lewis Gun to drive out enemy M.G's in A.24.b.central. This he successfully did in spite of heavy M.G. fire from the north. This post was then heavily attacked from the east and bombed by a party of enemy working up from the South. Surrounded by large parties of the enemy after firing off their ammunition his party withdrew to a point 100 yards East of SUPPORT COPSE. In view of the heavy M.G. fire coming from the left flank it was obvious that any attempt to establish a post here would result in heavy casualties and no further attempt was made until dark, when under cover of a short artillery bombardment a strong patrol pushed out and established a post well in front of our lines at about A.24.d.central. After three days' continuous fighting the Brigade was relieved the same night by the 175th Brigade and bivouacked on the battle-field of August 26th.

5. During the three days' fighting the Brigade captured over 500 prisoners and many M.G's. Throughout they were met with determined enemy resistance and large number of well-sited M.G's. Though they were not shelled on their assembly positions a fairly heavy enemy artillery fire was each day put down on their new positions and support lines after the objectives had been reached. The German Infantry, apart from the machine gunners, did not as a rule fight well and at times surrendered fairly easily, and our casualties were caused chiefly by enfilade machine gun fire and to a lesser extent by artillery fire.

6. Casualties.

Casualties August 25th/27th.

	Officers.	O.R.
6th Londons.	10	223
7th Londons.	13	275
8th Londons.	7	156
Total.	30	654

7. The approach for the attack of August 31st.

On the morning of August 30th the Brigade received orders to pass through the 175th Brigade and to proceed in advanced guard formation with three groups of the R.F.A. at the disposal of the Brigade. Orders were accordingly

/issued

Para. 7.
(contd.)
issued and busses provided for the Brigade to take them from MARICOURT to the Junction of roads by HEM WOOD in H.3 a. It soon transpired that the 175th Brigade had met with strong enemy resistance east of MARRIERES WOOD and that the advance could only continue by means of an organised attack. The battalions reached the embussing point after dark and marched to assembly positions in the valley in B.23.a. and B.23.c. An officer from each Battalion reported to Bde. H.Q. after his Battalion had reached their assembly positions and received the new orders for the attack that was to take place at 5.10 a.m. next morning. These orders could not be issued until 11.15 p.m.

8. The attack on August 31st.

The attack was carried out by the 6th Londons on the right and the 8th Londons on the left. On the right the 9th Australian Brigade and on the left the 47th Division also attacked. The starting line for the barrage was a line B.24.d.2.2. - B.18.b.2.0. west of MARRIERES WOOD and the objective the high ground immediately west of the RANCOURT - PERONNE Road. No guides were available for taking the troops to the starting positions and very little time for explaining the situation. The night was pitch dark and the country almost destitute of any guiding features.

All battalions, however, succeeded in reaching their forming up positions behind the barrage before Zero. Battalions had been ordered to assemble at least 400 yards behind the barrage line and this was done. The subsequent operation was also a most difficult one. MARRIERES WOOD was known to be strongly defended and was situate on the steep slope of a hill directly facing the line of advance. Beyond this again was a valley rising up to the slopes beyond, while the whole country east of the wood was dominated by the high ground N.E. of the village of BOUCHAVESNES. In spite of these difficulties the two assaulting Battalions, assisted by two companies of the 7th Londons, captured all their objectives. Nearly 400 prisoners were taken in MARRIERES WOOD and many Machine gunners who fired their guns to the last were killed with the bayonet. The units soon became mixed up but on reaching their objective, pushed out a strong patrol which established itself firmly at the Old QUARRY at C.20.central and got in touch with the Australians. The left of our line being at C.14.a.3.0. in touch with the 47th Division.

Great difficulty was experienced in re-organising, owing to heavy fire from east and North-east of BOUCHAVESNES, but this was done and at night the 173rd Brigade continued the attack, our troops remaining in their positions until relieved the following night by two companies of the Life Guards M.G. Battalion.

9. Captures.

Nearly 400 prisoners were captured in the day's operation two 4.2 Howitzers, two 77 mm. guns, a few Light Trench Mortars and many Machine Guns.
The prisoners included eight officers.

/10. Casualties.

10. Casualties, August 31st.

Our casualties were as follows :-

	Officers.	O.R.
6th Battalion.	3	90
7th Battalion.	2	20
8th Battalion.	7	150
Total.	12	260

11. General Conclusions.

The Brigade had been made up since the fighting of August 8/9th, mainly by young soldiers with four months' training only and no previous experience in the line. All Battalions were severely tested, but all ranks went unflinchingly to their objectives each day, carrying out four attacks in six days and on two occasions having a most difficult night approach march to do on unknown and difficult country. Our barrage was on each occasion good and as far as can be ascertained, accurate. On each occasion it remained on the Start Line for 15 minutes. This enabled the troops to correct their positions, as in no case was it possible to arrange for a taped assembly line.

Orders were, owing to the nature of the operations, received late in the day and were consequently issued very late to Battalion Commanders, thus making their task exceptionally difficult. Great credit must be given to Battalion Commanders and their Staff for having at short notice on August 26th and August 30th brought their Battalions to the correct place and in time to follow closely the barrage. The value of conferences in the field with Battalion Commanders was clearly demonstrated.

On every occasion it was found impossible, without heavy and undue casualties, to exploit our successes to any considerable extent. The enemy invariably holding commanding positions, expecially beyond our left flank. As a general rule his 77 mm. guns did not fire but he shelled our positions from 10 a.m. to 6 p.m. daily with 4.2's and 5.9's. Apparently he then withdrew his guns to new positions to deal with the next day's attack.

His machine gunners fought stoutly and fired their guns till surrounded, when they surrendered. Towards the close of operations, our men were not so willing to take the machine gunners prisoners, and in MARRIERES WOOD many were killed with the bayonet at or near their gun positions.

Col Causton's
comments on
the "Chipilly" spur
controversy
9/10 August 1918

58th Bn
P/a
27/8/'47.
Geo.

Col Causton
For Australians

NARRATIVE OF OPERATIONS.

Period 8th to 13th August 1918.

THE CONCENTRATION OF THE 58th DIVISION FOR THE ATTACK ON AUGUST 8th.

During the period August 1st - 6th, the concentration of the Division for the attack was carried out, the greatest secrecy being observed throughout. All movements of troops took place by night, and men, transport and guns remained carefully concealed in woods and villages during the day.

On the night of August 4/5th, the 173rd and 174th Brigades together with the 4th Suffolks, the 504 Field Coy and 511 Field Coy. and affiliated M.G. Companies were moved by bus and road to the FRANVILLERS area whence the 174th Brigade marched straight to bivouacs in deep Valley running up from the SOMME just west of SAILLY-LE-SEC.

On the following night, 5/6th, this Brigade relieved that portion of the front held by the 18th Division between CHIPP LANE (see map "C" attached) and the SOMME, and on the night of the 6th the 173rd Brigade moved into the Valley vacated by the 174th Brigade. The 175th Brigade were meanwhile being bussed up from VIGNACOURT to the BOIS ESCADOEUSE and completed their move on August 7th.

During this period all the Divisional Artillery together with three attached Brigades of Field Artillery who were to cover the attack, were moving up ammunition and preparing positions into which the guns were to be moved during the night before the attack.

On the evening of August 7th the concentration of the Division and its neighbours was complete.

The dispositions of the Division in detail at dawn on the 8th being as shown on the attached map.

GENERAL PLAN OF THE ATTACK.

The whole operation composed an attack to be made from MORLANCOURT to MOREUIL the primary objective being the old AMIENS Defence Line constructed in 1914, the recapture of which would release the important Railway and road junctions of AMIENS from gun fire. The front of the attack included the whole of the Fourth British Army under Sir H.RAWLINSON and of a French Army on their right.

The special role of the III Corps composed of the 18th and 58th Divisions was - operating North of the SOMME - to form a protective flank to the more extended advance of the Australian and Canadian Corps South of the river.

This was to be effected by capturing and holding a strong defensive position facing N.E. on the general line BOIS GRESSAIRE - BRIQUETERIE, and by forming a defensive flank along the heights overlooking MORLANCOURT from the South. The 58th Division was entrusted with the carrying out of the first part of the operation whilst the 18th Division on their left were ordered to form a defensive flank overlooking MORLANCOURT. The importance of the III Corps' operation, to a successful advance by the Australians South of the River, was obvious from a study of the ground.

The reaches of the SOMME between CORBIE and BRAY have very steep banks rising to cliffs in places and a resolute enemy

/entrenched

NARRATIVE OF OPERATIONS.

Period 8th to 13th August 1918.

THE CONCENTRATION OF THE 58th DIVISION FOR THE ATTACK OF AUGUST 8th.

During the period August 1st - 6th, the concentration of the Division for the attack was carried out, the greatest secrecy being observed throughout. All movements of troops took place by night, and men, transport and guns remained carefully concealed in woods and villages during the day.

On the night of August 4/5th, the 173rd and 174th Brigades together with the 4th Suffolks, the 504 Field Coy and 511 Field Coy. and affiliated M.G. Companies were moved by bus and road to the FRANVILLERS area whence the 174th Brigade marched straight to bivouacs in deep Valley running up from the SOMME just west of SAILLY-LE-SEC.

On the following night, 5/6th, this Brigade relieved that portion of the front held by the 18th Division between CHIMP LANE (see map "C" attached) and the SOMME, and on the night of the 6th the 173rd Brigade moved into the Valley vacated by the 174th Brigade. The 175th Brigade were meanwhile being bussed up from VIGNACOURT to the BOIS ESCADOEUSE and completed their move on August 7th.

During this period all the Divisional Artillery together with three attached Brigades of Field Artillery who were to cover the attack, were moving up ammunition and preparing positions into which the guns were to be moved during the night before the attack.

On the evening of August 7th the concentration of the Division and its neighbours was complete.

The dispositions of the Division in detail at dawn on the 8th being as shown on the attach map.

GENERAL PLAN OF THE ATTACK.

The whole operation composed an attack to be made from MORLANCOURT to MORUIL the primary objective being the old AMIENS Defence Line constructed in 1914; the recapture of which would release the important Railway and road junctions of AMIENS from gun fire. The front of the attack included the whole of the Fourth British Army under Sir H. RAWLINSON and of a French Army on their right.

The special role of the III Corps composed of the 18th and 58th Divisions was - operating North of the SOMME - to form a protective flank to the more extended advance of the Australian and Canadian Corps South of the river.

This was to be effected by capturing and holding a strong defensive position facing N.E. on the general line BOIS GRESSAIRE - BRIQUETERIE, and by forming a defensive flank along the heights overlooking MORLANCOURT from the South. The 58th Division was entrusted with the carrying out of the first part of the operation whilst the 18th Division on their left were ordered to form a defensive flank overlooking MORLANCOURT. The importance of the III Corps' operation, to a successful advance by the Australians South of the River, was obvious from a study of thegfound.

The reaches of the SOMME between CORBIE and BRAY have very steep banks rising to cliffs in places and a resolute enemy

/entrenched

- 2 -

entrenches anywhere along the heights on the North bank, between SAILLY LAURETTE and CHIPILLY would be able to enfilade with deadly effect troops advancing on the Southern Bank of the River.

THE SPECIAL PLAN OF THE 58th DIVISION.

The boundaries and objectives of the 58th Division and the 18th Division on its left are shewn on Map "C" attached.

The plan provided for the first objective the GREEN line being captured by the 174th Brigade and the 2/10th London Regt. attached, the latter under command of Lieut.-Colonel E.P.CAWSTON, were given the special mission of capturing SAILLY LAURETTE, whilst the assault on the GREEN line itself was entrusted to the 6th and 7th London Regts. with the 8th London Regt. moving in close support to the leading Battalions. That portion of the GREEN line allotted to the 18th Division was to be attacked by two Brigades, the 53rd and the 55th, each attacking with two Battalions leading.

After the capture of the GREEN line there was to be a pause of one hour after which the 173rd Brigade with the 53rd Brigade on their left were to pass through the Battalions of the 174th Brigade and capture the RED line, which comprised the whole of the CHIPILLY SPUR - a bare upland commanding a wide expanse of country South of the river.

The attack by the 173rd Brigade was entrusted to the 3rd London Regt. under command of Lieut.-Colonel SANDARS,MC. on the left and the 2/4th London Regt. under command of Lieut.-Colonel Grover,DSO. on the right with the 2/2nd London Regt. moving in close support. Simultaneously with the advance of the 173rd Brigade the 53rd Brigade of the 18th Division on their left were to complete the day's work by the capture of GRESSAIRE WOOD and the brickyard.

The attack was to be covered by a Field Artillery creeping barrage giving an average intensity of one gun to every 25 yds. (90 - 18-pdrs. and 30 - 4.5" Hows. were allotted to the 58th Division for the attack) whilst the deep valleys and gulleys running into the SOMME were to be dealt with by a Howitzer barrage jumping from valley to valley. The heavy artillery bombarding all known gun positions, machine gun nests and villages known to be strongly held.

The attack was further supported by 12 Tanks two were specially detailed to co-operate with the 2/10th London Regt. in their attack on SAILLY LAURETTE, subsequently assisting in the clearing of the Southern end of MALARD WOOD, whilst the remaining ten were detailed to co-operate with the 174th Brigade and subsequently to assist the attack of the 173rd Brigade on the CHIPILLY SPUR.

The 4th Suffolks, (Pioneer Bn.) of the 58th Division under the command of Lieut.-Colonel COPEMAN, CMG. were specially detailed to dig a series of strong posts along the BROWN line,(see map "C" attached) so as to provide a strong line of resistance in case of strong counter attacks forcing back the leading troops.

The Machine Gun Battalion were given such tasks as providing covering fire for the advancing Infantry and to assist in holding the ground when captured. In addition each of the assaulting Battalions was accompanied by one section of Machine Guns.

/Other

Other features of the attack were the use of Supply Tanks and of low flying aeroplanes both to drown the noise of the assembling tanks and for dropping ammunitions for the use of the leading troops and machine guns.

The 175th Infantry Brigade were in Corps Reserve for the attack and were concentrated in the BOIS ESCARDONEUSE at Zero on August 8th.

THE GERMAN ATTACK ON THE 18th DIVISION.

Before going on to describe the events of August 8th it is important to give some account of the German attack delivered on August 6th against the 54th Brigade.

At 4.15 am. the enemy put down a heavy barrage of shrapnel and trench mortars on our trenches from about 300 yards South of CRUMP LANE to about the line of the MORLANCOURT-CORBIE ROAD and followed it up with an attack with about 3 battalions.

At the time the 8th London Regt. were in process of relieving the 2nd Bedford Regt. from CRUMP LANE Southwards and the attack extended South of CRUMP LANE sufficiently far to involve the frontage occupied by the two left Companies. On this two Company frontage the enemy was repulsed, but North of CRUMP LANE about three lines of trenches were penetrated and number of prisoners taken by the enemy, and this penetration made it necessary to withdraw the outpost line on the Divisional front although the front line remained intact.

The immediate counter attack by troops of the 18th Division partially restored the situation but at 11.30 a.m. on August 6th the enemy still held AMMONS and CLONCURRY Trenches.

A further organised counter attack by troops of the 18th Division delivered at 4.40 a.m. on August 7th retook all the ground lost except a pocket towards the North end of CLONCURRY Trench.

The enemy's penetration of the 18th Divisional front admitted him into some of the forward dumps and gun positions awaiting occupation for the attack, and two men of the 50th Divisional Artillery in charge of these dumps were captured.

It seemed inevitable that the enemy would now become aware of the great attack that was impending either from his examination of prisoners or any way from the discovery of dumps and gun positions so far forward. As it turned out, however, the significance of these dumps appears to have completely escaped him and the statements of all prisoners agree that the attack on August 8th came as a complete surprise.

The only serious consequence of this attack was that the heavy losses incurred by the 54th Brigade both in the original attack and in their subsequent counter attacks to regain the lost trenches made it necessary to replace them by the 36th Infantry Brigade of the 12th Division for the attack on August 8th.

The withdrawal of the outpost line and the belief that the enemy might have recognized our gun positions made it necessary to recast the Artillery programme with new gun positions and a start line about 300 yards further West.

This was, however, successfully completed in spite of the shortness of time available.

HISTORY OF THE 58th DIVISION.

THE BATTLE ON AUGUST 8th.
(The capture of MALARD WOOD).

The hour for the attack (Zero) was fixed for 4.20 a.m. A dense mist prevailed at this hour and increased in density until about 8.30 a.m. after which it rapidly lifted so that by 10 a.m. it had entirely cleared. This mist undoubtedly saved us many casualties from machine gun fire, as all movements in the earlier stages of the attack were completely screened; on the other hand it just as certainly contributed to the loss of direction, and confusion, which took place after the first objective had been taken.

The Tanks were affected to an even greater extent than the Infantry, as their field of vision is limited at the best of times.

The 174th Brigade carried out their assembly undetected by the enemy and casualties during the forming up were slight.

The attack started punctually, with all troops moving forward close up to the barrage and although the enemy put up a stout fight his resistance in the front trenches was quickly overcome, and groups of prisoners were soon hurrying down the tracks leading from the front line, many running in their anxiety to get out of range of their own Artillery fire.

Identifications showed that we were opposed by the 27th WURTEMBURG Division - first class troops, who had only just come into the line after 8 weeks rest.

The chief resistance was encountered on the right where the 6th Battalion, assisted by one Tank had to fight hard all the way to MALARD WOOD, arriving there about 7.30 a.m. Very little opposition was actually encountered in the Wood and eventually the line was established along its Eastern edge.

The advance of the 174th Brigade was closely followed by the front Battalions of the 173rd Brigade so much so that in the dense fog some of their leading troops over-ran and became mixed up with the Battalions of the 174th Brigade.

The original intention had been for the leading Battalions of the 173rd Brigade (the 3rd and 2/4th Londons) to work round the Northern edge of MALARD WOOD to their assembly positions on the GREEN Line but owing to their being so mixed up with the 174th Brigade, this plan had to be abandoned and they passed through MALARD WOOD with the leading Brigade.

Immediately on debouching from the Wood both Battalions came under very heavy machine gun fire and were unable to reach their forming up line, in addition the 2/4th Londons in trying to overcome the opposition on their forming up line lost direction and became mixed up with units of the 18th Division.

In consequence of this difficulty in reaching the GREEN line only a few troops reinforced by the 2/2nd London Regt. were able to continue the advance when the barrage lifted, and only a few of those appear to have reached the steep cliff overlooking the SOMME.

The 2/2nd London Regt. moving forward to reinforce this line came under heavy machine gun fire from the CHIPILLY SPUR and after suffering severe loss had to retire to the cover of MALARD WOOD. Meanwhile on the right the enemy was still in

/possession

possession of the CHIPILLY SPUR from which he was interfering considerably with the advance of the Australians
South of the river. Many machine guns were installed on
this ridge and in some cases batteries of guns with their
triggers bound together were worked by single men from
the security of deep dug-outs. Any attempt to advance
towards CHIPILLY was met with a storm of machine gun fire.

No change in the general situation occurred during
the day and the line remained just outside MALARD WOOD.
The 2/10th London Regt. were therefore ordered to attack and
capture CHIPILLY at 7.30 p.m. so as to clear the way for the
Australians South of the river. Under cover of a heavy
bombardment the leading troops forced their way into the
outskirts of the Village but were unable to advance further
in the face of heavy machine gun and rifle fire and
eventually they had to withdraw to a position just outside
it. The attack by the 2/10th Londons on CHIPILLY brought
to an end the first day's fighting and the approximate line
held is shewn by the start line (in VIOLET) on attached
Map "C".

Although the full objectives of the day had not been
attained very considerable results had been attained and a
severe blow dealt to the enemy who was now considerably
disorganised. A large number of prisoners had been counted
and number of guns, Field and Heavy, not to mention hundreds
of machine guns, trench mortars and masses of equipment
abandoned by the enemy in his flight had been captured. Large
numbers of his dead and wounded were also scattered over the
newly captured ground.

In concluding this account of the first day's fighting
it will be of interest to record certain details of the
fighting not included above.

Although the contact aeroplanes constantly reported
the arrival of our men on the final objective it does not
appear in the light of subsequent knowledge that these reports
were correct, at the most only a handful of men could have
reached the bluff overlooking the SOMME and ETINEHEM and these
must speedily have either become casualties or been forced
to withdraw in the face of the heavy machine gun fire from
both CHIPILLY and GRESSAIRE WOOD.

The Tanks rendered very valuable assistance, and their
sudden appearance out of the mist in the middle of the enemy
infantry caused a panic in several cases. One Tank under
Lieut. Mc.GUIRE after losing its way in the mist came in
contact with enemy machine-gun nests S.E. of MORLANCOURT
and destroyed these taking 300 prisoners. Several Tanks were
knocked out by direct hits and at the end of the day only
six were fit for further action.

Captured enemy machine guns were used on several
occasions with good effect against retreating parties of
Germans.

The capture of SAILLY LAURETTE by the 2/10th Londons
under Lieut.-Colonel E.P. CAWSTON, was a very well executed
manoeuvre and by 6.30 a.m. not only had the whole village
been cleared but this Battalion had captured the QUARRY and
sunken road N.E. of the Village with a large number of local
reinforcements. In all it is estimated that this Battalion
accounted for 150 killed and about 500 prisoners of which
150 came from the QUARRY.

/The

The attack of the 18th Division was successful in attaining its first objective but as in the case of the 58th Division the confusion and loss of direction on the first objective prevented the attack being pressed home.

The attack by the Australians and Canadians on the right met with great success and all objectives were attained except on the left where resistance of the Germans on the CHIPILLY SPUR made an advance on the South bank of the SOMME past this Village very difficult.

The need for an immediate resumption of the offensive whilst the enemy was still in his present state of disorganization was paramount. Orders were, therefore issued for the attack to be resumed at dawn by the 175th Infantry Brigade and the 131st American Regt. on their right.

The 175th Infantry Brigade, although it had not been engaged in actual fighting on August 8th had, nevertheless done a considerable amount of marching. In the first instance the 9th and 12th Battalions were placed at the disposal of the 18th Division, and ordered by them to move up to the BALLARAT - ROMA Line. Later on, the 9th London Regt. were sent to the assistance of the 173rd Brigade and eventually dug themselves in on the Eastern edge of MALARD WOOD. The 12th London Regt. were sent at the same time to fill a gap on the front of the 36th Brigade (18th Div) but by the time they arrived it was dark and the gap had already been filled so they dug in behind the advanced troops of the 36th Brigade.

The attack ordered for dawn on the 9th had eventually to be postponed as in the darkness it was found impossible to collect the troops concerned or to move forward the American Regt. in time to co-operate.

THE CAPTURE OF GRESSAIRE WOOD AND THE CHIPILLY SPUR.

The attack that it had been intended should take place at dawn on the 9th was finally ordered for 5.30 p.m. on that afternoon. Orders to that effect could not be got out to the Brigades concerned until 12 noon, so very little time was available for making preparations. The assaulting troops consisted of the 131st American Regt. on the right and the 175th Brigade on the left whilst the 36th Brigade of the 18th Division attacked on the left of the 175th Brigade.

The boundaries and objectives of the day's attack are set forth on map "C" attached.

The 175th Brigade for the purpose of this action was composed of the 9th Londons and 12th Londons, 8th Londons and 5th Royal Berkshires, the latter two Battalions being lent by the 174th and 37th Brigades respectively.

The actual assaulting troops reading from left to right were the 8th Londons, 12th Londons, 3 Bn. 131st American Regt., 1st Bn. 131st American Regt.

In conjunction with this attack the 173rd Brigade were first to sideslip and take up a line between the QUARRY just East of MALARD WOOD and the SOMME to be in position by 3.30 pm. and then to advance and capture the RED line and CHIPILLY SPUR, at the same time as the attack further North, therefore forming a defensive flank for the Americans and clearing the way for the Australians South of the river.

The whole attack being covered by a creeping barrage which, after dwelling for 25 minutes on the Start Line was to creep forward at the rate of 10 yards in 4 minutes.

During the morning Brig.-General MAXWELL-SCOTT had to relinquish the command of the 175th Brigade owing to ill-health and was succeeded by Lt.-Colonel POWELL, Commanding the 9th London Regt.

Owing to the shortness of the notice received, verbal instructions had to be conveyed to all the Commanders concerned, neither was there any time to reconnoitre a forming up line, and to add to the difficulties the enemy continued to shell MALARD WOOD and its vicinity heavily throughout the day. The American Battalions taking part had to double the last mile in order to reach the forming up line in time. Notwithstanding all these difficulties, the assaulting troops were formed up only eight minutes after Zero, and went forward with great dash immediately the barrage lifted.

The Germans were completely surprised and many of their infantry seized with panic abandoned their arms and equipment and surrendered or ran away as soon as our men appeared. An hour after the attack started, the track running from the North end of MALARD WOOD to the line was thick with returning German prisoners many of these unaccompanied by any escort were running in panic to escape the heavy Artillery fire which the German Artillery was now directing on to this track, whilst the huddled heaps by the side of the track bore witness to the accuracy of this fire. By 8 p.m. it became clear that all objectives had been captured but both the 8th and 12th Battalions had suffered fairly severe casualties from machine gun fire and the 8th Londons had not obtained touch with the 12th Division.

In view of this situation the 5th Royal Berkshire were ordered to proceed to the assistance of the 8th Londons either by consolidating in depth behind them or by prolonging their

/left

left flank to join up with the 12th Division, and the 8th Londons were ordered forward in close support to the 12th Londons. Meanwhile the Battalions of the 173rd Brigade had reached the sunken road running North from CHIPILLY but had been unable to get further in face of enfilade machine gun fire from the terraces North of CHIPILLY. However the 2/10th Londons who were acting under their orders in close support working their way through CHIPILLY and all its Northern edge took the enemy machine guns on the terraces in flank and reverse. Fierce fighting took place for these guns but eventually they were all silenced, and the crews killed or captured, about 100 prisoners being taken in all.

The capture of CHIPILLY and the terraces soon brought about the fall of the whole SPUR and by 11 p.m. that night all objectives set for the day had been taken.

The artillery barrage for this action was very good and the enemy only retaliated with desultory shelling. Machine gun fire however was very intense and caused many casualties especially among the Americans. Most of the machine guns were installed in the sunken road near the brickyard and on the CHIPILLY terraces. The chief difficulty experienced was the keeping of direction in such featureless country. The Officer Commanding the 8th Londons to assist in preserving direction specially detailed officers to march in front of his attacking troops. These officers, however, were all killed or wounded and the whole attack edged off to the right causing a gap to appear on the left of our line.

The attack, however, was a complete success and the dash with which all ranks went forward in spite of the heavy marching and fighting of the previous day is deserving of the highest praise.

In one part the retreat of the Germans was so precipitate that the German Battalion Commander left his orders, maps, and telephone installation behind in his dugout.

THE CAPTURE OF TAILLES WOOD AND THE OCCUPATION OF THE OLD AMIENS DEFENCE LINE.

Early on the 10th information was received from the III Corps that the attack had been successful on the whole front and that the enemy was everywhere in retreat. The attack was to be continued without respite and the Division in conjunction with the 12th Division would push on at once and occupy the old Amiens Defence Line. The 9th Londons and the 131st American Regt. had already pushed out strong fighting patrols early in the morning and at noon these patrols sent back word that TAILLES WOOD was clear of the enemy, and the American patrols further reported the Old Amiens Defence Line trenches on their front empty. Owing to a strong gas concentration in the TAILLES WOOD however it was not possible to reach them on the 175th Brigade front. Arrangements were therefore made for these trenches to be attacked at 6 p.m. in conjunction with the 12th Division on our left, however news was received from the 9th Londons at 3 p.m. that they had already been occupied without opposition although the enemy was still holding them strongly opposite the 12th Division. The attack of the 12th Division therefore took place by itself and was successful except on a small portion of the front immediately on our left and this subsequently cleared by fighting patrols of the 9th Londons, so that by 11 p.m. the Old AMIENS Defences

/had

had been occupied on the whole front of the 58th and 12th Divisions.

On August 11th the line became stabilised, and certain reorganizations of the line were carried out, a part of the 12th Division's front was taken over and reorganized that night on a three battalion front held by the 12th, 9th and 2/10th London Regts from right to left. At the same time the Australians took over the 131st American Regt's front and this Regiment passed under their orders.

The 5th Yorkshires and 8th Londons returned to the command of their respective Brigades and the 173rd and 174th Brigades were withdrawn to the old trench system to reorganize.

The capture of the Old Amiens trench system brought to an end the First Phase of the 3rd Battle of the SOMME and on the night of August 12th the 175th Infantry Brigade was relieved by the 142nd Infantry Brigade and marched on the following day to the BOIS ESCARDONEUSE, the 173rd and 174th Brigades having moved on the previous day to QUERRIEU and ROUND WOOD respectively.

On August 10th Brig.-General COBHAM, DSO. arrived to take command of the 175th Brigade.

The Division had now been in action for 4 days during which they had made a total advance of 6,000 yards all in the face of strong opposition. 1,925 prisoners including 58 Officers had actually been counted through the cages and many more undoubtedly found their way back through other Divisional areas.

Some attempt has been made overleaf to record a list of the guns, machine guns and other booty captured during these four days but the Division was withdrawn from the area of the fighting before anything like a complete count could be made, neither was it possible to count the enemy dead, although all who subsequently examined the battle field are agreed that the numbers were unusually large.

In every way, therefore, the actions of August 8th - 12th deserve to rank as amongst the greatest and most successful fought by the 58th Division up to date, and on August 17th the Commander-in-Chief himself visited all Brigades of the Division and congratulated them on their performance, and to these congratulations must be added those of the Corps Commander, Sir A.BUTLER and Sir H.RAWLINSON, Commanding the Fourth Army.

----- o**o -----

The following is a list of part of the war material captured by this Division (and the 131st Regt. U.S. Infantry attached) since the commencement of operations on the 8th instant.

Some Trench Mortars and 77 mm. guns in addition are believed to have been taken away by Australian Troops, and there are probably more guns in the area which have not yet been located.

77 mm. Guns.

No.					Location.
8	...	...	...	...	K.33.b., along Western edge of BOIS CELESTINE.
4	...	...	...	...	K.29.a.5.5.
3	...	...	...	...	K.23.c.8.9. to K.23.d.1.8.
5	...	...	...	...	K.11.b.5.8.
1	...	...	...	...	K.22.a.2.1.
1	...	...	...	...	K.21.a.9.9.
3	...	...	...	...	K.28.d.3.4.
1	...	...	...	...	K.32.a.3.7.
1	...	...	...	...	K.26.b.
1	...	...	...	...	K.32.a.8.6.
2	...	...	...	...	K.27.a.3.5.
1	...	...	...	...	K.34.b.8.5.
4	...	...	...	...	Q.4.d.
2	...	...	...	...	N.W. end CHIPILLY.
37.					

4.1 inch Guns.

4	...	...	...	...	K.33.b.
5	...	...	...	...	K.27.d.9.1.
3	...	...	...	...	K.23.c.7.2.
1	...	...	...	...	K.18.a.5.0.
13.					

4.2 inch Howitzers.

2	...	...	...	...	K.33.d.8.8.
2	...	...	...	...	K.34.c.
2	...	...	...	...	K.34.a.3.8.
4	...	...	...	...	K.17.b.2.4.
10.					

5.9 inch Howitzers.

1	...	...	...	...	K.28.d.9.3.
3	...	...	...	...	K.18.c.
2	...	...	...	...	K.29.a.1.6.
5.					

5.9 inch Guns.

1	...	...	...	...	K.18.c.

8 inch Howitzers.

1	...	...	...	...	K.29.a.1.0.
1	...	...	...	...	K.29.a.3.9.
2.					

GRAND TOTAL - 68 Guns and Howitzers.

/It

It has only been possible to obtain the number of Trench Mortars and Machine Guns captured by the 174th Infantry Brigade.
The actual total captured by the Division is very much in excess of these, which are as follows :-

Trench Mortars.

Heavy. 9
Light. 27

Machine Guns.

Heavy. 39
Light. 133

In addition, an enemy aeroplane intact was captured in L.4.b.

Large quantities of S.A.A. and ammunition of all calibres were taken.

Also a large quantity of rifles, equipment and stores were taken, especially in CHIPILLY.

1,925 unwounded prisoners, including 58 officers, were captured by and passed through the cage of the Division (this includes those taken by 131st Regt. U.S. Infantry, but not any captured by other Divisions who passed through Corps Cage).

The number of wounded prisoners cannot yet be ascertained.

Many of the enemy were killed by the fire of the Artillery, Machine Guns and Infantry, and with the bayonet.

(Sd) C.M.DAVIES. Lt.-Colonel,
General Staff, 58th (London) Division.

12th August, 1918.

C.R.A.	6	copies.
C.R.E.	5	"
173rd Inf. Bde.	5	"
174th Inf. Bde.	5	"
175th Inf. Bde.	5	"
Signals.	2	"
58th Bn.M.G.C.	6	"
Div. Train.	4	"
A.D.M.S.	4	"
1/4th Suffolks.	2	"
"A" and "Q"	1	copy.
D.A.D.O.S.	1	"
D.A.D.V.S.	1	"
A.P.M.	1	"

Think 4.37 p.m. should read 4.37 a.m. Then III Corps orders were issued at 11.15 p.m. 24th and the 58th Division orders reached the 173rd Bde at 5.45 a.m. 25th.

NARRATIVE OF OPERATIONS.

Period 22nd August to 1st September 1918.

INTRODUCTORY.- The Division (less artillery) arrived in the QUERRIEU Area on relief by the 47th Division on August 14th.

Brigade Groups were disposed as follows :-

173rd Inf. Brigade.-	QUERRIEU.
174th Inf. Brigade.-	ROUND WOOD (W. of FRANVILLERS)
175th Inf. Brigade.-	BOIS ESCARDONNEUSE (S. of LA HOUSSOYE)

The Divisional Artillery was still left in the Sector N. of the SOMME and came under the orders of a Composite Force which was introduced to co-ordinate the operations of the III and Australian Corps across the SOMME Valley.

No definite instructions were forthcoming as to how long the Division would be in rest. The time was spent in reorganization, absorption of drafts and training.

On August 17th the Commander-in-Chief visited all Brigades during their training and expressed himself well pleased with the part the Division had taken in the operations just previously carried out.

GENERAL.- On August 18th a conference was held at which proposals were made for an attack by the III Corps with 47th, 12th and 18th Divisions. The objective was approximately a line running from the N. of BRAY to E. of ALBERT. The attack was to be carried out on August 22nd. in co-operation with attacks of the Fourth Army South of the SOMME and the Third Army in the direction of BAPAUME; the object of these attacks being to capture the country re-taken by the enemy on March 21st. so that he might not be able to destroy roads and railways in his intended withdrawal.

NARRATIVE.-
1918.
22nd AUGUST.- The Division (less artillery) was in Corps Reserve.

At Zero hour 175th Inf. Brigade with affiliated M.G. Coy. moved to position of assembly in rear of the old British Front Line W. of MORLANCOURT.

At Zero plus 1 hour 174th Inf. Brigade with affiliated M.G. Coy. moved from ROUND WOOD to a position E. of the HEILLY - FRANVILLERS Road.

23rd " The attack by the III Corps was continued by 47th, 12th and 18th Divisions.

173rd Inf. Brigade moved from QUERRIEU to the Valley S. of MERICOURT at dawn.

174th Inf. Brigade was placed at the disposal of 18th Division and remained in its assembly position E. of the HEILLY.- FRANVILLERS Road.

175th /

175th Inf. Brigade was placed at the disposal of the 47th Division for an attack at dawn on the 24th August, and moved up to assembly position about the North end of TAILLES WOOD.

At 10-30 pm. 173rd Inf. Brigade moved to assembly position in the Old AMIENS Defence Line.

24th August.—

At 1 am. on the 24th August the 175th Inf. Bde. on right and 140th Inf. Brigade (47th Division) on the left continued the attack under the 47th Division in conjunction with the 12th Division on the left and the 3rd Australian Division on the right.

The deep ravine running parallel to the objective line called the HAPPY VALLEY was crossed and "mopped up" in the moonlight and the objective was reached before dawn. Later in the day this valley was heavily shelled with gas and H.E. shells.

109 prisoners were captured representing 12 Coys. of each of the 116th and 117th Inf. Regts.

The 174th Inf. Brigade returned to command of G.O.C. 58th Division and were moved forward to the old British trenches 1500 yards S.W. of MORLANCOURT. The 1/4th Suffolks (Pioneer Battn.) and Field Coys. R.E. of the Division moved from BOIS ESCARDONNEUSE to the Valley S. of MERICOURT.

At 10 am. 58th Division took over the Headquarters of 47th Division and the Divisional Artillery of 47th Division and the command of the Right Divisional Sector of the Corps front passed to G.O.C. 58th Div. at the same time.

To exploit the successful attack carried out in the morning III Corps ordered the Division to make a further attack at 4 pm. on the same day (24th). This was later postponed until 2-30 am. the following morning.

25th   "

At 2-30 am. 175th Inf. Brigade and 140th Inf. Brigade attacked the objective shown on the attached map "B". The attack was carried out under a barrage moving at the rate of 100 yards in four minutes.

173rd Inf. Brigade moved forward in close support of the attack ready to carry either of the leading Brigades through to their objective if strong opposition was met.

On instructions received from III Corps at 4-37 pm. 173rd Inf. Brigade with 86th Army Bde. R.F.A. attached was ordered to be in readiness to form the advanced guard of the Division should the enemy's defence weaken.

Both Brigades gained their objective with little opposition and consolidated, pushing out patrols to the front. Divisions on the flanks also reported little resistance.

173rd Inf. Brigade was at once ordered to form the advanced guard of the Division and to advance on MARICOURT via BRONFAY FARM and North of BILLON WOOD

A Troop of Northumberland Hussars was at the

disposal /

disposal of 173rd Inf. Brigade.

Divisional Headquarters moved from HEILLY to South of MORLANCOURT at 9-30 am. but was obliged to return to HEILLY owing to a dump of gas shell being exploded near the site of the new Headquarters.

Divisional Headquarters was finally established South of MORLANCOURT about 11-30 am.

3rd Australian Division ordered their advance to proceed in conjunction with 58th Division, keeping touch with the 58th Division's Right.

12th Division on the left encountered little opposition and their action consisted chiefly in following up and keeping touch with the enemy.

140th and 141st Inf. Brigades reverted to the command of 47th Division at 11-44 am.

The C.R.A. 58th Division took over command of the artillery covering the Division from the C.R.A. 47th Division, 115th and 120th Heavy Batteries were placed under the 58th Division.

140th Inf. Brigade was to withdraw when 173rd Inf. Brigade had passed through their position.

The 2/4th Battalion which formed the vanguard encountered opposition when approaching BILLON WOOD and was compelled to deploy.

173rd Inf. Brigade reported the situation at 11am. to be as follows :- 2/4th Battn. attacking BILLON FM. 2/2nd Battn. about BRONFAY FARM, and the 3rd Battalion in Brigade Reserve. M.G. fire was reported from BILLON WOOD and the enemy shelling was becoming severe.

At 12-15 pm. the enemy was still in possession of BILLON WOOD, the 2/4th Battalion was then trying to work round the North side of the Wood.

At 1-30 pm. orders were issued for 173rd Inf. Brigade and 174th Inf. Brigade to push forward to the line COPSE "N" - A.26.c.5.0. - by BILLON AVENUE - SHEFFIELD AVENUE to LAPREE WOOD as soon as the relief of the 175th Inf. Brigade by the 174th Inf. Brigade was completed.

Very heavy fighting was experienced in BILLON WOOD and the vicinity. The enemy's artillery fire was also exceptionally severe. 173rd Inf. Brigade had troops in BILLON AVENUE during the early afternoon but were forced to withdraw owing to M.G. and Artillery fire. The greater part of the Wood was gained before evening but the situation in the South East corner was obscure until dark, and it is probable that the enemy held out there throughout the day.

At 4-30 pm. one Field Artillery Brigade was placed at the disposal of 174th Inf. Brigade.

26th August.- During the night it was thought that the enemy

were /

retiring on the trenches at the West edge of MARICOURT. His Main Line of Resistance was probably there but he still had troops West of COPSE Valley and in the trenches joining COPSE "E" and LAPREE WOOD.

Patrols of 174th and 173rd Inf. Brigades pushed out with the object of establishing a line running N.W. through COPSE "C" by dawn. They were however prevented in this by many isolated enemy M.Gs.

At 4-30 am. our artillery placed a heavy barrage on the trenches at the West edge of MARICOURT and on the trench line running S. from the village to CREST AVENUE. At the same time 174th and 173rd Inf. Bdes. advanced over the high ground E. of BILLON Wood and came under heavy M.G. and artillery fire chiefly from the village of MARICOURT. Several Field Guns were firing at close range and it is estimated that about 10 M.Gs. were firing from A.15.central and about 20 to 25 M.Gs. were pouring out fire from CREST AVENUE.

With the help of artillery attached to Brigades the advance was pressed on and by the afternoon a line running from "C" COPSE to a point 200 yards S. of OXFORD COPSE was established.

The 12th Division on the left had not cleared CARNOY and 173rd Inf. Brigade made a defensive flank facing North from OXFORD COPSE to LAPREE WOOD. South of "C" COPSE the line was not continuous but "D" COPSE and a bank 200 yards N. of it was manned by 174th Inf. Brigade who were in touch with 3rd Aust. Division on the Right. The Australian Patrols late in the evening pushed N.E. on the East side of the MARICOURT Valley towards CREST AVENUE and succeeded in driving the enemy back to cover in SPUR WOOD.

Arrangements for the following day's attack were made more difficult as no decision as to the Divisional Right boundary could be obtained.

After orders for the attack had been sent out it was decided by Australian Corps that the 3rd Australian Division would attack the Quarry in A.28.a. and FARGNY Mill but that III Corps must be responsible for FARGNY Wood.

It was then impossible, owing to the late hour, to alter the plan and detail sufficient troops to deal with FARGNY Wood. The 3rd Australian Division carried out the barrage as originally arranged.

27th August.— Three German Divisions had been identified as available to fight in the Sector. III Corps sent out a warning that stiff opposition was again to be expected in the MARICOURT Sector.

At 4-55 am in conjunction with the 3rd Australian Division on the right and the 12th Division on the left the 58th Division attacked under a creeping barrage. The barrage dwelt on the Start Line for 20 minutes and then moved forward at 100 yards in 4 minutes for 500 yards and then at the rate of 100 yards in 6 minutes.

174th Inf. Brigade attacked on the right and 173rd Inf. Brigade on the left.

The /

The Start Line, boundaries, and objectives are shown on the attached map "B". but 74th Inf. Brigade had to detach what troops were available to attack FARGNY Wood from the North.

News of the attack was not received until late owing to enemy shelling.

Both Brigades gained the general line of the objective but could not push forward to the line of exploitation owing to strong enemy resistance in the old German Front Line.

The situation on the right was obscure for some time and the enemy were not driven out of FARGNY Wood.

Front Line Battalions, especially those of 173rd Inf. Brigade, became very disorganised in the advance chiefly owing to mist and the high percentage of officer casualties.

Reorganization of troops on the objective was difficult owing to the accuracy of the enemy's snipers and artillery fire.

The 12th Division gained a general line North and South through the West edge of FAVIERE Wood. Touch with them on the objective was easily obtained.

The 3rd Australian Division gained objectives with the exception of FARGNY Mill. Front Line troops were unable to gain touch with them until late in the day.

A separate operation had to be arranged for the taking of FARGNY Wood, which was reported to be still occupied by the enemy at 9-5 pm.

28th August.— An attack with a creeping barrage was ordered to be carried out, the objective, Start Line etc. for which are shown on the attached Map "B"

Zero hour was 4-55 am. and the 173rd Inf. Brigade was to attack on the left with the 174th Inf. Brigade on the right.

This attack opened very successfully almost all over the Divisional Front. Enemy resistance was on the whole rather weak, though his barrage on the Old British Front Line and on MARICOURT during the attack was distinctly heavy.

By 8 am. the objective was reported as reached all along the Divisional front except at the Northern end, where more determined resistance was offered by the enemy in the BOIS D'EN HAUT. Here the attack entered the Wood but was temporarily held up by considerable enemy M.G. fire, especially from CLAPHAM Fm.

By 8-30 am. an International Post was established by the 8th Battalion Lon. Regt. and the Australians in A.30.b. and by 9-15 am. touch was still reported as definitely established by the two attacking Brigades, on the objective in SUPPORT COPSE.

The enemy M.Gs. in BOIS D'EN HAUT were also reported

by /

by the 12th Division as hanging up their advance at
about 10-30 am., but by 12-15 pm, the 173rd Inf. Bde.
had fought their way forward through the Wood and had
captured CLAPHAM FARM which had been the main point of
resistance in this area, and a joint post was established there with the 12th Division.

Other enemy Machine Guns had been causing annoyance and delay to the 174th Inf. Brigade and the
Australians on our right from the direction of A.24.b.
but by 11-7 am. the 174th Inf. Brigade were able to
report that two enemy Machine Guns in this neighbourhood
had been dealt with by an encircling movement.

Enemy shelling of the forward area was heavy
throughout.

At about 12-15 pm. the enemy was reported to be
dribbling back to the valley in B.13 and B.19, and the
Artillery was informed accordingly.

At 1-58 pm. the Australians reported the trenches
in B.25 and H.1.b.to be strongly held by the enemy with
forward M.Gs. near our forward posts.

At 7-30 pm. orders were issued for artillery
bombardments to be opened at 10-15 pm. to assist the
173rd and 174th Inf. Brigades in establishing posts at
B.13.c.0.0 and B.19.c.0.2. respectively - these posts
to be consolidated as soon as established.

29th August -
During the earlier part of the night 28/29th
August, forward posts were established as follows -

By 173rd Inf. Brigade at approximately A.24.b.9.9.
By 174th Inf. Brigade in the trench running from
A.24.d.4.2 to A.24.d.1.2.

After the establishing of the above posts those
two Brigades were relieved by the 175th Inf. Brigade
with the 4th Suffolks (Pioneers) attached, and the
whole Divisional front was then held by this "Composite"
Brigade.

After relief the 174th Inf. Brigade became the
Support Brigade, and was situated in A.22.a and c.
A.28.a and A.21., whilst the 173rd Inf. Brigade
passed to Divisional Reserve in L.4., the XXII Corps
Cavalry and Cyclists being attached.

Shortly after taking over, the 175th Inf. Bde.
established posts at A.18.d.8.8., A.24.b.9.9 and
A.24.d.4.2.

No organized attack with a barrage had been ordered
for the 29th, and the fighting resolved itself into a
series of patrol actions forward to tactical points,
followed by the advance of the infantry holding the
front line.

At 8-45 am. orders were issued for fighting
patrols to be pushed forward to follow up the enemy
who was believed to be withdrawing, and by 10-40 am.
a line of posts had been established on the general
line RED FARM - B.19.a.5.5 - B.13.c.2.0., and touch
was established on both flanks. Patrols were then

pushed /

pushed forward to BATTERY COPSE and reported the Copse clear of the enemy.

The enemy appears to have been somewhat demoralised as prisoners stated that during the previous night many ran away and were rounded up in PERONNE, where they were collected and sent back into the front line.

At 1-15 pm. 175th Inf. Brigade was ordered to endeavour to push forward to the trench running S.E. from the South end of MAUREPAS through B.21.central to B.28.a., where touch was to be established with the Australians.

At 1-50 pm. the XXII Corps Cyclists were placed under the orders of B.G.C. 175th Inf. Brigade.

At 3-50 pm. the 2nd Life Guards M.G. Battn. (less 2 Coys.) were moved forward to hold the line of trenches running N and S. through SUPPORT COPSE, and at 6-45 pm. 1 Squadron Northumberland Hussars was also attached to the 175th Inf. Brigade.

At 6-15 pm. 175th Inf. Brigade moved to A.23.b.2.0.

At 6-50 pm. enemy guns were located in MARRIERES WOOD.

At 8-15 pm. 175th Inf. Brigade reported that they had 2 Battalions in the trenches running S.S.W. from MAUREPAS and 2 Battalions in trenches running S.E. from MAUREPAS to B.28.a. where touch was established with the Australians in accordance with orders issued by Divisional Headquarters.

30th August.- Orders were issued on the 29th August for the advance to be continued on the 30th August as rapidly as possible and an advance guard consisting of the following units was ordered to move at dawn from the positions reached on the night of the 29th August.

       175th Inf. Brigade.
       4th Suffolk Regt.
       3 Brigades R.F.A.
       1 Section R.E.
       "C" and "D" Coys. 58th Bn. M.G.C.
       1 Coy. XXII Corps Cyclists.
       1 Sqdrn. Northumberland Hussars.

Divisions on both flanks had similar orders to push forward in co-operation.

During the night 29/30th August a copy of the 3rd Australian Division's Operation Orders showed that they intended to advance in a general N.E. direction, across the front of the 58th Division, cutting the Division out at C.14.central. The III Corps were asked if the boundary had been changed, but at the time they had no knowledge of the contemplated change.

At 5 am. a message was received from III Corps

stating /

stating that if the Australians were successful in crossing the SO..E further South the 3rd Australian Division's advance would be across the 58th Divisional boundaries, taking the system of trenches South of BOUCHAVESNES from the South flank.

The Advance Guard Commander - General COBHAM, 175th Inf. Brigade - was informed, but not sufficiently early to pass it on to the vanguard, which had already pushed ahead. At the same time the advance guard were ordered to continue their advance between the new boundaries as far as C.14.central.

The vanguard (consisting of 1 Squadron of Northumberland Hussars, 1 Coy. XXII Corps Cyclists, 1 Section of R.Es. 1 Section of 291st F.A. Brigade, and 2 Sections of M.G. Coy.) advanced at 5 am. The Cyclists selected the MAUREPAS - LE FOREST Road, the Cavalry Squadron were 1500 yards South of this road and encountered little opposition. One patrol of the cavalry were fired at from B.22.central, and another patrol of the same squadron had linked up with the Australian Cavalry. Both of the latter units reported opposition from B.23. c.5.5 (Hill 110) and considerable shell fire from MARRIERES Wood.

At 10-40 am. two fighting patrols were sent out towards MARRIERES Wood while the Main Guard at this time had reached the line N. and S. of B.22.a., where they were in touch with 47th Division on the left. At 11-10am. the 3rd Australian Division reported that their cavalry had reached Hill 150 (N.W. of MARRIERES Wood) and that squares B.18, 23, and 24 were clear of the enemy.

The advance was not altogether comfortable as the enemy shell fire was heavy in the general area between MAUREPAS and HEM Wood, and in addition long range M.G. fire was directed on our likely routes and avenues of approach.

At 11-50 am. nests of M.Gs. were located and with artillery support the Main Guard advanced towards MARRIERES Wood.

In the afternoon the Mainguard had progressed to the line of trenches from B.18.central to B.24.central, immediately West of MARRIERES Wood, in touch with Flank Divisions. Infantry patrols were forward of this line. The 175th Inf. Brigade were held up on this line by fire from M.Gs. and T.Ms. fired from within the Wood. During the day the line had advanced 3000 yards, the final line being just West of MARRIERES Wood from B.18.central to B.24.central (Map 62C)

In the meantime the Headquarters of the 58th Div. moved from the Quarry at L.1.b.3.0 to old Railway Siding at A.19.b.5.2., opening at the latter place at 3 pm.

At about 7 pm. arrangements were made between III Corps and Flank Divisions to continue the attack on the 31st. with the object of capturing the high ground East of MARRIERES Wood. Orders were issued for 174th Inf. Brigade to pass through 175th Inf. Brigade and to take over the advanced guard of the Division. This order was subsequently cancelled and an attack by the 174th Inf. Brigade accompanied by a creeping barrage was substituted.

At /

At 6-30 pm. the 174th Inf. Brigade moved forward by bus to CURLU, thence by march route to Valloy in B.22.

Two Companies of 2nd Life Guards M.G. Battalion were ordered to move to and defend the line B.28.a.5.0. to B.14.b.6.0. from 4 am. on the 31st August.

The Squadron of the Northumberland Hussars attached to the Division were ordered to pass to Corps Reserve but to remain in the forward area.

31st August.— On the morning of the 31st August the attack was launched by 174th Inf. Brigade at 5-10 am. The 3rd Australian Division co-operated on the right and the 47th Division on the left. The Start Line ran North and South about 400 yards West of MARRIERES Wood and the objective was the forward crest of the high ground overlooking BOUCHAVESNES.

The attack continued successfully, though the enemy's rearguards put up a good defence, chiefly with M.Gs. The ground in front of the objective lent itself particularly to defence by M.Gs. which the enemy concealed in the low scrub, ditches and quarries about the BAPAUME - PERONNE Road near BOUCHAVESNES.

The objective on the forward slope was reached under cover of the artillery creeping barrage and touch was maintained with flanking units.

The four Company Commanders of the left Battalion (8th Lon. Regt.) became casualties early in the attack, and most of the heavy casualties were sustained by the left Battalion as they came over the bare crest of the high ground out of the wood. The two weak Battalions - 8th Londons and 6th Londons - which formed the front line of the attack captured nearly 400 prisoners, two 4.2 Howitzers, two 77 mm. guns, a few Light Trench Mortars and many Machine Guns, with a certain amount of ammunition.

The flanking Divisions also captured several prisoners, representing the 447th, 445th and the Augusta Guard Regiments.

Later, the Australians pushed on, capturing Mt. ST. QUENTIN, a conspicuous high landmark which overlooked the back areas of our own and the enemy's front.

Early in the afternoon the enemy's resistance stiffened E. of the BAPAUME - PERONNE Road, and although he shelled our new positions and approaches with light and heavy pieces, no counter-attack developed On the other hand, Divisions of each flank, each repulsed a fairly well organized counter-attack during the afternoon.

Throughout the day, and it had been noticed on several days previously, the enemy aeroplanes made no show at all. Our superiority in the air was most marked by the numbers of our own planes over both lines and the total absence during the day of enemy machines.

At 2 pm. the 173rd Inf. Brigade were ordered to

move /

move forward by busses in readiness to attack on the morning of the 1st September. This was contrary to expectations as the Division had had a warning order that probably the 74th Division would relieve the 58th Division on the night of the 31/1st. During the afternoon orders were issued by the Division ordering the 173rd Inf. Brigade to attack through the 174th Inf. Brigade on the morning of September 1st, in co-operation with 3rd Australian Division on right and 47th Division on the left. The Start Line for the 173rd Inf. Brigade was roughly the BAPAUME - PERONNE Road, along which the barrage would fall at 5-30 am. The objective was the old German Reserve Line running South of MOISLAINS Wood.

The 175th Inf. Brigade moved back to the valley South of MARICOURT with their Headquarters at the QUARRY A.28.a. (Map 62.C)

1st September.- On the morning of the 1st September the attack was continued, the 173rd Inf. Brigade passing through the 174th Inf. Brigade, and attacking in conjunction with 3rd Australian Division on the right and the 47th Div. on the left. The plan was to capture BOUCHAVESNES and the ridge beyond, including the old British Front Line trenches in C.15.b and d. (Sheet 62C N.W.)

The approach march of the 173rd Inf. Brigade was considerably interfered with by the congestion of traffic along all roads and tracks in the forward area; but they reached their assembly positions at 3 am. without interference of the enemy.

At 5-30 am the attack began and troops moved forward under a creeping artillery barrage.

This attack was completely successful and the old British Front Line East of BOUCHAVESNES was captured without much difficulty. Touch with Divisions on each flank however was not made until some hours later. The enemy had opposed the advance by M.G. fire and his barrage put down in response to ours was prompt and heavy.

From the statements of prisoners captured during the day it was evident that it was the enemy's intention to hold the ridge East of BOUCHAVESNES at all costs. The exploitation of the successful attack was hampered by the fact that all movement forward was necessarily on the forward slope of the ridge, and therefore under full view of the enemy, and also that the Divisions on each flank were well in rear of the 58th Division and unable to co-operate. However, the 173rd Inf. Brigade established forward posts along the German trench line 800 yards in front of the final objective.

Considering the low strength of the 173rd Inf. Bde. the number of prisoners captured was large. In all 325 German Officers and men were captured as well as 8 Field guns, numerous M.Gs. and a Motor Ambulance complete with Driver.

The line as given above was handed over on the night of the 1/2nd September to the 74th Division. The Command of the Sector passed from G.O.C. 58th Division to G.O.C. 74th Division at midnight on September 1/2nd.

------oOo------

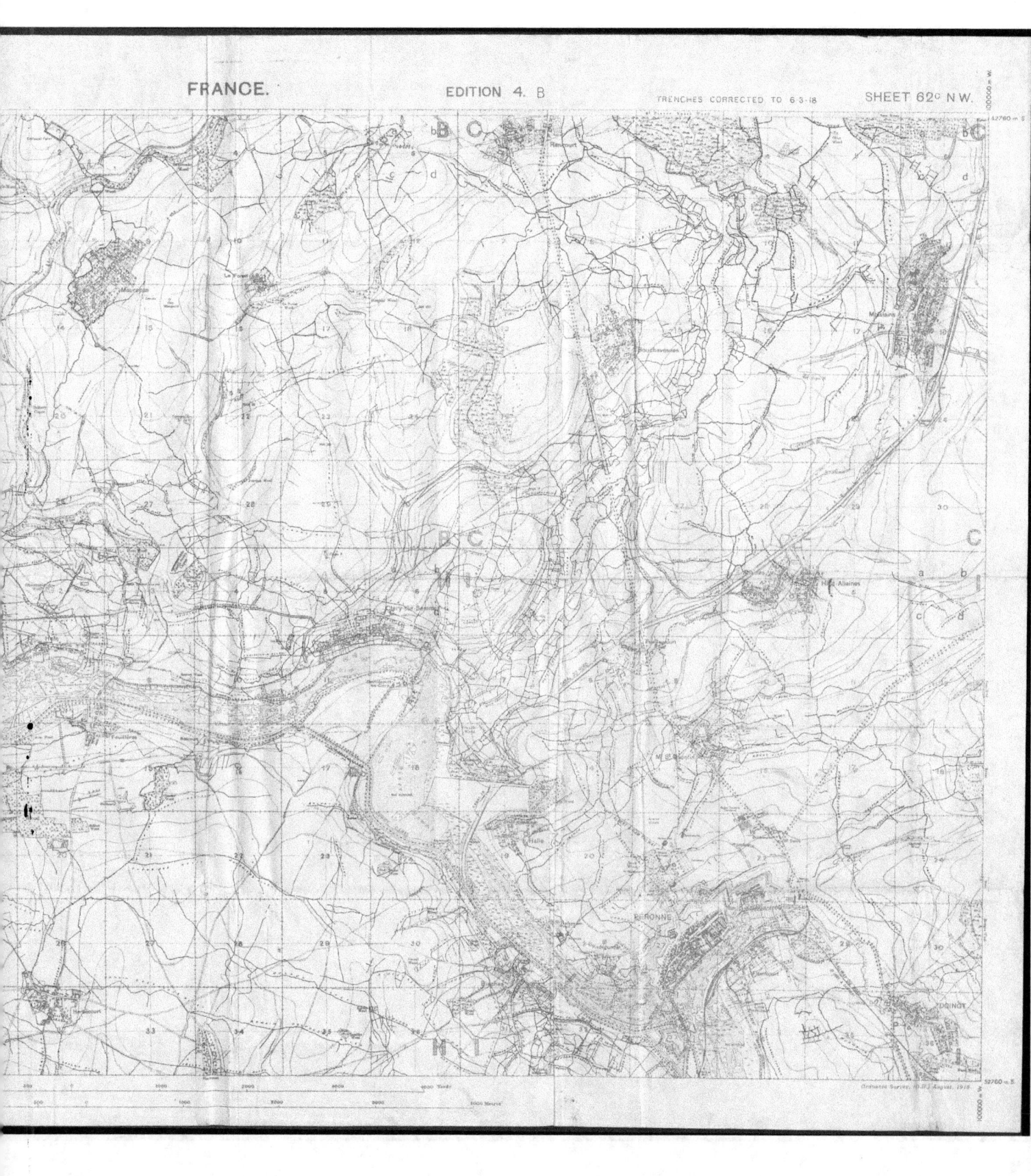

Instructions

for

forthcoming Operations

APPENDIX "A".

S.A.A.	300,000
M.G., S.A.A.	300,000
P.Webley.	3000
No.23 Grenade.	3000
" 5 Grenade.	3000
No. 36 Grenades.	4000
Stokes 3"	1500
V.P.A.White.	2000
do Red.	1000
S.S.O.	250
Flares.	2500
Petrol Tins (full)	300
L.G.Drums (full)	500
Box Respirators.	200

SECRET.

Copy No 20

FORTHCOMING OPERATIONS.

58th (LONDON) DIVISIONAL INSTRUCTIONS No. 1.

1. **GENERAL PLAN.-**

    The Fourth Army will attack the enemy's positions between the AMIENS - ROYE Road and MORLANCOURT on a date to be notified later.

    The III Corps will cover the flank of the main attack South of the SOMME by forming a defensive flank facing North-East between GRESSAIRE WOOD and the present front line in K.14.

    The 58th Division with one Coy. Tanks of 10th Tank Battn. will attack on the Right and the 18th Division with 2 Coys. Tanks of 10th Tank Battn. on the Left of the III Corps.

    The dividing line and objectives are shown on maps which have been already issued to Brigade Commanders.

2. **ZERO HOUR.-**

    As soon as it is light enough to see a man at 100 yards; exact time will be notified on the evening of "Y" day.

3. **BRIGADE GROUPS.-**

    For the operation Brigade Groups will be formed as follows -

173rd Inf. Bde. Group -	173rd Inf. Bde. 1/4th Suffolks (Pioneers) "A" Coy. M.G. Battn.
174th Inf. Bde. Group -	174th Inf. Bde. "B" Coy. M.G. Battn. 1 Battn. 175th Inf. Bde. (with Section of "C" (Coy. M.G. Battn.) (attached.)
175th Inf. Bde. Group -	175th Inf. Bde. (less 1 Battn.) "C" Coy. M.G. Battn.(less 1 Section.)

4. (a) The 174th Bde. Group will capture the first objective. One Battn. of 175th Inf. Brigade is placed at the disposal of 174th Inf. Bde. to deal with SAILLY-LAURETTE. On completion of the capture of SAILLY-LAURETTE this Battn. and and Section of M.G. Battn. will come under the 175th Inf. Bde. in Corps Reserve.

    (b) There will be a halt of one hour after the first objective has been gained at the end of which the 173rd Bde. will pass through the 174th Inf. Bde. and will capture the final objective.

    The 1/4th Suffolks will be used to consolidate the line marked BROWN on the map from K.29.c.5.0 to the Divisional boundary K.28.b.3.5.

    (c) The 175th Bde. Group will be in Corps Reserve and will probably be located in Wood in I 15.

    (d)

- 2 -

(d) "D" Coy. M.G. Battn. (less 2 Sections) will follow the left flank of the attack of the First and Second objectives and will be responsible for ensuring that no gap occurs between the 50th and 16th Divisions.

2 Sections "D" Coy. M.G. Battn. will remain in Divisional Reserve.

5. TANKS.-

Tanks will co-operate as follows :-

2 Tanks will assist the attack on SAILLY-LAURETTE and will move subsequently at 500 yards interval along the SAILLY-LAURETTE - CHIPILLY Road with a view to assisting in clearing the Southern end of MALARD Wood and the subsequent attack on CHIPILLY.

The remaining 10 Tanks will co-operate with the attack of the 174th Inf. Bde. After the first objective has been gained they will withdraw behind the Crest as soon as covering troops are established in position. They will then come under orders of 173rd Brigade and assist in the attack on the Second Objective. As soon as covering positions in and in front of the Second Objectives have been occupied the Tanks will be withdrawn into Corps Reserve.

6. ARTILLERY.-

The attack will be covered by a Field Artillery Creeping barrage (average of 1 gun per 25 yards of front) in accordance with the barrage map which will be issued as soon as possible.

The bottoms of Valleys which cannot be reached by 18-pdrs. will be dealt with by a Howitzer barrage, which will move from Valley to Valley to harmonize with the Creeping Barrage.

Heavy Howitzers will also bombard known gun positions, M.G. Nests, and certain Strong Points and Villages.

In order to help to mark the resumption of the advance from the first objective the barrage will be intensified for 3 mins. before it is again set in motion.

7. AEROPLANES.-

Low flying aeroplanes will co-operate in the attack.

8. HEADQUARTERS.-

Advanced Divisional Headquarters will be established for the operation in J 19.c.

Brigade H.Q. of 173rd and 174th Inf. Bdes at existing Battn. Headquarters in J.26.a.6.9 and J.22.d.2.3 respectively.

9. Further instructions will be issued later.

10. ACKNOWLEDGE.

Lieut-Colonel,
General Staff 50th (London) Division.

3rd August 1918.

Distribution - See Slip.

DISTRIBUTION.

```
Copy No. 1  Brig-Genl.    J.McC.MAXWELL C.B., D.S.O.    C.R.A.
     "  2      "          C.E.CONRAN. C.M.G. Cmdg. 173rd Bde.
     "  3      "          A.MAXWELL. D.S.O.      "    174th Bde.
     "  4      "          W. MAXWELL-SCOTT. D.S.O. "   175th Bde.
     "  5  Lt.Colonel     A.J.SAVAGE. D.S.O.     C.R.E.
     "  6      "          P.D.STEWART. D.S.O. Cmdg. M.G. Bn.
     "  7      "          A.G.P.McNALTY. C.M.G.  A.A. & Q.M.G.
     "  8      "          H.C.COPEMAN. C.M.G., D.S.O. Cmdg. 1/4th Suffolks
     "  9      "          E.A.WRAITH. D.S.O.     A.D.M.S.
     " 10  Major          C.M.HENDERSON. M.C.  O.C. Div. Sig. Coy.

    11-12  III Corps.
    13     Brig-Genl.     A.E.J.PERKINS. C.M.G. Cmdg. III Corps H.A.
    14     Major-Genl.    R.P.LEE. C.B. G.O.C. 18th Div.
    15     G. O. C.       Left Division Aust. Corps.
    16-17  Lieut-Col.     J.MICKLEM. D.S.O., M.C. Cmdg. 10th Tank Bn.
    18     18nd 95nd      Sqdrn. R.A.F.
    19.    5 to 3
```

S E C R E T.

ADMINISTRATIVE INSTRUCTIONS NO.1,
in accordance with Division Order No. 146

1. AMMUNITION.
Divisional Grenade Dump has been established at Road Junction near LA HOUSSOYE at I.2.d.7.3.

174th and 175th Brigades have already drawn S.A.A. to make up extra 50 rounds to be carried by the man.

Extra demands for ammunition should be wired to 58th Division Q.

S.A.A. Section D.A.C. is located in Wood at I.1.a.5.8.

2. SUPPLIES.
O.C. 58th Divisional Train will hold the following supplies on hand for use when required:-

One day's full ration of Rum.
5000 Rations of Oxo or Peasoup.
10,000 ozs of Solidified Alcohol.

No reserve dump of Iron Rations is maintained but Iron Rations can be had at short notice from III Corps.

3. PACK SADDLERY.
Pack saddles and water carrying crates on the scale of 16 Pack Saddles and 32 crates per Battalion have been demanded, and will be retained by D.A.D.O.S. at the disposal of Brigades.

4. WATER.
1000 Petrol Tins filled will be kept at Divisional Grenade Dump

The following Administrative Instructions issued by the 18th and 47th Divisions are published for information and guidance:-

	18th Divisional Sector.	47th Divisional Sector.
AMMUNITION.		
Divl. Bomb Store.	U.21.c.8.8.	J.7.d.5.2.
Bde. Dumps.	E.21.b.7.8.	K.16.c.9.4.
	E.21.c.7.4.	
R.E. STORES.		
Main Dump.	C.10.a.3.5.	J.17.c. (being formed)
RATION DUMP.	Refilling Point. CONTAY South (on Light Railway.) (6000 Iron Rations)	
VETERINARY AID POST.	HENENCOURT WOOD V.26.b.5.3.	J.22.a.

- 2 -

	18th Divisional Sector.	47th Divisional Sector.
WATER.	Water Tanks will be erected on ALBERT-AMIENS Road. Location will be notified later.	Horse trough and Dixie refilling point at J.16.d.8.0.
	Wells are known to exist in DERNACOURT and also in ALBERT and at E.4.b.7.0. and E.4.c.8.5.	It is hoped that well at Brickyard K.16.c. will be working by Zero day.
	No water must be consumed from Wells until tested by M.O.	
BATTLE STRAGGLER POSTS.	V.21.d.4.8. V.27.d.9.5. D.10.b.3.2. D.17.a.3.3.	J.16.d.7.0. J.10.c.8.0. J.18.d.0.1.
	Stragglers Collection Station:- Cage at BAIZIEUX C.6.b.5.3.	Stragglers Collection Station:- HEILLY Billet No.35.
P.of W.CAGE.	C.6.b.5.3.	HEILLY Billet No.35.
TROPHIES.	Trophy Dump is established at K.16.c. The Brickyard.	

E. Mynsell
Major,
for A.A.& Q.M.G.,
58th Division.

21/8/1918.

Copies to:-
"G"
C.R.A.
C.R.E.
Signal Coy.
173rd Inf. Bde.
174th do
175th do
58th Bn.M.G.C.
1/4th Suffolks.
Divl. Train.
A.D.M.S.

D.A.D.V.S.
D.A.D.O.S.
S.A.A.Sect.D.A.C.
D.B.O.
A.P.M.
S.S.O.
Camp Comdt.

S E C R E T.
                         FORTHCOMING OPERATIONS.   Copy No. _____

                  58th (LONDON) DIVISIONAL INSTRUCTIONS No. 2.

                         SYSTEM OF COMMUNICATIONS.

       A Map is attached (issued only to 173rd Inf. Bde. 174th Inf.
  Bde. C.R.A. Signals) shewing Main Routes of Communication.

1.   WIRES.-

     (a)   The only existing cable-bury which can help operations runs
         by a circuitous route from J.8.c.5.0 to Brigade Headquarters
         at J.22.d.2.4. This will be completed as far as Advanced Div.
         at J.19.c..
             This bury is very poor in places and cannot be relied upon
         as being 6'-6" in depth, but it is more protected than an over-
         land cable and provides an alternative route between Brigade
         and Advanced Division.

             Except for the above the Divisional System, including lines
         to flanking units, will consist entirely of overland cables.

             Routes will be laid as far as possible, so as to avoid
         points which are likely to be shelled.

     (b)   Forward of the present front line, the system adopted will
         be as laid down in S.S.191, i.e. R.A., Infantry and Machine
         Gun Signal personnel under orders of O.C. Divisional Signal
         Coy. will lay and maintain a common trunk route to a Brigade
         forward exchange, probably in K.27.a. Separate orders will
         be issued for the provision of the necessary personnel.
         174th Inf. Brigade will be responsible for the work on this
         line and will ensure that lines are maintained for the use
         of 173rd Inf. Brigade and R.A.- R.A., F.O.Os. and Battn.
         forward stations will be responsible for connecting themselves
         to this exchange.

             In the second phase of the battle a similar procedure will
         be adopted, and a second Brigade forward exchange will be
         established probably in K.29.c. The 173rd Inf. Brigade will
         be responsible for supervision of work on this section of the
         line.

2.   WIRELESS - (See Diagram)

         O.C. Divisional Signal Coy. will organize a complete wireless
     chain as follows :-

     (a)   Div. H.Q. (QUERRIEU) Trench Set working to Directing Station
         (WILSON Set and Luk iii tuner) at J.19.d.35.75., which station
         will also work forward to a trench set at J.28.a.80.99.

     (b)   At J.28.a.80.99 will also be installed a Power Buzzer and
         and Amplifier working to stations as follows :-

         (i)   Power Buzzer and Amplifier at J.35.d.8.0 (for reports
                on SAILLY-LAURETTE operation)

         (ii)   Power Buzzer and Amplifier at 174th Inf. Bde. Front
                Line Station (probably in K.19.c.)

                                                              (c)

(c) A Rear Loop Set will also be established at Front Line Station (K.19.c.) for communication with Brigade Forward Station (probably in K.27.a.) A Rear Loop Set will also be installed at this Brigade Forward Station to communicate with a Forward Loop Set to be allotted to an attacking Battn. of 173rd Inf. Brigade.

(d) Accumulator Dumps will be established before Zero hour at Trench Set Station at J.28.a.80.99 and at Brigade Front Line Station K.19.c.

(e) Trained Power Buzzer Amplifier and Loop Set Signallers will be detailed by Brigades to work under Divisional Wireless Officer as follows :-

174th Inf. Bde.- 2 men to work on P.B. and A. Station at J.28.a.80.99.
2 men to work on Rear Loop Set at Brigade Front Line Station.
2 men to work on P.B. and A. at Brigade Front Line Station.
2 men to work on Forward Loop at Brigade Forward Station (K.27).

175th Inf. Bde.- 2 men to work on P.B and A. at J.35.d.0.0.

173rd Inf. Bde.- 2 men to work on Rear Loop at Brigade Forward Station (K.27.a.)
2 men to work on Forward Loop with Battn. Commander of 173rd Inf. Brigade.

The Divisional Wireless Officer will arrange direct with Inf. Brigades the time and place at which these men are to report.

(f) Personnel for the Station at about K.27.a.3.6 and K.29.c.3.6. will go forward with the leading Companies of their respective Brigades.

3. PIGEONS.-

Eight birds per day have been allotted each to 173rd and 174th Inf. Brigades. These will be delivered at Brigade Headquarters Y day about 6 pm. for distribution to Battalions and Companies.

4. VISUAL.-

All Stations have been sited as far as possible, so as to afford a complete chain of communication forward into captured ground (see map).
All Visual Stations, West of the existing Front Line will be on the Divisional Telephone System.
Forward of the Front Line a Visual Station has been sited (approx.) at K.27.a.3.6. to work to the Station at K.19.c.4.1. and to work back to the latter and a further Station has been sited (approx.) at K.29.c.3.6.
Personnel for the Station at about K.27.a.3.6. will be detailed by 174th Inf. Bde. from Battn. Signal personnel and for the Station at about K.29.c.3.6. by 173rd Inf. Brigade. The personnel will go forward with the leading Companies of their respective Brigades.

5.

- 3 -

5. D.Rs AND RUNNERS.-

   (a) Mounted and Motor Cycle Despatch Riders will provide continuous communication from Advanced Divisional Headquarters to Brigade Headquarters; lateral communication, if not direct will be procured through the next higher formation.

   (b) Runners will be organized under orders of Brigade Commanders for communication forward from Brigade Headquarters down to Platoons.

6. CONTACT 'PLANES.-

   A Dropping Station will be established near Advanced Divisional Headquarters at about J.19.a.9.2. Brigades and Battalions will be prepared to use Popham Panels under instructions to be issued later.

7. ACKNOWLEDGE.

[signature]

Lieut-Colonel,
General Staff 58th (London) Division.

5th August 1918.

Distribution.

Copy No.	Rank	Name	Command
1	Brig-Genl.	J.McC. MAXWELL, C.B., D.S.O.	C.R.A.
2	"	C.E. CORKRAN, C.M.G.	Cmdg. 173rd Bde.
3	"	A. MAXWELL, D.S.O.	" 174th Bde.
4	"	W. MAXWELL-SCOTT, D.S.O.	" 175th Bde.
5	Colonel	E.A. WRAITH, D.S.O.	A.D.M.S.
6	Lt. Col.	A.J. SAVAGE, D.S.O.	C.R.E.
7	"	C.J. WILEY, D.S.O.	Cmdg. M.G. Battn.
8	"	A.G.P. McNALTY, C.M.G.	A.A. & Q.M.G.
9	"	H.C. COPEMAN, C.M.G., D.S.O.	Cmdg 1/4 Suffolks.
10	Major	C.M. HENDERSON, M.C.	O.C. Div. Signals.
11-12		III Corps.	
13	Brig-Genl.	A.E.J. PERKINS, C.M.G.	Cmdg. III Corps H.A.
14	Major-Genl.	R.P. LEE, C.B.	G.O.C. 18th Div.
15	"		G.O.C. 3rd Aust. Div.
16-17	Lt. Col.	J. MICKLEM, D.S.O., M.C.	Cmdg. 10th Tank Bn.
18	Major	K.F. BALMAINE,	Cmdg. 35th Sqdrn. R.A.F.
19.			G.O.C. 4th Aust. Div.

----------oOo----------

SECRET.   FORTHCOMING OPERATIONS.   Copy No.

58th (LONDON) DIVISIONAL INSTRUCTIONS No.3.

TANKS.

A map is attached (issued only to formations and units marked with an asterisk) showing forming up places and approximate routes to be taken by Tanks.

1. The Coy. of Tanks allotted to the 58th Division is "C" Coy., 10th Bn. Tank Corps.

2. The Coy. consists of 3 Sections, each of 4 Mark V Tanks.

3. Forming up places and approximate routes of the Tanks are shown on the attached map.
   Each Section is shown in a different colour.

4. (a) The rôle of the Tanks is to form part of the firing line and thus assist the advance of the leading parties of Inf.

   (b) Each Section advances normally with 3 Tanks in line and 1 in support.

   (c) The whole keep as close to the barrage as possible and try to form a screen in front of the leading troops.

   (d) To fulfil the above rôle, Tanks cannot wait to "mop up" until after the final objective has been gained except as arranged in para: 7 (b) and para: 11, below. This work must be done by infantry.

   (e) Tanks will wait to assist any part of the firing line which may be held up.

   (f) The following points must be clearly impressed on all ranks of the infantry :-

      (i) That they are on no account to wait for Tanks.
      (ii) That regardless of the direction taken by any Tank they (the infantry) must keep their own direction.

5. B.Gs.C. 173rd and 174th Inf. Bdes. will each detail six specially intelligent N.C.Os., one to ride in each Tank.
   Each of these N.C.Os. will be responsible for continuously informing the Tank Commander of the progress of the infantry and any signals which they may make. They will accompany the Tanks until they rendezvous after the capture of the final objective.

6. For the advance from the first objective and until the commencement of the advance to the second objective the Tanks will be under the command of the B.G.C. 174th Inf. Bde.

7. ACTION OF TANKS UP TO COMMENCEMENT OF ADVANCE ON THE SECOND OBJECTIVE.-

   (a) BLUE and RED Sections as shown will operate against Western edge of Valley in K.27 a and b. and Western edge of MALARD Wood. On the infantry reaching this obstacle RED and BLUE Tanks will all turn North, cross the Valley at the most Southerly point at which it is passable and wheel into position on East edge of MALARD Wood. On the infantry joining them they will advance to GREEN Line assist in its capture and return to rallying point as shown on map.
                                                                    O.C.Tanks ...

Forthcoming Operations
58th (London) Divisional Instructions No 3

Page 2 Appears To Be Missing

13. The following signals will be used between Tanks and Inf :-

(i) <u>From Infantry to Tanks</u> :-

A steel helmet raised on a fixed bayonet denotes -

"TANK ASSISTANCE REQUIRED"

(ii) <u>From Tanks to Infantry</u> :-

GREEN and WHITE Flag denotes	-	COME ON.
RED and YELLOW Flag "	-	OUT OF ACTION.
TRICOLOUR Flag "	-	COMING BACK.

14. Tank Headquarters during the battle will be :-

10th Tank Battn. H.Q.   MILL J.7.b.3.7.

"C" Coy. 10th Tank Battn. H.Q. -   Till GREEN Line is taken, with Brigadier of attacking Brigade.

When Tanks are rallying, after taking GREEN Line, with Tanks.

After attack on RED Line is launched, K.26.c.4.9.

15. ACKNOWLEDGE.

Lieut-Colonel,
General Staff 58th (London) Division.

5th August 1918.

<u>Distribution.</u>

Copy No.	1	C.R.A.
	2	173rd Inf. Bde. * (2 copies)
	3	174th Inf. Bde. * (2 ")
	4	175th Inf. Bde. * (1 copy)
	5	C.R.E.
	6	58th Bn. M.G.C. * (1 copy)
	7	A.A. & Q.M.G.
	8	1/4th Suffolks.
	9	A.D.M.S.
	10	O.C. Signals.
	11-12	III Corps.
	13	III Corps H.A.
	14	18th Division.
	15	3rd Aust. Div.
	16	4th "
	17	10th Tank Battn.
	18	"C" Coy. 10th Tank Battn.
	19	35th Sqdrn. R.A.F.

Tank
Roads

SECRET.

Copy No. _____

FORTHCOMING OPERATIONS.

58th (LONDON) DIVISIONAL INSTRUCTIONS No. 4.

MACHINE GUNS.

1. The Machine Guns will support the attack by covering fire and put down protective barrages during consolidation. They will as far as possible be employed in sections during the advance and where necessary, after the final objective is reached, distributed in pairs in the Forward Zone.

2. For the attack on SAILLY LAURETTE, a section of "C" Coy. will be attached to the 2/10th London Regt. The task allotted to this section will be to prevent any enemy movement along the Spur and the roads approaching the village through K.31. and K.32.

3. During the advance of 174th Inf. Brigade on the first objective, "D" Coy. of the M.G.Bn. and one section of "C" Coy. will be allotted the task of searching by intense fire, the wood and ravines running in a S.W. direction from K.27 central.
    The final barrage line for these guns will correspond to the outpost line of the first objective. Fire will cease on this line when our troops are due to reach the western edge of MALARD WOOD.

4. "B" Coy. of the M.G.Bn. attached to 174th Inf. Brigade will follow the advance of the Brigade as quickly as possible and take up positions to be able to carry out (a) the defence of the ground gained, and (b) to cover the advance of 173rd Inf. Brigade to the final objective.
    The O.C. "B" Coy. M.G.Bn. will arrange the details under orders of 174th Inf. Brigade in consultation with 173rd Inf. Brigade.
    8 guns of "D" Coy. on completion of their task will move forward to assist in the above in accordance with para.6 below.

5. "A" Coy. of the M.G.Bn. will be under the orders of the B.G.C. 173rd Inf. Brigade for the purpose of consolidating the ground between the First and Second Objectives.
    Arrangements should be made for harassing fire on the area E. of the SOMME between MERICOURT-sur-SOMME and ETINEHEM.

6. 8 guns of "D" Coy. in addition to the task allotted in para.3, will be required to fill any gap which might take place on the Northern flank of the DIVISION as the attack progresses. These 8 guns will consequently be in position on the left flank of the Division to carry out their first task as in para.3., and when they move forward to assist "B" Coy. will take up a position for the purpose about K.27.a.0.7. The remaining 8 guns of "D" Coy. will remain in position in Divisional Reserve.

7. 8 guns of "C" Coy. will be with 175th Inf. Brigade in Corps Reserve. The other 8 guns of this Coy. will rejoin them as soon as they can be released.

8. Full details as to duration of fire, timings, safety limits, etc., will be issued to all concerned by the O.C., Machine Gun Battalion.

9. ACKNOWLEDGE.

CW Davis
Lieut.-Colonel
General Staff, 58th (London) Division.

5th August, 1918.

Distribution - See slip attached.

SECRET.   Copy No.

FORTHCOMING OPERATIONS.

58th (LONDON) DIVISIONAL INSTRUCTIONS No.5.

ARTILLERY.

1. **ALLOTMENT OF FIELD ARTILLERY.** -

    Five Brigades of Field Artillery are allotted to the 58th (London) Division, viz:-

	18-pdrs.	4.5 Hows.	6" Newtons.
58th D.A.	36	12	12
30th D.A.	36	12	12
86th Army Bde.) R.F.A.	18	6	-
	90	30	24

    As soon as the creeping barrage is timed to lift from the Protective Barrage for the First Objective, one Bde. R.F.A. will be transferred from 58th Division to 18th Division.

2. **ARTILLERY FIRE BEFORE ZERO.** -

    No more artillery, either Field or Heavy, than was active, on III Corps front on 1st August will be disclosed before Zero.

3. **CREEPING BARRAGE.** -

    A frontal Creeping Barrage will be formed by 18-pdr. guns (average one gun per 25 yards of front) and will precede the Infantry and Tanks.
    The first lift will be at Zero plus 4 minutes.
    The barrage will creep by lifts of 100 yards and conform to the times shown on amended Barrage Map herewith.

    The numbers on the map give the times in mins. after Zero at which the barrage will lift from the lines referred to.

4. **RATES OF FIRE FOR CREEPING BARRAGE.** -

    First 4 mins. ... ... Intense.
    First 4 mins. after leaving
        Protective Barrage for 1st Objective.. Intense.
    Remainder of Creeping Barrage ... Normal.

5. **ACTION OF 4.5"HOWITZERS** is given in Table "A" attached.

    Table "B" for Heavy Artillery will follow as soon as possible.

6. **PROTECTIVE BARRAGES.** -

    (a) For the First Objective. - On reaching the Protective Barrage Line, fire of each unit will remain stationary for 20 minutes, after which it will search to a depth of 500 yards once in every 10 mins. Fire on the Protective Barrage Line will be continued in the intervals between bursts of searching fire.

(b).....

- 2 -

(b) <u>For the Final Objective.</u> - The protective Barrage Line for the Final Objective extends across the front and Left Flank of the 18th Division on our Left but does not extend Southwards across the front of the 58th Division.

(c) <u>Rates of Fire for Protective Barrages.</u> -

18-pdrs.

During Searching.	Normal.
From 15 mins. before the Protective Barrage for the First Objective is timed to lift to 12 mins. before this time.	Intense.
Remaining 5 mins. of this barrage.	Normal.
All other times when the barrages are stationary.	Slow.

7. <u>MOBILE RESERVE ON WHEELS.</u> -

The Fifth Army Brigade R.H.A. will move forward at Zero along the CORBIE - BRAY Road and come into action by this road and Tracks to the South of it, in positions about K.26. This move will be timed so as not to interfere with the advance of the 173rd Inf. Brigade.

1 Section of 18-pdrs. will be attached to the 173rd Inf. Bde. and will come under the orders of the B.G.C., 173rd Inf. Brigade from the time of leaving the First Objective to capture of Final Objective.
It will be in Mobile Reserve East of the River ANCRE and will move forward under the orders of B.G.C., 173rd Infantry Brigade.

The C.R.E., in consultation with the C.R.A. and B.G.C., 174th Infantry Brigade will arrange that tracks across our trenches and gaps in wire are prepared for the advance of these sections.

1 Section of 18-pdrs. will be detailed to support the Battn. of the 175th Inf. Bde. placed at the disposal of the 174th Inf. Bde. to deal with SAILLY-LAURETTE. This Section will come under the orders of the Battalion Commander concerned from Zero until the conclusion of the operation.

8. <u>SUPERIMPOSED BATTERIES.</u> -

1 Battery in each F.A. Brigade covering the 58th Divisional Front will be superimposed on the Barrage Line.
These Batteries will be ready to answer L.L. Calls.

9. <u>MOVES OF HEAVY ARTILLERY.</u> -

The following moves will be made by the H.A. in the 58th Divisional Area :-

1-60 pdr. and 1 6" How. Battery will advance immediately the Final Objective is captured to position about SAILLY-LAURETTE.

1-60 pdr....

1-60 pdr. and 1 6" How Battery will advance on the evening after the attack to positions about J.24 or the Valley running North from SAILLY-LAURETTE.

10. **6" NEWTONS.** -

6" Newtons will be employed to assist in the capture of SAILLY-LAURETTE.

11. **LIAISON.**

A F.A. Liaison Officer not under the rank of Captain will be attached to each of 173rd and 174th Infantry Brigades. They will be in communication with the F.A. covering the Divisional Front and with the Heavy Artillery through D.H.Q.

Artillery Liaison Officers will join the Headquarters to which they are attached at least 24 hours before Zero.

There will be no Liaison Officers attached to Battn. H.Q.

12. **RIGHT FLANK CORPS BARRAGE.** -

F.A. Barrage maps of the Australian Corps co-operating on the Right of the 58th Division are attached for the information of 173rd and 174th Infantry Brigades. *

13. **ACKNOWLEDGE.**

Lieut.-Colonel,
General Staff, 58th (London) Division.

5th August, 1918.

Distribution as per Instruction No. 4.

* Map issued with Divisional Instruction No. 7.

A

15+

21+

0.6 0.10 0.30 0.42 0.54 1.6 1.18 1.30 1.42 1.34 2.30 3.0

NOTE.—(1). These traces are intended to facilitate the communication of information as to the position of targets, which
(2). The squares on this trace are 500 yards in length on the 1/10,000 scale, 1,000 yards in length on the 1/20
on the 1/40,000 scale.
(3). The squares on the trace are fitted to the squares of the map showing the targets, which are then
letters and numbers must also be added to enable the recipient to place the trace in the correct position
may also be traced, but this is not essential. The name and scale of the map to which the trace refers
can be used for the 1/10,000, 1/20,000, or 1/40,000 scale.

G.S.G.S. 3023.

"A" Form
MESSAGES AND SIGNALS.

Army Form C. 2121
(In pads of 100.)

Prefix	Code	m.	Words	Charge	This message is on a/c of:	Recd. at ......m.
Office of Origin and Service Instructions			Sent		......Service.	Date..........
			At ......m.			From ....
			To			
			By		(Signature of "Franking Officer")	By..........

TO	3 Corps	MGRA Sig	DSO	47 Div
	173	CRE	10.55 pm	74 Div
	174	CRE	3 Aust Div	18 Div
		army sig		

| Sender's Number. | Day of Month. | In reply to Number. | AAA |

Command of our troops
right sector will pass
from GOC 5th to GOC
2nd Corps at midnight
17/18 September and
advise all concerned

From: 5 Corps
Place:
Time: 9.35

The above may be forwarded as now corrected. (Z)

Censor.   Signature of Addressor or person authorised to telegraph in his name
* This line should be erased if not required.

Order No. 1625. Wt. W3253/ P 511 27/2 H. & K., Ltd. (E. 2634).

"A" Form
MESSAGES AND SIGNALS.

Army Form C. 2121
(In pads of 100.)

Prefix....Code......m.	Words	Charge.	This message is on a/c of:	Recd. at......m.
Office of Origin and Service Instructions	Sent At ......m.		......Service.	Date........
	To			From ....
	By........	(Signature of "Franking Officer")	By........

TO —

Sender's Number.	Day of Month.	In reply to Number.	AAA
GX 318	30		

Dw HQ closed at
L1B30 and opened at
A19B52 at 3 pm AAA
Addee all recipients of
00153

From 58 Dw
Place
Time 3 Pm

Signature of Addressor: Go to m Kitchen
Mayn

W.D.

GX.334   30   —   AAA

174th Bde. will pass through 175 Bde. and will attack tomorrow at 5.10 a.m. aaa Start line for F.A. Barrage due N and S line from B.18.b.2.0. to B.24.d.2.2. aaa Barrage will dwell 20 mins. on start line lifting at 5.30 at rate of 100 yards in 6 mins. aaa Barrage will dwell 15 mins. on Eastern edge of MARRIERES WOOD then lifting again at rate of 100 yards in 6 mins. up to objective which will be a line from C.14.a.3.0. on left through C.14.c.0.0. to edge of WOOD C.19.d.3.0. thence edge of WOOD C.19.d.1.5. aaa All troops East of barrage start line will be withdrawn West before Zero aaa. 175 Bde. will hold position on SPUR B.18.central - B.24.central after 174 Bde. have passed through aaa Acknowledge aaa Added all recipients of O.O 153

→ Barrage will dwell for 15 minutes 300 yards beyond the objective at a slow rate of fire aaa.

58th Divn.
9 p.m.

G.E.W. Harrison
for Lt.-Col.
G.S.

"A" Form
MESSAGES AND SIGNALS.

Army Form C. 2121
(In pads of 100.)

TO: W.D.

Sender's Number: YX 346
Day of Month: 31
AAA

58 Div is probably to be relieved by 74th Div tonight aaa No further details yet available aaa Addsd Bde CRA CRE Sig Q APM Train 258 DADOS DADMS C Comdt Reception Camp -MGBn

From: 8 Div
Place:
Time: 10.30 am

Censor: Lt Col W W Harrison

W.D.

G.X. 353　　　31　　--　　AAA

173rd Inf. Bde. will move forward by busses
this evening and will attack tomorrow morning
aaa Details later aaa Division will not
be relieved until after the attack aaa
Added. all recipients O.O.'s. Within the
Division -.

58th Divn.
2 p.m.

　　　　　　　　　　　　　　　　　[signature]
　　　　　　　　　　　　　　　　　Lt.-Col. G.S.

GX 358.   31.   AAA

173rd Bde. will move forward by bus this evening and
attack through 174 Bde. tomorrow in conjunction with
47th Division on left and 3rd Australian Div. on
right AAA Dividing line on North a straight line from
O.14.a.3.0. to C.10.central on South from O.20.central to
O.16.d.0.5. AAA Objective O.10.c.6.8. to C.10.d.8.4.
thence South by trench line to O.16.d.0.5 AAA Barrage will
fall at 5.50 a.m. on line RANCOURT - Mt. ST. QUENTIN Road as
far South as O.20.b.0.04.and thence on a line to O.20.b.3-1.5.2
AAA It will dwell on start line for 15 minutes and then
make lifts parallel to the road at the rate of 100 yards in
five minutes up to the objective AAA Protective barrage will
be maintained beyond the objective for 15 minutes after the
barrage reaches the furthest point of the objective AAA
All troops East of the Start Line within the Divisional
Boundaries will be withdrawn before Zero AAA 174 Bde. will
continue to hold present position on eastern slopes of
Spur O.13.d. O.19.a. In touch with Australian Div. at Old
QUARRY O.20.central AAA 173 Bde. H.Q. Hill 110 AAA Added
all recipients O.O. 152 plus 74th Division.

C.W.B.Amos
Lt.-Colonel,
G.S.

58 Btvn.
4.15 pm.

D.R. L.S.

GX 330   31   AAA

175. Bde. Group will move as soon as possible to A.22 - A.28. Bde. H.Q. QUARRY A.28.a. South of MARICOURT AAA 175 Bde. will ensure that traffic on the MARICOURT - CLERY Rd. is not delayed in any way by their troops or transport AAA Transport Lines 175 Bde. remain in present location tonight. AAA Addsd 175 Bde. reptd all recipients O.O. 153 plus 74 Div.

[signature]

Lt.-Colonel,
G.S.

58 Divn.
4.50 pm.

Urgent Ops.
Priority to
173 Bde. 3rd Aust Div.
47 Div

GX359.   31   ..   AAA

Ref. GX358 AAA Barrage will fall at 5 am
and not 5-30 am AAA It will dwell on Start
Line for 10 mins. and not for 15 mins. AAA
ACKNOWLEDGE AAA Added. all recipients of
GX358

                                      [signature]
                                      Lt-Col
                                      GS.

58th Div.
9 pm.

174.   APM.   35 Bgdr RAF
175.   AOMS   2nd L.Bn. M/Gun
CRA   3 Tanks   74 Divn
CRE   3 — HQ.
M/gun   3 — Div.
Sig   Bgdn. Corps Cav.
Arty   Coy — Cyclist

File

Urgent Operations
Priority to 173 Bde.

G.X. 374   31   --   AAA
Reference G.X. 358 Barrage will dwell on
Start Line 5 mins. and not 15 mins aaa
Added all recipients G.X. 358

58th Divn.
10.30 p.m.

G. J. Gough Capt.
Lt.-Col.
G.S.

The following is a list of part of the war material captured by this Division (and the 131st Regt. U.S. Infantry attached) since the commencement of operations on the 8th instant.

Some Trench Mortars and 77 mm. guns in addition are believed to have been taken away by Australian Troops, and there are probably more guns in the area which have not yet been located.

77 mm. Guns.

No.				Location.
8	....	....	....	K.33.b., along Western edge of BOIS CELESTINE.
4	....	....	....	K.29.a.5.5.
3	....	....	....	K.23.c.8.9. to K.23.d.1.8.
5	....	....	....	K.11.b.5.8.
1	....	....	....	K.22.a.2.1.
1	....	....	....	K.21.a.9.9.
3	....	....	....	K.28.d.3.4.
1	....	....	....	K.32.a.3.7.
1	....	....	....	K.26.b.
1	....	....	....	K.32.a.8.6.
1	....	....	....	K.27.a.2.5.
2	....	....	....	K.34.b.8.5.
1	....	....	....	Q.4.d.
4	....	....	....	
2	....	....	....	N.W. end CHIPILLY.

37.
====

4.1 inch Guns.

4	....	....	....	K.33.b.
5	....	....	....	K.27.d.9.1.
3	....	....	....	K.23.c.7.2.
1	....	....	....	K.18.a.5.0.

13.
====

4.2 inch Howitzers.

2	....	....	....	K.33.d.8.8.
2	....	....	....	K.34.c.
2	....	....	....	K.34.a.3.8.
4	....	....	....	K.17.b.2.4.

10.
====

5.9 inch Howitzers.

1	....	....	....	K.28.d.9.3.
2	....	....	....	K.18.c.
2	....	....	....	K.29.a.1.6.

5.
====

5.9 inch Guns.

| 1 | .... | .... | .... | K.18.c. |

8-inch Howitzers.

| 1 | .... | .... | .... | K.29.a.1.9. |
| 1 | .... | .... | .... | K.29.a.3.9. |

2.
===

GRAND TOTAL - 68 guns and Howitzers.

It has only been possible to obtain the number of Trench Mortars and Machine Guns captured by the 174th Infantry Brigade. The actual total captured by the Division is very much in excess of these, which are as follows:-

Trench Mortars.

Heavy 9
Light 27

Machine Guns.

Heavy 57
Light 133

In addition an enemy aeroplane intact was captured in Q.4.b.

Large quantities of S.A.A. and ammunition of all calibres were taken.

Also a large quantity of rifles, equipment and stores were taken, especially in CHIPILLY.

1,925 unwounded prisoners, including 58 officers, were captured by and passed through the cage of the Division (this includes those taken by 131 Regt. U.S. Infantry, but not any captured by other Divisions who passed through Corps Cage).

The number of wounded prisoners cannot yet be ascertained.

Many of the enemy were killed by the fire of the Artillery, Machine Guns and Infantry, and with the bayonet.

Lieut.-Colonel,
General Staff, 58th (London) Division.

12th August, 1918.

C.R.A.	6	copies.
C.R.E.	5	"
173rd Inf.Bde.	5	"
174th Inf.Bde.	5	"
175th Inf.Bde.	5	"
Signals.	2	"
58th Bn. M.G.C.	6	"
Div. Train.	4	"
A.D.M.S.	4	"
1/4th Suffolks.	2	"
"A" and "Q"	2	"
Camp Commandt.	1	copy.
D.A.D.O.S.	1	"
D.A.D.V.S.	1	"
A.P.M.	1	"

Copy to 58 D.A. (Rear)   194/389

58th (LONDON) DIVISION.

Information about the enemy during the Battle of 8th - 11th August, 1918.

----

1. On the morning of the 8th August, the enemy Order of Battle, N. to S. was :-

    233 Divn. (448 I.R.
             (449 I.R.   ALBERT SECTOR.
             (450 I.R.

    54 Res. Divn. (246 R.I.R.
                  (247 R.I.R.   to VILLE-sur-ANCRE.
                  (248 R.I.R.

    27th Divn. (120 I.R.
               (123 Gren. Regt.   MORLANCOURT SECTOR.
               (124 I.R.

    43rd Res. Divn. (201 R.I.R.
                    (202 R.I.R.   Astride R. SOMME (in process of relief
                    (203 R.I.R.   by 108th Division.)

    13th Divn. (13 I.R.
               (15 I.R.   HAMEL SECTOR.
               (55 I.R.

2. The brunt of the attack on 58th Divisional Front on the morning of the 8th inst. was borne by the 27th Division (a good fresh WURTEMBERG Division), by the 202 I.R. (43rd Res. Divn.) and by the 265th I.R. (108 Divn.), who were relieving the 202 R.I.R.

3. A very large number of prisoners of the 265th I.R. were taken, and also some of the 202nd I.R. A considerable number of prisoners were taken from the 120 I.R. and 123 Gren. Regt.

4. Artillery and Machine Gunners of the 107th Divn. had not yet left the Sector after the relief of their Division by the 27th Division, and men of these units were captured.
    In addition, artillerymen and other Divisional troops of other Divisions were captured including Heavy Artillerymen and men of a Wireless Detachment belonging to the XI Army Corps.
    During the fighting of the 9th and 10th August various Regiments and Battalions of the Divisions in Line were moved up from Reserve. In addition two Battalions of 450 I.R. (233rd Divn), in reserve to the ALBERT Sector, reinforced the front, and also one Battalion of the 479 I.R. (243 Divn) from Corps Reserve.
    Other artillery units were also identified and further Divisional and sector troops.
    In addition the 26th Res. Divn. was moved up from rest.

IDENTIFICATIONS.   (i) Elements of 7 Divisions have been identified on the front MORLANCOURT - R. SOMME, during the first three day's fighting.
    (ii) Of these :-
        3 were normally holding the front.
            54th Res. Divn, 27 Div, 43 Res. Divn.
        1 was in process of relieving astride the R. SOMME -
            108 Divn.
        1 was in reserve to this front -
            243rd Divn.
        1 was holding the ALBERT Sector and contributed two Battalions from reserve in the MONTAUBAN Area.
            233 Divn.
        1 was in rest and has re-inforced the front -
            26 Res. Divn.

5. Elements of 14 Regiments (a German Regt. approx. = a British Brigade) have taken part in the battle on the front MORLANCOURT-R. SOMME.

4. Approx. 27 Battalions have been identified on the above front. Though many of these Battalions were engaged entirely against this Division it cannot be concluded that the total fighting strength of 27 Battalions has been engaged against this Division.

5. Below are the total identifications obtained by this Division (in conjunction with the 33rd American Division).

COMPLETE LIST OF IDENTIFICATIONS MADE BY THIS DIVISION (in conjunction with 33rd American Division).

54th Res. Divn. (246 R.I.R. (3rd Bn)
(247 R.I.R. (2nd and 3rd Bns.)
(248 R.I.R. (3rd Bn.)

233 Divn.   450 I.R. (2nd and 3rd Bns.)

243 Divn. (479 I.R. (3rd Bn.)
(233 F.A.R.
(443 Minenwerfers.

27 Divn. (120 I.R. (1st, 2nd and 3rd Bns.)
(123 Gren Regt (1st, 2nd and 3rd Bns.)
(124 I.R. (1st, 2nd and 3rd Bns.)
(13 F.A.R.
(27 Minenwerfers.

43 Res. Divn. (201 R.I.R. (? 2 Bns.)
(202 R.I.R. (1st Bn.)
(43 Res. F.A.R.

108 Divn. (97 I.R. (1st, 2nd, and 3rd Bns.)
(137 I.R. (1st, 2nd and 3rd Bns.)
(265 R.I.R. (3rd Bn.)
(Res. Pion. 33.

107 Divn.   213 F.A.R.

26 Res. Divn. 119 R.I.R. (1st Bn.) (identification made by Australi..

SECTOR TROOPS. (LANDWEHR FUSSARTILLERIE Bn. 4.
(FUSSARTILLERIE Bn. 16.
(FUNKERABTEILUNG 144.
(SCHARSCHUTZEN M.G. ABT. 6.

TOTAL PRISONERS and GUNS CAPTURED BY THIS DIVISION (in connection with 132st American Infantry Regt.) (up to 4 pm 11th August, 1918)

Prisoners through Divl. Cage (unwounded) ... 56 Officers.
Prisoners through A.D.S. (wounded) ... 1950 O.R. About 100 - 200.

TOTAL GUNS CAPTURED. 77mm ... 37.; 105mm ... 23.; 150mm ... 6, 21cm ... 2.   Total ... 68.

The above have actually been counted and map references taken.

T.G. Hughes. Lieut
for Lieut.-Colonel,

13th August, 1918.   General Staff, 58th (London) Division.

Copies to :-   G.O.C.   33rd Amer Divn. (12).
G.S.O. I.   173rd I. Bde. (5).
Filo.   174th I. Bde. (5).
"Q". (1).   175th I. Bde. (5).
Hand over (5).   1/4th Suffolks (1).
III Corps "I". (1).   M.G. Bn. (5).
C.R.A. (8).   Spare. (6).
C.R.E. (1).
A.D.M.S. (1).

Originals

1 - 31st August 1918.

War Diary

App. "B"

Locations.

S E C R E T.   58th (LONDON) DIVISION.   Copy No....

LOCATION OF UNITS 6 a.m. 2nd August, 1918.

Reference Sheets 62D N.E. and 62D N.W. 1/40,000.

Divisional H.Q.	BEAUCOURT CHATEAU.
58th Div. Arty. H.Q.	BEAUCOURT CHATEAU.
290th Bde. R.F.A.	C.7.c.7.8.
291st -do-	BAVELINCOURT.
58th D.T.M.O.	WARLOY.
58th D.A.C.	Chateau, BEHENCOURT.
25th Div. R.A., H.Q.	-do-
110 Bde. R.F.A.	BEHENCOURT.
112 -do-	D.7.a.8.7.
25th Div. Amm. Col.	B.17.c.6.9.
25th D.T.M.O.	D.4.c.2.4.
5th Army Bde. R.H.A.	D.21.c.90.30.
86th Army Bde. R.F.A.	The Chateau, BAVELINCOURT.

Right Sub-sector.   K.7.b. - E.19.b.0.2.
173rd Inf. Brigade H.Q.   D.27.a.0.3.
  2nd Bn. London Rgt.   Line Left Sub-section H.Q. D.29.b.2.4.
  6th   -do-   Brigade Reserve H.Q. D.27.a.0.3.
  1st Bn. 132 A. Regt.   (Line Right Sub-section H.Q. J.11.a.7.7.
  3rd   -do-   (Support. H.Q. J.5.d.8.5.
  173rd T.M. Bty.   D.27.a.0.3.

Left Sub-sector.   E.19.b.0.2. - E.8.a.3.2.
175th Inf. Brigade H.Q.   D.21.b.5.1.
  9th Bn. London Rgt.   Support H.Q. D.17.b.15.40.
  10th   -do-   ST. LAURENT FM. H.Q. C.18.d.2.5.
  12th   -do-   Line Left Sub-section. H.Q. D.12.d.5.6.
  3rd Bn. 132 A. Rgt.   Line Right sub-section H.Q. D.24.a.1.7.
  175th T.M. Bty.   LINE. H.Q. D.21.b.5.1.

Reserve Brigade.
174th Inf. Brigade H.Q.   EBART'S FARM C.1.c.5.1.)
  6th Bn. Lon. Rgt.   ROUND WOOD C.20.b.7.1.   ) Moving to
  7th   -do-   "   "   C.20.b. and d.) CANAPLES Area
  8th   -do-   BAIZIEUX.   ) 2nd inst.
  174th T.M.Bty.   BOIS ROBERT C.11.   )

1/4th Suffolk Rgt, Pnrs.   BAIZIEUX.   Moving to VILLERS BOCAGE
                                            on 2nd inst.
C.R.E.   BEAUCOURT CHATEAU.
  503rd Field Coy. R.E.   C.5.b.2.3.
  504th -do-   D.26.b.2.8.
  511th -do-   C.5.b.7.8.

58th Bn. M.G.C. H.Q.   EBART'S FARM C.1.c.5.1.
  "A" Company.   D.21.b.3.1.   (moving to HALLOY-LES-PERNOIS.
  "B"   "   D.27.a.3.3.   2nd inst.)
  "C"   "   EBART'S FARM C.1.c.5.1.
  "D"   "   FRANVILLERS.

                                            Lieut.-Colonel,
                                   General Staff, 58th (London) Division.
) 1st August, 1918.

S_E_C_R_E_T.   Copy No.....

58th (LONDON) DIVISION.

LOCATION OF UNITS 6 a.m. 3rd August, 1918.

Reference Sheets 62D N.E. and 62D N.W. 1/20,000. Sht. LENS 11. 1/100,000.

		Moving after 6 am. 3rd to :-
<u>Divisional H.Q.</u>	BEAUCOURT CHATEAU.	
<u>58th Div. Arty. H.Q.</u>	BEAUCOURT CHATEAU.	
290th Bde. R.F.A.	C.7.c.7.8.	
291st -do-	BAVELINCOURT.	
58th D.T.M.O.	WARLOY.	
58th D.A.C.	Chateau, BEHENCOURT.	
<u>25th Div. R.A. H.Q.</u>	-do-	
110th Bde. R.F.A.	BEHENCOURT.	
112th -do-	D.7.a.8.7.	
25th Div. Amm. Col.	B.17.c.6.9.	
25th B.T.M.O.	D.4.c.2.4.	
5th Army Bde. R.H.A.	D.21.c.90.30.	
86th Army Bde. R.F.A.	The Chateau, BAVELINCOURT.	
<u>173rd Inf. Brigade H.Q.</u>	BERTEAUCOURT.	
2nd Bn. Lon. Rgt.	ST. LEGER.	
3rd -do-	BERTEAUCOURT.	
4th -do-	PERNOIS.	
173rd T.M. Bty.	BERTEAUCOURT.	
<u>174th Inf. Brigade.</u>	CANAPLES.	
6th Bn. Lon. Rgt.	CANAPLES.	
7th -do-	HALLOY-LES-PERNOIS.	
8th -do-	WARGNIES.	
174th T.M. Bty.	CANAPLES.	
Line Loft Sub-sector.	E.19.b.0.2. - E.8.a.3.2.	
<u>175th Inf. Brigade. H.Q.</u>	D.21.b.5.1.	)
9th Bn. Lon. Rgt.	Support H.Q. D.17.b.15.40.	)
10th -do-	ST. LAURENT FM.	)
	H.Q. C.18.d.2.5.	) VIGNACOURT Area.
12th -do-	LINE. Left Sub-section.	)
	H.Q. D.12.d.5.6.	)
3rd Bn. 132 A. Rgt.	LINE. Right sub-section.	)
	H.Q. D.24.a.1.7.	)
175th T.M. Bty.	LINE. H.Q. D.21.b.5.1.	)
1/4th Suffolk Rgt. Pnrs.	VILLERS BOCAGE.	
<u>C.R.E.</u>	BEAUCOURT CHATEAU.	
503rd Field Coy. R.E.	C.5.b.2.3.	VIGNACOURT.
504th -do-	BERTEAUCOURT.	
511th -do-	HAVERNAS.	
<u>58th Bn.M.G.C. H.Q.</u>	EBART'S FARM. C.1.c.5.1.	
"A" Company.	HALLOY-LES-PERNOIS.	
"B" "	D.27.a.3.3.	FLESSELLES.
"C" "	BERTEAUCOURT.	
"D" "	FRANVILLERS.	FLESSELLES.

for Lieut.-Colonel,
General Staff, 58th (London) Division.

2nd August, 1918.

S_E_C_R_E_T. Copy No. 41

58th (LONDON) DIVISION.

No. 3.

LOCATION OF UNITS 6 a.m. 4th August, 1918.

Reference Sheets 62D N.E. and 62D N.W. 1/20,000. LENS Sht.11.1/100,000.

		Moving after 6 a.m. 4th to:-
Divisional H.Q.	BEAUCOURT CHATEAU.	QUERRIEU CH.
58th Div. Arty. H.Q.	BEAUCOURT CHATEAU.	QUERREIU CH.
290th Bde. R.F.A.	C.7.c.7.8.	
291st -do-	BAVELINCOURT.	
58th D.T.M.O.	VARLOY.	
58th D.A.C.	Chateau, BEHENCOURT.	
25th Div. Arty. H.Q.	-do-	
110th Bde. R.F.A.	BEHENCOURT.	
112th -do-	D.7.a.8.7.	
25th Div. Amm. Col.	E.17.c.6.9.	
25th D.T.M.O.	D.4.c.2.4.	
169th A. Bde. F.A.	D.21.c.90.30.	
86th A. Bde. F.A.	The Chateau, BAVELINCOURT.	

173rd Inf. Brigade H.Q.	BERTEAUCOURT.
2nd Bn. Lon. Rgt.	ST. LEGER.
3rd -do-	BERTEAUCOURT.
4th -do-	PERNOIS.
173rd T.M. Bty.	BERTEAUCOURT.

174th Inf. Brigade H.Q.	CANAPLES.
6th Bn. Lon. Rgt.	CANAPLES.
7th -do-	HALLOY-LES-PERNOIS.
8th -do-	WARGNIES.
174th T.M. Bty.	CANAPLES.

175th Inf. Brigade H.Q.	VIGNACOURT.
9th Bn. Lon. Rgt.)	
10th -do-) VIGNACOURT.	
12th -do-)	
175th T.M. Bty.)	

| 1/4th Suffolk Rgt. | VILLERS BOCAGE. |

C.R.E.	BEAUCOURT CHATEAU.	QUERRIEU CH.
503rd Field Coy.	QUERRIEU.	
504th -do-	BERTEAUCOURT.	
511th -do-	HAVERNAS.	

58th Bn. M.G.C., H.Q.	FLESSELLES.
"A" Company.	HALLOY-LES-PERNOIS.
"B" "	BEHENCOURT
"C" "	BERTEAUCOURT.
"D" "	BEHENCOURT.

G.D. Gough Capt
Lieut.-Colonel,
General Staff, 58th (London) Division.

3rd August, 1918.

58th (LONDON) DIVISION.

Copy. No. 19

LOCATION OF UNITS 6 a.m. 5th August, 1918.

Reference Sheets 62D N.E., N.W. 1/20,000. Sht. LENS 11 1/100,000.

Divisional H.Q.	QUERRIEU CHATEAU.
58th Div. Arty. H.Q.	QUERRIEU CHATEAU.
290th F.A. Brigade.	C.7.c.7.8.
291st -do-	BAVELINCOURT.
58th D.T.M.O.	WARLOY.
58th D.A.C.	Chateau, BEHENCOURT.
173rd Inf. Brigade.	BEHENCOURT.
2nd Bn. Lon. Rgt.	I.15.a.
3rd -do-	I.15.c.
4th -do-	I.21.a.
173rd T.M. Bty.	BOIS ESCARDONNEUSE I.15.
174th Inf. Brigade.	LAHOUSSOYE.
6th Bn. Lon. Rgt.)	
7th -do-)	J.21.c. and 27.a
8th -do-)	
174th T.M. Bty.)	
175th Inf. Brigade.	VIGNACOURT.
9th Bn. Lon. Rgt.	VIGNACOURT.
10th -do-	J.25.b., J.26.a.
12th -do-	VIGNACOURT.
175th T.M. Bty.	VIGNACOURT
1/4th Suffolk Regt. Pnrs.	I.15.a.
C.R.E.	QUERRIEU CHATEAU.
503rd Field Coy. R.E.)	
504th -do-)	I.15.a. and b.
511th -do-)	
58th Bn. M.G.C. H.Q.	PONT NOYELLES.
"A" Company.	I.15.
"B" "	J.21.c.
"C" "	BERTEAUCOURT.
"D" "	BEHENCOURT.

4th August, 1918.

Lieut.-Colonel,
General Staff, 58th (London) Division.

Copy No. 1	A.D.C. for G.O.C.	11 & 12	III Corps.
2	173rd Inf. Brigade.	13	18th Division.
3	174th Inf. Brigade.	14	10th Tank Bn.
4	175th Inf. Brigade.	15	"C" Coy. 10 Tank Bn.
5	C.R.A.	16	A.D.M.S.
6	C.R.E.	17	1/4th Suffolks.
7	Signals.	18 & 19	War Diary.
8	58th Bn. M.G.C.	20	File.
9 & 10	"A" and "Q".		

58th (LONDON) DIVISION.   Copy No.

LOCATION OF UNITS 6 a.m. 5th August, 1918.

Reference Sheets 62D N.E. and N.W. 1/20,000 Sht. LENS 11 1/100,000.

Divisional H.Q.	QUERRIEU CHATEAU.
58th Div. Arty. H.Q.	QUERRIEU CHATEAU.
290th F.A. Brigade.	0.7.c.7.8.
291st —do—	BAVELINCOURT.
58th D.A.C.	Chateau, BEHENCOURT.
173rd Inf. Brigade H.Q.	BEHENCOURT.
2nd Bn. Lon. Rgt.	
3rd —do—	J.21.c. and 27.a.
4th —do—	
173rd T.M. Bty.	
174th Inf. Brigade H.Q.	LAHOUSROYE.
6th Bn. Lon. Rgt.	
7th —do—	LINE.
8th —do—	
174th T.M. Bty.	
175th Inf. Brigade.	VIGNACOURT.
9th Bn. Lon. Rgt.	VIGNACOURT.
18th —do—	J.25b., J.26.a.
12th —do—	VIGNACOURT.
175th T.M. Bty.	VIGNACOURT.
1/4th Suffolk Rgt. Pnrs.	I.15.a.
C. R. E.	
503rd Field Coy. R.E.	
504th —do—	I.15.a. and b.
511th —do—	
58th Bn. M.G.C. H.Q.	PONT NOYELLES.
"A" Company.	I.16.
"B" "	J.21.c.
"C" "	BERTEAUCOURT.
"D" "	BEHENCOURT.

G. F. Gough Capt
Lieut.-Colonel,
General Staff, 58th (London) Division.

5th August, 1918.

Copy No.			
1	A.D.C. for G.O.C.	13	18th Division.
2	173rd Inf. Brigade.	14	3rd Aust. Divn.
3	174th Inf. Brigade.	15	"C" Coy. 10th Tank Bn.
4	175th Inf. Brigade.	16	A.D.M.S.
5	C.R.A.	17	10th Tank. Bn.
6	C.R.E.	18	1/4th Suffolk Rgt.
7	Signals.	19 & 20	War Diary.
8	58th Bn. M.G.C.	21	File.
9 & 10	"A" & "Q".		
11 & 12	III Corps.		

SECRET

W.D.

58th (LONDON) DIVISION.

Copy No 19

LOCATION of UNITS 6 a.m. 14th August, 1918.

Reference Sheets 62D N.E. and N.W. 1/20,000.)

Divisional H.Q.	ST. GRATIEN.
58th Divl. Arty.	(with LIAISON FORCE).
173rd Inf. Brigade, H.Q.	Chateau, QUERRIEU.
2nd Bn London Rgt.)	
3rd -do-)	QUERRIEU.
4th -do-)	
173rd T.M. Bty.)	
174th Inf. Brigade H.Q.	FRECHENCOURT.
6th Bn. London Rgt.)	
7th -do-)	ROUND WOOD C.20.b. & d.
8th -do-)	
174th T.M. Bty.)	
175th Inf. Brigade H.Q.	FRECHENCOURT.
9th Bn. London Rgt.)	
10th -do-)	BOIS ESCARDONNEUSE. I. 15.
12th -do-)	
175th T.M. Bty.)	
1/4th Suffolk Rgt. Pnrs.	BOIS ESCARDONNEUSE. I.15.
C. R. E.	ST. GRATIEN.
503rd Field Coy. R.E.)	
504th -do-)	BOIS ESCARDONNEUSE I. 15.
511th -do-)	
58th Bn. M.G.C., H.Q.	PONT NOYELLES.
"A" Company.)	
"B" ")	WOOD I.14. a. & c.
"C" ")	
"D" ")	

Lieut.-Colonel,
General Staff, 58th (London) Division.

13th August, 1918.

Copy No.
1 A.D.C. for G.O.C.
2 173rd Inf. Bde.
3 174th Inf. Bde.
4 175th Inf. Bde.
5 C.R.A., 58th Divn.
6 C.R.E.
7 Signals.
8 M.G. Bn.
9 & 10 "A" & "Q".
11 & 12 III Corps.
13 47th Division.
14 12th Division.
15 18th Division.
16 63rd Division.
17 A.D.M.S.
18 1/4th Suffolk Regt.
19) War Diary.
20)
21 File.

SECRET.   58th (LONDON) DIVISION.   Copy No 18

LOCATION OF UNITS 6 a.m. 18th August, 1918.

Reference Sheets 62D N.E. and N.W. 1/20,000.

<u>Divisional H.Q.</u>	ST. GRATIEN.
<u>58th Divl. Arty. H.Q.</u>	(with LIAISON FORCE).
<u>173rd Inf. Brigade H.Q.</u>	Chateau, QUERRIEU.
2nd Bn. Lon. Rgt.	QUERRIEU.
3rd -do-)	
4th -do-)	PONT NOYELLES.
173rd T.M. Bty.)	
<u>174th Inf. Brigade H.Q.</u>	FRECHENCOURT.
6th Bn. Lon. Rgt.)	
7th -do-)	ROUND WOOD C.20.b. & d.
8th -do-)	
174th T.M. Bty.)	
<u>175th Inf. Brigade H.Q.</u>	FRECHENCOURT.
9th Bn. Lon. Rgt.)	
10th -do-)	BOIS ESCARDONNEUSE. I.15.
12th -do-)	
175th T.M. Bty.)	
<u>1/4th Suffolk Rgt. Pnrs.</u>	BOIS ESCARDONNEUSE. I.15.
<u>C. R. E.</u>	ST. GRATIEN.
503rd Field Coy. R.E.	I.15.a.5.5.
504th -do-	I.15.a.9.6.
511th -do-	I.14.a.4.6.
<u>58th Bn. M.G.B. H.Q.</u>	KEY WOOD I.14.c.
"A" Company.)	
"B" ")	KEY WOOD I.14.a. and c.
"C" ")	
"D" ")	

E.W.Harrison Major
(?) Lieut.-Colonel,
17th August, 1918. General Staff, 58th (London) Division.

Copy No. 1. A.D.C. for G.O.C.   14 12th Division.
     2 173rd Inf. Bde.   15 18th Division.
     3 174th Inf. Bde.   16 A.D.M.S.
     4 175th Inf. Bde.   17 1/4th Suffolk Regt.
     5 C.R.A., 58th Divn.   18)
     6 C.R.E.   19) War Diary.
     7 Signals.   20 File.
     8 M.G. Bn.
  9 & 10 "A" & "Q".
 11 & 12 III Corps.
    13 47th Division.

SECRET.   Copy No. ....

58th (LONDON) DIVISION.

LOCATION OF UNITS at 5 p.m. August 24th, 1918.

Reference Sheets 62D N.W. and N.E. 1/20,000.

58th Divisional H.Q.	HEILLY.
12th Divisional H.Q.	D.26.b.8.2.
47th Divisional H.Q.	QUERRIEU.
47th Div. Arty. H.Q.	HEILLY.
58th Div. Arty. H.Q.	(With Liaison Force).
173rd Inf. Brigade H.Q.	K.14.b.2.2.
2nd Bn. London Rgt.)	
3rd -do-)	K.6.c. and d. K.12.a. & b.
4th -do-)	
173rd T.M. Bty.	K.14.b.
174th Inf. Brigade H.Q.	K.14.b.2.2.
6th Bn. London Rgt.	K.13.a.6.3.
7th -do-	K.13.d.1.8.
8th -do-	K.13.b.4.3.
174th T.M. Bty.	K.14.b.
175th Inf. Brigade H.Q.	K.14.b.2.2.
9th Bn. London Rgt.	LINE, about F.27.central.
10th -do-	LINE, about L.2.central.
12th -do-	LINE, about L.3.d.
175th T.M. Bty.	K.14.b.
1/4th Suffolk Rgt.	J.9. and J.15. (Moving to K.10.b. & d. at about 10.30 p.m. 24th).
C.R.E.	HEILLY CHATEAU.
503rd Field Coy. R.E.)	
504th -do-)	J.8.b. (Moving to J.24.b. at 4 p.m. 24th August).
511th -do-)	
Horse Lines Field Coys. R.E.	J.8.b.
140 Inf. Brigade H.Q.	K.17.a.5.5.
141 -do-	K.17.a.5.5.
142 -do-	J.11.d.5.5.
22 Corps Cavalry.	LAHOUSSOYE.
Coy. of 22 Corps Cyclists.	-do-
2 Coys. 2nd (L.G.) M.G. Bn.	One Coy. at K.15.d.6.1. One Coy. K.25.d.7.3.

C.K. Spence, Capt.
for
Lieut.-Colonel,
24/8/18.   General Staff, 58th (London) Division.

Copy No.1	A.D.C. for G.O.C.	15	47th Division.
2	173rd Inf. Brigade.	16	3rd Aust. Divn.
3	174th Inf. Brigade.	17	18th Division.
4	175th Inf. Brigade.	18	A.D.M.S.
5	C.R.A. 47th Division.	19	1/4th Suffolk Regt.
6	C.R.A. 58th Division.	20	XXII Corps Cavalry.
7	C.R.E.	21	2nd (L.G.) M.G. Bn.
8	Signals.	22	1st Tank Bn.
9	M.G. Bn.	23 & 24	War Diary.
10 & 11	"A" & "Q".	25	File.
12 & 13	III Corps.		
14	12th Division.		

War Diary

(6339) Wt. W160/M3016 1,500,000 10/17 McA & W Ltd (E 1898) Forms W3091.   Army Form W.3091.

Cover for Documents.

Nature of Enclosures.

Notes, or Letters written.

WD/

GX.211. 12   AAA.

Ref. 55 Div. GX.206 AAA.

142nd Inf. Bde. H.Q.

for "J.26.c.0.8. road K.26.c.0.8".

55 Div.
7 p.

A. Durrit Lt.Col.
     G.S.

S E C R E T.

Copy No. 23

58th (LONDON) DIVISION ORDER No. 145.

1. The following moves will take place on 13th August. -

   (a) 175th Inf. Brigade to BOIS ESCARDONNEUSE.
   No restrictions as to route.
   Move to commence 4-30 pm.
   Brigade Headquarters - FRECHENCOURT.

   (b) 174th Inf. Brigade to ROUND WOOD, C.20.
   No restrictions as to route.
   Move to commence at 8-30 pm.
   Brigade Headquarters - FRECHENCOURT.

   (c) M.G. Coys. at present with 175th Inf. Brigade on relief and other Coys. 58th Bn. M.G.C. under orders from O.C. 58th Bn. M.G.C. to Wood in I.14.a and c.
   No restrictions as to route or time of move except -

       (a) As above for Coys. with 175th Inf. Bde.
       (b) That M.G. Coy. with 174th Inf. Bde. will not move before 8-30 pm.

   (d) 1/4th Suffolks (Pioneers) and Fd. Coys. R.E. to bivouacs in BOIS ESCARDONNEUSE.
   No restrictions as to route, but to be clear of bivouacs by 4 pm.

2. Battle Surplus 175th Inf. Bde. will move to BOIS ESCARDONNEUSE by 4 pm. tomorrow, 13th inst.
   " 174th Inf. Bde. has already been ordered to ROUND WOOD.
   " 173rd Inf. Bde. will rejoin its Brigade tomorrow morning, 13th inst.

CMDavies
Lieut-Colonel,
General Staff 58th (London) Division.

Issued at 5-15 pm

Distribution.

As for O.O. 143. 40' Div. Reception Camp
142nd Inf Bde

W.D.

GX.226.   13.   AAA.

173   Bde   will   move
today   at   5pm.   to
billets in   QUERRIEU and
not   as   stated   AAA.
Brigade H.Q.   CHATEAU QUERRIEU
AAA   Added   all recipients
of   OC.145

58 DIV.
1.10. pm.

T. O. Goodn— Capt

Lt Col
G.S.

"W.D."

GX.227   13.   AAA.
Ref. O.O.145 para. 1(b)
move will commence at
5 pm. instead of 8-30 pm.
AAA. 175 Bde. on
arrival at BOIS ESCARDONEUSE
will be Bde. in
Corps Reserve in place
of 173 Bde AAA.
Added all recipients of
O.O.145.

58 Div.
1.10 pm.

G.J. [illegible] Capt.

SECRET.

G.S.3455.

III Corps

174th Inf. Brigade is placed at the disposal of G.O.C. 18th Division for Tactical purposes from 12 midnight 20/21st August.

The Brigade will remain in the vicinity of ROUND WOOD. Its role will be that of support or counter-attack brigade to the 18th Division.

Except for counter-attack purposes it will not be employed East of the LAVIEVILLE LINE.

In the event of the Brigade being used by the 18th Division the Battle Surplus will march to join the Reception Camp at MIRVAUX immediately.

174th Inf. Brigade to ACKNOWLEDGE.

CW Davis
Lieut-Colonel,
General Staff 50th (London) Division.

20th August 1918.

Copy to List "B".

List "B".

"Q"   A.D.M.S.
S.R.A.   D.A.D.O.S.
C.R.E.   D.A.D.V.S.
173rd Inf. Bde.   O.C. Train.
174th Inf. Bde.   S.S.O.
175th Inf. Bde.   A.P.M.
58th Bn. M.G.C.   58th Div. Recptn. Camp.
O.C. Signals.   249th Emp. Coy.
1/4th Suffolk Regt.   Camp Comdt.
                       D.G.O.

G.O.1595

G.S.3456

MOVEMENT IN THE DIVISIONAL AREA.

All officers and other ranks reconnoitring and moving IN the forward area will observe the following instructions :-

1. Maps may not be carried exposed to view. On reconnaissances they should be unfolded under cover and then compared with the ground from memory.

2. In the forward area, two persons at most, not groups of several persons, may move about together.

3. Assemblages and conferences at observation posts on commanding ground or at points on the ground overlooked by the enemy are forbidden.

4. Every possible advantage will be taken of cover, and open country overlooked by the enemy will be avoided. There should be no hesitation in making a detour where necessary. For reconnaissances, guides will be requisitioned from the infantry of the sector, unless the individuals concerned belong to a unit which forms an integral part of the Division and are thoroughly familiar with the ground.

Lieut-Colonel,
General Staff 58th (London) Division.

21st August 1918.

Copy to III Corps.
       18th Div.
       47th Div.

SECRET.   Copy No. 24

58TH (LONDON) DIVISION ORDER NO. 146.

21st August 1918.

---

1. The attached secret map shows the objectives and positions of Headquarters of formations of the III Corps for the forthcoming attack.

2. The 58th Division (less Artillery) will be in Corps Reserve.

3. The Division will be located before Zero hour as given in 58th Division location of units dated 14th August 1918.

4. 174th and 175th Infantry Brigades with their affiliated Machine Gun Coys. will be prepared to make the following moves at Zero hour on Z day :-

    (a) 174th Infantry Brigade with its affiliated M.G.Coy. ("B" Coy) to a position of assembly N. of the river ANCRE near HEILLY.

    (b) 175th Infantry Brigade with its affiliated M.G.Coy. ("C" Coy) to a position of assembly in rear of the old British front line West of MORLANCOURT.

    Transport Lines of the above Brigades will not move.

5. Provided the moves forecast in para. 4 are confirmed, Brigade Headquarters of the above Brigades will be established by 6 a.m. on Z day as follows :-

        174th Inf. Brigade   HEILLY.

        175th Inf. Brigade ... J.11.d.5.5. at position to be vacated by 140th Brigade (47th Div) at 6 a.m.

    H.Q., 173rd Infantry Brigade will remain at QUERRIEU Chateau.

6. The completion of the moves ordered in para. 4 and the establishment of Brigade Headquarters mentioned in para. 5 will each be wired to Divisional Headquarters.

7. 173rd Infantry Brigade and the 58th Bn. M.G.C. (less 2 Coys) will be ready to move at 2 hours notice.

8. Zero day 22nd

    Zero hour ...... 4.45 am

9. 58th Division G.S. No.3455 dated 20th August, 1918 is cancelled.

10. ACKNOWLEDGE.

                                         B.W.Harrison Major

                                         for Lieut.-Colonel,

                               General Staff, 58th (London) Division.

Issued at .. 1.30 pm.

    Battle Surplus of 174th and 175th Brigades will remain at ROUND WOOD and BOIS ESCARDONNEUSE respectively pending further orders.

                                                                  P.T.O.

DISTRIBUTION of O.O.146.

Copy No. 1. A.D.C. for G.O.C.
2. 173rd Inf. Brigade.
3. 174th Inf. Brigade.
4. 175th Inf. Brigade.
5. C.R.A. 58th Div.
6. C.R.E.
7. Signals.
8. 58th Bn. M.G.C.
9 & 10. A & Q.
11. A.P.M.
12. O.C. Train.
13. S.S.O.
14. D.A.D.O.S.
15. A.D.M.S.
17. 1/4th Suffolk Regt.
18. Camp Comdt.
19 & 20. III Corps.
21. 12th Division.
22. 18th Division.
23. 47th Division.
24 & 25. War Diary.
26. File.
16. ~~Spare~~ Reception Camp

SECRET.

58th Divn.
G.S. 146/1.

C. R. A.
C. R. E.
58th Bn. M.G.C.
1/4th Suffolk Regt.
173rd Inf. Brigade.
174th Inf. Brigade.
175th Inf. Brigade.
"A" & "Q".
A.D.C. for G.O.C.

Reference Map issued with Divisional Order No. 148.

12th Division are attacking with 35th Brigade on the Right and 36th Brigade on the Left, both Brigades going to final objective.

Lieut-Colonel,
General Staff, 58th (London) Division.

21st August, 1918.

"O" Form.
MESSAGES AND SIGNALS.

Prefix	Code	Words 3	Received From	Sent, or sent out At	Office Stamp
Charges to Collect £ s. d.			By Powell	To	
Service Instructions H 41				By	

Handed in at 58 Div Office 5.38 m. Received 6.12 p.m.

TO Corps

Sender's Number	Day of Month	In reply to Number	A A A
4500	21		

174	and	175	Bdes
will	move	as	detailed
in	paras	4	and
5	of	58	Divl
Order	No	146	except
th	as	follows	aaa Time
that	174	Bde	moves
will	be	one	hour
later	than	stated	aaa
174	and	175	Bde
HQ	will	be	established
one	hour	later	than
stated aaa		174	175
Bdes	and	146	Bn
to	acknowledge		aaa
added	receipts		of
OO = 146			

FROM PLACE & TIME 58 Div 5.20 pm

W.D.

G.500. 21st. AAA.
174 and 175 Bdes.
will move as detailed
in paras. 4 and
5 of 58 Divl.
Order No 146. except
as follows AAA Time
that 174 Bde moves
will be one hour
later than stated AAA
174 and 175 Bde
H.Q. will be established
one hour later than
stated AAA 174 175
Bdes and M.G. Bn
to acknowledge AAA Addsd
recipients of O. 146
58 Div.
5.20 pm.

SWWHarris
Major GS

W.D.

G. 503   21   —   AAA

Reference Divisional Order No. 146 para. 5 line 6 for "12th Divn." read "47th Divn." aaa Added all recipients O.O 146

58th Divn.

                                              Lt.-Col G.S.

G.S. 1447

III Corps orders attack to be continued tomorrow by 47th Div. in conjunction with 3rd Australian Division. Zero hour to be notified later. Objective - old trench line L.5.b.4.0 - F.29.b.3.0 - F.23.c.2.0 - F.28.b.0.8 - F.28.a.0.7 - F.27.b.0.8. 47th Division will effect junction with 3rd Aust. Division at road junction L.5.b.4.0. On remainder of Corps front line will be advanced to general line F.21.a.0 - F.20.b.3.5 - F.14.central - F.13.b.9.8 - E.12.b.5.0 - E.6.b.7.0 - W.30.d.8.4 - W.30.b.6.3 - W.24.d.7.9 where 38th Division (V Corps) will join with 18th Div. 12th Division will mop up F.19 and 20 and secure high ground in F.13.a.

Copies to all recipients OO146.

BMWHannon Major
for Lieut-Colonel,
General Staff 58th (London) Division.

5 P.M.
22nd August 1918.

WD

G.562   22nd

173rd Bde will move tomorrow starting at 4 am to valley S. of MERICOURT in T.9. and T.15. Position of Bde H.Q. will be notified later aaa Addsd all recipients of OO 146 aaa Ref. above "A" Coy. 58 L Bn M.G. will move with 173rd Bde

58d Div
9.45 pm

C.M.W. Harrison Major
for Lt. Col.
G.S.

W.D.

G. 572   22   AAA

175th Inf. Bde. is moving under orders of 47th Division to occupy the old AMIENS DEFENCE Line in K.6. and K.12. Brigade H.Q. is being established at K.14.b.2.2. aaa 142nd Brigade is moving to position S.W. of MORLANCOURT with H.Q. at J.11.d.5.5. to reorhanise aaa Added List "B" less Corps and Flank Divns.

58th Divn.

11.50 p.m.

                         Major
                         G.S.

"OD

G.585   23   -

174th Bde is placed forthwith
at disposal of 18th Div.
for operations if necessary.
aaa Added recipients OC
146. Less Corps & Flank
Divs.

58th Div

Mitchin
Major

(2)

G. 596.   A.A.A.
23. 58 Bde will take over the
Bde front from 47 Bde. Eastern
Bde front at 10 p.m.
tomorrow A.A.A. 58 Bde H.Q.
will close ST GRATIEN 10 p.m.
tomorrow and open HEILLY
same time A.A.A.
47 Bde will continue to
command artillery of Eastern
Bde A.A.A. 173 Bde marched
at 8.45 p.m. today to
position rendezvous in K.6.c.
and d. and K.12.a and b.
A.A.A. 173 Bde H.Q. will
be established at K.14.E.2.2.
A.A.A. D.G. Bn less 3 Coys
174 Bde. 1/4 Suffolks and

. Field Coys will
    ready wire 6 a.m.
    tomorrow A.A.A. ACKNOWLEDGE A.A.A.
    ADDT Lieut B.

S.J. Dan.
10.15 p.m.

(Sgd) W Harrison
Brig. Gl.
for Lt-Col. S.S.

M.G. Bn.
1/4 Suffolks

G.606   23   AAA

1/4 Suffolks and D coy M.G.Bn leave
BOIS ESCARDONNEUSE at 6am. today
and proceed to VALLEY South
of MERICOURT in J.9. and J.15.
AAA. OC. Pioneer Bn will arrange
order of march and allot areas
for bivouacking in VALLEY AAA
Arrival of Units to be wired
to DHQ AAA M.G. Bn. HQ. will
be established at HEILLY by
10 A.M. at which hour O.C.
M.G. Bn will report D.H.Q.
HEILLY to see Divl Comdr
AAA Addsh Front 1/4 Suffolks
and M.G.Bn refth fet B
less Corps and flank
Divs plus 47 Div.

55 Bn.   ESW Harrison
1.50 A.M.   Lt Col E.S.

"A" Form
MESSAGES AND SIGNALS.

Army Form C. 2121 (In pads of 100.)

Sender's Number.	Day of Month.	In reply to Number.	AAA
G.612	24		

Zero hour given in para one of 58 Divl Order 147 is cancelled HAA Zero hour will now be 2.30 AM on 25th inst AAA Remainder of DO No 147 stands AAA added AAA DO 147 plus 141 Bde AAA ACKNOWLEDGE

From 58...
Place
Time 12 Noon

"C" Form.
MESSAGES AND SIGNALS.

Army Form C. 2123.
(In books of 100.)

No. of Message _____

Prefix	Code	Words 67	Received	Sent, or sent out	Office Stamp
	£ s. d.		From LH	At ___ m.	
Charges to Collect			By	To	
Service Instructions		To Gadds		By	5-186
58 Div					

Handed in at _____ Corps Office ___ m. Received ___ 96.

TO

*Sender's Number	Day of Month	In reply to Number	A A A
G.20	140th	143rd	and
175th	Bdes	will	be
established	as	follows	instead
of	as	ordered	in
OO144	para	11	aaa
175th	Bde	L1B32	aaa
140th	Bde	K6B91	aaa
143rd	Bde	in	A
position	to	be	selected
by	Bde	Comdr	close
to	HQ	of	either
140	or	175	Bdes
aaa	exact	position	to
be	reported	early	aaa
added	all	recipients	OO
147			

FROM PLACE & TIME: 58 Div 4.30 pm

* This line should be erased if not required.

SECRET.   Copy No. _____

58th (LONDON) DIVISION ORDER No. 147.

                                                24/8/18.

1.   The 58th Division with 140th Inf. Brigade attached will
attack today, 24th, in conjunction with the 3rd Australian Divn.,
on the right and the 12th Division on the left.
        Approximate start line, dividing lines and objective are
shown on attached map.
        Zero hour will be ~~4 p.m.~~ 2.30 a.m. 25th Aug.

2.   175th Inf. Brigade will attack on the right and 140th Inf.
Brigade on the left, each with 1 M.G. Coy. attached.
        173rd Inf. Brigade in Support with 1 M.G. Coy. and 1 Troop
Northumberland Hussars attached.
        174th Inf. Brigade in Reserve, with 1 M.G. Coy. attached, in
trenches S.W. of MORLANCOURT, in K.14.a. and c. and K.13.

3.   The attack will be covered by a creeping barrage advancing
at the rate of 100 yards in 4 minutes.
        Barrage maps showing exact start line, lifts and objective
will be issued by noon.
        As the start line in the centre of the Divisional front is
more advanced than on either flank, the barrage will lift from the
flanks first, remaining stationary in the centre until the troops
on the flanks are level with the centre.

4.   175th and 140th Inf. Brigades will advance close behind
the barrage each with two battalions in the front line and one in
close support up to the final objective where they will consolidate.
        They will send out strong fighting patrols to exploit
success to the utmost beyond the objective.

5.   173rd Inf. Brigade will advance from assembly position
K.6.c. and d., K.12.a. and b. at Zero hour in rear of 175th and 140th
Inf. Brigades. Should either 175th or 140th Inf. Brigades be held
up before reaching the final objective, B.G.C.; 173rd Inf. Brigade
will send forward one or more battalions as he may consider necessary,
to carry them forward to the final objective without awaiting orders
from Divisional Headquarters.

6.   1 Squadron, 22nd Corps Cavalry will move from present position
- LA HOUSSOYE at an hour to be named by the O.C. so that they will
reach an assembly position in the HAPPY VALLEY in F.27.c. at Zero
plus one hour.
        The O.C. will send out patrols to keep himself informed of
the situation of the infantry, and will with his whole squadron
take advantage of any opportunity of pushing through the infantry
after they have reached the objective to exploit the success and
keep touch with the enemy.

7.   1 Company 22nd Corps Cyclists will move from present position
near LA HOUSSOYE under orders of the O.C. at such an hour that they
will reach an assembly position in K.18.a. by Zero plus one hour
where they will be in Divisional Reserve.
        The O.C. will detail 6 selected men to report to 173rd Inf.
Brigade Headquarters, K.14.b.2.2. at 12 noon today to act as orderlies.

8.   Unit Commanders will take all possible precautions to prevent
their troops from being observed by hostile aircraft when on the
move and when in position of assembly.

- 2 -

9. 175th Inf. Brigade will arrange to have a Liaison Officer with the 10th Australian Brigade, 3rd Division who will be on their right.
    140th Inf. Brigade will similarly arrange to have a Liaison Officer with the 37th Inf. Brigade, 12th Division who will be on their left.

10. 175th, 140th and 173rd Inf. Brigades will arrange to have a mounted Officer from each of their battalions at Brigade Headquarters to convey orders to their battalions.

11. 175th and 140th Inf. Brigades will establish advanced Headquarters in the HAPPY VALLEY in F.27.c. by Zero minus 1 hour.
    173rd Inf. Brigade Advanced Headquarters will be established at K.17.a.5.5. by Zero minus 1 hour and will move forward at Zero hour with the 173rd Inf. Brigade up to the HAPPY VALLEY where they will establish Advanced Headquarters close to those of 175th and 140th Inf. Brigades in F.27.c.
    174th Inf. Brigade Headquarters will be at K.14.b.2.2.

12. O.C. Signal Coy. will arrange Signal Report Centres and D.R. Relay Posts at K.14.b.2.2., K.17.a.5.5. and Cross Roads K.6.d.9.7. from which urgent messages will be forwarded from Infantry Brigades, O.C. Sqdn. Cavalry and O.C. Coy. Cyclists to Divisional Headquarters.

13. Divisional Headquarters open at HEILLY at 10 a.m. today.

14. ACKNOWLEDGE.

C.M. Davis

Lieut.-Colonel,
General Staff, 58th (London) Division.

Issued at 1 a.m.

Copy No. 1. A.D.C. for G.O.C. *
2. 173rd Inf. Brigade. *
3. 174th Inf. Brigade. *
4. 175th Inf. Brigade. *
5. C.R.A. 47th Div. *
6. C.R.E. *
7. Signals.
8. M.G. Bn. *
9 & 10. "A" and "Q"
11. A.P.M.
12. O.C. Train.
13. S.S.O.
14. D.A.D.O.S.
15. D.A.D.V.S.
16. A.D.M.S.
17. 1/4th Suffolks.
18. Camp Comdt.
19 & 20. III Corps.
21. III Corps H.A. *
22. C.R.A. 58 Div.
23. Reception Camp.
24. 47th Divn.
25. 3rd Aust. Divn. *
26. 12th Divn. *
27. 1st Bn. Tanks. *
28. 140th Inf. Brigade. *
29. File. *
30 & 31. War Diary.
32 & 33. 22nd Corps Cavalry. *
(copy for Sqdn. & Coy. Cyclists
34. 35th Sqdn. R.A.F. *

Maps.

SECRET.   Copy No. 30

58th (LONDON) DIVISION ORDER No. 148.

                                      24/8/18.

Continuation of O.O. 147.

1.   Field Arty. Barrage Map herewith.
      Heavy Arty. will shell the following areas lifting 500 yards in front of the F.A. barrage -
      (a) Road F.15.
      (b) old trenches F.22.b and d.
      (c) old trenches F.30.a, F.29.d. and L.5.
      After the protective F.A. barrage ceases the H.A. will continue protective harassing fire from 900 to 1,400 yards in front of final objective.

2.   174th Inf. Brigade will move at zero minus 1 hour to position of assembly to be vacated by 173rd Inf. Brigade in K.6.c and K.12.a and b.
      174th Inf. Brigade Headquarters will remain at K.14.b.2.2.

3.   In addition to the M.Gs. already detailed 1 Coy. Life Guards M.G. Battn. will be attached each to 140th and 175th Inf. Brigades for the purpose of consolidating the objective when gained by means of direct fire.
      O.C. Coys. have been directed to report   to Bde. Commanders.

4.   Contact Aeroplanes will fly over as soon after dawn as it is light enough. The leading line of the Infantry will signal their position by means of discs and rifles laid on the ground in groups of three. 1 Counter-attack aeroplane will remain over the Corps front for the whole of the 25th.

5. ~~As soon as it is light enough to distinguish friend from enemy 6 Tanks will move up to assist the Infantry in mopping up. Three being allotted each to 140th and 175th Inf. Brigades.~~ [Cancelled / No tanks allotted]

6.   Cancel para: 6 of O.O. 147 and substitute -

   "6   1 Sqdrn 22nd Corps Cavalry will move from present position [LA HOUSSOYE] at an hour to be named by the O.C. so that they will reach an assembly position in K.18.a. at Zero plus 1 hour where they will be in Divisional Reserve."

7.   ACKNOWLEDGE.
                              ChrDavies   Lieut-Colonel,
                              General Staff 58th (London) Division.

Issued at 2.45 pm.

Distribution as per O.O. 147. also maps
plus Coy 2nd Life Gds M.G.Bn } with OO147
141st Inf Bde.

"C" Form.
MESSAGES AND SIGNALS.

Army Form C. 2123.
(In books of 100.)
No. of Message

| Prefix | Code | Words | Received. From YEH By 26a | Sent, or sent out. At ___ m. To ___ By 10/f | Office Stamp. 24.VIII.18 |

Charges to Collect
Service Instructions

Handed in at 38 Div. Office 6 10/f m. Received 7 9/f m.

TO 3rd Corps

*Sender's Number	Day of Month	In reply to Number	AAA
G623	24		

Para 3 of OO148 is cancelled aaa no tanks are available for this divn aaa These tanks have been allotted to 12th Divn to deal with enemy in F20 aaa add all recipients OO148

FROM 38 Div.
PLACE & TIME 5.45 pm

* This line should be erased if not required.

"A" Form
MESSAGES AND SIGNALS.

Army Form C. 2121
(In pads of 100.)

TO 173 Bde.

Sender's Number: G 147/1
Day of Month: 24

AAA

Reference O.O. 147 issued herewith AAA Since 140 Bde are attacking at 1-0 am this morning it is possible that they may not be in a fit condition to carry out the attack as ordered AAA In this case you will be ordered to carry out the attack in place of them with two Coys in front line and one in support with 175 Bde on your right and 12th Div on your left AAA You will make all preparations and have draft orders prepared for both eventualities ~~...~~ also the necessary reconnaissances will be made for both.

From: 58 Div
Place:
Time: 12-50 am

C.R.E.

G.605. 24. AAA.

Field Coys R.E. will leave
Bois ESCARDENNOISE at
6.30.a.m. 24th inst. and
~~will~~ march to J.8.b.
West of MERICOURT AAA.
Added priority CRE
re 8th flst B less Corps
and flank Divs plus
47 Div.

58. Div.   (SN)
1.40. A.m.   Lt Col.
                              G.S.

ADMINISTRATIVE INSTRUCTIONS.
in accordance with Divisional Order No. 147.

GENERAL.

(1)　　General Administrative arrangements as already notified in A.I. Nos. 1 & 2 for 47th Divisional Sector.

AMMUNITION.

(2)　　Main Ammunition Dump is at Cemetery Copse. For contents see Appendix "A".
　　　　Small forward dump at Brickyard K.16.c.9.4. where there is also a dump of picks and shovels.
　　　　S.A.A. Section will be at HEILLY HALTE J.13.b. O.C., S.A.A. Section will detail 1 officer and 6 limbers to proceed to and stay at CEMETERY COPSE J.24.b.5.5., relieving similar party of 47th Division by 3 p.m. 24th instant These 6 limbers will first collect 1000 full petrol tins from Grenade dump at LA HOUSSOYE and retain them at CEMETERY COPSE.
　　　　12 to 16 pack saddles will be taken over from 47th Division at this Location
　　　　D.B.O. will proceed with his personnel (less 3 other ranks) to take over ammunition dump at CEMETERY COPSE by 4 p.m. 24th 3 Other Ranks will be left in charge of the dump at LA HOUSSOYE. CEMETERY COPSE is on the telephone.

SUPPLIES.

(3)　　Divisional Train will take over dump of Iron Rations etc. near BONNAY (This dump was handed over to 47th Division by this Division on relief) Location will be notified later. There is a dump of about 2000 Iron Rations at the Brickyard K.16.c.9.4.
　　　　Railhead will remain at POULAINVILLE for the present.

ORDNANCE.

(4)　　D.A.D.O.S. will be located on HEILLY -FRANVILLERS road on the evening of the 24th

REINFORCEMENTS.

(5)　　Railhead for reinforcements remains CANAPLES till 26th, when it changes to FLESSELLES. Reception Camp for the present remaining at MIRVAUX.

BATTLE SURPLUS KITS.

(6)　　Reception Camp will make arrangements for kits dumped in ROUND WOOD and ESCARDONNEUSE WOOD to be conveyed to MIRVAUX.

BATHS.

(7). Baths in Reserve Divisional Area are being handed over to Area Commandants.

O.C. Reception Camp will arrange to run PIERREGOT Water-point baths for use of Battle Surplus. One ton of coal is being delivered under Corps arrangements for immediate use.

Baths at HEILLY (6-spray) at Saw-mills J.7.b.3.7.

GAS RESERVE.

(8) S.D. and clean underclothing, now at QUERRIEU, will be transferred to HEILLY as soon as possible. 200 S.D. suits are at the Brickyard K.16.c.9.4., which will be taken over from 47th Division.

CASUALTIES.

(9) Estimated casualties must be wired twice a day to D.H.Q. They will be calculated as follows:-

    For Infantry Battalions -   By Fifties.
    " M.G.Battalion.   By Twenty-fives.

(b) Accurate casualty reports will follow as soon as possible. In the case of Staff and Senior Regimental Officers, attention is drawn to this office letter A4/3237 of 22/8/18. In the case of other officer casualties, care must be taken to give -
(a) Exact Regiment or attachment.
(b) Name, verified by A.1.
(c) Date of casualty.

All casualty wires to be marked PRIORITY and addressed to 58th Division NOT to Rear H.Q.

ARMY REST CAMP AND COOKERY COURSES.

(10) Personnel already detailed will proceed according to instructions already issued.

(11) P. of W. CAGE AT CEMETERY COPSE.

(11)

CEMETERIES IN FORWARD AREA.

(12)   J.24.b.9.9.   K.20.c.0.3.
       J.24.b.9.0.   K.20.b.5.6.
       J.24.a.0.0.   K.2.d.8.3.

(13) MAIN SALVAGE DUMP.   I.24.c.13.

24/8/18.

J. Mitchell,
Major,
for A.A. & Q.M.G. 58th Divsn.

"A" Form
MESSAGES AND SIGNALS.

Army Form C. 2121
(In pads of 100.)

TO: 140 Bde

Sender's Number: G623
Day of Month: 24
AAA

Ref barrage map accompanying 58 Divn OO 148 road in F 20 b - 21 a - 15 c. will be exclusive to 140 Bde and inclusive to 371R Bde.

From: 58 Divn
Place:
Time: 5.5 pm

(sd) L K Spencer Capt

MESSAGE FORM.

_____ Division.

Map Reference or Mark
on Map at Back.

1. I am at_____
2. I am at_____ and am consolidating.
3. I am at_____ and have consolidated.
4. Am held up by M.G. at_____
5. I need: Ammunition
                   Bombs
                   Rifle Grenades
                   Water
                   Verey Lights
                   Stokes Shells

6. Counter-attack forming up at _____

7. I am in touch with _____ on Right at _____
                                    Left

8. I am not in touch on Right.
                        Left.

9. Am being shelled from _____

10. I estimate my present strength at _____ rifles.

11. Hostile { Battery
             Machine Gun } active at _____
             Trench Mortar

Time_____ m.   Name_____

                    Platoon_____

Date_____   Company_____

                    Battalion_____

G625 24.   AAA.

Para 5 of OO 148 is cancelled aaa No Tanks are available for this Divn. aaa Three Tanks have been allotted to 121R Divn to deal with enemy in F.20. aaa Addsd all recipients OO 148.

58 Divn.
5-45 pm.

Mitchinson
Lt Col GS.

SECRET.   Copy No.......

58th DIVISION OPERATION ORDER No. 149.

25/8/18.

1. ✓   The 140th and 141st Inf. Brigades revert on receipt of this order to command of 47th Division.

2. 2   The 47th Division will be responsible for Defence of the Ridge BECORDEL Loop Station.

3. 3   The Coy. 2nd Life Guards M.G.Bn. at present attached to 175th Inf. Bde. will come under 47th Division and will be temporarily attached to 140th Inf. Brigade, through whom they will receive orders from 47th Division.

4. 4   The 173rd Inf. Brigade will relieve 140th Inf. Brigade in the position now held by them by direct arrangement between Brigadiers.
    140th Inf. Bde. on relief will assemble in squares 22 a & c. until orders are received from 47th Division.
    The 174th Inf. Bde. will relieve the 175th Inf Bde. in the Right Sector as soon as possible by direct arrangement with B.G.C. 175th Inf. Brigade.

5. 5/   Acknowledge.

C M Davies
Lieut.-Colonel,
General Staff, 58th (London) Division.

Issued at 1.30 p.m.

Distribution :-

As per attached slip.

Position to which 175 Bde will withdraw will be notified by wire later.

WD

G. 193   25   —   AAA

Reference G. 141 and Move of Divl. H.Q. aaa
Advanced H.Q. will open at 12 noon aaa AdEnd all recipients G. 001

0815 (time.

11.25 a.m.

(Sd) L. . Jackson Capt.

Army Form C. 2121
(In pads of 100.)

SIGNALS. No. of Message............

| Office of Origin and Service Instructions | Charge. Sent At To By | This message is on a/c of: ....Service. (Signature of "Franking Officer") | Recd. at......m. Date............ From .... By............ |

TO { 173 Bde ~~140 Bde~~ 140 Bde

| Sender's Number. | Day of Month. | In reply to Number. | AAA |
| GX 105 | 25 | | |

It is to be clearly understood that relief of 140 by 173 Bde ~~done~~ ordered in O.O. 149 of today does not ~~appear~~ entail any withdrawal by 143 Bde AAA 173 Bde will occupy the sectors now held by 140 Bde and will push on to E as rapidly as possible but on no account will any unit of 173 Bde withdraw AAA When 140 Bde are satisfied that 173 are covering their front they will be withdrawn under orders of 47 Divn Guard

From
Place 58 Div 140 173 Bdes
Time

The above may be forwarded as now corrected. (Z)
....
Censor. Signature of Addressor or person authorised to telegraph in his name
* This line should be erased if not required.

Order No. 1625. Wt. W3253/ P 511. 27/2. H. & K., Ltd. (E. 2634).

MESSAGES AND SIGNALS.

Army Form C. 2121
(In pads of 100.)

Prefix......Code......m	Words	Charge	This message is on a/c of:	Recd. at......m
Office of Origin and Service Instructions				
	Sent		......Service	Date.........
	At......m			From.........
	To			
	By		(Signature of "Franking Officer")	By.........

TO

| Sender's Number. | Day of Month. | In reply to Number. | AAA |
| 10E | 23 | | |

Ref Coy AAA The
artillery line between Bty is
will be a staged
line from Fay to F
A 21 at the thence to FMD
A 22 etc. keep the Fay
AAA Then must have
will NOT B2 with
have with 173 Bty
any thence Bosun way
of the AAA
[illegible] 173 2nd F
A [illegible] 173 AAA

From
Place
Time

The above may be forwarded as now corrected. (Z)

Censor. Signature of Addressee or person authorised to telegraph in his name
* This line should be erased if not required.

Order No. 1625. Wt. W3253/ P 511. 27/2. H. & K., Ltd. (E. 2634)

"A" Form
MESSAGES AND SIGNALS.

Army Form C. 2121
(In pads of 100.)

Prefix........Code........m.	Words	Charge	This message is on a/c of:	Recd. at......m.
Office of Origin and Service Instructions	Sent		..........Service.	Date..........
106/	At.........m.			From..........
	To..........			
	By..........		(Signature of "Franking Officer")	By..........

TO	3 Corps. 12 DW	3rd Aust DW. CRA		

Sender's Number.	Day of Month.	In reply to Number.	AAA
GX.107.	25.		

2nd Londons are on line COPSE H - A.19.b.5.9. AAA. Heavy fire reported from BILLON AV. - Eastern edge BILLON WOOD and direction MARICOURT AAA. 2 Coys 2nd Londons ordered to turn the East of BILLON WOOD from the North AAA Addsd Corps report flank Divs CRA.

From 58 DW
Place
Time 2.30 pm.

The above may be forwarded as now corrected.   ECWW Harrison
                                                    Major

Censor.   Signature of Addressor or person authorised to telegraph in his name
* This line should be erased if not required.

Order No. 1625. Wt. W3253/   P 511. 27/2   H. & K., Ltd. (E. 2634).

"A" Form
MESSAGES AND SIGNALS.

Army Form C. 2121
(In pads of 100.)

TO		CRA		
		174 Bde		

Sender's Number.	Day of Month	In reply to Number.	AAA
GX113	25		

One	7A	Bde	will
be	placed	at	disposal
174	Bde	forthwith	and
the	Group	under	will
report	at	once	to
Bde	174	Bde	at
at 630 am		AAA	CRA
174	Bde		

From: 5 Div
Place:
Time: 4.20?

GX104   AAA

On relief of 175th and 140th Bdes, respectively the role of the 174th and 173rd Bdes will be to push forward at every opportunity and as rapidly as possible keeping in close touch with the 3rd Aust. Div. on the right and the 12th Div. on the left AAA They will endeavour to establish forthwith a line from COPSE N - A.28.c.5.0 by BILLON AVENUE - SHEFFIELD AVENUE to LAPREE Wood inclusive A.14.c.7.5 AAA At any part of the line which is not in touch with the enemy fighting patrols will be sent forward at once to gain touch with and report position of the enemy. AAA Added. 174th 173rd Inf. Bdes. reptd all recipients O.O. 149.

58th Div.
1-30 pm.

C.W. Davies
Lt. Col.
G.S.

3 Bdes.   Q.   47 Div.
CRA.   aDMS.
CRE.   12 Div.
Sig.   3,5 Aust Div.

GX 115.   25th   AAA

At 4 a.m. tomorrow a standing F.A. barrage
will be placed on the trench line CREST Av.
- A.27.d.8.7. to A.28.a.4.9., thence along
trench from A.22.c. to cross roads at
22.a.8.4. thence along road to A.21.b.9.5.
thence N. along trench from A.15.d.8.1. to
A.15.d.3.4. thence N. to A.15.b.4.9. AAA
At 4.30 a.m. the barrage will lift to a line
300 yards beyond above line where it will remain
for 15 minutes   searbhing in
                                            depth during this
                                                   period AAA
During the night 173 and 174 Bdes will push
forward strong fighting patrols followed by
formed bodies of troops up to the barrage
start line and will endeavour to enter the
enemy trenches when the barrage lifts from
them xxx and subsequently to push forward from
the trench system to the General Line A.30.a.
0.0. - A.24.a.4.8. - A.18.a.0.4. AAA Corps
H.A. will xxxx co-operate by bombarding
MARICOURT and the trench system in A.22. and
A.29.a. and will time their lifts in accordance with F.A. barrage AAA Divisions on
flanks are being asked to co-operate AAA
Inter-Divisional and Brigade boundaries as
already laid down AAA C.R.A. will co-ordinate
barrage using groups attached to 173 and 174
Bdes. which revert to the Brigade to which
now affiliated at 4.45 a.m. tomorrow. AAA
Added 173, 174, 175 Bdes. C.R.A. reptd all
concerned

58th Div.

8.40 p.m.
                                    Lt.-Colonel,
                                       G.S.

"A" Form
MESSAGES AND SIGNALS.

Army Form C. 2121
(In pads of 100.)

No. of Message..........

Prefix..........Code..........m.	Words	Charge.	This message is on a/c of:	Recd. at......m.
Office of Origin and Service Instructions	Sent		..........Service.	Date..........
	At ....m.			From ....
	To			
	By		(Signature of "Franking Officer")	By..........

TO { Squadron 22nd Corps Cav
Cyc 22nd Corps [illegible]

Sender's Number.	Day of Month.	In reply to Number.	AAA
G.X.118	25		

Squadron 22nd Corps Cav and Cyc 22nd
Corps Cyclists attached 58th Div will
move [illegible] to reach position of
readiness about F 21 d by 5 a.m.
tomorrow AAA O.C. Squadron will
[illegible] 12th
Div on left flank about [illegible]
[illegible] of that place AAA Squadron
and Cyc [illegible]
[illegible]
[illegible] F 21 d [illegible]
[illegible]
[illegible]
[illegible]
[illegible] 173rd [illegible]

From 58 D
Place
Time 11 pm

The above may be forwarded as now corrected. (Z) [illegible]

..........Censor. Signature of Addressor or person authorised to telegraph in his name

* This line should be erased if not required.

Order No. 1625. Wt. W8253/ P 511. 27/2 H. & K., Ltd. (E. 2634).

WD

G.645   25th.

Should the final objective be reached
& opposition not be serious 173rd
Bde: with 86th Bde RFA attached
will follow up the enemy on
MARICOURT acting as Advanced
Guard aaa 175th & 140th Inf.
Bdes will remain in position on
objective aaa Heavy Arty
protective barrage will cease at 7am.
aaa Addsd all recipients C/O
148th

CWDavis

58th Div.

4-37am

Lt Col
GS.

WB.

G649   25th.

174th Bde will move on receipt
of these orders to an assembly
position in Z.3. in readiness
to advance in support of 173rd
Bde. if ordered to do so aaa
Addsd all recipients O.O. 148

5th Div   C W Davis
6.5 am   Lt Col
               GS

W.D.

G.651. 25.

Cav. HQ. will be established at K.14.c.22. South of MORLANCOURT at 9.30 a.m. AAA Added all recipients of OO748.

55 Div.
6.30. A.m.

[signature] for LHQSS.

W.D.

G. 101   S5   —   AAA

Reference G. 651 aaa Move of Divisional H.Q. postponed aaa H.Q. re-opened HEILLY aaa Added all recipients G. 651

58th Divn.

10.40 a.m.

(Sd) C.H. DAVIES Lt.-Col. G.S.

SECRET. Copy No. 19

58TH (LONDON) DIVISION ORDER NO. 150.

26/8/1918.

1. The Division will attack with a creeping barrage tomorrow in cooperation with the 3rd Australian Division on the right.
   Zero Hour will be 4.55. a.m.
   Objective, line of exploitation and dividing lines are shewn on attached map.

2. 174th Brigade will attack on the right, 173rd Brigade on the left.

3. Barrage maps will be issued as soon as possible.
   The Barrage will stand on the start line for 20 minutes lifting from that line at the rate of 100 yards in 4 minutes for 500 yards and thence on to a line 300 yards beyond the objective at the rate of 100 yards in 6 minutes.
   A protective barrage will search in depth for 30 minutes up to the line of exploitation.
   Corps H.A. will cooperate by bombarding targets to the East of the F.A. Barrage with which its lifts will conform.

4. After the protective barrage ceases F.A. Bdes. will again come under the orders of the Brigadiers Commanding the Brigades to which they were attached before the operation and strong patrols will be pushed forward to the line of exploitation shewn on map.

5. ACKNOWLEDGE.

OMDavies
Lieut. Colonel,
General Staff 58th (London) Division.

Issued at 8.5 p.m.

Distribution.

Copy No. 1. A.D.C. for G.O.C.
2. 173 Bde. (4 Maps)
3. 174 Bde. (4 Maps)
4. 175 Bde. (1 Map)
5. C.R.A.
6. 58 Bn. M.G.C.
7. C.R.E.
8. Suffolks.
9. A and Q.
10. A.D.M.S.
11. Signals.
12. III Corps (1 Map).
13. III Corps H.A. (1 Map).
14. 12th Div. (1 Map).
15. 3rd Aust. Div. (1 Map)
16. 22nd Corps Cav. (1 Map).
17. 35 Sqdn. R.A.F. (1 Map)
18. Corps Cyclists.
19.) War Diary.
20.)
21. File.
22. 47 Div.

SECRET

58TH (LONDON) DIVISION ORDER NO. 151.

Copy No: 20

27/8/1918.

1. The Division will attack in conjunction with the 3rd Australian Division on the Right and the 12th Division on the Left.
   Zero hour will be 4-55 am. at which hour the barrage will open on the Start Line.
   Map is attached showing Start Line, Dividing Lines, Objective and Line of Exploitation. (Maps issued as per C.O.150)

2. 174th Inf. Brigade will attack on the Right and 173rd Inf. Brigade on the Left.

3. The attack will be covered by a Creeping Artillery Barrage at the rate of 100 yards in 6 minutes, commencing at the Start Line at Zero and lifting in accordance with barrage map which will be issued as soon as possible.
   As the Barrage Start Line is crooked, the more westerly portions of it will lift first and will move forward until the whole barrage is on a N & S line through the most Easterly portion of the Start Line. From this line the whole barrage will move forward on parallel N & S lines at the rate of 100 yards in every 6 minutes.

4. A protective barrage will search in depth for 30 minutes up to the line of exploitation.
   Corps Heavy Artillery will co-operate by bombarding targets to the East of the Field Artillery barrage, with which its lifts will conform.
   After the protective barrage ceases Field Artillery Brigades will again come under orders of Brigadiers Commanding the bdes. to which they were attached before the operation and strong patrols will be pushed forward to the line of exploitation shown on map.

5. 174th Inf. Brigade will take steps to ensure close co-operation with the 9th Australian Inf. Brigade on the right.
   A joint post will be established on the objective - A.30.a.2.8 Trench Junction and subsequently a joint post on the line of exploitation in QUARRY in A.20.b.7.5.

6. Watches will be synchronized at Divisional Headquarters at 6 pm., at Headquarters 174th Inf. Brigade at 7 pm. and at Headquarters 173rd Inf. Brigade at 7-30 pm.

7. ACKNOWLEDGE.

C.M.Davis
Lieut-Colonel,
General Staff 58th (London) Division.

Issued at 4.55 pm.

Distribution as per attached slip.

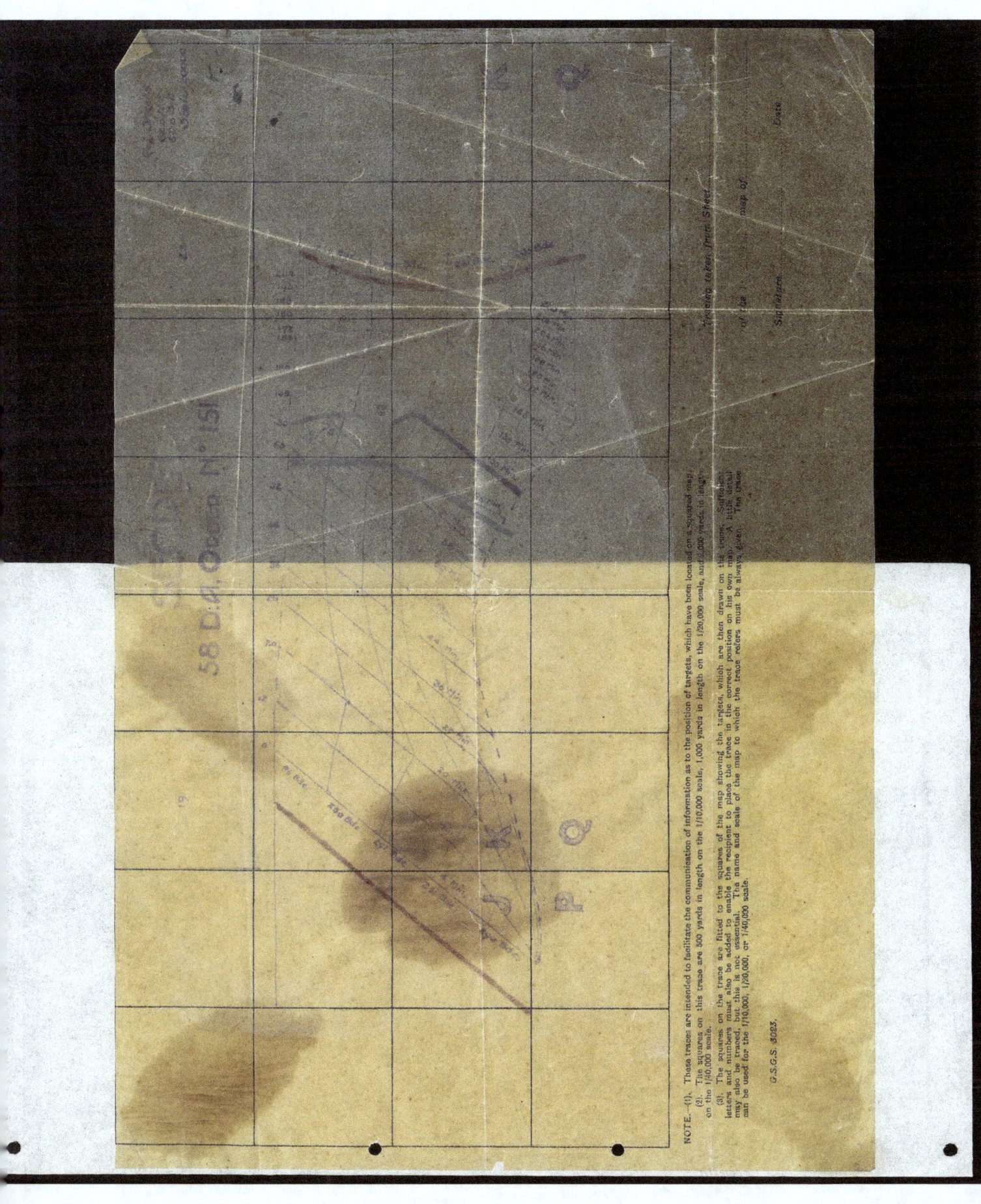

G.S. 151/1.

Amendment to 58th Division O.O. 151.

1. The objective allotted to 173rd Inf. Brigade will be increased so as to include the trench running from A.18.c.4.6. N. Eastwards to A.18.b.4.2. where junction will be established with troops 12th Division who will have taken HARDECOURT by the time that the barrage lifts from the new objective.
    The creeping barrage will continue through the BOIS D'ENHAUT up to this new objective until it reaches a protective line 300 yds outside the objective.

2. The exploitation will be carried out by Companies specially detailed beforehand as follows :-

    (a) 1 Coy. from 173rd Inf. Bde. to establish a Post about A.18.d.9.1.

    (b) 1 Coy. from 174th Inf. Bde. to establish a Post about A.24.d.9.4.

    (c) 1 Coy. from 174th Inf. Bde. to establish a joint post with the 9th Australian Inf. Brigade at the QUARRY A.30.b.7.5.

3. Reference para. 4, line 1 of O.O.151 :-

    All fire on the protective barrage will cease at Zero plus *1 hour and 42 minutes*

4. 173rd Inf. Brigade to acknowledge.

                                        M Davis
                                        Lt.-Colonel,
                            General Staff, 58th (London) Division.

27/8/18.

    To all recipient of O.O. 151.

```
SEEN BY :-
G.O.C........
G.S.O.I........
G.S.O.II.......
G.S.O.III......
```

S E C R E T. Copy No. 33

58th (LONDON) DIVISION ORDER No. 134.

31/7/18.

ORDERS FOR RELIEF.

1. The 58th Division (less Artillery) will be relieved in the Centre Sector of the III Corps by the 12th Division (less Artillery) in accordance with attached Table, commencing August 2nd. The relief will be complete by dawn August 4th.

2. 173rd Infantry Brigade will be relieved by the 35th Infantry Brigade in the Right Sector on the night August 2/3rd.
    The 1st American Bn. of the 132nd. Regt., in the line on the Right, will be handed over on relief and come under the orders of the G.O.C., 35th Infantry Brigade.

3. The 175th Infantry Brigade will be relieved in their present dispositions (two battalions in the Left Sector and one battalion at ST.LAURENCE Farm) by the 37th Infantry Brigade on the night 3rd/4th Aug. The 3rd American Bn. 132nd Regt. will be handed over on relief and come under the orders of the G.O.C., 37th Infantry Bde.

4. The positions of the 174th Inf. Brigade will be used as staging area for the 35th and 37th Inf. Brigades. The 36th Inf. Bde. will finally take over the positions of the 174th Inf. Bde.

5. _Machine Gun Battalion._ The Company covering the Left Brigade will be relieved on the night 2nd/3rd Aug. and the two Companies covering the Right Brigade will be relieved on the night 3rd/4th Aug. All details of relief will be arranged direct between Machine Gun Battalion Commanders.

6. R.E. reliefs will be arranged direct between C.R.E's.

7. Field Ambulances will be relieved under arrangements to be made between A.D's.M.S.

8. The relief of the 58th Divisional Artillery by the 25th Divisional Artillery will be completed on Aug. 2nd. The Divisional Artillery will then be at their present wagon lines in Corps Mobile Reserve.
    Command of the Divisional Artillery covering the Centre Sector will pass from C.R.A. 58th Division to C.R.A. 25th Division at 10 a.m. 4th Aug.

9. Defence Schemes, Maps, Aeroplane Photographs and documents relating to the Brigade Sectors, also S.O.S. Signal Message Carrying Rockets and S.A.A., A.P. will be handed over on relief.

10. Infantry Working Parties of 58th Division at present attached to Tunnelling Companies will be relieved by similar numbers by 12th Division.

11. Completion of all reliefs will be reported to Divisional H.Q.

12. B.G's.C. 173rd and 175th Infantry Brigades will hand over the command of their respective Sectors on completion of the Infantry relief

13.

13. Command of Centre Divisional Sector will pass from G.O.C., 58th Division to G.O.C., 12th Division at 10 a.m. on August 4th, 1918, at which time command of the following Artillery and Machine Gun Bn. will pass to G.O.C., 12th Division :-

        25th Divisional Artillery.
        5th Army Brigade R.H.A.
        86th Army Brigade R.F.A. (in Mobile Reserve)
        50th Machine Gun Battalion ~~(less 2 Companies)~~ [1 Coy]

ORDERS FOR EMBUSSING AND MOVE TO VIGNACOURT AREA.

14. As relieved the Division (less Artillery) will move to the VIGNACOURT area, dismounted personnel by bus and transport by march route.

    Detail tables for embussing, and billeting in the VIGNACOURT area are attached in "Administrative Arrangements".

    The composition of Brigade Groups will be as detailed in the "Administrative Arrangements" and Brigades will issue orders for embussing and the march of transport to the units of their Brigade Group.

15. Transport will march on the following dates :-

        174th Inf.Bde.Group - Aug. 2nd.
        173rd Inf.Bde.Group - Aug. 3rd.
        175th Inf.Bde.Group - Aug. 4th.

There will be no restrictions as regards routes or times. Distances will be observed as in Fourth Army Routine Order No.2039.

16. 174th Inf. Brigade Group [less 2 Bns] will be concentrated ready to embus at 4 p.m. on 3rd Aug. To enable them to do this the Pioneers and two Companies in the LAVIEVILLE Line will withdraw to the BAIZIEUX Line before dawn on the 2nd August. If ordered however, to Man Battle Stations between the time of withdrawal to the BAIZIEUX Line and time of embussing, these units will return to their Battle Stations in the LAVIEVILLE Line.

17. The 173rd and 175th Inf. Brigades and Machine Gun Companies in the line will march to embussing point on relief.

    Advanced parties of 12th Division will in some instances have to take over the dispositions of Field Companies and Field Ambulances.

18. Orders as regards the 'Battle Surplus' at MIRVAUX will be issued later.

19. Divisional Headquarters will close at BEAUCOURT Chateau at 10 a.m. 4th August and open at VIGNACOURT (QUERRIEU CHATEAU) at the same hour.

20. ACKNOWLEDGE.

                                                    EGMW Harrison
                                                       Major,
Issued at 1 am 1/8/18.   General Staff, 58th (London) Division.

        Distribution on page 3.

DISTRIBUTION :-

Copy No	1.	A.D.C. for G.O.C.
	2.	173rd Inf. Brigade.
	3.	174th Inf. Brigade.
	4.	175th Inf. Brigade.
	5.	C.R.A.
	6.	C.R.E.
	7.	Signals.
	8.	58th Bn. M.G.C.
9 & 10.		"A" and "Q".
	11.	A.P.M.
	12.	A.D.M.S.
	13.	1/4th Suffolks.
	14.	Divnl. Train.
	15.	S.S.O.
	16.	D.A.D.O.S.
	17.	Camp Comdt.
18 & 19.		III Corps.
	20.	12th Division.
	21.	47th Division.
	22.	33rd American Divn.
	23.	18th Division.
	24.	132nd American Regt.
	25.	66th American Brigade.
	26.	D.A.D.V.S.
	27.	180th Tunnelling Co.R.E.
	28.	2nd Tank Bn.
	29.	"B" Coy. 2nd Tank Bn.
30 & 31.		War Diary.
	32.	File.

To all recipients of
    Administrative Arrangements issued with
    58th Division Order No. 134

    Reference Location Table (Appendix "C"), the M.G. Battalion will not have Headquarters and 2 Companies in FLESSELLES. They will be accomodated in HAVERNAS instead. The 8th Bn. London Regt.(174th Bde.) will be accommodated entirely in WARGNIES, the accommodation in HAVERNAS being handed over to the M.G. Battalion.

    The Divisional Reception Camp will for the present remain at MIRVAUX.

1/8/18.
LFL.
                      Major.
    for A.A.& Q.M.G., 58th Division.

G. 257 1st.

In para. 13 of O.O.134 for "50th M.G.Battn. less 2 Coys." read " 1 Coy. 50th M.G.Battn. AAA Addsd All recipients of O.O.134

Order amended BR

58th Div.

E.S.W. Harrison
Major,
G.S.

G.266   1   --   AAA

174 Brigade Group less 2 Battalions will
now ombus at 4 p.m. on 2nd inst aaa Para.
16 and Relief Table of 56th Division
Order No. 134 will be amended accordingly
AAA The two battns. are ombussing earlier
under separate instructions being issued
to 174th Bde. AAA Added. all recipients of
O.O.134.

Order
Amended
BR

56th Div.

BMWN Harrison
Maj:
G.S.

"A" Form. Army Form C. 2121.
MESSAGES AND SIGNALS.

Ref.	para:	16	of
O.O.134	dated	31/7/18	AAA
174	Bde.	Group	will
be	concentrated	ready	to
ombus	at	6 pm.	on
2nd	Aug;	and	not
as	stated	AAA	Addsd.
all	recipients	O.O.134.	

From 58th Div.

Time 9-45 am.

E M W Harrison
Major.

No.	Date.	Unit.	From.	Embussing Point.	Debussing Point.	Destination.	Relief.
6	Aug. 3rd	Personnel 36th Bde. Group.	VIGNACOURT FLESSELLES.	On VIGNACOURT - FLESSELLES Rd. tail of Col. facing E. at E. edge VIGNACOURT 7 pm.	As in Serial No. 1.	ROUND WOOD Reserve Bde. Area.	Replaces 37th Bde.
7	3/4th	37th Brigade.	ROUND WOOD Reserve Brigade Area.			Left Front Line.	175th Bde.
8	4th	Personnel 175th Bde. Group. *(less 503rd Cy R.E. move to Querrieu Area under WArs of Bde)*	BEHENCOURT.	As for Debussing Point Serial No. 1, after 1 am.	As for Embussing Point Serial No. 6.	VIGNACOURT FLESSELLES.	
			Routes for busses EASTWARDS will be FLESSELLES - MOLLIENS-au-BOIS - CONTAY Cross-roads 1½ miles S.W. BAIZIEUX.				
			Routes for busses WESTWARDS - CONTAY - HERISART - VILLERS-BOCAGE.			**	

RELIEF TABLE issued with O.O.154.

No.	Date.	Unit.	From.	Embussing Point.	Debussing Point.	Destination.	Relieve.
1	Aug. 2nd	Personnel 35th Bde. Group and Pioneers.	CANAPLES Area.	Head of Col. facing S. at N. edge HAVERNAS on HAVERNAS-CANAPLES Rd. 4 pm.	Head of Col. facing W. at E. edge BEHENCOURT on RAIZIEUX-BEHENCOURT Rd.	ROUND WOOD.	174th Bde. Group.
2	2nd	Personnel 174th Bde. Group. (Bn 2 Bn) 2 Bn (except to return to Rd.)	ROUND WOOD.	As for Debussing point in Serial No. 1. 8 pm.	Head of Col. facing E. at W. edge HALLOY on HALLOY-BERTEAUCOURT Rd.	CANAPLES Area.	?
3	2nd	Personnel 37th Bde. Group.	BERTEAUCOURT.	As for debussing point Serial No. 2, 9 pm.	As in Serial No. 1.	ROUND WOOD.	
4	2/3rd	35th Brigade.	ROUND WOOD (Reserve Bde. Area.)	"	"	Right Front Line.	173rd Bde.
5	3rd	Personnel 173rd Bde. Group.	BEHENCOURT.	As for debussing point in serial No. 1. After 1 am.	As in Serial No. 2.	BERTEAUCOURT.	

=========
S E C R E T.   Copy No. 25
=========

58TH (LONDON) DIVISION ORDER NO. 152.
=*=*=*=*=*=*=*=*=*=*=*=*=*=*=*=*=*=*=

28/8/1918.

Reference Warning Order No. G.X. 207.

1. 175th Inf. Bde. with 1/4th Suffolks (Pioneers) attached will relieve the 173rd Inf. Bde. and 174th Bde. on the whole Divisional Front on the night 28th/29th August.

2. On relief:-

   (a) The 174th Inf. Bde. will be in support and will be disposed in squares A.22.a and c, A.28.a., A.21.
   One Battalion may go to the VALLEY in A.20.d. and A.26.b. if desired.

   (b) The 173rd Inf. Bde. will be in Divisional Reserve and will occupy the accommodation about L.4.

3. Brigade Hd. Qrs. will probably be established as under:-definite notification will be made later:-

   173rd Inf. Bde. - F.21.d.4.0.
   174th Inf. Bde. - L.30.c.3.0.(present location).
   175th Inf. Bde. - A.19.b.4.2.(vacated by 173rd Bde.)

4. Affiliated M.G. Coys. will remain with their Brigades.
   "D" Coy. 58 M.G. Bn. is placed at the disposal of 175 Inf. Bde.

5. Secs. of Field Coys. R.E. at present with the 173 and 174 Bdes. are being withdrawn and C.R.E. is detailing 1 Sec. of a Field Coy. R.E. to be attached to 175 Bde.

6. In case of counter-attack the rôle of the 174th Bde. will be -

   (i). To defend in depth the line A.28. central - A.22.c.5.0. - A.22.a.8.0. and thence Western Outskirts of MARICOURT.

   (ii). To counter-attack to regain our front line if ordered by the Division.

7. Two Coys. of the 2nd Bn. Life Guards M.G. Battn. have been placed at the disposal of 58th Division.
   They will be disposed to defend the BILLON Line. in A.20.a. and c. and A.26.a. and c. under orders to be issued by O.C. 58 Bn. M.G.C.

8. Divisional Hd. Qrs. will close at K.14.b.2.2. at 3 p.m. and open at L.1.b.3.0. at the same hour.

9. ACKNOWLEDGE.

Issued at 11.35 a.m.

                                    Lieut. Colonel,
                        General Staff 58th (London) Division.

                                            Distribution overleaf.

DISTRIBUTION OF O.&O. 152.

1. A.D.C. for G.O.C.
2. 193rd Inf. Bde.
3. 194th Inf. Bde.
4. 175th Inf. Bde.
5. 1/4th Suffolks.
6. 58 Bn. M.G.C.
7. 2/Life Gds. M.G. Battn.
8. C.R.A.
9. C.R.E.
10. A.D.M.S.
11. O.C. Signals.
12. A and Q.
13. A.P.M.
14. Train.
15. S.S.O.
16. D.A.D.O.S.
17. D.A.D.V.S.
18. III Corps.
19. 3rd Aust. Div.
20. 12th Div.
21. 47th Div.

"A" Form
MESSAGES AND SIGNALS.

Army Form C. 2121
(In pads of 100.)

Prefix........ Code............ m | Words | Charge
Office of Origin and Service Instructions

This message is on a/c of:
.... Service.
(Signature of "Franking Officer")

Sent At .... m
To ....
By ....

Recd. at .... m
Date ....
From ....
By ....

TO: 173 Bde
174 "   XXII   Corps Mounted Troop
175 "

Sender's Number	Day of Month	In reply to Number	AAA
AA 22	20		

Ref AO 132. todays date
one Squadron 22nd Corps
Cavalry and Coy 22nd Corps
Cyclists will on relief be
attached 173 Bde and will
be located in L.L. area
addsd 173 Bde reply 174
175 Bdes & 22nd
Corps Mounted Troops

From 22 Div
Place
Time 7.5 pm

Censor. Signature of Addressor or person authorised to telegraph in his name
*This line should be erased if not required.

Order No. 1025. Wt. W3253/ P 511 27/2 H. & K., Ltd. (E. 2634).

"A" Form
MESSAGES AND SIGNALS.

Army Form C. 2121
(In pads of 100.)

Sender's Number.	Day of Month.	In reply to Number.	AAA
Ref	OO 1536	AAA	The
See	Fd	Coy	RE
with	174	Bde	with
remain	with	the	Bde
for	the	present	

From 58 Dn

Major

S E C R E T.
=========
G.S.152/1.

Reference paragraph 3 of 58th (London) Division Order
No:-152, after relief Brigade Headquarters will be established
as under :-

173rd Inf. Brigade   :   F.21.d.4.0.
174th Inf. Brigade   :   F.50.c.3.0.
175th Inf. Brigade   :   A.20.b.9.2.

                                    Lieut-Colonel,
                            General Staff 58th (London) Division.

28th August 1918.

Copies to all recipients of Division Order No. 152.

W.D.

30

29/8/1918.

58th (LONDON) DIVISION ORDER No. 153.

1. The advance will be continued tomorrow as rapidly as possible.

2. (a) The Advance Guard will consist of the following under the command of the B.G.C. 175th Inf. Brigade :-

> 175th Inf. Brigade.
> 1/4th Suffolks.
> 3 Bdes. R.F.A.
> 1 Section R.E.
> C & D Coys. M.G. Battn.
> 1 Coy. XXII Corps Cyclists.
> 1 Squadron Northumberland Hussars.

(b) The mounted troops and cyclists will be pushed ahead at dawn closely supported by Artillery.

(c) The Infantry in formed bodies and the remainder of the Artillery will follow the mounted troops as quickly as possible and will attack the enemy wherever he is met.

(d) Every endeavour will be made to keep touch with Divisions on the flanks but loss of touch will not be allowed to delay the advance.

(e) Headquarters 175th Inf. Brigade have been established at A.23.d.8.8

3. (a) 174th Inf. Brigade with "B" Coy. M.G. Battn. and 1 Section R.E. attached will be in readiness to move by bus tomorrow 30th inst. in the afternoon. They will debus as close to the front Line of the 175th Inf. Brigade as possible and will advance through the 175th Inf. Brigade at dawn.

(b) B.G.C. 174th Inf. Brigade will take over the duties of Advanced Guard Commander from 4 am. 31st inst. at which hour 3 Brigades R.F.A. and Coy. XXII Corps Cyclists will come under his orders.

(c) The Squadron XXII Corps mounted troops will be attached to 174th Inf. Brigade from 10 am. tomorrow 30th inst. The O.C. Squadron will report to 174th Inf. Brigade by 9 am. 30th inst. for orders.

4. 173rd Inf. Brigade will remain in present position in readiness to move at two hours notice after 12 noon tomorrow 30th inst.

5. C.R.A. will detail the Brigades R.F.A. to act under the orders of B.Gs.C. 175th and 174th Inf. Brigades respectively as detailed in paras. 2 and 3 above. The fourth Brigade R.F.A. will be in readiness to move forward if required to support an attack but men and horses will be rested as far as possible.
The C.R.A. will move forward the H.A. attached to the Division
6. as the ground is made good by the Artillery.

6. Field Coys. R.E. will move tomorrow to A.25.d. C.R.E. will open Headquarters at A.19.b.8.0 at 3 pm. tomorrow 30th inst.

7. Divisional Headquarters will close at L.1.b.4.0 at 3 pm. tomorrow 30th inst., reopening at A.19.b.8.0 at the same hour.

C Hutchin Major for

Lieut. Colonel,
General Staff 58th (London) Division.

Issued to Signals at 7.35 pm

Distribution overleaf.

DISTRIBUTION.

```
Copy No.  1  A.D.C. for G.O.C.
          2  173rd Inf. Bde.
          3  174th Inf. Bde.
          4  175th Inf. Bde.
          5  C.R.A.
          6  C.R.E.
          7  1/4th Suffolks.
          8  58th Bn. M.G.C.
          9  Signals.
      10-11  A & Q.
         12  A.P.M.
         13  Train.
         14  S.S.O.
         15  D.A.D.O.S.
         16  D.A.D.V.S.
         17  A.D.M.S.
      18-19  III Corps.
         20  III Corps H.A.
         21  47th Div.
         22  3rd Aust. Div.
         23  12th Div.
         24  XXII Corps Cavalry.
         25  Coy. XXII Corps Cyclists.
         26  Sqdrn. N/Hussars.
         27  35th Sqdrn. R.A.F.
         28  2nd. L/Gds. M.G. Bn.
         29  File.
      30-31  War Diary.
         32  Camp Comdt.
```

"A" Form.
MESSAGES AND SIGNALS.

Army Form C. 2121.
(In pads of 100.)

Prefix......Code......m.	Words.	Charge.	This message is on a/c of:	Recd. at......m.
Office of Origin and Service Instructions.				Date......
	Sent At......m.		W.D.	From......
	To......		Service.	By......
	By......		(Signature of "Franking Officer.")	

TO

Sender's Number.	Day of Month.	In reply to Number.	
* GX260	29	—	AAA

Col HQ will move
tomorrow to A.20.b.2.2.
at 3pm and add to
all reports OO 152

From: 58 Div
Place:
Time: 29 1104

The above may be forwarded as now corrected. **(Z)**

Censor. Signature of Addressee or person authorised to telegraph in his name.

* This line, except **AAA**, should be erased if not required.
Wt. W 8253/P511. 500,000 Pads. 1/18. B. & S. Ltd. (E2389.)

W.D.

G.X. 278.   29   --   AAA

Following from Right Flank Corps begins aaa
Prisoners state mines laid ready to blow up
PERONNE Station and that retirement is
eventually intended to reach old CAMBRAI -
ST. QUENTIN line but they believe
temporary stand will be made at PERONNE AAA
Surrounding villages stated to have been
cleared of stores material etc. aaa
aaa Added all recipients of O.O's.

58th Divn.
10 1 a.m.

Chitchingham
Bt.-Col for
G.S.

W.D.

G.X. 306   30   --   AAA

Reference G.X. 294 the sweep Northwards of the
Australians is only temporary aaa 58th Divl.
Boundaries viz - : East and West lines through
B.29. 30 central on the South and B.17.18.
central on the North hold good although Australians
will be operating in our area today aaa
O.O. 153 holds good in all respects aaa Added
all recipients O.O. 153

Priority to 175 Bde & CRA.

58th Divn.
11.25 a.m.

ESHW Harrison
Lt.-Col.

Appendix "C"

LOCATIONS IN NEW AREA

Unit	Location	Takes over from
Divl. Headquarters	VIGNACOURT	
A.D.M.S.	do.	
C.R.E.	do.	
Train H.Q.	do.	
A.P.M.	do.	
D.A.D.V.S.	do.	
D.A.D.O.S.	do.	
D.G.O.	do.	
Sen. Chaplains	do.	
French Mission	do.	
Div. Reception Camp	~~CANAPLES~~ MIRVAUX	
173rd Bde. Group	BERTEAUCOURT Area	
173rd Bde.H.Q.	BERTEAUCOURT	37th Bde.H.Q.
2/2nd Ldn.Regt.	ST. LEGER	6th R.W.Kents
3rd do.	BERTEAUCOURT	6th Buffs
2/4th do.	PERNOIS	6th Queens
173 L.T.M.B.	BERTEAUCOURT	37 L.T.M.B.
2/1st H.C.Fd.Amb.	do.	36th Field Amb.
510 Coy.A.S.C.	do.	Coy. 12th Div. Train
174th Bde. Group	CANAPLES Area	
174th Bde.H.Q.	CANAPLES	35th Bde.H.Q.
6th Ldn.Regt.	do.	Cambridgeshires
7th do.	HALLOY LES PERNOIS	7th Norfolks
8th do.	WARGNIES (~~1 Coy. HAVERNAS~~)	9th Essex
174 L.T.M.B.	CANAPLES	35th L.T.M.B.
2/2nd H.C.Fd.Amb.	HAVERNAS	38th Field Amb.
511 Coy.A.S.C.	CANAPLES	Coy. 12th Div.Train
175th Bde. Group	VIGNACOURT Area	
175th Bde.H.Q.	VIGNACOURT	36th Bde.H.Q.
9th Ldn. Regt.	do.	9th Royal Fusrs.
2/10th do.	do.	7th Royal Sussex
12th do.	do.	5th Royal Berks
175 L.T.M.B.	do.	36 L.T.M.B.
2/3rd H.C.Fd.Amb.	do.	37th Field Amb.
512 Coy.A.S.C.	do.	Coy. 12th Div.Train
1/4th Suffolk Pioneers	VILLERS BOCAGE	2 M.G.Coys. 12th Div. & any necessary tentage
58th M.G.Bn. H.Q.	~~FLESSELLES~~ HAVERNAS	H.Q.Pnrs. 12th Div.
"A" Coy.	HALLOY LES PERNOIS	"A" Coy.12th M.G.Bn.
"C" Coy.	BERTEAUCOURT	"C" Coy. do.
"B" Coy.)	~~FLESSELLES~~ HAVERNAS	Coy.Pnr.Bn. 12th Div.
"D" Coy.)		do.
503 Field Co.R.E.	VIGNACOURT	70th Field Co.R.E.
504 do.	BERTEAUCOURT	87th do.
521 do.	HAVERNAS	69th do.
S.A.A.Sect.D.A.C.	CANAPLES	

58th (LONDON) DIVISION.

ADMINISTRATIVE ARRANGEMENTS
(In connection with 58th Div. Order No.134)

RAILHEAD. First day at new railhead, VIGNACOURT, 3rd August. The Divisional Artillery will continue to draw from POULAINVILLE by light railway, and will be attached to 12th Division Pack.

SUPPLIES Supplies will be issued as follows:-

Bde. Group	Last day of issue in present area.	First day of issue in new area
174th Bde. Group	1st Aug.	3rd Aug.
173rd do.	1st Aug.	3rd Aug.
175th do.	2nd Aug.	4th Aug.

All units will consume their day in hand during the move.

EMBUSSING PROGRAMME See attached Appendix "A".

LORRY PROGRAMME See attached Appendix "B".

WATER WAGONS 2 Water Wagons held by 175th Inf. Bde. will be handed over to relieving Brigade.

ATTACHED UNITS Units attached for rations will be taken over by 12th Division. Details to be arranged by S.S.O.

STORES Ammunition Dumps, Trench and Area Stores, including fireworks, water tins, extra water bottles, pack-saddlery surplus to establishment, reserves of ammunition, water and rations, tarpaulins for covering ammunition, and reserve S.D. clothing, will be handed over to 12th Division on relief.
Receipts will be taken and copies forwarded to 58th Division "Q".

TENTAGE All tentage in possession will be handed over in situ, whether standing or in store, receipts being taken and forwarded to this office. Tentage in possession of the Divisional Artillery will be retained.

(2)

BATHS

Brigade baths will be handed over to corresponding Brigades of the 12th Division. The Divisional Baths Officer will hand over, on Aug. 3rd, the baths at MIRVAUX Water Point, AGNICOURT, BEAUCOURT, BEHENCOURT, BOIS ROBERT, BAIZIEUX (P. of W.Cage), to the Baths Officer, 12th Division.

The 2/2nd H.C. Field Ambulance will hand over the ST.GRATIEN WOOD bath to the incoming Field Ambulance.

Irons, Primus Stoves, and Clothing, will NOT be handed over.

TOWN MAJORS

The 12th Division will relieve the Town Major, BAIZIEUX, on Aug. 2nd, and provide a clerk for the Town Major, BEHENCOURT.

RECEPTION CAMP

The Reception Camp at MIRVAUX will be handed over to the 12th Division. The staff will be accommodated at CANAPLES by arrangement with the 174th Inf.Bde.

AREA PERSONNEL

On relief the 12th Division will take over the duties of Traffic Police, Stragglers Posts, etc.

LOCATIONS IN NEW AREA

See attached Appendix "C".

A. McNalty

31/7/18.
LFL.

Lieut.Colonel,
A.A. & Q.M.G., 58th Division.

Copies to:-

A.D.C. to G.O.C.	Camp Cdt.D.H.Q.	A.C. BEAUCOURT
"G"	58th Div.M.T.Coy.	T.M. BEHENCOURT
173rd Inf.Bde.	D.A.D.O.S.	T.M. BAIZIEUX
174th do.	D.A.D.V.S.	T.M.MIRVAUX
175th do.	Claims Officer	
C.R.A. C.R.E.	Baths Officer	
O.C.Signals	S.A.A.Sect. D.A.C.	
58th M.G.Bn.	Employment Coy.	
A.P.M.	Salvage Offr.	
A.D.M.S.	O.C.Reception Camp	
1/4th Suffolks	R.D.O.	
Divl.Train	12th Division	
S.S.O.	III Corps	

APPENDIX "A".

EMBUSSING PROGRAMME.

Embussing Point.   BERENCOURT – BAIZIEUX Road, with head
of Column facing West at Eastern outskirts
of BERENCOURT.

174th Brigade Group.

Serial No.	Unit	Strength for Embussing.	No. of Busses.
1	H.Q. 174th Bde. and L.T.M. Bty.	150	6
2	6th London Regt.	750	30
3	7th do	650	26
4	8th do	650	26
5	1/4th Suffolks	800	32
6	2/2nd Field Ambce.	200	8
7	D Coy. M.G. Battn.	200	8
		3400	136

Time of Embussing.   4 p.m. 2nd August 1918.

Debussing Point.   Head of Column facing East at West
edge HALLOY on HALLOY – BERTEAUCOURT
Road.

EMBUSSING PROGRAMME.

Embussing Point. BEHENCOURT - BAIZIEUX Road with head of Column facing West at Eastern outskirts of BEHENCOURT.

175th Brigade Group.

Serial No.	Unit	Strength for Embussing	No. of Busses.
1	H.Q. 175th Bde. and L.T.M. Bty.	225	9
2	9th London Regt.	800	32
3	2/10th London Regt.	675	27
4	12th London Regt.	750	30
5	~~503 Field Coy. R.E.~~	~~150~~	~~6~~
6	2/3rd Field Ambce.	200	8
7	Divl. Headqrs.	225	9
8	B Coy. M.G. Battn.	200	8
9	D Coy. M.G. Battn.	200	8
10	H.Q. M.G. Battn	100	4
		3525	141

Time of Embussing. 2 a.m. 4th August 1918.

Debussing Point. On Vignacourt - Flesseles Road, tail of Column facing East at East edge VIGNACOURT.

LORRY PROGRAMME.
--*-*-*-*-*-*-*

Date	Time	No. of Lorries	Unit to which to report.	RENDEZVOUS.	Duty.	Destination.	Remarks.
2nd Aug.	7 a.m.	4	174th Bde.	No.38 Billet CONTAY.	Stores.	CANAPLES Area	
2nd Aug	7 a.m.	1	174th Bde.H.Q.	ESARTS FARM	do	CANAPLES	
3rd Aug	7 a.m.	5	173rd Bde.	U.22.c.3.3. on CONTAY - WARLOY Road.	do	BERTEAUCOURT Area.	
3rd Aug	7 a.m.	5	58th Reception Camp.	MIRVAUX	do	CANAPLES Area.	
3rd Aug.	7 a.m.	5	58th Divl.Baths Officer	Clothing Dump BEAUCOURT.	do	VIGNACOURT.	
4th Aug.	6 a.m.	14	H.Q. 58th Divn.	BEAUCOURT Chateau.	do	VIGNACOURT.	To include C.R.E. Gas Officer, Concert Party, French Mission, etc.
4th Aug.	7 a.m.	5	175th Bde.	Church BAVELINCOURT	do	VIGNACOURT Area.	

S E C R E T.

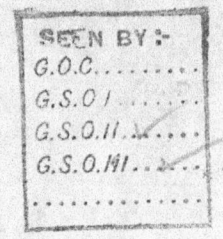

58th Divn.
G.S. 134/1.

Reference 58th Divisional Order No. 134 dated 31st July, 1918.

1. Divisional Headquarters will close at BEAUCOURT CHATEAU at 10 a.m. 4th August and open at QUERRIEU CHATEAU at the same hour.
   Para. 19 will be amended accordingly.

2. 503rd Field Company R.E. will, on relief, move to the QUERRIEU area under orders to be issued by C. R. E. 503rd Field Coy. will therefore be deleted from the 175th Infantry Brigade Group.

E.J.W.Harrison Major
for Lieut.-Colonel,
General Staff, 58th (London) Division.

3rd August, 1918.

Copies to all recipients of 58th Division Order No. 134.

SECRET.   Copy No. _____

58th (LONDON) DIVISION ORDER No.135.

                                                3rd August, 1918

1.   The 173rd and 174th Infantry Brigade Groups, composed as under, will move from their present billets, night 4th/5th August, by bus and march route, in accordance with the March Table overleaf.

2.   Infantry Brigade Groups will be constituted, for the purpose of this move only, as follows :-

   173rd Infantry Brigade Group.

         173rd Inf. Brigade.
         1/4th Bn. Suffolks (Pioneers)
         504th Field Coy. R.E.
         511th Field Coy. R.E.
         "A" Coy. 58th Bn. M.G.C.

   174th Infantry Brigade Group.

         174th Inf. Brigade.
         1 Section "C" Coy. 58th Bn. M.G.C.

3.   Orders for the move of transport will be issued later.

4.   ACKNOWLEDGE.

                                          [signed]
                                          Lt.-Colonel,
                             General Staff, 58th (London) Division.

Issued at 5.50pm.

Copy No.			
1.	A.D.C. for G.O.C.	16.	D.A.D.O.S.
2.	173rd Inf. Brigade.	17.	D.A.D.V.S.
3.	174th Inf. Brigade.	18.	Camp Comdt.
4.	175th Inf. Brigade.	19 & 20.	III Corps.
5.	C.R.A.	21.	12th Division.
6.	C.R.E.	22.	18th Division.
7.	Signals.	23.	47th Division.
8.	58th Bn. M.G.C.	24.	Tank Bn.
9 & 10.	"A" and "Q".	25.	Coy. Tank Bn.
11.	A.P.M.		
12.	A.D.M.S.	27 & 28.	War Diary.
13.	1/4th Suffolks.	29.	File.
14.	Div. Train.		
15.	S.S.O.		

TABLE TO ACCOMPANY 58TH DIVISION OPERATION ORDER NO. 135 DATED 3RD AUGUST, 1918.

Serial No.	Date.	Unit.	From.	To.	Route.	Embussing Point.	Debussing Point.	Remarks.
1.	Night 4/5th Aug.	174th Inf. Bde. Group.	CANAPLES Area.	FRANVILLERS Area.		HAVERNAS – CANAPLES Road Head of Column facing south at N. edge of HAVERNAS.	AMIENS – ALBERT Road Head of Column facing East at South end of FRANVILLERS (G.28.d.9.0.)	By Bus Embus at 9 p.m.
2.	Night 4/5th Aug.	173rd Inf. Bde. Group. (less 1/4R Suffolk Regt (Pioneers))	BERTEAU-COURT Area.	FRANVILLERS Area.		BERTEAUCOURT – HALLOY Road Head of Column facing East of HALLOY.	– do –	By Bus Embus at 10 p.m.
3.	Night 4/5th Aug.	1/4th Suffolk Regt.(Pioneer Bn)	VILLERS BOCAGE Area.	FRANVILLERS Area.		FLESSELLES – VILLERS BOCAGE Road. Head of Column facing East at Road Junction W. of VILLERS BOCAGE.	– do –	By Bus Embus at 10.30 p.m
4.	Night 4/5th Aug.	174th Inf. Bde. Group.	FRANVILLERS Debussing Point.	BIVOUACS J.27.a. and c.	HEILLY – VAUX-sur-SOMME.			By March Route To be clear of debussing point half an hour after debussing. Move to be completed before dawn.
5.	Night 4/5th Aug.	173rd Inf. Bde. Group.	FRANVILLERS Debussing Point.	WOOD. I.15.	Via LA HOUSSOYE.			By March Route to be completed by dawn.

S E C R E T.

Copy No. 26

58th (LONDON) DIVISION ORDER No.136.

4th August, 1918.

58th (London) Division Order No.135 dated 3rd August 1918 is cancelled and the following substituted :-

The 173rd and 174th Infantry Brigade Groups, composed as under and 1/4th Bn. Suffolks (Pioneers) will move from their present billet night 4th/5th August, by bus and march route, in accordance with the March Table overleaf.

2.   Infantry Brigade Groups will be constituted, for the purpose of this move only, as follows :-

173rd Infantry Brigade Group.

    173rd Inf. Brigade.
    504th Field Coy. R.E.
    511th Field Coy. R.E.
    "A" Coy. 58th Bn. M.G.C.

174th Infantry Brigade Group.

    174th Inf. Brigade.
    1 Section "C" Coy. 58th Bn. M.G.C.

3.   There must be no delay in embussing.

4.   173rd Infantry Brigade will allot accommodation to 1/4th Bn. Suffolks (Pioneers) in WOOD, I.15.

5.   Brigade Headquarters - 173rd and 174th Infantry Brigades at LA HOUSSOYE.

6.   ACKNOWLEDGE.

Lt.-Colonel
General Staff, 58th (London) Division.

Issued at 7 a.m.

Copy No. 1. A.D.C. for G.O.C.   16. D.A.D.O.S.
    2. 173rd Inf. Brigade.   17. D.A.D.V.S.
    3. 174th Inf. Brigade.   18. Camp Camdt.
    4. 175th Inf. Brigade.   19 & 20. III Corps.
    5. C.R.A.   21. 12th Div.
    6. C.R.E.   22. 18th Div.
    7. Signals.   23. 47th Div.
    8. 58th Bn. M.G.C.   24. 10th Tank Bn.
    9 & 10. "A" and "Q".   25.   Coy. Tank Bn.
    11. A.P.M.   26 & 27. War Diary.
    12. A.D.M.S.   28. File.
    13. 1/4th Suffolks.
    14. Div. Train.
    15. S.S.O.

TABLE TO ACCOMPANY 58th DIVISION ORDER NO. 138, DATED 3rd AUGUST 1918

Serial No.	Date.	Unit.	From.	To.	Route.	Embussing Point.	Debussing Point.	Remarks.
1.	Night 4/5th Aug.	174th Inf. Bde. Group.	CANAPLES Area.	FRANVILLERS Area.		HAVERNAS - CANAPLES Rd. Head of column facing East South at N.E. edge of HAVERNAS.	AMIENS-ALBERT Rd. Head of column facing East at X Rds. 500 yds. South of FRANVILLERS (C.28.d.9.0.)	By Bus. Embus at 9 p.m.
2.	Night 4/5th Aug.	1/4th Suffolk Rgt. (Pioneers)	VILLERS BOCAGE Area.	FRANVILLERS Area.		FLESSELLES - VILLERS BOCAGE Rd. Head of column facing East at Road junction N.W. of VILLERS BOCAGE.	Same as Serial No. 1.	By Bus. Embus at 9.45 p.m. Will proceed at head of bus column of 174 Brigade Group.
3.	Night 4/5th Aug.	173rd Inf. Bde. Group.	BERTEAUCOURT Area.	FRANVILLERS Area.		BERTEAUCOURT - HALLOY Rd. Head of column facing E. at West edge of HALLOY.	ALBERT-AMIENS Rd. Head of column facing E. at West edge of LA HOUSSOYE.	By Bus. Embus at 9.45 p.m.
4.	Night 4/5th Aug.	174th Inf. Bde. Group.	FRANVILLERS Debussing Point.	BIVOUACS J.27.a. and c.	HEILLY-VAUX-sur-SOMME.			By march route. To be clear of debussing point half an hour after debussing. Move to be completed before dawn.

P.T.O.

- 2 -

Serial No.	Date.	Unit.	From.	To.	Route.	Embussing Point.	Debussing Point.	Remarks.
5.	Night 4/5th Aug.	1/4th Suffolks. (Pioneers)	FRANVILLERS Debussing Point.	WOOD I.15.	Via LA HOUSSOYE.			To clear the road at debussing point for 174 Inf. Bde. Group and wait until it is clear before moving off. Accommodation from 173rd Inf. Brigade
6.	Night 4/5th Aug.	173rd Inf. Bde. Group.	LA HOUSSOYE Debussing Point.	WOOD I.15.	Via LA HOUSSOYE.			By march route. Move to be completed by dawn.
7.	Night 4/5th Aug.	Transport 174th Inf. Bde. Group.	CANAPLES Area.	WOOD I.9.a & b	VILLERS BOCAGE –MOLLIENS–au– BOIS– ST. GRATIEN– QUERRIEU.			Starting point S. edge HAVERNAS at 11 pm. To follow busses of 173rd Inf. Bde.
8.	Night 4/5th Aug.	Transport 173rd Inf. Bde. Group.	BERTEAU– COURT Area.	–do–	–do–			Starting point N.S. edge HAVERNAS at 12 M.N.
9.	Night 4/5th Aug.	Transport 1/4th Suffolks. (Pioneers)	VILLERS BOCAGE.	–do–	–do–			Starting point E. edge VILLERS BOCAGE at 8.30 pm.

G350   4

Ref: 58th Div: Order No: 136 AAA
Owing to alteration in routes
bus columns at debussing
point will face West instead
of East AAA Debussing point
for Serials No 1 and 2 is
altered from Head of column
FRANVILLERS to Head of
Column LA HOUSSOYE AAA
ACKNOWLEDGE AAA Addrd.
all recipients of OO 136

58 Div
9.30 am

G. F. Gough Capt
for Lieut Col.

"C" Form.
MESSAGES AND SIGNALS.

Army Form C. 2123.
(In books of 100.)

No. of Message

Prefix	Code	Words 24	Received From YEH	Sent, or sent out. At m.	Office Stamp
Charges to Collect			By	To	0 - 4.VIII.18
Service Instructions				By	

Handed in at .... Office ...... m. Received ...... m.

TO Troops

*Sender's Number	Day of Month.	In reply to Number	A A A
G/535	4		

Amend para 5 OO
136 aaa Headqrs 173rd
Inf Brigade at CHATEAU
BETTENCOURT aaa Added all
recipients of 136.

Locations

FROM 58 Div.
PLACE & TIME

* This line should be erased if not required.

S E C R E T.

Copy No. 1

58th (LONDON) DIVISION ORDER No.137.

Ref: 1/20,000 Trench Map.   4/8/18.

1. On the night 5/6th August 174th Inf. Brigade Group, 58th Division will take over from the 18th Division that portion of the Corps front from CRUMP LANE (inclusive to the 58th Division) K.23.b. 5.7. to the SOMME.
    58th Division to have the right of way via the COOTAMUNDRA - CRUMP LANE C.T.
    Inter-Divisional boundary will be as shewn on attached tracing.

2. All details of relief will be arranged direct between B.Gs.C. concerned.

3. Brigade Groups as laid down in 58th Divisional Instructions No. 1, dated 3rd August.

4. Command of the area taken over by the 58th Division will pass from G.O.C. 18th Division to G.O.C. 58th Division at 10 am. 8th August.

5. Completion of relief will be notified to Divisional Headquarters by the code word "RABBIT"

6. On the night 6/7th August the 173rd Inf. Brigade Group will move from the Wood I.15 to the bivouacs vacated by 174th Inf. Brigade about J.27.a & c.
    No restrictions as to routes.
    Not to move before 9-30 pm., and to be complete by dawn.

7. ACKNOWLEDGE.

                                          Lieut-Colonel,
                            General Staff 58th (London) Division.

Issued at 5 pm.

```
Copy No. 1 A.D.C. for G.O.C.  *    13 1/4th Suffolks.
         2 173rd Inf. Bde.    *    14 Div. Train.
         3 174th Inf. Bde.    *    15 S.S.O.
         4 175th Inf. Bde.    *    16 D.A.D.O.S.
         5 C.R.A.             *    17 D.A.D.V.S.
         6 C.R.E.             *    18 Camp Comdt.
         7 Signals.           *  19-20 III Corps.
         8 58th Bn M.G.C.     *    21 18th Div.
      9-10 A & Q.             *    22 10th Tank Bn.
        11 A.P.M.                  23 "C" Coy. 10th Tank Bn.
        12 A.D.M.S.                24 File.
                                25-26 War Diary.
```

* Tracings only to those marked *

REF. SHEET 62ONE 1/20,000

SECRET
To accompany 4th Cdn Arty Intr 101

Sailly-le-Sec

J P
36 6

I J
O P
  5

Identification Trace for use with Artillery Maps.

Tracing taken from Sheet .... of the 1: .... map of ....
Signature ....
Date ....

WD

G.360.   5.

Ref. 58th Div Order
137 AAA Para one
AAA. third line AAA.
For (inclusive to the
58th Div) read (exclusive
to the 58th Div)
AAA. added. all concerned.

58th Div.   R. Burnett
7.5 pm   Col. GS

S E C R E T.

18th. Div. No. G. 66.

58th. Division.

Attached Tracing showing dispositions of 3rd. Australian Division passed to you, please.

(sd) A.H.Hopwood, Major.

5th. Aug. 1918.
for
Major-General,
Commanding 18th. Division.

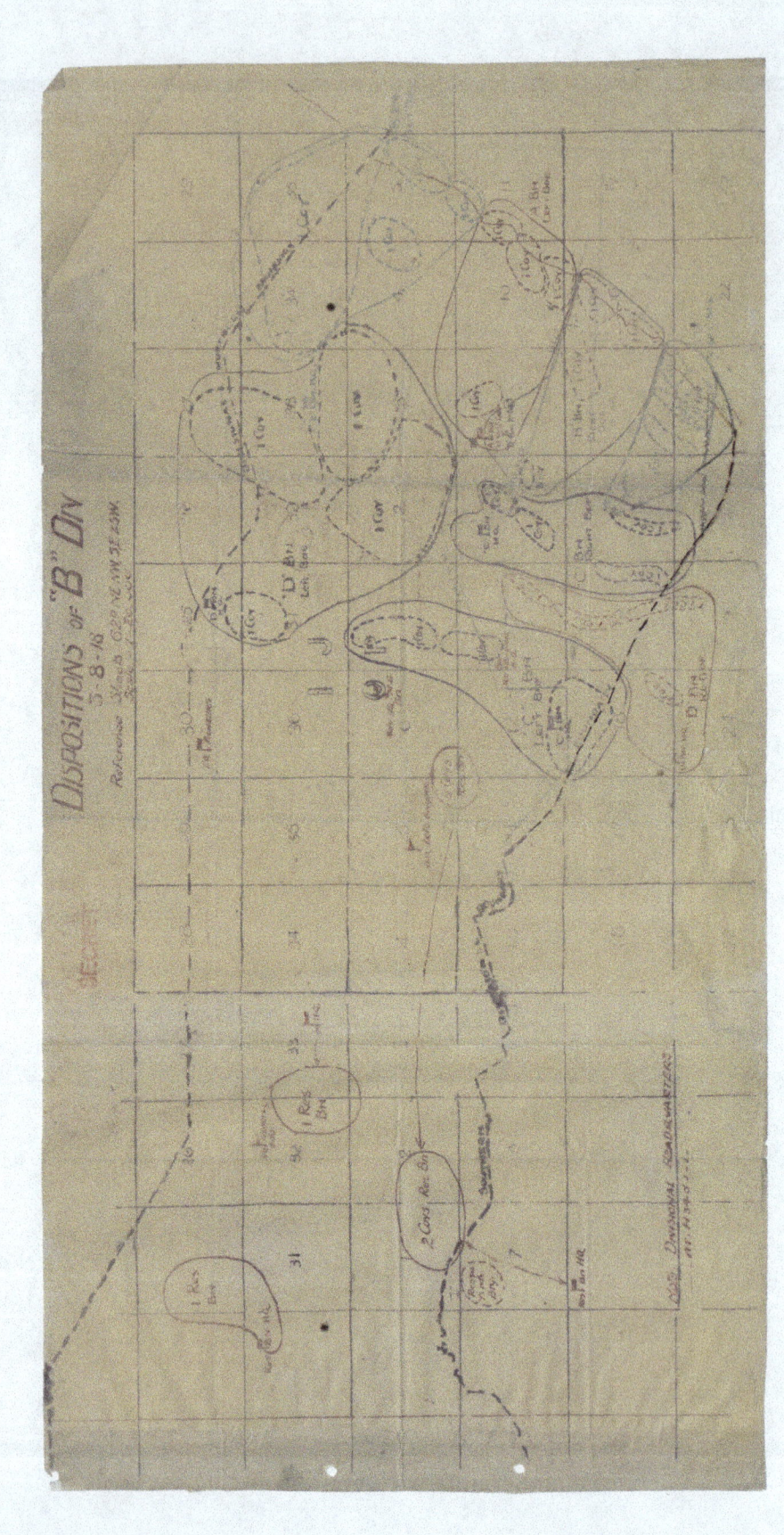

COPY

Appendix 1

SECRET.   FORTHCOMING OPERATIONS

58th (LONDON) DIVISIONAL INSTRUCTIONS No. 4.

MACHINE GUNS.

1. The Machine Guns will support the attack by covering fire and put down protective barrages during consolidation. They will as far as possible be employed in sections during the advance and where necessary after the final objective is reached, distrbuted in pairs in the Forward Zone.

2. For the attack on SAILLY LAURETTE, a section of "C" Company will be attached to the 2/10th London Regt. The task allotted to this Section will be to prevent any enemy movement along the Spur and the roads approaching the village through K 31 and K 32.

3. During the advance of 174th Inf.Brigade on the first objective, "D" Company of the M.G.Bn. and one Section of "C" Company will be allotted the task of searching by intense fire, the wood and ravines running in a S.W. direction from K 27 central.

    The final barrage line for these guns will correspond to the outpost line of the first objective. Fire will cease on this line when our troops are due to reach the western edge of MALARD WOOD.

4. "B" Company of the M.G.Bn. attached to 174th Inf.Bde willl follow the advance of the Brigade as quickly as possible and take up positions to be able to carry out (a) the defence of the ground gained and (b) to cover the advance of 173rd Inf.Bde. to the final objective.
    The O.C. "B" Coy M.G.Bn will arrange the details under orders of 174th Inf.Bde in consultation with 173rd Inf.Brigade.
    8 Guns of "D" Coy. on completion of their task will move forward to assist in accordance with para 6 below.

5. "A" Coy of the M.G.Bn will be under the orders of the B.G.C. 173rd Inf.Bde for the purpose of consolidating the ground between the First and second objectives.
    Arrangemenas should be made for harassing fire on the area E of the SOMME between MERICOURT-sur-SOMME and ETINEHEM.

6. 8 guns of "D" Company in addition to the task allotted in para.3 will be required to fill any gap which might take place on the Northern flank of the DIVISION as the attack progresses. These 8 guns will consequently be in position on the left flank of the Division to carry out their first task as in para.3 and when they move forward to assist "B" Coy. will take up a position for the purpose about K 27.a.0.7. The remaining 8 guns of "D" Coy will remain in position in Divisional Reserve.

7. 8 guns of "C" Coy will be with 175th Inf. Brigade in Corps Reserve. The other 8 guns of this Coy. will rejoin them as soon as they can be released.

8. Full details as to duration of fire, timings, safety limits, etc will be issued to all concerned by the O.C. Machine Gun Battalion.

9. ACKNOWLEDGE.

                    (Sgd) C.M.DAVIS, Lieut Colonel.
                General Staff. 58th (London) Division.

5th August 1918.

S E C R E T.

Copy No. 27

58th (LONDON) DIVISION ORDER No. 138.

5/8/18.

Ref: 1/20,000 Trench Map.

1.   58th (London) Division Order No. 137 - para. 1, third line, for "(inclusive to the 58th Division)" amend to read "(exclusive to the 58th Division)".

   Tracing issued with above order should be amended accordingly.

2.   Headquarters, 174th Infantry Brigade will move tonight, 5th/6th August, from LA HOUSSOYE to J.19.c.

3.   ACKNOWLEDGE.

R. Burritt
Colonel,
General Staff, 58th (London) Division.

Issued at 1.30 p.m.

Copy No. 1. A.D.C. for G.O.C.
    2. 173rd Inf. Bde.
    3. 174th Inf. Bde.
    4. 175th Inf. Bde.
    5. C.R.A.
    6. C.R.E.
    7. Signals.
    8. 58 Bn. M.G.C.
  9-10. "A" & "Q".
   11. A.P.M.
   12. A.D.M.S.
   13. 1/4th Suffolks.
   14. Div. Train.
   15. S.S.O.
   16. D.A.D.O.S.
   17. D.A.D.V.S.
   18. Camp Comdt.
  19-20. III Corps.
   21. 18th Div.
   22. 3rd Avat. Div.
   23. 10th Tank Bn.
   24. "O" Coy. Tank Bn.
   25. File.
  26-27. War Diary.

SECRET.   Copy No 26

FORTHCOMING OPERATIONS.

58TH (LONDON) DIVISIONAL INSTRUCTIONS NO. 10.

GENERAL INSTRUCTIONS.

1. **CUTTING ENEMY TELEPHONE WIRES.** - Steps will be taken to ensure that all enemy telephone wires are cut by the first troops to reach them. The lateral wires are of particular importance.

2. **CONSOLIDATION.** -
   (a). 174th Inf. Bde. will consolidate a position to be selected by the B.G.C., on the GREEN Line as shewn on map issued with Division Instructions No. 1, and 173rd Inf. Bde. on the BROWN Line, with an outpost line overlooking the SOMME on the East side of CHIPILLY Spur.

   (b). If either of these lines are found to be for any reason unsuitable or if the tactical situation does not admit of their consolidation 174th and 173rd Inf. Bdes. will each consolidate a line on a good defensive position as close in rear of the leading troops of each Brigade as is possible.

   (c). The consolidation will be commenced by the construction of strong works at selected points. These may later be joined up by a continuous trench line.

   (d). The 1/4th Suffolks will act under orders of 173rd Inf. Bde. and will be used for consolidation. Any men of the 1/4th Suffolks who cannot be usefully employed by 173rd Inf. Bde. will be sent to 174th Inf. Bde. for work on consolidating GREEN Line as soon as B.G.C. 173rd Inf. Bde. considers that the tactical situation permits their withdrawal. Similarly, those men of 1/4th Suffolks who are employed by 173rd Inf. Bde. will be sent back to come under 174th Inf. Bde. as soon as their task is completed. Transfer of men of 1/4th Suffolks from 173rd Inf. Bde. to 174th Inf. Bde. will be reported to Divisional Headquarters.

3. **ROYAL ENGINEERS.** - A R.E. Liaison Officer is being attached by C.R.E. to each of 173rd and 174th Inf. Bdes. Demands for R.E. assistance will be made through this Liaison Officer unless the attachment of one or more sections of a Field Company is required, in which case requirements will be notified to Divisional Headquarters.

4. **COUNTER-ATTACK.** - As a counter-attack in force is more likely from the North-east than from the East or South-east, 173 and 174th Inf. Bdes. will be ready to support the 18th Division in meeting such attack if required.

5. **LIAISON** - Brigades will take steps to keep in touch with Brigades on their flanks and will impress on Battalion Commanders the necessity of close touch being maintained with units on their flanks.
   This is of especial importance in selecting lines to be consolidated, and also for notifying the position of reserves.

6......

- 2 -

6. <u>LIAISON WITH TANKS.</u> - The Officer Commanding "C" Coy. 10th TANK Bn. will report direct to 173rd and 174th Inf. Bdes.
All tactical information emanating from tanks will therefore be sent back by D.G's. C. Brigades to Divisional Headquarters.

7. <u>RESERVE TANKS</u> - On completion of the tasks allotted to them by Divisions, a total of one company and one section of tanks (i.e. 16 fighting tanks) will remain in their rallying positions in the valleys in K.27. and K.26. ready to engage any hostile counter-attack.
These counter-attack tanks will come under the orders of the 18th Division. The remainder of the fighting tanks will return to HEILLY Tankadrome.

8. <u>MAPS.</u> - Sheets 62 D. N.E. and 62 D. S.E., 1/20,000 map, of which the message maps to be issued is a facsimile will be used for all references.

Lieut. Colonel
8th August, 1918.   General Staff 58th (London) Division.

Distribution (see attached slip).

"A" Form.
MESSAGES AND SIGNALS.

Army Form C. 2121 (In pads of 100.)

Prefix....Code....m	Words.	Charge.	This message is on a/c of:	Recd. at ....m
Office of Origin and Service Instructions.	Sent			Date............
....	At........m		........Service.	From............
....	To........			By..............
	By........		(Signature of "Franking Officer.")	

TO { C Coy. 58th M.G.B.
     175 Inf Bde
     .... M.G. Bn }

Sender's Number.	Day of Month.	In reply to Number.	A A A
G.345	5		

A	det	C Coy	58 M.G.B.
will	move	as	thus
to	tonight	PONT	NIEVELLES
and	forward	guns	and
collect	guns	as	many
S.A.A.	boxes	as	possible
by	lorry	transport	by
mans	point F	MMM	Some
.....	to	be	brought
by	MTO Q	who	will
notify	time	of	entraining
direct	MMM	the	move
to	be	completed	by	dawn
6 inst	MMM	added MMM	C Coy 58 MGB
to Q	copies	175 Inf Bde	and
58th M.G.Bn			

From 58 Bn
Place
Time

The above may be forwarded as now corrected. (Z) .... Captain
                                                Censor.   Signature of Addresser or person authorised to telegraph in his name.

* This line should be erased if not required.

SECRET.   58th BATTALION MACHINE GUN CORPS.

            ADDENDUM No. 1 to ORDER No. 24.

                                            6th August 1918.

1.   The following firework signals will be employed:-

        (1) No. 32 Grenade, GREEN over GREEN over GREEN.... S.O.S.
        (2) No. 32 Grenade, WHITE over WHITE over WHITE... SUCCESS SIGNAL.
                                            i.e. OBJECTIVE GAINED.

2.   O's.C. Companies and Sections will obtain ZERO hour from
        Brigades to which they are attached and will be responsible that
        watches are synchronised.

3.   Battalion H.Q. will be with Advance Divisional H.Q. at J. 19.c.
        where all reports will be sent.

                                        C.J. WILEY. Lieut. Colonel.

Distribution.

   All recipients of Order No. 24.

WD/

SECRET.

Copy No. 28

58th (LONDON) DIVISION ORDER No. 138.

Ref. 1/20,000 Map.   6th August 1918.

----

1.   The 173rd Infantry Brigade Group will move by march route, night 6th/7th August, from WOOD I.15. to Valley J.28.a and c.

2.   Move not to begin before 9 p.m. and to be completed before dawn. No restrictions as to route.

3.   One Troop, Northumberland Hussars attached to 58th Division, will move by march route 7th August from MONTONVILLERS to WOOD J.19.c. No restrictions as to time or route.

4.   ACKNOWLEDGE.

                                        R. Burritt
                                                Colonel,
                                General Staff, 58th (London) Division.

Issued at ....1 a.m....

        Copy No. 1. A.D.C. for G.O.C.
                2. 173rd Inf. Brigade.
                3. 174th Inf. Brigade.
                4. 175th Inf. Brigade.
                5. C.R.A.
                6. C.R.E.
                7. Signals.
                8. 58th Bn. M.G.C.
           9 & 10. "A" and "Q".
               11. A.P.M.
               12. A.D.M.S.
               13. 1/4th Suffolk Rgt.
               14. Div. Train.
               15. S.S.O.
               16. D.A.D.O.S.
               17. D.A.D.V.S.
               18. Camp Comdt.
          19 & 20. III Corps.
               21. 18th Division.
               22. 3rd Aust. Divn.
               23. 4th   "   "
               24. 10th Tank Bn.
               25. "C" Coy. 10th Tank Bn.
               26. File.
          27 & 28. War Diary.
               29. Troop Northumberland Hussars.

SECRET

D.R.L.S.

173, 174, 175 Bdes. M.G. Bn. Q
ARW. Sigs. ADMS.

G.861   6

175 Inf Bde less one Bn will march tonight to BOIS ESCARDONNEUSE I.15 in accordance with orders issued direct by 3 Corps. AAA 'C' Coy M.G. Bn less 2 sections and remainder of 175 Bde Group will march to same area under orders of 175. Inf Bde.

58 Div.

R. Burritt
Col. GS

"A" Form
MESSAGES AND SIGNALS.

Army Form C. 2121
(in pads of 100).

No. of Message..............

Prefix......Code......m.	Words.	Charge.	This message is on a/c of:	Recd. at..........m.
Office of Origin and Service Instructions.	Sent			Date.............
....	At........m.	...............Service.	From.............
....	To...............		By...............
....	By...............	(Signature of "Franking Officer.")	

TO	173)	Odes	MGBn	Signals
	174)		Q	ADMS
	175)			

Sender's Number.	Day of Month.	In reply to Number.	AAA
G 861	6		

Ref. 58R Divn. G.861 of today AAA Personnel up to 1,400 will move by lorry evening 6th and 7th August in accordance with orders issued direct to 175th Inf Bde by 3rd Corps.

From
Place 58 Divn.
Time 3.7

Censor. Signature of Addressor or person authorised to telegraph in his name.

R. 58 Divn Colonel

SECRET.   58th BATTALION MACHINE GUN CORPS.   Copy No. 1

ORDER No. 24.

Ref. Map. 62 D. N.E. 1 20000.   August 6th 1918.
Local Map. B 1 20000.

1. Reference 58th Divisional Instructions No 4 dated 5th August. The attached map shows the tasks allotted to the Machine Guns detailed to support the advance by covering fire and the approximate positions of the Batteries.

2. For the attack on the First Objective fire will be opened at ZERO and maintained at the rate of 100 rounds a minute until the task is complete at ZERO plus 20 minutes.

3. The Section attached to 2/10th London Regiment will complete its task at ZERO plus 15 minutes.

4. During the consolidation of the First Objective the rate of fire will be 50 rounds a minute. This will be increased to 100 rounds a minute for 10 minutes when 173rd Infantry Brigade are passing through 174th Infantry Brigade for the advance on the final objective.
    Fire will cease at ZERO plus 145 minutes.

5. Officers Commanding Batteries in accordance with the above will prepare necessary charts and arrange for ammunition and water supply.

6. ACKNOWLEDGE.

                                    C.J.WILEY. Lieut.Colonel.

Copy 1. to 58th Div G.
     2.   173 Inf.Bde.
     3.   174 Inf.Bde.
     4.   175 Inf.Bde.
     5.   O.C."A" Co 58 Bn.M.G.C.
     6.   O.C."B" Co   do.
     7.   O.C."C" Co   do.
     8.   O.C."D" Co   do.
     9.   18th M.G.Bn.
    10.   C.M.G.O.
    11.   3rd Australian M.G.Bn.
    12.   4th   do.
    13.   O.C.58th M.G.Bn.
    14.   2nd in Command 58 M.G.Bn.
    15.   Signal Officer.
    16.   War Diary.
    17.   File.
    18.19. Spare.

SECRET.

Copy No. 25

58th (LONDON) DIVISION ORDER NO. 159.

Ref. 1/20,000 Map.
Sheets 62 D. N.E.
62 D. S.E.

7th Aug. 1918.

1. The 58th (London) Division will attack the enemy's positions approximately between the SOMME and an East and West line running through K.25.b.9.7. and K.29.a.9.7. on a day and hour to be notified later.

2. Divisional boundaries and objectives are shown on maps which have already been issued.

3. The attack will be carried out in accordance with the various Instructions for Forthcoming Operations which have been issued from 58th Divisional Headquarters.

4. The 174th Inf. Brigade Group will capture the first objective.

5. One Battn. of the 175th Inf. Brigade, one Section of 18-pdrs., and one Section of "C" Coy. M.G.Battn. are placed at the disposal of the B.G.C., 174th Inf. Brigade to deal with SAILLY-LAURETTE.

6. The 173rd Inf. Brigade Group will pass through the 174th Inf. Brigade after the first objective has been gained and capture the final objective.
One Section 18-pdrs. is attached to the 173rd Inf. Brigade for this operation.

7. The 175th Inf. Brigade (less 1 Battn.) and "C" Coy. M.G.Battn. (less 2 Sections) will be in Corps Reserve, and will be at PONT NOYELLES and WOOD I.15.

8. The 174th Inf. Brigade will consolidate a position on the GREEN Line and the 173rd Inf. Brigade a position on the BROWN Line.

9. The 1/4th Suffolks will act under the orders of the 173rd Inf. Brigade and will be used for consolidation.

10. "D" Coy., and one Section "C" Coy. M.G.Battn. will cover the advance of the 174th Inf. Brigade on the first objective. In addition, 8 guns of "D" Coy. will be ready to fill any gap which might take place on the Northern flank of the Division as the attack progresses, and will move forward to assist in covering the advance of 173rd Inf. Brigade to the final objective.
The remaining 8 guns of "D" Coy. will remain in position in Divisional Reserve.

11. Tanks will co-operate in the attack. -

    (a) For the advance to the 1st objective and until the commencement of the advance to the 2nd objective, all Tanks will be under the command of the B.G.C., 174th Inf. Brigade.

    (b) As soon as the advance to the 2nd objective commences all available Tanks will come under the orders of the B.G.C. 173rd Inf. Brigade.

12. The C.R.A., 58th Division will arrange in consultation with G.O.C., R.A. III Corps, for the required Field Artillery support for the attack.

13........

- 2 -

13.   The 503rd, 504th and 511th Field Coys. R.E. will remain at Wood I.15. in readiness to move at half an hour's notice and one Troop Northumberland Hussars in Wood at J.19.c. ready to move at short notice.

14.   Divisional and Brigade Headquarters will be located as follows:-

173rd Inf. Bde. Adv. Headquarters will be at J.28.a.8.9.
174th   "   "   "   "   "   " " J.22.d.2.3.
175th   "   "   "   "   "   " " QUERRIEU.

Advanced Divisional Headquarters will open at 7 p.m. August 7th at J.19.c.3.1.

15.   ACKNOWLEDGE.

[signature]

Lieut. Colonel,
General Staff 58th (London) Division.

Issued at 1 p.m.

DISTRIBUTION.

Copy No.	
1	A.D.C. for G.O.C.
2	173rd Inf. Brigade.
3	174th Inf. Brigade.
4	175th Inf. Brigade.
5	C.R.A.
6	C.R.E.
7	Signals.
8	58th Bn. M.G.C.
9 & 10	"A" and "Q"
11	A.P.M.
12	A.D.M.S.
13	1/4th Suffolk Regt.
14	Troop Northumberland Hrs.
15	35 Sqdn. R.A.F.
16 & 17	III Corps.
18	18th Division.
19	3rd Aust. Divn.
20	4th " "
21	10th Tank Bn.
22	"C" Coy. 10th Tank Bn.
23	File.
24 & 25	War Diary.

SECRET.

G.S.139/2

C.R.A.
C.R.E.
173rd Inf. Bde.
174th Inf. Bde.
175th Inf. Bde.
58th Bn. M.G.C.
O.C. Signals.
1/4th Suffolks.
A.D.M.S.
A & Q.
A.P.M.
"C" Coy. 10th Tank Bn.
1/1st N. Hussars.

Copy

Reference 58th (London) Division Order No. 139.

1. Zero day is 8th August 1918.

2. Zero hour is ...4-20..am

3. ACKNOWLEDGE.

C M Davies
Lieut-Colonel,
General Staff 58th (London) Division.

7th August 1918.

S E C R E T.

G.S. 139/1.

C.R.A.
C.R.E.
173rd Inf. Brigade.
174th Inf. Brigade.
175th Inf. Brigade.
58th Bn. M.G.C.
Signals.
"A" and "Q".
"C" Coy. 10th Tank Bn.
A.P.M.

Reference 58th (London) Division Order No. 139.

1. The 36th Infantry Brigade of the 12th Division has been attached to the 18th Division for the operation.
Two Bns. of the 36th Inf. Brigade on the Right and the 55th Inf. Brigade on the Left will attack the first objective.
The 53rd Inf. Brigade with one Bn. of the 36th Inf. Brigade attached, will pass through to the attack of the final objective.

2. Headquarters, 36th Infantry Brigade - FRECHENCOURT, (V.29.b.2.4.).

3. ACKNOWLEDGE.

C.W.Davis
Lieut.-Colonel,
General Staff, 58th (London) Division.

7th August, 1918.

SECRET   Copy No...4...

R.E. INSTRUCTION No. 1
by
C.R.E. 58th. Division.

Reference map :-   August 7th. 1918.
Sheet 62D. 1/40000.

1. The 3 Field Companies will remain in the BOIS ESCARDOTNEUSE, I.15 ready to move forward for work at half hour's notice.

2. The 253 Tunnelling Co.R.E. now working on the CORBIE - SAILLY Road will continue to do so and will carry forward the work of improvement as far as operations permit; their task therefore, will be the improvement of the SAILLY - CHIPILLY Road in front of SAILLY, and the keeping open of the SAILLY - CORBIE Road in rear of SAILLY.

3. The maintenance of the 3 lateral communications from VAUX will be effected as under :-
   (a) From VAUX to the main CORBIE - BRAY Road by 503rd Field Co.R.E.
   (b) From SAILLY-le-SEC passing through J.28.b. and J.22.d. as far as the Divisional boundary by 504th Field Co.R.E.
   (c) SAILLY-le-SEC to the same main road passing through J.29.a. and b, J.23.d. as far as the Divisional boundary by 511th Field Co.R.E.

No more men than are absolutely necessary will be detailed for this work.

4. R.E.Stores.
   (a) The following R.E. materials are being carried up by each Supply Tank, vide Administrative Arrangements No.2:-
         60 Long Screw Pickets
        120 Short   "   "
         30 Coils Barbed Wire
         50 Shovels
         50 Picks

   Destinations of these Tanks are K.29.a.0.1., K.34.b.2.5., K.28.a.5.1. These places are subject to alterations according to circumstances under orders of B.G.C. Infantry Brigades.

   (b) In addition an advanced R.E.Dump will be formed tomorrow at J.28.c.3.7. consisting of :-
        200 Coils Barbed Wire
        400 Long Screw Pickets
        800 Short   "   "
       1000 Shovels
        400 Picks
         40 Coils French Concertina Wire.

   (c) Small Dumps of R.E.Material are at the following places:-
        KOWLOON Dump -   J.26.d.9.2.
        SPUD VILLA Dump - J.29.c.
        On the Road in J.29.a.
        On the Road in J.22.d.

   (d) The main Divisional R.E.Dump is in BONNAY.

   R.E.Stores from this dump can be drawn on the indent of O.C. 1/4th Suffolk Pioneers, Field Company Commanders, R.E. Liaison officers, O.C. 253 Tunnelling Co.R.E., and any other officer in cases of urgent necessity: any large quantities of material drawn from BONNAY Dump to be notified to Rear H.Q. as soon as possible so that arrangements may be made for replenishment.

5. C.R.E's Advanced H.Q. will be at J.19.c.
    Rear H.Q. at QUERRIEU CHATEAU.

6. The M.O. i/c Divisional R.E. will remain at Rear H.Q. until further orders.

7. ACKNOWLEDGE.
    done

                                        Lieut. Colonel R.E.
    Issued at 11 a.m.   C.R.E. 58th Division.

Copy No. 1 - 503 Fd Co.R.E.   Copy No. 9 - 1/4th Suffolk Pioneers
  "   " 2 - 504 Fd Co.R.E.   "   " 10 - A.D.M.S.
  "   " 3 @ 511 Fd Co.R.E.   "   " 11 - O.C. Signals
  "   " 4 - 'G' 58th Divn.   "   " 12 - S.S.O.
  "   " 5 - 'Q' 58th Divn.   "   " 13 - M.O. i/c 58th Divl.R.E.
  "   " 6 - 173 Inf.Bde.   "   " 14 - O.C.253 Tunnelling Co.R.E.
  "   " 7 - 174 Inf.Bde.   "   " 15 - C.E. III Corps.
  "   " 8 - 175 Inf.Bde.   "   " 16 - War Diary
                                      "   " 17 - File.

SECRET.   Copy No. 4

Addendum No.1 to R.E. Instructions No. 1
by
C.R.E. 58th Division.

7th August, 1918.

1. Delete para. 5 and substitute the following:-

   "5.   C.R.E.'s Headquarters will remain for the present at QUERRIEU CHATEAU."

2. O.C. 253 Tunnelling Co. R.E. will attach forthwith to each of 173rd and 174th Infantry Brigades a party of about 1 Officer and 6 or 8 men to go forward under Brigade arrangements and search for possible 'booby traps' and report on all dugouts found.

                                              Lieut. Colonel R.E.
Issued at 3.45 p.m.   C.R.E. 58th Division.

Copy to all recipients of R.E. Instructions No.1

SECRET.

Copy No. 5

R.E. INSTRUCTIONS NO. 2
by
C.R.E. 58th Division.

Ref: Map.
Sheet 62D. 1/40,000.

8th August. 1918.

1. Para. 3 of R.E. Instructions No.1 is cancelled; para 2 will be amended in accordance with following paras.

2. From 6 p.m. on the 8th instant Lieut. Colonel HEARN D.S.O. (C.R.E. Rear Zone Defences) under the Chief Engineer, III Corps, will be responsible for the upkeep of roads West of SAILLY-le-SEC - MERICOURT Road inclusive.

3. O.C. 504th Field Co.R.E. will forthwith assume responsibility for the upkeep of the SAILLY-le-SEC - MORLANCOURT Road as far as J.23.d.8.8.

4. Further Instructions will be issued later as the situation developes.

5. ACKNOWLEDGE.

Issued at 10.30 a.m.

Lieut. Colonel R.E.
C.R.E. 58th Division.

Copy No.1 - 503 Fd Co.R.E.   Copy No.5 - 'G' 58th Divn
"   " 2 - 504 Fd Co.R.E.   "   " 6 - 'Q' 58th Divn
"   " 3 - 511 Fd Co.R.E.   "   " 7 - C.E. III Corps.
"   " 4 - 253 Tunnelling Coy. "   " 8 - File
                               "   " 9 - War Diary

S E C R E T.

Copy No. _____

58th (LONDON) DIVISION ORDER No. 140.

8/8/1918.

1. The 58th Division with 131st American Regt. attached will attack tomorrow. A Composite Bde. under Brig-Genl. MAXWELL-SCOTT, D.S.O. will be on the Right, 131st American Regt. on the Left. 12th Division will attack on the Left of 131st American Regt.

    Zero hour will be 5.30.a.m.

2. (a) The First objective K.24.c.3.4 - K.17.central - Rd. junction K.10.b.2.5.
    Second Objective K.24.d.6.8., K.18.d.9.5. along old trench system through K.12.d and b. - K.12.d and b. K.6.c. to railway in K.6.a.3.2. which will form junction with 12th Div.

    (b) Dividing line 131st American Regt. and 12th Division K.14.d.8.3. (trench junction) K.10.b.2.5. (Rd. junction) K.6.a.3.2. (railway).
    Dividing Line between Gen. MAXWELL'S Composite Bde. and 131st American Regt. - A straight Line from K.22.a.0.0. through X Rds. K.17.central to 2nd Objective about K.12.d.8.8.

3. The attack will be covered by a creeping barrage advancing 100 yards in 4 mins. Start Line on which barrage will open at Zero from K.15.a.7.1. through X Rd. K.21.b.6.8 to K.35.a.7.9.
    Barrage will lift from Start Line Zero plus 20 and by successive lifts of 100 yards. in 4 mins all parallel and to the Start Line. Barrage will halt for 30 mins. on a line 300 yards N.E. of First Objective, and will then proceed by similar lifts of 100 yards in 4 mins. until a line 300 yards beyond the 2nd Objective is reached. On this Line the protective barrage will remain 30 mins.

4. 12 Tanks will co-operate 2 of which will advance between GRESSAIRE Wood and the SOMME, the remaining 10 being evenly spaced between GRESSAIRE Wood and the Left of the 131st American Regt.

5. Composition of Brig-Genl. MAXWELL-SCOTT'S Brigade will be :-

    9th Battn. Lond. Regt.
    12th. do.
    2/2nd. do.

    Two or more Battns. 12th Division to be attached under orders to be issued later.

6. M.Gs. will be attached as follows :-

    8 guns of "C" Coy. now with 175th Bde. to Genl. MAXWELL-SCOTT'S Brigade.
    8 guns of "B" Coy. now with 174th Bde. will be attached to 131st American Regt.

    O.C. 58th M.G. Battn. will arrange for all other M.G. fire.

7. 12th Division are providing guides who will conduct 131st American Regt. to Start Line.

2.

8. Arrangements for co-operation with aircraft as ordered for operations carried out to-day.

9. 131st American Regt. will have two Battns. in front line and one in support. The two Battns. in front line will go through to 2nd objective.

10. 173rd Inf. Bde. less 2/2nd Battn. London Regt. will be responsible for forming a line overlooking the SOMME from K.35.central to first objective at K.24.c.7.5.

11. 174th Inf. Bde. with 10th Battn. London Regt. attached, will be responsible for forming a defensive line in K.34.c and d. thence along Ridge to SOMME at K.35.central and will endeavour to clear CHIPILLY and the CHIPILLY Spur.

12. ACKNOWLEDGE.

C.M. Davies

Lieut-Colonel,
General Staff 58th (London) Division.

Issued at 12-30 am. 9th June.

Distribution attached.

DISTRIBUTION.

Copy No, 1 A.D.C. for G.O.C.
2 173rd Inf. Bde.
3 174th Inf. Bde.
4 Brig-Genl. MAXWELL-SCOTT'S Composite Brigade.
5 C.R.A.
6 C.R.E.
7 Signals.
8 58th Bn. M.G.C.
9-10 A & Q.
11 A.P.M.
12 A.D.M.S.
13 1/4th Suffolks.
14 Troop Northumberland Hussars.
15 35th Sqdrn R.A.F.
16-17 III Corps.
18 18th Division.
19 3rd Aust. Div.
20 4th Aust. Div.
21 10th Tank Battn.
22 "C" Coy. 10th Tank Bn.
23 File.
24-25 War Diary.
26 131st American Regt.

"A" Form.
MESSAGES AND SIGNALS.

Army Form C. 2121.
(In pads of 100.)

Prefix	Code	m.	Words	Charge			
Office of Origin and Service Instructions.				This message is on a/c of:		Recd. at ...... m.	
Urgent Operation Priority			Sent At ...... m. To By	W D (Signature of "Franking Officer.")		Date From By	

TO

Sender's Number.	Day of Month.	In reply to Number.	AAA
9x 56	9		

Ref OO 140 aaa. Hour of attack is postponed and will be notified later aaa 1st and 2nd Bns. 131st American Infty Regt will move E of Pw R to vallay running NE from SAILLY LAURETTE in 131 c and b and K 25 d. aaa 16 R Div are providing guides aaa Move must be completed by daylight and every precaution for concealment from enemy observation during daylight taken aaa 58 Div will continue to hold line in accordance with orders current before issue of OC 140, but will

From
Place
Time

The above may be forwarded as now corrected. **(Z)**

Censor. Signature of Addressor or person authorised to telegraph in his name.

* This line, except **AAA**, should be erased if not required.
Wt. W 3253/P511. 500,000 Pads. 1/18. B. & S. Ltd. **(E2389.)**

"A" Form.
MESSAGES AND SIGNALS.

Army Form C. 2121.
(In pads of 100.)
No. of Message............

Prefix....Code....m.	Words.	Charge.	This message is on a/c of:	Recd. at ..... m.
Office of Origin and Service Instructions.	Sent			Date..........
....	At....m.		..............Service.	From..........
....	To *			
....	By		(Signature of "Franking Officer.")	By

TO				
Sender's Number.	Day of Month.	In reply to Number.		A A A

be in readiness to carry
out the attack as ordered
in OO-140 at short notice
aaa Acknowledge aaa
added all recipients
OO 140

From
Place 58 Div.
Time

SECRET.

Copy No. 25

59th (LONDON) DIVISION ORDER No. 141.

9/9/1918.

1. The Division is to attack ~~to-morrow.~~ today

   The present line will be re-organized as follows forthwith :-

   173rd Inf. Bde. On the Right from the SOLAK to the QUARRY K.27.d.9.0 inclusive.

   174th Inf. Bde. QUARRY exclusive to junction with 18th Division.

2. The following units will be withdrawn at the earliest possible moment and assemble in Valley K.26.c., and K.25.d. where they will come under the orders of B.G.C. 175th Inf. Brigade. -

   9th Battn.
   12th Battn.
   8th Battn.
   1/4th Suffolks.
   175th Trench Mortar Bty.
   "C" Coy. M.G. Bn.

   These Battns. will not await relief but will move immediately on receipt of orders; M.Gs. remaining in position to cover the front.

   10th Battn. will be attached to 173rd Inf. Bde.

   Completion of relief of each of above units will be reported by the Brigade to which they now belong, and at arrival of each Assembly position by 175th Inf. Bde.

   173rd Inf. Bde. H.Q. will be established   J.30.d.0.0.

   174th   do.   K.31.c.9.2.

   175th Inf. Bde. and 131st American Regt. will select Head-quarters in K.32.b. or K.26.d to which they will move by 4 pm. to-day.

3. ACKNOWLEDGE

   Lieut-Colonel,
   General Staff 59th (London) Division.

Issued at.

Distribution.

As per O.O. 140.

"A" Form.
MESSAGES AND SIGNALS.
Army Form C. 2121.
(In pads of 100.)
No. of Message............

Prefix......Code......m	Words.	Charge.	This message is on a/c of :	Recd. at .... m.
Office of Origin and Service Instructions.	Sent		............Service.	Date............
	At............m.			From............
	To............		(Signature of "Franking Officer.")	By............
	By............			

TO { 173 Bde / CRA 58 Div
     Coy H.A.

| Sender's Number. | Day of Month. | In reply to Number. | A A A |
| GX 10 | 9 | — | |

In event of our patrols not having
established themselves on RIDGE K 35 c + a
K 29 c. The ridge will be bombarded by
Coy HA + Div Arty at 2-30 pm AAA
173 Bde will notify DHQ not
later than 1 pm whether they have
occupied the RIDGE in order that the
bombardment may be postponed if
necessary AAA Bombardment will
cease at 3-30 pm when the 173 Inf Bde
Bde will immediately move + occupy
the ridge K 35 c + a K 29 c AAA
This order does NOT cancel attack
referred to in OO 141 Addsd 173
Inf Bde repd Coy HA + 175
Bde + 58 Div

From: 58 Div
Place:
Time: 12 noon

The above may be forwarded as now corrected.   (Z)
Censor. | Signature of Addressor or person authorised to telegraph in his name

ND

SDR
Urgent Ops
Priority 131st
Am

131st Am'n Regt. 173, 174, 175
Bdes. Sigs. O. CRA. ADMS

G X 71.   9
The 131st Am. Regt will move
at once via SAILLY LAURETTE – K.32.t.8.0.
and into GULLY in K.32.t. AAA. Report Hour of
Starting so that Smoke may be put on
CHIPILLY Spur to conceal the movement
AAA Acknowledge.   AAA Added
131st Am. Regt   repto
Bdes. Sigs. O. CRA. ADMS.

SDR to 131st Am. Regt.

58 Div.   R. Burritt
12.30 pm.   Col
                           for HCE

"A" Form.
MESSAGES AND SIGNALS.

Army Form C. 2121.

| Sender's Number. | Day of Month. | In reply to Number. | AAA |

GX 74   9

Continuation O.O. No 142 aaa
173 Bde will be responsible
for protecting right flank
of 131 American Regt by holding
a line overlooking SOMME from
K 35 central northwards to
objective aaa 174 Bde will
be responsible for the CHIPILLY
SPUR South of grid line
through K 33. 34. 35 central
aaa Bde HQ 175 and Regt
HQ 131 American Regt are
being established about
J 36 central aaa Addsd
173. 174. 175 Bdes and 131
American Regt reptd all
recipients of 58 Div OO 142

Place: 58 Div

S E C R E T.   Copy No.

58th (LONDON) DIVISION ORDER NO. 142.

9/8/18.

1. The 58th Division with 131st American Regt. attached will attack to-day. The 131st American Regt. on the Right the 175th Inf. Bde. (less 10th Battn.)(but with ~~~~~~~ 1 Bn. 174th Bde. and 1 Bn. R. Berks attached) on Left. The 12th Division will attack on the Left of the 175th Inf. Bde.
   Zero hour will be ~~5 p.m.~~ 5-30 p.m.

2. (a) The objective K.24.d.1.5. - K.18.c.0.0. - K.17.central - K.11.c.3.0. - (Railway) - K.11.a.1.4 (Rd. junction).

   (b) Dividing Line 175th Inf. Bde. and 12th Division K.15.c.5.2. Rd. junction K.11.a.1.4. - K.6.a.3.1.

   Dividing Line between 175th Inf. Bde. and 131st American Regt., K.27.b.2.8. - K.22.central. - K.17.central. - K.12.d.6.9.

3. The attack will be covered by a Creeping Barrage advancing 100 yards in 4 mins. Start Line on which barrage will open at Zero - K.15.d.0.5. - K.28.a.8.5.- K.35.c.6.5.

   Barrage will lift on the Right at Zero plus 8, and on the Left at Zero plus 20. Subsequent lifts being at the rate of 100 yards in 4 mins. and parallel with the general line of the first objective. Protective barrage will halt for one hour on a line 300 yards N.E. of the objective.

4. 10 Tanks of 10th Tank Battn. will co-operate - 5 on the front of the 131st American Regt. 5 on the front of the 175th Inf. Bde.

5. "C" Coy. 58th M.G. Battn. will be attached to 175th Inf. Bde.
   131st American Regt. has its own M.G. Coy.
   O.C. 58th M.G. Battn. will arrange for all other M.G. fire.

6. 174th Inf. Bde. will get in touch with 131st American Regt. and will provide any guides required.

7. 131st American Regt. will have two Battns. in front Line, One Battn. in support and to mop up.

8. ACKNOWLEDGE.

   Lieut-Colonel,
   General Staff 58th (London) Division.

Issued at 1-30 pm.

Distribution as for O.O. 140.

"A" Form.
MESSAGES AND SIGNALS.
Army Form C. 2121. (In pads of 100.)
No. of Message..............

Prefix......Code......m	Words.	Charge.	This message is on a/c of:	Recd. at......m
Office of Origin and Service Instructions.	Sent		..........Service.	Date.........
	At......m			From.........
	To......			
	By......		(Signature of "Franking Officer.")	By.........

TO { Newton NCO 142

Sender's Number.	Day of Month.	In reply to Number.	A A A
VX 73	9		

Nest Havers spot enemy line -
K21 c 87 K22 a 21 K22 c 55
K22 c 08 K20 a 81 K34 [illegible]
AAA 131 [illegible] Bgt will take
steps to clear any enemy west of
start line w[ith] assistance of Tanks
AAA addr Rec point 00 142

From 58
Place
Time 1.30 pm

The above may be forwarded as now corrected. (Z)
Censor. Signature of Addressor or person authorised to telegraph in his name.
* This line should be erased if not required.

"A" Form.
MESSAGES AND SIGNALS.

Urgent Operations
Priority

SX 75

Reference OO142 aaa ZERO hour 5.30 pm NOT 5 pm aaa Acknowledge aaa Addsd all recipients OO142.

From 56 Div
Place 5 pm
Time

173,174,175 Bdes. 131st American Regt.
A Coy. Tanks, R.F.A. 58 M.G.Bn.

G.X.76   9

A contact aeroplane will fly over objective
at ZERO plus two hours AAA added all concerned

58th Div.

                                              Capt.

"A" Form.
MESSAGES AND SIGNALS.
Army Form C. 2121.
(In pads of 100.)

Prefix	Code	Words	Charge	This message is on a/c of:	Recd. at m.
Office of Origin and Service Instructions.		Sent			Date
		At m.		Service.	From
		To			
		By		(Signature of "Franking Officer.")	By

TO 175, 173, 174 Bdes.

Sender's Number.	Day of Month.	In reply to Number.	
GA 77	9		**AAA**

¼ Suffolks when withdrawn from line will become Divl reserve in Assembly Positions in VALLEY K.26.c. and K.25.d. AAA AAAA 3 Bdes reford other respond of do 1+1.

From 58 Dn
Place
Time 3.30p.

G.X.81.   9

C.R.E. 58th Div. will assume command of 1/4th
Suffolks and 8th R.Sussexs (Pioneers) 18th
Div) ordered to assemble in 58th Div. Reserve
in K.26.c. AAA He will move them forward after
the objective of 131 American Rgt. and 175
Bde. has been gained and will consolidate a
position across the Div. front will Right
on SOMME and left in touch with 12th Div.
in rear of the objective on the best line he
can select AAA 131 American Rgt. and 175 Bde
will consolidate the front line when gained
AAA Addsd all recipients O.O.142

58 Div.

5.45 pm.

Lt.Col.

"A" Form.					Army Form C. 2121. (In pads of 100.)
MESSAGES AND SIGNALS.					No. of Message............
Prefix.........Code.........m		Words.	Charge.	This message is on a/c of:	Recd. at.........m.
Office of Origin and Service Instructions.		Sent At.........m. To......... By.........		..........Service. (Signature of "Franking Officer.")	Date......... From......... By.........

TO	3rd Corps

Sender's Number.	Day of Month.	In reply to Number.	AAA
GX82	9		

Success Signal 6-10 pm at CHIPILLY SPUR

From	58 Div.
Place	
Time	6-10 pm

GX.90.   9.
Ref. GX 81. AAA 1310th Am Regt.
and 175 Bde will push forward strong
patrols with M.G's to cover the working
parties of pioneers consolidating AAA Patrols
will also be sent forward to report as
early as possible whether Trench Line
K.24. central through K.24.b. K.18.d.
and b. K.12.d a.&b. and a. K.5.d.
is occupied by enemy AAA If not our
outpost line will be put in that
line AAA. SOS Barrage will fall
300 yards beyond above old Trench
line until Brigade Commds: report
exact line of their most advanced
troops. AAA Addsd all recipients
of OO142

58 DIV.
8.40 p.m.

Gphayl Capt.
for Lt Col.

Spare

73, 74, 175 Bdes. CRA MGBn
12, 18 d, 4 d & 3 Aust Divs 3 Corps.
33 American Div CRE.
Y. 91   9   -

Map timed 8/pm 25pm dropped by
Aeroplane shows 175 Bde & 12 d Div
on or in front of their objective with
small gap it K.11.a. aaa Another
map received later & untimed shows
12 Div & 175 Bde on their objectives
as far as K.17 central aaa South
of this line shown to run K.23
central K.29 & 2.5. Added
3 Bdes referred CRA MGBn 12, 18,
Divs 3 & 4 d Aust Divs 3 Corps
33 American Div CRE.

58 Div.
9 pm
                                 Maybe Capt.

173, 174, 175 Bdes CRA CRE
Q. AA/MS A/QM 4 Suffolks
131st Am Reg 58th Div G.C.

GX 96   9.

Intercepted Wireless message timed
9.15 pm from GRESSAIRE WOOD
begins AAA send at
once for fresh reinforcements
AAA 3rd Bn 479
I.R. almost knocked out
by Tank attack no
longer in position to
hold AAA 243 Res.
Div. South East of
CHIPILLY AAA We are
across River SOMME AAA
If enemy follows on
HILL 85 strong firing
line.

58 Div
10. pm

                        Offbrit Capt
                        T.K.Col

O.H.M.S.

Urgent Ops.
Priv to
Cliv Davies
Lt Col.
175 Bde. 131st Am. Regt.

9 x 99   9
Owing to successes in South enemy reported retiring everywhere AAA Army Comd has ordered old Trench line K.24 central, K.18.d and c. K.12 d and c and a to be occupied forthwith AAA You will push forward at once and seize this line AAA Close touch will be kept between 131st Regt and 175 Bde and with 12 Div on left AAA Junction with 12 Div will be at K.12.c.9.3 (CROSS RDS) AAA Addsd. 175 Bde 131st Am Regt reptd 173, 174 Bdes Flank Divs. Sigs 58 Div MGC. Q. CRA CRE. 1/4 Suffolks. 18 Div

58 Div
11.15 pm
                Cliv Davies
                    Lt Col.

173, 174, 175 Bdes, CRA CRE Q
ADMS, APM, 1/4 Suffolks.
131st Amer. Regt. 53rd M.G.Bn.

4X103. 9'
174 Bde. report that they have
gained objective and are on
the ridge overlooking SOMME
and in touch with Americans
on left. AAA. Staff Offr. has
been round line of 175 Bde.
and 131st Amer. Regt. and reports
that they are on their objectives

58th Divn.
11-55p.

The date of this message should apparently be 10th? because G.X 103 was sent off at 11.15 p.m 9th and the number of this message is G.X 117 and was apparently timed 9.30 am

mm.

30/5/33.

173, 174. CRA.
175. CRE. 4th Aust Divn
131st American Regt.

GX 117.   9

B.G.C. 173 Bde will hand over
to B.G.C. 174 Bde command
of all troops on the CHIPILLY
SPUR. S. of K29 cent. and
174th Bde will arrange to withdraw
all American troops in this
as early as possible and send
them to rendezvous. K28 a 7.5.
where 131st American Regt. will
send them orders.

58th Divn
9-30am   [signature]

Gx 146. 10.
175 Bde will take
over from 131st Bger.
Regt. the trenches held
by the latter in South
K.12.d. K.12.d.80. holy direct
in K.12.d. to 131st Amer.
movements with ART — An international
Regt. will be established
at K.12.d.S.O. K&A — 173.
and — 174 Btls with
attached M.G.s at present
under command of 174
will withdraw in
accordance with orders
to be sent direct by
174 Bde hy.

②

Must Gen AAA They
are not like to
withdrawn before tomorrow
the AAA Nthn. 3 Bdes
morning. reptd. Getts — GHQ
MGB by ADMS 44th
to Supplies
Asst. Div.

Gilroy Capt
NT LCol.

58 Div
7.30 pm

173rd 175th Bdes.
174th C.R.A   58th Bn M.G.Br.
       C.R.E.

GX.161   11.   AAA.

It is the intention to continue
the advance to the BRAYE —
MEAULTE Road as the next step
AAA. 175 Bde will carry out
active patrolling to keep in touch
with the enemy and make every
endeavour to seize tactical
points with a view to the
above advance AAA 173
and 174 Bdes will reorganize
AAA. ACKNOWLEDGE. AAA.
Added List A

58th Div.
9. AM.   C.W.Davies
                           Lt Col GS

GX 162   11   —

10th Bn. now under 174 Bde will march forthwith to assembly position about K.20.b. K.21.a. where they will come under orders of 175 Bde aaa. As soon as can be arranged 175 Bde will withdraw 5 Berks who will be sent back to rejoin their Division aaa All units 173 + 174 Bdes & M.G. Coy M.G. Bn now under orders 174 Bde whether relieved or not will be withdrawn from line & march under orders 174 Bde to areas as follows aaa 174 Bde & A Coy. M.G. Bn. K 14 & K 15 a &c aaa Units 173 Bde Squares J.18 & K 13 a &c. where they will come under command of 173 Bde aaa Move to be completed by 6 pm aaa 8th Bn now attached 175 Bde will be withdrawn by 175 & will rejoin 174 Bde in areas South of MORLANCOURT. aaa Bde H.Q. will be notified later aaa
Addsd. List B.
    58 Div.

10. am.

C.W. Davis Lt. Col.

Sk 163.
In continuation of Sk 162
Bde H.Qrs. will
remain in present position
173. move to QUARRY
T.9.E.9.2. and 174. move
to J.H.a. called and thence
to be contact by
7pm with Bteo. wide
the ready to open
Adv. H.Q. all positions
to be notified near
BRATE - CORSIE Road at
short notice it required.
Exact positions will be
notified by Div. H.Q.
ANTI Aircraft Lookout "B"

5th Bn
10.10. A.M.

C W Davis
Lt Col S.

"A" Form.   Army Form C. 2121.
MESSAGES AND SIGNALS.   (In pads of 100.)   No. of Message ......

Prefix ..... Code ..... m.	Words.	Charge.	This message is on a/c of:	Recd. at ..... m.
Office of Origin and Service Instructions.	Sent			Date .....
Urgent Ops	At ..... m.		.... Service.	From .....
Priority	To			
C in D / L	By		(Signature of "Franking Officer.")	By .....

TO   173, 174, 175   Bdes

Sender's Number.	Day of Month.	In reply to Number.	
GX 165	11		AAA

Cancel my GX 163 AAA

Bde HQ will remain

in present positions until

further orders RWH Bde d

3 Bdes

From 58 Div

Place

Time 11 5 A.m.

The above may be forwarded as now corrected.   (Z)   JW Davis Lt Col

Censor.   Signature of Addressor or person authorised to telegraph in his name.

* This line, except **A A A**, should be erased if not required.
Wt. W 3253/P511. 500,000 Pads. 1/18. B. & S. Ltd. (E2389.)

"A" Form.
MESSAGES AND SIGNALS.

Army Form C. 2121.
(In pads of 100.)

Sender's Number.	Day of Month.	In reply to Number.	
GX170	11.		A A A
Corps	notify	that	Division
is	likely	to	be
relieved	tomorrow	night	and
to	proceed	to	LA HOUSSOYE
Area	AAA	Battle	Surplus
will	be	prepared	to
move	at	short	notice
same	area	tomorrow	morning
AAA	Addsd	10th	B
Reception	Camp	two	3 Corps
Flank	Div	plus	Camp
Cdr			

From: 56 Div
Time: 12 30 pm

C M Davies Lt Col

"A" Form
MESSAGES AND SIGNALS.

Army Form C. 2121
(In pads of 100.)

Prefix........Code........m.	Words	Charge	This message is on a/c of :	Recd. at......m.
Office of Origin and Service Instructions	Sent		..................Service.	Date............
WD/	At........m.			From..........
	To............			
	By............	(Signature of "Franking Officer")		By............

TO 1/3 174 Bdes 175 Bde CRACKER
Sender's Number. Day of Month. In reply to Number. AAA
                                3 Corps Frank Bde

GK 1/3 11   AAA
Area allotted in my
GK 162 now reported as
being shelled AAA Bde 174
will at his discretion divert
his Btn to J.24.C and d and
173 occupy square J.18
only AAA Corps have
been asked to move
troops now reported to
be there AAA Report
exact locations when decided

From 58 Dw
Place
Time

GX.173.   H.   AAA

Following from Fourth Army AAA Attack
last night by Aust. Corps astride
SOMME gained general N. and S.
line thro' L.20.b. N. of River AAA
S. of SOMME W. and N.W. of PROYART
and along main FOUCAUCOURT Road.
AAA No details as yet AAA Last night
Canadians line ran approx LA CATBUSE -
L.26.a.5.0.- L.17 central - FOUQUESCOURT -
CHILLY - W. half HALLU (doubtful)
to railway A.9. central AAA 10 E.A.
crashed 10 out of control AAA One
Div. 3rd Corps estimated over 50 guns
taken AAA 4 guns with limbers
captured by right Div. Canadian
Corps W. of LACAMBUSE AAA Added
list ~~III div~~ 3 Corps and Flank Divs.
~~58 Div.~~

1.15 p.m.   P.Rowett(?)
                              for Lt Col.

SIGNALS. Army Form C. 2121.

TO	4 Australian Div	

Sender's Number: GK
Day of Month: 11
AAA

Reference Conversation with
O.C. 58th Div (name of
soldier in question
Pte Johnson 3325
36 Battalion
4 Australian Div)

Man placed under arrest &
handed over to artillery at
K 26 C 3.5.

From: 58 Div
Time: 11 AM

"A" Form
MESSAGES AND SIGNALS.

Army Form C. 2121
(In pads of 100.)

TO: CRA

Sender's Number: Gx185
Day of Month: 11

Following from 3rd Corps AAA 18th A.F.A. Bde with 1 Pack Section is being transferred from 3rd to 5th Corps and will march night 11th/12th to 0.35.6 and d an 0.36.c (Sheet 57d) N.E. HARPONVILLE AAA to report for Billets to Town Major VARENNES AAA any route but not to enter CONTAY before 10 pm AAA Ends AAA Acknowledge

From: 58 Div
Time: 6-55 p

S E C R E T.

Copy No. _____

58th (LONDON) DIVISION ORDER No. 143.

12/8/18.

and 2 Coys. M.G. Bn.
1. 175th Inf. Brigade/will be relieved in the line by the 142nd Inf. Bde. (47th Div.) during night 12/13th, and on relief will proceed to Bivouacs vacated by 174th Inf. Brigade in J.24.
Brigade Headquarters to VAUX Sur SOMME.

(a) Details of relief will be arranged direct between B.Gs.C. concerned.

C.R.E.
(b) /O.C. Signals and A.D.M.S. will arrange details direct with C.R.E. O.C. Signals and A.D.M.S. 47th Division.

(c) Command of the Sector will pass to the G.O.C. 47th Division Headquarters at HEILLEY at 10 am on the 13th inst.

2. (a) 174th Inf. Brigade will move on August 12th to ROUND Wood. C.20.
No restrictions as to route but the movement will not commence before 8-30 pm.

(b) Brigade Headquarters probably BEHENCOURT Chateau.

3. 1 Coy. M.G. Battn. now at VAUX Sur SOMME, and 1 Coy. now attached to 174th Inf. Bde. will move to Wood I.14.a and c. where they will come under orders of O.C. M.G. Battn. No restrictions as to route. Move not to commence before 8-30 pm.

4. 173rd Inf. Bde. will remain in its present position.

5. Field Coys. R.E. and 1/4th Suffolks (Pioneers) will return to former bivouacs in BOIS D'ESCARDONNEUSE to be clear of present bivouacs by 7-30 pm. No restrictions as to route.

7. Divisional Headquarters in J.19.c. will close at 10 am on the 13th inst. and re-open at the same hour at ST. GRATIEN Chateau.

8. ACKNOWLEDGE.

Issued at 11.50 am

Lieut-Colonel,
General Staff 58th (London) Division.

Distribution.

Copy No. 1 A.D.C. for G.O.C.
2 173rd Inf. Bde.
3 174th Inf. Bde.
4 175th Inf. Bde.
5 C.R.A.
6 C.R.E.
7 Signals.
8 58th Bn. M.G.C.
9-10 A. & Q.
11 A.P.M.
12 A.D.M.S.
13 1/4th Suffolks.
14 Troop N/Hussars.
15 35th Sqdrn. R.A.F.
16-17 III Corps.
18 12th Div.
19 47th Div.
20 Liaison Force.
21 10th Tank Bn.
22 File.
23-24 War Diary.
25 131st American

W.D.

GX 200   12

Para. 4 of OO 143 is cancelled aaa
173 Bde will move as soon as
accommodation can be arranged
to area B of MERICOURT L'ABBE
J 9, 13, 14, 15. where they will be in
Corps Reserve aaa Bde H.Q.
~~...~~ aaa Addsd all
recipients OO 143.

(will be notified later)

58 Div.
12.25 pm

                    ChrDavis
                    2 Col. GS

W.D.

GX 201.   12
Ref para 1. OO 143 aaa
2 M.G. Coy attached 175
Bde will not be relieved
tonight but will be
relieved night 13/14th
by direct arrangement
between O's C. M.G. Bns.
aaa Addsd all recipients
OO 143.

58 Div.
1 pm.

P. Barrett Lt Col.

WB

GX 202.   12

Cancel para 6 of OO 143 aaa
Field Coys RE and 1/4 Suffolks
will work on front line tonight
aaa details later aaa added
all recipients oc 143.

58 Div.
1.30 pm.

A. J. Croup Capt

WP/L

Sx.203   12.

Operation Order 143 is
cancelled AAA further
orders will be issued
later. AAA Addr to all
recipients of O.O.143

58 Div.   CM Davies
1.50 p.m.   Lt Col
                             58.

SECRET.   Copy No 24

58TH (LONDON) DIVISION ORDER NO. 144.

12th August, 1918.

1. 175th Inf. Bde. will be relieved in the line by the 142nd Inf. Bde. (47th Div.) during night 12/13th, and on relief will proceed to Bivouacs vacated by 173rd Inf. Bde. in J.19.
   Brigade Hd. Qrs. 175 Bde. will be notified later.
   Brigade Hd. Qrs. 142 Bde. will be at J.17.b.3.7.

   (a). Details of relief will be arranged direct between O.C's. Concerned.

   (b). M.G's. will be relieved on night 13/14th by direct arrangement O.C. M.G. Bns.

   (c). C.R.E., O.C. Signals and A.D.M.S. will arrange details direct with C.R.E., O.C. Signals and A.D.M.S. 47th Division.

   (d). Command of the Sector will pass to the G.O.C. 47th Division Hd. Qrs. at SEILLY at 10 a.m. on the 13th inst.

2. (a). 174th Inf. Bde. with Coy. of M.G. Battn. attached will remain in present position.

3. 173rd Inf. Bde. will move as soon as accommodation can be arranged to area J.9., J.13., J.14., J.15., with Brigade Hd. Qrs. at J.13.b.5.9. and will be in Corps Reserve.

4. 1/4th Field Coys. R.E. and the Suffolk Pioneer Bn. will work tonight on wiring the front line under orders of 175th Inf. Bde. On completion of work Field Coy. R.E. and 1/4th Suffolk Regt. will return to present billets at J.24.
   All arrangements for work and guides will be the same as arranged for night 11/12th.
   175th Inf. Bde. will provide covering parties which will be relieved by 142nd Inf. Bde. as early as possible.

5. Divisional Hd. Qrs. in J.19.c. will close at 10 a.m. on the 13th inst. and re-open at the same hour at ST. GRATIEN Chateau.

6. ACKNOWLEDGE.

                                    Lieut. Colonel,
                            General Staff 58th (London) Division.

Issued at 3 p.m.

                Distribution as per O.O. 143 plus 142nd Inf. Bde.

GX 206   12

Cancel lines 4 and 5 of para 1. OO 144 and substitute following aaa Bde HQ 175 Bde will be in J.11.d and of 142nd Bde J.26.c.0.8 aaa added all recipients OO 144

58 Divn.
3.40 pm.

CMD Davies
Lt Col.

www.ingramcontent.com/pod-product-compliance
Lightning Source LLC
Chambersburg PA
CBHW081427300426
44108CB00016BA/2315